PROFITABLE FOOD AND BEVERAGE OPERATION

PROFITABLE FOOD AND BEVERAGE OPERATION

Edited By

JOSEPH BRODNER

Certified Public Accountant, Member American Institute of Accountants; Member of the firm of Harris, Kerr, Forster & Company (New York)

HOWARD M. CARLSON

Certified Public Accountant, Member American Institute of Accountants; Member of the firm of Harris, Kerr, Forster & Company (Chicago)

HENRY T. MASCHAL

Certified Public Accountant, Member American Institute of Accountants; Member of the firm of Harris, Kerr, Forster & Company (San Francisco)

AHRENS PUBLISHING COMPANY, INC.

NEW YORK

PROFITABLE FOOD AND BEVERAGE OPERATION

First Edition, 1951

Second Revised Edition, 1955

Third Revised Edition, 1959

Fourth Revised Edition, 1962

Library of Congress Card Catalogue Number: 62-12462

Manufactured in U. S. A.

The editors dedicate this work to the thousands of men and women everywhere who devote their lifetime efforts to the service of food and beverages to a hungry and thirsty clientele, whether in commercial restaurants, hotel dining rooms, schools and colleges, hospitals, clubs, or institutional cafeterias. They hope that its contents may unlock some of the so-called deep, dark secrets which too long have made such a mystery of this subject.

Joseph Brodner
Howard M. Carlson
Henry T. Maschal

CONTENTS

Charts and Illustrations xi

Foreword by the Publisher xv

Preface xvii

I. THE SCOPE AND IMPORTANCE OF THE INDUSTRY 1

Number of units—number of employees—sales—economic importance—educational opportunities—industry press.

II. MANAGEMENT 4

Supervision of departments—tracing operating losses—interdepartmental relationships—organization of the catering department—accounting controls—statistical references—check lists—legal considerations—accident prevention—employee relations.

III. PRINCIPLES OF MENU-MAKING 28

Importance of sales analysis—stock on hand—the market—time of year—time of day—location—capabilities of preparation staff—appearance of food—price.

IV. MENU SUGGESTIONS 39

Appetizers—soups—entrees—seafood—fish—meat—poultry and game — desserts — beverages — breakfast suggestions — off-hour menus.

V. MERCHANDISING THE MENU 57

Format—copy—importance of variety in arrangement of copy—value of limited menus—knowledge of patrons' economic status—importance of quality and service.

VI. FOOD PURCHASING GUIDES 68

The food buyer—choice of buying procedure—purchasing methods and sources—relations with purveyors—the market—quality buying—specification buying—kitchen tests—Federal grading and standards for meat—grades of pork, poultry, eggs, butter, canned fruits and vegetables, fresh fruits and vegetables, fish—buying routine.

VII. RECEIVING PROCEDURES 100

Requirements—mechanics—standard specifications—responsibility of the accounting department—records.

VIII. STORING FOOD 111

Requirements—refrigeration—canned goods—inventories—storage time and temperatures for fruits and vegetables.

IX. ISSUING FOOD 125

Mechanics of issuing—tagging meat—pre-packaging—requisitions—forced issues—controls.

X. FOOD PREPARATION 130

Basic requirements—fish and meat cookery—vegetable cookery—soups—baked goods—use of leftovers—salads.

XI. EMPLOYEE TRAINING 145

Analyzing training needs—training procedure—job breakdown—job analysis.

XII. FOOD AND BEVERAGE SERVICE 153

Types of dining room service—scope of employees' duties—techniques of service—room service—beverage service—merchandising wine.

XIII. CAFETERIA AND COUNTER SERVICE 181

Types of cafeterias—appeal of counter service—techniques—gratuity problems—take-out service—payroll.

XIV. INDUSTRIAL, HOSPITAL, INSTITUTIONAL, SCHOOL AND CLUB FOOD SERVICE 188

Discussion of problems not common to commercial restaurants—types of service—menu planning—staggered service—food purchasing—basic controls—inventories—payroll—community help.

XV. AMERICAN PLAN FOOD SERVICE IN HOTELS 207

Special menu structure—sample menus—portion sizes—controls—special features—food checking—transient meal service.

XVI. ADVERTISING AND PROMOTION 228

Eight keys to successful advertising—advertising media—suggestions for publicity—the advertising manager or agency—the importance of advertising.

XVII. SANITATION AND HYGIENE 245

Health and hygiene of employees—sanitation in food storage and preparation—equipment—general kitchen maintenance—dishwashing—handling and storage of food—disposal of waste—pest control—sanitation check lists—check list for methods of cleaning—false economy of filth.

XVIII. BEVERAGE PURCHASING GUIDES 269

Basic ingredients—inventories—categories of alcoholic beverages—European wines—wines of the United States—beer, ale, porter and stout—distilled beverages—American whiskies—Scotch whisky—Irish whiskey—rums—brandies—gins—miscellaneous spirits—catering to a brand-minded public.

XIX. WINE CELLAR OPERATION 293

Physical requirements—receiving clerk—storage—inventories.

XX. BANQUETS 301

Personnel duties—interdepartmental functions—guarantee—seating space—menu pricing—profit in selling function rooms—checking their productivity—banquet sales office—index files—clipping service—control of banquet revenue.

XXI. MUSIC AND ENTERTAINMENT 317

Types of entertainment—cost—break-even point—schedule problems—selection of entertainment—schedule changes.

XXII. BUDGETING FOR A FOOD AND BEVERAGE OPERATION 327

The prime purpose of business—sales volume required—amounts available for costs and expenses—payroll costs—direct operating supplies cost—raw food and beverage cost—summary of the budget—budgeted operating expenses.

XXIII. KITCHEN PLANNING 337

Value of sound basic planning—seating capacity and seating space—how to determine each—general principles of layout—cafeteria or preparation kitchen—hospital kitchen—special restaurants—layout pitfalls to avoid—check list for pre-planning—dishwashing and silver cleaning—locker rooms and wash rooms—offices.

XXIV. SOME ASPECTS OF FOOD CONTROL 359

Departmental interrelationships—purchasing control—receiving control—storage control—issuing control—production control—inventory control—food cost control—sales control—daily reports—food cost analysis.

XXV. PRE-COST PRE-CONTROL PROCEDURES 376

Scope and purpose—restaurant portion sales history—format of sales records—ratio of sales—variation in days of the week—sell-out items—standard specifications—standard portion sizes—daily price board—standard recipe card—"forecast" and "actual" pre-cost and abstract—summary of food costs and potential savings.

XXVI. WINE AND LIQUOR CONTROL 396

Purchasing—receiving—storing—issuing—bar control—selling price control—inventory control.

XXVII. PAYROLL ANALYSIS 414

Analyzing work loads—methods of analysis—staffing problems—remedial measures.

XXVIII. PAYROLL CONTROL 427

Basic staffing table—the payroll analyst—preliminary procedures in payroll control system—daily report—weekly payroll cost control—monthly payroll summary—employment turnover.

XXIX. VENDING MACHINES AND FOOD SERVICE 436

History of vending machines—advantages—size of market—planning for food service vending—merchandising—employees—lessons for the operator.

BIBLIOGRAPHY 445

INDEX 449

CHARTS AND ILLUSTRATIONS

Pro-Forma Statement of Income, Profit and Loss 14
Typical Standard Purchase Specifications 79
Meat Inspection and Grading Stamps 84
Grade and Inspection Labels for Canned Goods 90
Weights and Yields of Canned Vegetables 91
Weights and Yields of Canned Fruits 91
Calendar of Fresh Fruits and Vegetables 93
Steward's Market Quotation List 97
Purchase Order 98
Meat Tag 103
Blind Purchase Order 106
Receiving Clerk's Daily Report 107
Individual Receiving Ticket 108
Request for Credit Memo 109

The following illustrations are grouped between pages 110 and 111

Proper Way to Hang Fresh Meats in Refrigerated Boxes
The Receiving Clerk
Storeroom with Improper Arrangement
Well Arranged Meat Box
Pantry with Modern Self-Service Equipment
Dining Room Service Stand
Kitchen Service Bar
Table Set-Up for Coffee Shop or Informal Service
Buffet Table Set-Up
Table Set-Up for Six Persons

Refrigeration Chart 115
Citrus Fruit and Egg Storage 117
Requisition 128
Meat Cuts for Roasting 133
Meat Cuts for Broiling 133
Meat Cuts for Braising 134
Meat Cuts Cooked in Water 134
Sample Work Chart for Waitresses 156

The following illustrations are grouped between pages 176 and 177

Formal Dining Room
Coffee Shop
Lunch Counter
Commercial Cafeteria
Industrial Cafeteria
Outmoded Warewashing Unit
Modern Warewashing Unit
Use of the Wine Basket
Beverage Storeroom Showing Use of Bin Cards

American Plan Meal Checking Sheet 219
"Introduction to Dining Room" Card 219-220
Guest Order Check 221
Extra Meal Charge Voucher 222
Restaurant Check 223
Transient Meal Ticket 224
Dining Room Cash and Charge Record 225
Room Service Charge Voucher 226

The following illustrations are grouped between pages 244 and 245

Examples of Elevator Cards
Complete Promotion Pieces for a New Restaurant
Promotion Pieces Illustrating Program for Entertainment in a Hotel Dining Room
Internal Promotion Displays Used at Elevator Floor Landings
Sanitation Check List 258
"Methods of Cleaning" Chart 264
Banquet Pricing Tables 308-309-310
Monthly Banquet Sales Record 311
Banquet Details Record 312
Banquet Check 314
Function Room Inspection Report 315
Weekly Entertainment Sheet 319
Daily Food Cost Control Sheet 370
Daily Food Cost Report 372
Food Purchase Distribution and Inventory Turnover 373
Purchase Price Comparison 374
Food Cost Analysis 375
Table Showing Comparisons "Before" and "After" Installation of Pre-Control 377
Portion-marked Menu 380
Segment of Typical Sales Analysis Book 381
Daily Unit Sales and Ratio Record 382

Butcher Test Card 386
Standard Recipe Card 388
Menu Pre-Cost and Abstract (Forecast) 391
Menu Pre-Cost and Abstract (Completed) 392
Summary of Food Costs and Potential Savings 393
Recapitulation of Pre-Cost Pre-Control Results 394
Beverage Receiving Record 396-397
Beverage Purchase Order 398
Bin Card for Beverage Storeroom 399
Service Bar-Kitchen Requisition Form 400-401
Bar Inventory and Requisition 402
Bottle Sales and Differential Form 403
Summary of Beverage Operations 408
Beverage Perpetual Inventory Record 410
Analysis of Covers Served for Test Period 416
Work-Productivity Analysis 417
Warewashers' Work Schedule before Analysis of Work-Loads 419
Hourly Distribution of Work-Loads 419
Work Schedule 420
Daily Payroll Report 430
Master Control Sheet 431
Weekly Payroll Cost Control Report 432
Monthly Payroll Summary 433
Labor Turnover Analysis 434

FOREWORD

To THIS fourth edition of Profitable Food and Beverage Operation, there has been added an extremely important chapter. The title is "Vending Machines and Food Service."

This additional chapter brings the reader important information on the rapid advance being made by these machines in food service. The traditional operator might find many economies in this type of service if only for partial use.

In my humble opinion, this fourth edition of Profitable Food and Beverage Operation represents the most authoritative and comprehensive reference work on successful modern day hotel and restaurant operation.

In less than ten years more than 15,000 copies of "Profitable Food and Beverage Operation" have been sold. If this isn't a record for a full length industry book covering the hotel, restaurant and allied business, we are much surprised. It is a further personal tribute to the authors Messrs. Joseph Brodner, Howard M. Carlson and Henry T. Maschal, long time partners as well as to their internationally known and respected firm—Harris, Kerr, Forster & Company.

The industry owes them a debt of gratitude for making possible the dissemination of such valuable and practical information about the successful operation of a hotel and restaurant.

Don Nichols

PREFACE

IN RECENT YEARS there has been a virtual avalanche of technical books and texts on specialized subjects—covering practically every field of endeavor, including certain phases of food and beverage operations. Notwithstanding the apparent availability of essential and basic material dealing with these operations, inquiries on subjects relating to food and beverage operational problems continue to be received by our various offices. In addition, as consultants to the American Hotel Association, members' questions are directed to our firm for answering. Such inquiries and questions are never-ending, yet a majority do not involve intricate problems but rather simple queries of a fundamental character on day-to-day operations. Many requests are received for source material, speeches, articles and books wherein may be found the answers to these questions.

Interestingly enough, queries are received from every type of food and beverage service establishment: commercial restaurants, hotels, hospitals, clubs, industrial and institutional feeding operations, schools and colleges, department stores and others. The need has been made obvious, in these many inquiries and requests, for a broad manual of information on present-day methods, practices and policies aiming at the successful *business* management of food and beverage operations.

The purpose of this book is to present in organized form not alone the information as to current practices and methods, but a comprehensive perspective of these practices and methods as they relate and tie in with each other as factors in the attainment of *profitable* food and beverage operations as a business. The book serves only in part the needs of those concerned with the technical aspects of such things as the nutritive values of foods, the arts and techniques of cookery, service facilities, and a myriad of other matters of similar nature. This is what in common usage today is called a "business book."

In this light, and insofar as it fulfills that purpose, it should be useful and of value to all those engaged in any form of commercial serving of food and beverages whether as a primary business in itself, as a major department of business as in hotels, or, as a secondary service facility to the conduct of other primary operations, as in industrial feeding, hospitals, schools, colleges, clubs or other institutional operations.

The book should also fill a recognized lack now existing in the literature available for students in the field of hotel, restaurant and institutional management operation.

In this book the editors have attempted to prepare a work that would meet the needs not only of restaurant managers and operators, but also department heads and staff employees, as well as laymen interested in this great business of public and quasi-public feeding. It should serve as a practical working tool for all those who have occasion to delve into the intricacies of food and beverage operations. The material has been presented in simple, understandable language, intelligent use of which should serve also the purpose of acquainting restaurant and catering personnel with the duties and responsibilities of their respective positions.

The compiling of this material was no easy task. Information and data were gathered from hundreds of accounting and survey reports; from speeches made by our partners and associates; from their articles written for trade magazines and other periodicals, and from our own house organ, The Transcript. Use has also been made of government publications, particularly the manuals prepared by the War Shipping Administration on food standards and specifications. The editors and their research associates have reviewed many of the existing books and other publications on related subjects. These are included in the bibliography on page 436. Illustrative photographs are used by courtesy and permission of the Lexington and Commodore Hotels in New York; Simtex Mills, and Nathan Straus-Duparquet, Inc.

It would be a happy circumstance if we could list in detail the names of all those whose contributions and efforts have made this book possible. The list would be too long. Yet, we would be remiss indeed if we did not single out for credit those of Harris, Kerr, Forster & Company who pioneered in new and advanced methods and procedures, and did so much to reduce to practical application the philosophy of theoretical food and beverage operating procedures. Among these are our partners Mr. Murray Rappaport, C.P.A., and Mr. Edmund Miller, C.P.A., both in New York, whose experience is countrywide and who have, for many years, been spreading the gospel of Profitable Food and Beverage Operation; Mr. G. Carroll Weaver, Manager of special Services in our Chicago office. Credit goes also to our partners, Messrs. Fred W. Eckert, C.P.A. of Chicago and Allan C. George, C.P.A. of New York, who have spoken to numerous groups throughout the country on the importance of operating their food and beverage outlets on a sound business basis. We have made good use of the subject matter of many of their addresses and technical papers. For his contribution in revising and amplifying the chapter on Advertising and Promotion, our sincere thanks to H. Victor Grohmann. And to Mr. David J. Berge, President of the Brass Rail Organization we are indeed appreciative for his contribution in the form of the new chapter on "Vending Machines and Food Service."

We would like it known that we are deeply grateful to the associates and staff members in all of our offices whose written material has been used, whose suggestions have been incorporated and whose time was given to research, numerous conferences and discussions on how best to present the subject matter of this book. For, after all, we are only the conduit through which flows the broad knowledge of this subject to those who would know more about the fundamentals of this great business.

In this fourth printing and revised edition we wish to acknowledge our sincere thanks to all those readers who were kind enough to take the time to write to the editors giving their ideas and suggestions for additional material to be included in this work. To the extent that we considered it would improve the presentation and serve the purpose for which the book is intended such new material is now included.

The editors consider that this work will be a helpful beginning in formulating the structure for sound business management in this field and the development of further intensive studies in particular phases involved in the ultimate goal of profitable food and beverage operation.

JOSEPH BRODNER
HOWARD M. CARLSON
HENRY T. MASCHAL

New York, N. Y.
February, 1962.

Chapter I: THE SCOPE AND IMPORTANCE OF THE INDUSTRY

THE BUSINESS OF FEEDING, housing, and serving alcoholic beverages to the American public away from the home is important business. It is big business and one that plays a vital part in the economic scheme of America.

How important and big is it? Current sales figures of the U.S. Department of Commerce indicate that approximately 23 per cent of all food and drink in the United States is consumed away from home. This is done primarily in the 230,929 commercial restaurants and in the 29,439 hotels that, sales-wise, take in the lion's share of the total eating, drinking and living-out market. The country's commercial eating establishments are broken down as follows:

TYPE OF COMMERCIAL ESTABLISHMENT	ANNUAL SALES
* Restaurants (Food (84.1%) and Beverage Sales)	$11,460,000,000
** Hotels (Sales—All Sources)	2,912,000,000
* Drinking Places (Beverage (76.8%) and Food Sales)	3,916,000,000
Drug Stores (Food Sales Only)	606,443,000
Industrial Restaurants (Food Sales Only)	585,479,000
Variety Stores (Food Sales Only)	197,576,000
Tourist Courts (Food Sales Only)	93,731,000
Department Stores (Food Sales Only)	132,451,000
Confectionery Stores (Food Sales Only)	64,861,000
Miscellaneous Stores (Food Sales Only)	79,454,000
TOTAL	$20,047,995,000

* Bureau of the census, 1960.
** 1960 Industry Sales percentages applied to 1958 Census Sales of $2,827,023,000.
All others from "1961 Analysis of the Food Service Industry."

What is the character of these commercial eating establishments? The 1958 Census of Business placed the number of commercial restaurants at 230,929. These included table service restaurants, cafeterias, caterers, lunchrooms, lunch counters, refreshment stands, fountains and diners that derive the bulk of their income from the sales of meals. The same Census showed a total of 29,439 hotels and 114,925 taverns, bars, and other drinking places. In addition, in-plant feeding operations, hospitals, clubs, schools and colleges, drug stores, steamships and railroads, among others, represent important food outlets away from the home.

Perhaps no business in America has grown more rapidly, and in some respects, more solidly, than these have. It was not too many years ago that ownership of a hotel or a restaurant was characterized by "ye-hail-fellow-well-met" host. Too often the "boss" was a convivial soul—long on friendship and short on management methods.

As recently as 1936, Department of Commerce figures show that only three billion, twenty million dollars was spent for food and beverages consumed outside the home. This compares with a current annual expenditure of more than twenty billion dollars. This means that in the past twenty-three years the outside-the-home market for food and beverages has increased almost 560 per cent.

Take hotels alone. They employ over 400,000 people, serve two hundred and seventy-five million registered guests annually in one million, seven hundred thousand rooms. Hotel property today is conservatively valued at more than six billion dollars.

Restaurants and taverns represent the fourth largest retail business in America. In California, it is the largest single retail business.

From the standpoint of importance in our economic scheme of things, the contribution to the war effort by the hotel and restaurant business is sufficient evidence. It played a dominating role in taking care of the essential and important war-time traveling needs. It housed and fed business executives, government expediters, service men in transit, as well as the general, day-to-day working public. It made available instantaneous and permanent housing and feeding facilities in crowded war areas. It automatically was able to house and feed uncounted war workers. The hotel, the restaurant, and the club usually was the mobilization center for important war drives.

Obviously, the several hundred establishments converted by the Army and the Navy from commercial use, represented a marked contribution to the war effort—and represented facilities which would have taken months to create, had it been necessary to erect new buildings.

There are a number of valid reasons why this industry of housing and feeding the American public away from the home should have prospered and developed. Here are some of the obvious ones.

The many schools and colleges with courses on hotel and restaurant administration have attracted a fine type of man- and woman-power to the industry. Graduates from Cornell University, Michigan State College, Penn State College, University of New Hampshire, Mississippi State College, the University of Chicago, the University of Denver, the University of Oklahoma, San Francisco Junior College, and perhaps another dozen nationally known colleges, have brought a new caste and tone to hotel and restaurant operation.

There are far more women in business today than there were twenty-five years ago. There are certain types of work which women can do more efficiently than men. There is no likelihood in the foreseeable future that the trend of the American girl to work, will be curtailed. Whether or not there are more women in business, there is a strong aversion on the part of women in this country to standing at the range in their own homes. This encourages more eating-out in hotels, restaurants, clubs, and other such establishments.

The American public is extremely travel-conscious. The travel industry today is a vital one. It is estimated that, for every travel dollar spent, about 45 cents of it goes into the hotel and restaurant cash register.

Such industry associations as the American Hotel Association and the National Restaurant Association have contributed much to the welding of a strong industry.

The efficient food and beverage control methods developed by specialists in the accounting field of the industry can be pointed to as a vital contribution to more profitable operation.

The industry press, represented by the strong magazines serving the hotel, the restaurant, the hospital, the school, and the club fields, to name a few, has been an important educational influence.

In short, the operators of the places of business where the public is housed and fed away from the home, contribute much to the welfare of our scheme of life. They represent an industry which has grown more than three-fold in the last twenty years.

It is the editors' opinion that the opportunities for further expanding hotel and restaurant services have, by no means, reached their limits. To enable forward-looking executives among hotels, restaurants, hospitals, schools, clubs, and other such establishments to capitalize on their business opportunities, is the primary purpose of this book.

Chapter II: MANAGEMENT

ALL RESTAURANTS or food service establishments where meals are provided have practically the same problems. This is true whether they serve only food, or food and beverages, or whether they are part of a hotel, club, hospital, school, or institution. Although they may differ as to grade of food served, type of service and clientele, they have the same basic problems—purchasing, receiving, storage, preparation, and service. The extent to which these functions are carried out wisely and efficiently, measures the success or failure of each operation. There are many issues which enter the picture with commercial operations such as advertising, training and supervision of personnel, and methods for obtaining satisfied patrons. The five main problems, however, remain common to all places where meals are served. How to help solve these problems efficiently and with the greatest resulting profit to the food establishment will be directly dealt with in this book.

While it is intended that this book be general in character as applied to the various phases of restaurant operations, there are frequent references to hotels as differentiated from other types of operations, commercial or industrial. This could not be avoided as hotels do present problems peculiarly their own in the catering field. The very nature of hotel operations requires a high degree of departmentalization, and an interlocking interdependence among the various departments. Consequently, it was deemed advisable to point out, wherever necessary, any problems encountered by hotels not necessarily common to other types of feeding operations.

In hotels of large and medium size, the supervision of the entire food and beverage operation is generally the responsibility of the catering manager. In small hotels, the manager is the one in charge. This same division of work is true of large and small clubs. In commercial restaurants, the duties are divided in about the same way although the titles may differ. In large chain operations, the individual in charge of food and beverages is often called the food supervisor with a subordinate supervisor for each unit in the chain. Large restaurants may have a catering manager or a food supervisor but in the small operations, the responsibility for food, from its purchase to its service, rests with the manager.

In schools, hospitals, and institutions of various kinds, the person in charge of food usually has the title of dietician.

RESPONSIBILITIES

Departmental Supervision. The head of a food operation serving the public is concerned with many different functions of the establishment: the banquet sales office, the wine cellar, the service and stand-up bars, the cocktail lounges, the storerooms, the kitchens, the public dining rooms, banquet rooms, and the service to guest rooms. Although the latter function is strictly confined to hotels, many restaurants specialize in "take-out" service. The smaller operations do not have all these departments, although they often do accommodate groups for luncheon and private parties for dinner.

Strict supervision must be maintained over the purchasing, receiving, storing, preparing, and serving of food and beverages. Working supervision is delegated to subordinate department heads but the ultimate responsibility for all phases of the food and beverage operation rests in the hands of one person whether he be the manager, catering manager, food supervisor, or whatever the title. It is obvious that supervision involving so many different departments cannot be handled entirely from an office. Frequent inspection and continuous checks must be made of each separate operation. Department heads may make what appear to be very full reports but they will seldom report on their own shortcomings. These must be unearthed, studied, and corrected by the "head man."

This individual is not required to perform specific tasks personally but he should know how they are accomplished. He is not expected to unpack crates and put food away in the storeroom but he should know the best way to do it and the most efficient location for each type of food. He should know the proper temperatures for ice boxes and many other technical details. He should be able to locate the trouble spots when the food or beverage costs are too high. He must have a knowledge of the planning of a well-balanced menu and the standards of purchasing, preparation, sanitation, and service, and he must see to it, by constant inspection and checking, that these standards are adhered to.

He must be able to settle disputes arising from rivalries or misunderstandings between department heads and between service and preparation personnel. These employees are quite apt to blame each other for various shortcomings in quality of food or service. He must be able to go into the kitchen or any point where jobs overlap, and determine whether one individual employee, or group of employees, is taking advantage of another individual or group. Many times he will find that money and time are being wasted simply because of an unwillingness on the part of some employees to cooperate with others. Unfortunately, examples of this sort are endless. In one kitchen, a new vegetable slicer had been installed, yet when the manager went into the kitchen he discovered the vegetable woman slicing the vegetables by hand. Upon inquiry, he found that the people in the salad section would not allow her to use the slicer. In addition to the investment in the slicer, he was paying her for hours of unnecessary work during which she could have performed other duties. In another location, arguments always arose at the ice cream counter between the attendant and the waitresses. The girls brought their dishes from another part of the kitchen to have them filled at the dessert station. One girl might have four orders for ice cream and she would bring over four ice cream dishes, going on to another serving station for coffee. When she returned, only two dishes were ready for her, the attendant declaring that was all she had brought to be filled. Probably some other waitress had taken the other two. The manager stopped these arguments by moving the ice cream dishes to the dessert station.

Such examples are all too prevalent and these useless arguments can be stopped if the authorized person has enough discernment to find the cause and make the changes. Many times, if he will talk with the people in the kitchen and dining room, he will get many ideas for short cuts in both time and labor.

Often the duties of two people can be combined. This is something the person in charge of the food operation will never learn unless he remains in the kitchen during the entire meal period on frequent occasions. Department heads will not often voluntarily suggest giving up any of the people in their department for fear of being under-staffed.

In addition to this thorough knowledge of the working of the food department, the person in charge must know, in a general way, the local and state regulations regarding the sale of food and beverages and have a working knowledge of the tax laws. He should also know something about advertising and promotion. Last, but by no means least, he must know how to handle people, both employees and patrons. The majority of those who have made a success in this business can credit about 85 per cent of that success to the knack of getting other people to do what they want them to do.

Sales Volume. This is the barometer of every business and of vital importance to the management. If the sales volume is unsatisfactory, certain changes are necessary. What these changes should be depends upon a careful analysis of the operation. Usually an inadequate volume is due to one of the eight reasons given below. A possible explanation follows each one.

(1) *Prices are out of line with competition.* This may be due to careless purchasing, waste, or excessive staffing.

(2) *Menus are monotonous.* This may be the result of poor planning, or lack of imagination or just plain indifference.

(3) *Food is of poor quality.* A number of reasons may account for this situation—an incompetent or indifferent staff, purchasing of low-grade food, excessively long storage of food, and/or cooking the food in large batches and permitting it to stand for hours before serving, either in the steam table or at room temperature.

(4) *Service is faulty or slow.* This may be the result of improper supervision; lack of training of the service staff; inadequate equipment both in the kitchen and the dining room; friction between service and kitchen staff; too-great distances for the waiters to travel between kitchen and dining room, and/or poor kitchen layout. When the distance from the kitchen is great, some of the facilities for service, such as the coffee service, should be moved into the dining room. If inefficient kitchen layout slows up the service, it is advisable to have outside experts study the layout and rearrange the equipment in a way to get rid of bottlenecks and smooth the flow of work.

(5) *Conditions are unsanitary.* Lack of cleanliness is usually the result of negligence, poor training, or inadequate cleaning schedules.

(6) *The dining room is unattractive and noisy.* An unattractive room is usually colorless or dark or both. This can be easily remedied by painting the walls in more attractive colors, by gay hangings and possibly by the addition of mirrored panels. An improved lighting system will do wonders for many rooms and colorful uniforms on the service staff will please the employees as well as the guests. Sound proofing materials for the ceiling of the dining room many times proves an excellent investment. If the service staff is trained to handle china and silverware carefully, it will reduce the clatter to a minimum.

(7) *The location is poor.* An attractive street entrance will do much to overcome the disadvantages of a bad location. A modern, well-

designed store front is like an invitation promising good things inside. For the average hotel, a street entrance directly into the restaurant has proved of great sales value, as very few passers-by find their way into the hotel dining room if they must pass through the lobby.

(8) *The promotion is inadequate or, in some way, is failing to do its job.* This is such a broad and varied subject that it is treated in a separate chapter of this book.

Operating Costs and Profits. Food and payroll costs are the two principal costs of the food department. High food costs may be accounted for by a number of causes, such as: poor purchasing, waste, over-production, pilfering or, sometimes, poor judgment in menu pricing. Waste is the result of incompetence, poor menu-planning, inadequate supervision or improper training. A campaign of employee training and posted house rules may help with this problem. If house rules are posted, however, they must be enforced. Pilfering can be overcome by proper controls.

At the back-door, a responsible employee must be on guard. A timekeeper can maintain a close check of all out-going parcels, particularly if house rules require an authorized pass for every out-going package. Garbage that is being removed as well as linen being sent to the laundry, should be subjected to periodic test checks. Both of these have been used by some unscrupulous employees as a means of "covering" unauthorized removal of foodstuffs and liquor.

Tracing Operating Losses. The beverage department is usually profitable and is all too often expected to "bail out" the food department. This is particularly true in hotels, since many commercial restaurants do not have bars and must make money on their food sales or close their doors. Because so many restaurants are successful when they sell only food, there is all the more reason why the hotel's food department, if properly supervised, should be a profitable venture.

Many of the losses the hotels incur can be charged to tradition. Formal dining rooms in city hotels are sometimes very well patronized and, to "keep up with the Joneses," small hotels try to copy their big city brothers. As a result, they have a formal dining room resembling the old fashioned parlor that was opened only for funerals and weddings. It has been only within recent years that many hotels have seen the light and turned their formal dining rooms into coffee shops, put in street entrances and showed a profit in their food departments. Too many are still clinging to the old ways just to please an occasional guest.

Inter-departmental Relationships. The food and beverage operation is not a self-contained unit. Its overlapping relationships with other departments require functional coordination and cooperation. This is equally true whether in a hotel, club, hospital or industrial plant. The full potential of the operation is rarely realized unless there is the fullest cooperation of all departments and a functional coordination that will make for efficiency in every operating phase.

The accounting department is responsible for the control of the funds and pertinent records of the entire establishment. Because of this, food and beverage checkers and cashiers are directly responsible to the chief accountant and not to the manager of the food department. However, the food checkers and cashiers come into close working contact with the waiters or waitresses. This contact must be one of cooperation, and the manager of the food department should work with the chief accountant to see that petty differences are not permitted to grow to the extent where they can cost the operation money. Waiters, sometimes to satisfy a grudge against a checker, purposely jam up the traffic around the checker's stand. This prevents efficient work and costly mistakes can result. The maitre d'hotel or head waiter or hostess should keep an eye on a situation of this kind and see that such traffic difficulties are smoothed out.

As an aid to the accounting department, waiters should be instructed to obtain legible signatures on all charge checks or themselves block print the name of the patrons, asking for proper spelling. This will reduce errors in posting that often lead to uncollectible debts.

In a hotel, the food and beverage operation is in close contact with the rooms department insofar as the cleaning operations are concerned in connection with room service and banquet functions. Even though a banquet department may be assigned its own banquet housemen, close cooperation with the housekeeper is necessary so that these housemen will not be idle between banquets. Cooperation is necessary in regard to the use of service elevators. Here the man in charge of the food department must work with the superintendent of service. This situation arises particularly in the case of banquets. Sometimes, one service elevator is sufficient, but it may happen that the banquet is of such size as to tie up several of the service elevators. In this case the housekeeper should be notified so that she may post notices in all the service elevator entrances. Rooms department employees will then know which elevators are available and will not stand around waiting for elevators that do not arrive.

The superintendent of service should also be instructed to have his elevator operators in passenger elevators announce meal service when they carry a load of passengers down to the lobby, in the morning, at noon, or during the dinner hour. This can influence the volume of sales quite considerably.

The food department must also work with the chief engineer as he must be notified of the need for heat and light for banquet functions. Close cooperation here can prove a saving in power bills.

There are maintenance and repairs needed in the food and beverage department since equipment and furnishings must be kept in good condition. This involves the work of several departments—sometimes the engineering staff, often the housekeeping department in a supervisory capacity, and the upholstery and furniture repair department. A regular schedule of inspection should be worked out to see that all equipment is kept in good condition.

ORGANIZATION OF THE CATERING DEPARTMENT

Organization Charts. The plan of organization of the food and beverage operation will depend, to a great extent, upon the size of the establishment. The important consideration, regardless of size of operation, is the existence of an organization chart. When this exists only in the manager's head, he must be consulted every time a question arises and he is frequently not available. An organization chart on paper facilitates proper channeling of authority and aids in planning the schedule of working shifts. It is valuable also in delegating authority, in eliminating the danger of by-passing the head of a station, and in making adjustments when an employee of special skills leaves the establishment.

An auxiliary of the organization chart is the function chart which indicates the work of the various employees.

Division of Subordinate Supervision. The day-by-day operation of the various sections and subsections of the food and beverage department should be left to the department heads, section, and station heads. However, the person in charge of the operation must continually supervise and check the manner in which the various sections are being operated. Each of these employees must report to an immediate superior. There is no set rule as to the best way to determine just where to place that responsibility. Much depends upon the type and size of the operation.

Some food operations may function best if the supervision of the preparation staff is in the hands of an executive chef, in which case he must be the type of man who can maintain satisfactory control over this staff. Frequently such a man is not sufficiently imaginative to be a good menu planner. A food production manager is sometimes most suitable for menu planning and production control but not as well qualified as a chef to hire and supervise preparation employees. In some establishments, a food production manager will also take over many of the steward's duties and can, therefore, be considered a modified replacement for the steward. In other operations, a food production manager has direct supervision over both the chef and steward and is a virtual replacement for the catering manager except for supervision of service.

Frequently a man, if given the title of executive chef, is lost in a welter of desk work but as a working chef he might be excellent. The extent to which the organization structure should be modified to accommodate the special talents of key preparation personnel is a problem that only the one in complete charge of the food operation can solve.

Similarly, in the steward's department, purchasing and floor supervision must frequently be segregated. In larger operations, the steward's department is often more efficiently operated if the dishwashing is supervised by a head dishwasher or head dish machine operator.

Supervision of public dining room and banquet service is frequently subject to periodic changes. The principal problem is the danger of leaving a dining room in the hands of a hostess who does not have the authority to supervise service properly. In all supervisory positions, it is a cardinal principle that *authority must match responsibility*. If the hostess is responsible for dining room service, she must have the authority to enforce her orders.

Responsibility can and should be delegated and department heads should not be interfered with if they are doing their work properly. They do need firm supervision, however, to be sure everyone is kept in line. It is impossible to give this type of supervision from an office. Either the manager or a well-trained subordinate attached to the catering department, but reporting to the manager, should work at as many stations as possible to get the actual "feel" of the job. Intelligent supervision is very difficult unless the supervisor knows how long any job takes and how it should be done.

ACCOUNTING CONTROLS

Uniform System of Accounts. The basic system of accounting classification for food and beverage operations in hotels has been embodied in the book titled, "Uniform System of Accounts for Hotels." This classification was formulated by joint committees of accounting and management representatives with the idea that if all hotels used the same classification, comparisons could be made as to costs and profits. The committee decided, however, that it would be impractical to provide for any suitable allocation of overhead, on a uniform basis, to each different department —food, rooms, etc. Therefore, in this system, only direct department costs are allocated to the operation of each department and general overhead and fixed charges such as rent, advertising, light, heat, water, repairs, and such expenses, are grouped together as administrative or overhead classifications and deducted from the sum total of all departmental profits. Although the Uniform System has been successful in permitting a comparison of the expenses of all hotels that maintain their records in accordance with the classifications there laid down, and in the accumulation of statistical data, many hotel men are beginning to realize that each department should share in the overhead expenses. Some have made up supplementary statements providing for allocation of overhead expenses. As they quite logically argue, commercial restaurants which serve only food and beverages must carry the overhead expenses as part of the operating cost which gives them a true picture of their profit or loss results.

Where hotels provide such supplementary statements, it is advisable to append the method of calculating the allocation of overhead to facilitate comparisons with other hotels.

There is a definite trend toward the use of a Uniform System of Accounts for commercial restaurants as well as other types of feeding operations, particularly hospitals and clubs. The evolution to uniformity is not rapid but is gradually gaining momentum. It is hoped that uniform accounting practices in all catering fields will one day enjoy the same universal adoption as has been experienced in hotels.

Monthly Statements. The monthly statement of the food and beverage operation should show a comparison of the month's operation with the corresponding month of the previous year. It should also provide a comparison of the operation of the current fiscal year to date with that of the prior fiscal year. These figures should indicate where a further analysis is needed and where remedial steps are necessary. When any expense items show a marked increase or any sources of revenue show a decline, careful investigation into the causes should be made.

The monthly statement is the "fever chart" of an operation. Marked changes should be studied until the conditions causing them are located. Increasing expenses and dwindling revenue do not occur without reason. Sometimes they are due to a national financial upheaval, but usually the reasons are more likely to be right within the confines of the establishment itself.

If kitchen fuel, laundry, guest supplies or other expenses show marked increases, carelessness somewhere may be the direct cause. A new employee may not have been properly trained in methods of conservation.

If sales from a particular outlet show a pronounced decline, a day-by-day and meal-by-meal analysis of comparative sales may ferret out the trouble. For example, if one outlet indicates an abrupt loss of 1000 covers compared to a prior year, both months under comparison should be analyzed in terms of average sales for each day of the week to determine whether certain days are reflecting greater losses or whether the downward trend is evenly distributed over each day of the week. This breakdown should also be carried out for each meal of the day. It may be found, for example, that Friday dinner, Saturday lunch, and Sunday lunch and dinner are sagging badly. Comparison of current menus with those of last year would then be in order. Perhaps the current selections are much less appealing or the price structure may be out of line. A Sunday buffet may be advisable to bring in a new stream of family patronage. Or "loss leaders" might be advisable if patrons appear to be sharply price-conscious. Or the menu-pricing structure may be very badly balanced with too many low-priced items depressing the total volume or too many high-priced items driving patronage elsewhere. Perhaps new competition has developed during the year.

Two major types of food and beverage statements are in use at present. One reflects a combined statement of food and beverage sales, expense and profit; the other separates the two. The use of the latter entails more work for the accounting department but it provides a much better picture of the operation. Among other things, it prevents a favorable beverage business from obscuring the weaknesses of a poor food business. A form for this type of statement appears on page 14.

Control Employees. There are four categories of control employees, (1) food and beverage controllers, (2) cashiers, (3) checkers, and (4) receiving clerks. The food and beverage controllers record the purchases and issues, reconcile inventories, analyze sales, and determine cost of merchandise sold. They should also check portion sizes, make butcher tests, analyze purchases and test-check the receiving of food and bever-

STATEMENT OF INCOME, PROFIT AND LOSS

	November, 1950		
	Food	Beverages	Total
Gross Sales			
(List separately individual service outlets)	$	$	$
Total Gross Sales	$	$	$
Less: Allowances			
Total Net Sales	$	$	$
Cost of Merchandise Consumed	$	$	$
Less: Cost of Employees' Meals			
Net Cost of Sales	$	$	$
Gross Profit on Sales	$	$	$
Add: Cover Charges			
Minimum Charges			
Corkage			
Sundry Banquet Income			
Total Revenue	$	$	$
Expenses:			
Salaries and Wages	$	$	$
Payroll Taxes			
Employees' Meals			
Uniforms			
Music and Entertainment			
Laundry			
Kitchen Fuel			
Linen			
China and Glassware			
Silverware			
Utensils			
Dry Cleaning			
Contract Cleaning			
Cleaning Supplies			
Guests' Supplies			
Paper Supplies			
Menus and Wine Lists			
Printing and Stationery			
Banquet Expense			
Banquet Commissions			
Advertising			
Licenses and Permits			
Plants and Decorations			
Electricity and Lighting			
Ice and Refrigeration			
Telephone, Telegrams & Postage			
Repairs and Maintenance			
Rent			
Water			
Heat			
Insurance			
Real Estate Taxes			
Interest			
Depreciation			
Amortization of Leasehold			
Amortization of Leasehold Improvements			
Miscellaneous			
Total Expenses	$	$	$
Net Profit or (Loss)	$	$	$

ages. The food controller is in a key position to render valuable assistance informulating menu policies. The chapter on the Pre-Cost Pre-Control Procedures will make this more apparent.

When a food controller does not fulfill all these duties it may very well be that he is bogged down with excessive detail, sometimes not too vital. He may be putting into his daily food report too many calculations that are not of first importance. A streamlined report might give him time for far more valuable work such as that mentioned above. The chapter on Food Control indicates how reports can be kept to a serviceable minimum.

Cashiers are responsible for collecting cash or charging restaurant patrons for all restaurant checks. In some bar operations, the bartenders make their own change and ring up the beverage sales on the cash registers. Unless the bar operation is very small, this practice should be discouraged. It places a tempting opportunity for tampering in the hands of the bartender. Where feasible, it is wiser to combine the position of beverage checker and cashier.

Checking beverage service at a stand-up bar presents the same type of problem as checking food in a coffee shop. Unless the beverage checker is stationed at a location that is near the bartender's working area, each bartender will have to cover considerable distance in bringing every drink order to the checker's station. In a busy bar, this creates cross-traffic and slows down the service.

Checking food in a kitchen requires that the flow of service from range to patron be directed to the outlet controlled by a checker. Any access to service elevators for room service and banquet service without direct control by a checker can become an open invitation to pilfering. Fire laws in some communities require easy access to a fire door. If this is not guarded in any way, it allows dishonest employees to by-pass the checker and, in some instances, the watchman at the employees' entrance. The fire door should have some type of seal which is easily broken but with an alarm attachment. This will prevent the illegal passage of food through this door.

The duties and responsibilities of the receiving clerk are fully covered in the chapter dealing with the receiving of food and beverages.

SUPPLEMENTARY REPORTS

Daily Food and Beverage Cost Reports. When daily food and beverage cost reports can be completed by noon of the following day, there is ample time to take necessary steps to remedy errors. Because issues from the store room must be allocated—to the bar, dining room, or banquet department—these daily reports cannot be an exact indication of a day's costs but they do indicate trends and tendencies that merit attention.

The cumulative figures in the month-to-date column on the daily food cost report become quite an accurate guide after the third or fourth day of each month. If the first of the month occurs on a week end, part of the food that is used on the first or second day of the month is likely to be requisitioned on the last day of the prior month. This will tend to understate the actual consumption for the first day or two of the new month but as the month progresses, this understatement of consumption will have a less direct bearing on the absolute accuracy of the food cost percentage.

Daily Payroll Report. A daily payroll report is also a valuable instrument of management control. This should record payroll costs in terms of man-days or man-hours of work rather than in dollars and cents. Comparisons with other periods are more easily related in terms of hours or days, since wage rates vary from year to year and even from month to month.

This report has a profound psychological effect on department heads when they are obliged to submit a summary of the number of regular and extra employees required by their departments. It serves as a check on over-staffing and chronic absenteeism. It also permits close study of fluctuations in payroll in relation to volume of business. The need for changing employees' days off to correspond to changes in volume becomes more apparent with a daily payroll report. The development and uses of a daily payroll report is further explained in the chapter dealing with payroll control.

Portion Analysis. Every manager of a food service operation should have at his disposal a complete set of records indicating how many portions of each entree were sold and the cost of each, day by day. The cashier or checker can maintain a tabulation of the number of portions of each item sold or a transcription may be made from the patrons' checks in the food controller's office. A recapitulation of the number of portions sold and the cost of each, is easy reference material and is invaluable in ironing out menu weaknesses. The relative selling strength of high-cost and low-cost items will be revealed at a glance. For further details, see the chapter on Pre-Cost Pre-Control Procedures.

Without this report, no one can know for certain how many portions of each entree are being sold and over-production is more difficult to control. A simple symbol on the menu should indicate which items are ready for serving and which ones are prepared to order. When congestion exists near the range, a change in the number of items that are prepared to order may help resolve kitchen bottlenecks. Many patrons do not know which items require waiting. If menus indicate this fact, the flow of service may be speeded up.

Special Studies. Whenever cost or profit figures show a marked change, a special study of the facts behind the changing figures is warranted. It is seldom that the person in charge of the food department can ferret out the reasons for these changes himself; he will need the help of the accounting department. Before asking for this, however, he and the chief accountant should determine by personal consultation which problems are most important and merit a special study. Many times one problem hinges on another and the chief accountant may be able to put his finger on the one that is the key to the situation. This will save the accounting department many hours of work. Most chief accountants are eager to present necessary figures to help correct any flaw in the operation. If they know exactly what the management is looking for or what the problem is, they are in a much better position to give competent assistance.

Undistributed Expenses. Returning to the subject of the Uniform System of Accounts, since this system at present does not provide for inclusion of a portion of the overhead expense in the food and beverage statement, many managers make the mistake of treating these expenses as though they were non-existent. In hotels, the principal sources of revenue are the rooms and the food and beverage departments. It is quite obvious that all overhead expenses are incurred primarily by these departments. While the income ratios among these departments will vary considerably as will any formula for allocation, every effort should be made to arrive at a satisfactory formula. These expenses are very real and should be taken into account by every manager.

Advertising and promotion budgets should be studied closely even though they are not charged directly to the hotel catering operation. Payroll taxes and employee relations expense constitute another overhead expense that is a real part of the payroll cost. These costs should also be kept in mind when evaluations are made of the direct payroll costs on the departmental statement.

Heat. light, power, and water are other undistributed expenses in hotels. These can be greatly reduced by an alert staff. Here are a few of the common ways in which these expenses are unnecessarily increased:

(1) Failure to report the need for minor repairs, such as leaking faucets;
(2) The habit of pot washers and vegetable cleaners of letting the water run continuously;
(3) Failure to check on waste in public and employee washrooms;
(4) Failure of dish machine operators to close tank drain valves and tank water supply valves;
(5) Failure to reclaim water used in air conditioning systems;
(6) Electric lights left burning unnecessarily in banquet rooms, dining rooms, and kitchen;
(7) Failure to turn off power equipment when it is not in use;
(8) Failure to close doors to refrigerators, plate warmers and steamers;
(9) Improper care of equipment.

STATISTICAL REFERENCES

The statistical references generally appended to the monthly financial statement constitute a sort of barometer of the operation. However, there is the danger of placing too much reliance on these references because the month or the season may be exceptional for any number of reasons.

Cost of Food and Beverages. The food cost percentage is a valuable guide. If it is too high, this condition is certainly caused by defects in operation—unwise purchasing, waste of materials, spoilage because of over-long or careless storage, pilfering, or over-production. If the food cost is too low, it may mean that the quality of the food is poor. Poor food will usually drive away a large percentage of the customers. A low food cost may look well on paper, but if the dining room is half empty and the staff of employees working at only a fraction of a reasonable potential, a too-low food cost loses its attraction.

Similarly, a low beverage cost is not always an indication of a successful operation. Some bars serve a two-ounce drink at the same price as another bar that serves an ounce-and-one-half. The two-ounce drink sometimes attracts so much additional business that the profit in terms of dollars will be greater even though the percentage of profit will be smaller.

Covers Served. In hotels, the number of covers served in the restaurant should be studied in relation to two important factors—the house count (i.e. number of guests in the hotel) and the capacity of the dining room.

In a commercial restaurant, the latter only is important. The house count may be high but very few of the guests are eating in the hotel, or the dining room may be used only to about 50 per cent of its capacity. In either case, revisions should be made in the merchandising policy. Better internal merchandising will bring more of the hotel guests into the dining room; better local advertising will bring people in from the outside. The menus may be at fault. These should be studied and a portion analysis instituted. A field study of nearby competitors should be made. These problems are treated in the chapter on business promotion.

Payroll. Most financial statements contain a percentage figure that indicates the ratio of departmental payroll to the volume of sales. This statistical reference should indicate at a glance what percentage of each revenue dollar is expended for payroll. However, a high payroll percentage does not always mean that the staff should or can be cut. It may be at a minimum but the volume of business may be so low that the staff is turning out only a fraction of its potential.

The schedule of salaries and wages in the monthly financial statement generally indicates how many persons were employed in various classifications. In the average payroll report, the breakdown of classifications is not complete enough to indicate weak spots in the payroll structure. Every separate job title should be listed as well as the number of employees in that classification. A general listing of the number of employees in the steward's section, for example, is not sufficient. The breakdown into dishwashers, cleaners, yardmen, icemen, and other classifications should be made. This type of job classification with a daily payroll report, will prevent any disparity between accounting department records and those of the department heads. Frequently, when an employee is transferred from one job to another by the department head, notification of that change is not sent to the accounting department. Such discrepancies can be misleading to the manager who is trying to keep a close control over payroll costs.

An analysis of the number of employees in each section of the food department—receiving, storage, preparation, and service—required to handle 100 covers a day can be extremely helpful in spotting payroll weaknesses.

Profit. A food and beverage operation that shows an overall profit is not necessarily beyond improvement. Food expenses and profit or loss should be separated from beverage expenses and profit. Certain arbitrary allocations should be carefully indicated. By means of this separation between food and beverages, the profit gained by the latter will not be covering up a loss in the food department.

In hotels, appended to the financial statement, there should be a memorandum indicating what the profit or loss figures would be if a reasonable portion of the undistributed overhead expenses mentioned previously were allocated to the food and beverage operation.

Hidden expenses resulting from deficiencies in operation should not be confused with undistributed expenses. The former cannot always be segregated or calculated. These are the result of many of the factors that bring about high food costs—unwise purchasing, faulty receiving, improper storing, pilfering, spoilage, waste of materials, faulty sanitation, poor menu planning, inadequate control and/or over-production—all of which defy measuring. They affect the profit figures and can only be controlled by close study of every job and function on the part of the management.

CHECK LISTS

It is practically impossible for any manager to remember when each phase of the food and beverage operation was last inspected. Since it is not advisable to have inspection follow a fixed pattern on the calendar, a check list is the only satisfactory means of making sure that every part of the catering operation is inspected within a given time.

Special Inspection. Food operations do not usually go bad over night. They deteriorate gradually. One day is not noticeably worse than the previous day. For that reason, changes for the worse are hard to detect by anyone close to an operation. A check list that indicates the dates of previous inspections and the faults found at that time will help prevent this slow degeneration. The principal checks, discussed at greater length in other chapters are:

- Surprise Receiving Tests
- Storeroom Inspection
- Wine Cellar Inspection
- Sanitation Check List
- Internal Promotion Displays
- Market Research
- Public Dining Room Inspection
- Banquet Service Inspection
- Beverage Service Inspection
- Refrigeration Inspection
- Between-Meal Steam Table Inspection

The foregoing represents a basic minimum. Many other inspections can be added. When such check lists are properly dated, they will do much to reduce hidden costs and increase general efficiency. In many of the large operations, these check-ups will have to be made by various supervisors. In these cases, the persons making the check-up should initial the chart and indicate the date. Generally an employee with the status of supervisor will not initial a chart until he has made the necessary inspection. These charts then form a ready reference on what inspections have been made and the ones that still remain to be made.

Periodic Reviews. Every part of a catering operation, whether large or small, should be subject to periodic review and analysis. Notes, comments, new regulations, new experiments, and changes in methods should be set down in a record book. Having an available history of conferences, suggestions, actions to be taken, and comments on past changes can aid in any further changes that may be deemed necessary. It is also valuable in the event of any change in key personnel. Unfortunately, key personnel have a habit of keeping many things connected with their work in their heads with no record or job analysis to aid their successors. This means that a new man, unfamiliar with the work of the people under him, will have to take time to familiarize himself with his department and staff. This could mean a bad break in the continuity of the work and it may be reflected in the quality of the food and service.

LEGAL CONSIDERATIONS

There are certain legal requirements to be met by a food and beverage department. Although a manager cannot be expected to concern himself with all of the legal fine points, he should have a working knowledge of the main features, at least to the extent of knowing when legal advice from qualified counsel is needed.

Licenses and Permits. Various licenses and permits are required in different states regarding the sale of beer, liquors, wines and food. Some states have established sanitation laws that are required to be posted on the premises. The manager of a food and beverage establishment should be familiar with these requirements, particularly if he contemplates changing the mode of operation.

Local Regulations. There are a number of local regulations regarding the sale of alcoholic beverages. Their infraction can result in heavy fines. The sale of beverages to minors can bring about a most embarrassing and expensive situation. Pleading that he does not know the law will not help the operator at such a time, so it behooves him to acquaint himself with his responsibility in such instances.

General Laws. There are many general laws with which a manager should be familiar. These pertain to hours of labor, employment of females, protective requirements, washroom facilities, public safety, minimum wages, workmen's compensation insurance requirements, food handling, and health inspection.

ACCIDENT PREVENTION

Accident prevention deserves serious consideration in the modern restaurant. It requires continual study of improved equipment and safety programs. In addition to the human suffering accidents cause, the restaurant is penalized through increased compensation insurance costs, loss of a possible key employee and, if the accident is serious, a very bad break-down psychologically, among the employees. Industry generally has put into effect some very excellent safety programs and every manager should study these and choose one that best fits his own situation or modify one until it does. A good safety program is no longer work left to the reformer—it is just good business sense.

Many restaurants have found it advisable to select one responsible employee and place him in charge of the safety program. It would be his business to make certain that all employees are properly instructed on what to do in the event of fire. All new employees should receive these instructions as part of their early training and the date they received this instruction should be recorded on their personal history cards.

Employee Hazards. One of the major causes of accidents in both the kitchen and dining room of a restaurant is slippery floors. This is easy to understand in a busy operation where a certain amount of spillage is inevitable and difficult to control. House rules requiring prompt action when liquids or food are spilled on the floor must be enforced, but whoever wields the mop or broom must be careful not to collide with other employees and cause further trouble.

Most kitchen floors are extremely hazardous when wet. They require a daily mopping and this should be done at night after the kitchen is closed. Otherwise, there will not be sufficient time for the floor to dry before the kitchen is opened for breakfast service, especially if ventilation is poor. There are on the market now a number of excellent flooring materials for kitchens. Among these are slate and quarry tile. These are more impervious than other types of kitchen flooring to normal kitchen stains such as grease, soap, and water. No floor is proof against slips and falls unless it is dry and clean. In areas around sinks or dish machines or ranges where the slip hazard is greatest due to spilled water or grease, wooden grills should be used during working hours. Waxes should never be used on kitchen floors.

Employee training and inspection of equipment will do much to reduce the number of burns received by kitchen employees. For small burns usually the administering of first aid by a qualified person will suffice. If the burns are serious, a physician should be summoned at once.

All cuts, however slight, should receive first aid treatment to prevent infection. Knife cuts are often caused because the operator's hand slips from the handle to the sharp blade. This can be prevented if every knife is equipped with a guard. There are several types of these guards on the market, inexpensive and easily applied. Knives should be purchased carefully and those with round, smooth handles avoided. Handles that are corrugated are much less likely to slip and cut the hand.

When not in use, the knives must be kept in a carefully constructed guard and never be permitted to lie about, even for a short time. Nothing should be cut that requires extreme pressure, such as frozen meats. They should be at least partially thawed before cutting.

Butchers or other workers using sharp knives should have plenty of room in which to work and should not be in the traffic lane of hand trucks or personnel with trays. Knives with exposed cutting surfaces should never be carried from place to place. A sheath of leather, wood, aluminum, or plastic should be placed on a knife unless it can be replaced immediately in a permanent guard.

When knives are sharpened, a wire mesh glove and leather wrist protector should be worn on the hand which holds the sharpener. An artery can be severed or partial paralysis result from a cut caused by the slip of a knife. An abdominal apron guard should be worn during boning operations.

The immediate removal of broken glass is necessary but it should never be picked up with the bare hands. Gloves should be worn if the glass must be handled but a broom or dust pan is the best method of removing it from the floor. It should be placed in a box or can, used only for this purpose, never in a basket with other refuse.

Employees handling refuse containers should be obliged to wear gloves and wrist guards. Open tins or broken bottles can cause badly infected wounds. If the containers cannot be picked up and emptied all at one time, then the contents should be removed with a scoop shovel.

Structural Defects. It is the duty of the safety director to study the kitchen layout for structural defects that may cause accidents. Following are a few of the danger points to watch:

(1) The main traffic aisles in the kitchen should be free of permanent stations. The ranges, fry kettles, salad section, etc., should face away from the main traffic aisles.

(2) Other aisles should be wide enough to permit the workers to stand comfortably at their stations and with ample room to pass each other when that is necessary.

(3) When ovens are below the range tops, there should be ample room for stooping to get the roasts or other cooked foods out of the ovens.

(4) The large bake ovens with their long pans should be set in an area large enough to permit the baker to swing around and place the cakes or pies on a table or on cooling racks behind him.

(5) The area which is taken up by a door opening inward should be painted a distinct color as a warning not to loiter within that area.

(6) Sharp corners should be rounded or padded.

(7) Stairs should be inspected frequently. Metal strips on the steps wear smooth and become slippery or they may break and cause a tripping hazard. Stairs must be well lighted.

(8) The kitchen and all working areas should be well lighted. A light kitchen is a clean kitchen. Refuse seldom collects in brightly lighted corners.

(9) Poor ventilation increases fatigue and workers that are not alert are much more prone to have accidents.

(10) The line which trucks must follow should be carefully plotted to avoid collision with workers.

In spite of all kinds of safety devices, carelessness still takes its toll in the kitchen. Clear instructions should be given about the necessity of turning off the power on all power-driven equipment such as beaters, slicers, and grinders when any kind of an adjustment is made. Knives, forks, ladles or any elongated objects should never be used to push food into power-driven food grinders. Only cylindrically-shaped objects, such as wooden mallets, should be used for this purpose. High heels should not be permitted in the kitchen and haste through busy traffic aisles should be prohibited. Overloading of trays is another major cause of accidents. Many times, if trays are properly stacked, they will hold more than those that appear to be over-loaded. Waiters, waitresses, and bus help should be well trained in how trays should be stacked.

Dollies and handtrucks should be in sufficient supply and used for transporting heavy objects. This avoids the injury caused by carrying heavy loads and also the danger of collision because the worker's vision is obscured. Workers using these trucks should not walk backwards but always face in the direction in which the truck is moving. When not in use, trucks should be stacked out of the way.

Public Safety. The safety of the patrons in a restaurant is the responsibility of the management even though they may be careless and give way in panic easily in times of danger. All fire regulations regarding drapery and hangings should be strictly observed. The layout of the tables should be such as to give easy access to an exit. All waiters, waitresses, captains, and bus help should be trained to be on the alert for neglected cigarettes. Suitable facilities should be available for hanging coats and hats in a place out of the line of traffic so they will not be an obstruction in case a hasty exit is necessary. Exit signs should be conspicuously posted and emergency doors tested periodically.

All service people should be trained in the proper way of handling trays, particularly those containing hot fluids, to avoid spilling on the patrons.

Chairs and tables should be tested periodically. Those used for banquets require careful tests as they are set up for temporary use and are often handled very roughly.

Alcohol lamps or canned heat appliances should be handled only by qualified employees and should be kept away from doors, windows, fans, or other equipment that may create a draft.

Chipped, cracked or broken tableware should be discarded. This should be the regular job of the safety inspector. Otherwise, chipped china and glassware will return to the dining room again and again.

Stairways should be inspected regularly as well as carpets or rugs which may have worn places that become tripping hazards.

EMPLOYEE RELATIONS

Poor work is not always caused by lack of training or knowledge on the part of employees. It is frequently traced to disgruntlement with the job, the management or fellow employees. A high turnover of labor is an indication of poor employee relations as well as one cause of decreased profits. Each new employee's breaking-in period is a hidden expense. It takes time for each one, regardless of his experience, to learn the ways and the policies of a new establishment. This means his productivity for a time is low. The most efficient staffs, as a rule, are those with low turnover records.

Discord. There are three main sources of discord that an employee is likely to encounter, (1) his contact with his immediate superior, (2) his contact with other employees in his own department, and (3) with the employees in other departments. Where the rate of turnover is much higher in one department than another, it may be the fault of that department head unless difficult working conditions are at fault. A restaurant with the kitchen on a floor above or below the dining room and only a steep flight of stairs connecting the two might have great difficulty keeping its waiters.

Where discord exists within a department, the answer may be found in a meeting of the entire personnel of that department. At such a meeting it may be possible to find out what is wrong and why. Once the issues have been aired, the department head can probably determine for himself the justice of the complaints and work out a solution. Usually trouble occurs because of shirking or an unfair division of work. If a department head works closely with his people he can usually tell where the trouble lies and what should be done about it.

If the difficulty is personal in nature, it may not be so easy to correct. It frequently happens that two good workers have antagonistic personalities and cannot adjust to each other. In this case, it might be worth while to move one of them to another station if this can be done. However, people can usually be made to see that their personal feelings cannot be allowed to interfere with their work.

With regard to discord or friction between employees in different departments, it may be necessary for the department heads involved to work out some solution jointly. Frequently this trouble is not the fault of any individual but the fault of one station that is over-burdened. Often there is trouble between the waitresses and kitchen employees—perhaps the steam table attendants. The waitresses may not be getting their orders through fast enough. Perhaps there is too much work for the number of people at the steam table. That is something for the manager or the department heads to figure out.

The point is that discord between employees should not be shrugged off as something that is bound to happen and about which nothing can be done. Usually there is a reason for it and, whether the reason is justified or not, if it is brought out into the light and examined, the result may be a happy solution for everyone.

Grievances. Unresolved grievances can be the cause of great dissatisfaction on the part of employees, resulting in poor work, careless handling of equipment, waste of materials and accidents. Every employee who feels he has a grievance should be permitted to present his case and feel that he will get a fair hearing and just treatment. Some very large establishments have "grievance committees," the members of which are elected by ballot by the entire staff. In smaller places, the department head or the manager should be able to handle such matters and welcome the opportunity to straighten out any real or imaginary grievance. One that is disregarded can do incalculable harm.

Recognition. Appropriate recognition of a job well done is vital to good employer-employee relations. Department heads should be instructed to commend employees whose work performance lives up to their expectation or surpasses it. It is helpful too if some public notice is given to an outstanding employee. This may be in the form of a suitable notice in the house publication, at a staff meeting where the employee is commended, or even a notice on the bulletin board. Such attention and recognition pleases employees out of all proportion to the effort involved. Anyone who has any doubts about this should try it. A house bulletin of some kind, if it is only one or two mimeographed sheets, is an excellent good-will builder among employees.

Exit Interviews. Every employee, upon leaving an establishment permanently, should be called in for an exit interview. Frankness can usually be depended upon at this time and the information obtained, if catalogued, can be of help in later similar problems that arise. There is always a reason why an employee leaves. If that reason concerns his work or his fellow employees or his department head—whether his reason is justified or not—it is a serious omission if the manager neglects to learn the entire story from the employee. Exit interviews often reveal serious flaws in the work structure of an establishment that might not be learned in any other way.

Chapter III: PRINCIPLES OF MENU-MAKING *

A MENU SHOULD BE MORE than merely a listing of dishes that the chef prepares with the hope that some of them will appeal to the palates of the customers. Although many chefs are capable of writing excellent menus, it is impossible for one man, regardless of his experience and capabilities, to give proper supervision to the operation of the kitchen and, at the same time, do the analytical work, study, and research necessary to do a complete job of menu construction. Without such analyses, he is in no position to know what the customers want.

In a department store, the men and women who select the merchandise to be sold have sales analysis staffs that are busy studying sales charts, sales reports and research material. Only after a careful study of the available sales data, is a decision made on what should be offered to the public and how much of certain kinds of merchandise should be provided for resale. In restaurants and hotels, this very important work is usually left entirely to the chef with occasional suggestions from the management.

If the chef is to do this work, management should furnish him with the necessary sales information so that menus will reflect the eating habits and desires of the patrons. Menu-making cannot be reduced to a sure-fire formula that will work day in and day out. Tastes of customers vary from day to day and from season to season. A large transient trade imposes certain problems while a repeat trade will raise other difficulties. In the latter case, no customer should be taken for granted. Even though he may return six or seven times, there is no positive assurance that he will continue this practice unless he is continually sold and resold on the food that the menu offers.

* The subject of menus has been divided into three parts, (1) the principles, (2) the merchandising, and (3) the actual menu suggestions. However, these subjects frequently overlap and a reading of all three chapters as a unit is suggested to clarify the inter-relationship of various menu problems.

The principles and procedures described in this and the next two chapters represent the composite result of many studies, and their application under actual operating conditions. Menu-making should be *business-making* in any well managed food establishment.

SALES ANALYSIS

A practical method of accumulating sales data is to have the food checker or cashier keep score on a copy of the menu, of the sales of entree items. A record should be kept of these menus showing the sales experience of each entree item for each day of the week on which it appears on the menu.

Menu studies have shown that 75 per cent of all entree sales on luncheon and dinner menus are concentrated on not over seven items. In spite of this, menus are continually offered having as many as 14 to 18 entrees, with resultant waste from over-production, shrinkage from storage, and the expense of a large staff necessary for the preparation.

The menu should fulfill for a food service establishment much the same function that show windows do for a department store. They must encourage the customer to take notice of the merchandise offered for sale and channel the customer's desire to buy in certain well-planned directions. A high-class store selling women's wear will, in January and February, show clothes for Southern wear because they have learned, through analyzing sales, that a large number of their customers want that type of merchandise at that time. In the spring, a department store will feature all manner of gadgets for clothes closets—shelf paper, fancy boxes, moth proof bags. The management knows that during the season for house cleaning such suggestions will induce people to buy. A hardware store in a small community will display a window full of gardening tools and paint supplies during this same season. Similarly, a restaurant should use its menu as its "show window" and give to its customers the items they want at a time when they are most likely to buy them. The best way to obtain this information is through an analysis of the daily sales.

Sales analysis may also be furthered by keeping abreast of competition. Every restaurant man should know what his competition is doing. If there are not several places of the same grade of service in his own community, it takes very little effort to get menus from out-of-town establishments. He can ask his friends who travel to bring him menus from the places they patronize when they are away from home. He should read his trade papers. They are full of ideas on menu planning. A comparison of menus will suggest new ideas. The chef should be encouraged to visit competitive eating places. The analysis of a successful competitor's menu is very important.

A menu is necessarily influenced by available facilities. Under facilities belong dining room furnishings and decor, whether waiters or waitresses are used for service, the amount and kind of kitchen equipment available, the number of kitchen employees, and the extent of their experience. A tea room could not serve the same type of meal as could be served in the dining room of a large metropolitan hotel. The kitchen of a coffee shop, planned only for that type of service, could not turn out an elaborate meal nor would its employees, trained for coffee shop service, be able to handle such a meal.

PRIMARY PRINCIPLES OF MENU WRITING

Having decided the average type of clientele and the available facilities, there are eight major considerations which the menu writer should have in mind when he actually sits down to do the work. These are, (1) the refrigerator, (2) the market, (3) the calendar, (4) the clock, (5) the neighborhood or clientele, (6) the kitchen, (7) the appearance, and (8) the price.

The Refrigerator. The contents of the refrigerators should be the first consideration of the menu writer because they are fundamentally a place of temporary storage, not a low temperature storeroom. *Stock must move,* even in the storeroom. That is one hard and fast rule. It is no coincidence that successful restaurants carry a relatively small stock that is turned over quickly. It was planned that way.

While an inventory of left-overs is helpful and necessary for the menu writer, a personal inspection of the contents of the refrigerators is also advisable. Careless checking before writing the menu results in three bad conditions:

(1) Direct loss of money through spoilage;

(2) Inferior taste because of over-long storage;

(3) Ultimate over-loading of the menu with left-over items.

The left-overs, if worked off every day, will lower food costs without lessening the sales appeal of the menu. Daily work-offs lighten the job of menu making. A good menu from the patrons' standpoint, and an economical menu from the restaurant's standpoint, is not possible unless the refrigerator is checked before menu-making is undertaken.

The Market. The menu writer must know what is available in the local market or at least within range of easy transportation and the probable prices of these items. Air express has widened the horizon for deliveries considerably, but air express is dependent on weather and substitutes for foods shipped in by air should always be on hand. To avoid complications in deliveries, it is a basic rule to use as much of the seasonal and locally grown foods as possible. Their condition is usually better and they are less expensive. Easy availability is a basic consideration of menu-writing. It is asking for trouble, when writing Friday's menu on Wednesday, to put down salmon steaks unless it has been ascertained where the steaks are coming from and that they will be on hand. Many circumstances may make food unobtainable—storms in winter, floods in spring or a truckers' strike any time of the year.

Several good restaurant operators advocate the blocked out menu where each day's main items are listed for a week in advance—appetizers, soups, entrees, salads and desserts—with sufficient space left blank to fill in with dishes that are to be made up from left-overs. This blocked-out menu is merely a guide that may be changed as the need arises but there is no doubt that it is of great assistance to the food purchaser because it enables him to watch the market for favorable "buys."

This advance information is also necessary in planning a banquet menu. Here, especially, the amount of food needed must be figured carefully in order to maintain a proper margin of profit. A few wasted portions can soon eat up the profit. To be sure, the chef may contrive to use up the left-overs but there is a vast difference between the selling price of breast of chicken for a banquet and chicken cutlets on the next day's menu. An empty refrigerator after a banquet spells success to a prudent operator.

The Calendar. Recently, when someone asked a chef what was a good item to order from the menu he said he did not know because he "never ate anything from the menu—that's for the customers." That is a basic weakness of many menus when "meat-potatoes-and-pie" chefs write menus and follow the line of least resistance. Some menus offer heavy soups, stews, roasts and rich desserts the year around with no deviation for the summer months when appetites need a bit of coaxing with cool drinks, crisp salads, and light desserts. Any tendency toward a static, unchanging menu throughout the year can prove disastrous and result in considerable loss of patronage, over-production, and waste. Furthermore, there are great profit possibilities in fruits, vegetables, and salad entrees for summer. Sandwich plates, cold cuts, and jellied soups are popular and have a low food cost. Special attention should be given to blue plates, chef's specials, and daily specials for late spring and summer consumption since the majority of people tend to eat lighter meals during the summer.

When daylight-saving time is in effect, many persons go from their places of business to some form of outdoor recreation. A centrally located food outlet featuring special dinner snacks might easily attract early dinner trade shortly after five o'clock. Fruit plates, arranged with an eye to harmony in color, can feature in-season fruits and hold trade that might otherwise go to a competitive place that is known for serving light lunches.

Holidays afford an excellent opportunity for specialities. It is advisable to recognize holidays and special occasions in some form in preparing the menu, if for no other reason than the favorable community comment it creates.

St. Valentine's Day, Washington's Birthday, St. Patrick's Day, Easter, Fourth of July, Hallowe'en, Election Day, Thanksgiving, and Christmas are observed on a national scale and provide an interesting challenge for the menu-writer. In addition, there are other days of special regional interest. Following are a few suggestions for holidays. There are scores of others which an imaginative menu-writer can create.

St. Valentine's Day—Subject: Hearts. Color: Red. Suggestions: Red aspic salads molded in the shape of hearts; heart-shaped cookies or mints; honey buns; white cake with pink icing.

Washington's Birthday—Subject: Cherries. Suggestions: Cherry fruit cocktail; cherry pie; cherry sauce and cherry garnishes.

St. Patrick's Day—Subject: Shamrocks and Ireland. Color: Green. Suggestions: Green aspic salad molded in the shape of shamrocks; Irish stew; pistachio ice cream; cakes with green icing.

Easter—Subject: Springtime and Eggs. Suggestions: Egg specialties; spring lamb; brightly colored eggs as a table decoration.

Fourth of July—Subject: American Flag. Colors: Red, White and Blue. Suggestions: Ideas honoring the original thirteen states, perhaps featuring on the menu items for which they are noted: Massachusetts cranberries, New Hampshire apples, Rhode Island capon, Connecticut berries, New York grapes, New Jersey tomatoes, Pennsylvania cabbage, Delaware crabmeat, Maryland melon, Virginia ham, North Carolina beans, South Carolina yams, and Georgia peaches. Salads or desserts might be served with small flags on a toothpick standing up in the center.

Election Day—In those years when national elections are taking place and the entire nation is going to the polls, in addition to featuring on the menu items from only the thirteen states, many other items might be added such as Oregon turkeys, California grapes, Maine lobster, Texas grapefruit, Wisconsin cheese, New Mexico carrots, Michigan cherries, Idaho potatoes, Iowa corn, Florida oranges, Utah celery, Louisiana shrimp,

Colorado lake trout and many others to emphasize the far-flung products of our country. The point is to feature the state name on the menu. A salad on such a day might be called "Congressional Salad" or "Presidential Salad" with an explanation of what it contained.

Admission Day, which is celebrated in many states, can be used as a time to feature products of the home state, giving the name of the particular county or locality of origin within the state.

Thanksgiving and Christmas have their well-established culinary traditions.

The Clock. The time of the day should have great bearing upon the selections of the menu-maker. Breakfasts are taken very much for granted and tend to become standardized. Very few establishments make any provision at all for the late riser. Many patrons who arrive in the dining room after eleven o'clock have difficulty in finding anything available resembling breakfast foods.

It is not possible for restaurants to serve breakfast in complete conflict with luncheon, but one dish at least should be included in the luncheon menu for the late riser or the light eater. In some establishments it may be possible to arrange the cooking equipment so that the preparation of egg dishes and griddle cakes will not interfere with the luncheon preparation or service.

Luncheon listings should not contain the same number of heavy dishes as the dinner menu. Because patrons usually have much less time for lunch, menus should be written to provide quick turnover. That means minimizing made-to-order items for luncheon. It should be possible, in a busy restaurant, to serve three turnovers of patrons during luncheon if they can have a complete luncheon within 40 minutes.

Where dinner is the basic meal for an establishment, it automatically receives the greatest attention. However, if there is a major sporting event or some other reason that makes speed of service important, dishes that are quickly and easily served should be provided and labeled as such for the benefit of patrons who may be in a hurry.

Supper menus may easily go awry. The most judicious analysis of sales should be made to determine the actual number of prepared dishes that are sold in comparison to snacks. If the sale of dishes requiring expensive staffing is low, it may be wise to limit supper items to snacks only, with short orders added for week-end evenings when trade is more brisk.

The Neighborhood. It is a fairly safe assumption that over 90 per cent of the luncheon customers will come from no more than five minutes' walking distance. There are exceptions but being in the minority, they may be disregarded. Therefore, to know the potential customers means to be acquainted with all the sources in the neighborhood where they might originate. If the restaurant is located amid large office buildings, that means the patrons will be business executives and office workers. Good food, a dignified atmosphere, and top-notch service are the magnets for the executives. Office workers generally want good value and speedy service. A formal dining room and coffee shop, if the volume of business warrants it, might be the solution in this location.

If the restaurant is located in a shopping center, the clientele will be made up of women shoppers and possibly some business executives. The women will probably prefer tea room or coffee shop service with moderate prices and a general atmosphere of daintiness in the decorations and selection of dishes.

A restaurant located near a railway station or a bus terminal is likely to have patrons who have limited time and perhaps limited budgets at their disposal. A clearly visible and easily accessible coffee shop may prove most satisfactory to them.

If a restaurant is in or near a residential neighborhood, where the residents make a general practice of eating their meals at home, there may be relatively little business for the restaurant except on Sundays. Sunday buffet and a few invitation meals "on the house" to several key people may help develop greater week-day business. The average rent paid in the neighborhood will provide a clue to the spending habits of the residents.

If the neighborhood is made up of couples and both husband and wife go to business, dinner business might be very good. An actual count of customers emerging from the nearest grocery store or market during the hours from four to six in the afternoon is revealing evidence of the type of people in the neighborhood. If there is a large number of baby carriages in the vicinity, proper provision for qualified personnel to supervise the small tots from noon until two o'clock may attract the mothers in for lunch. It is baby-sitting on a group scale but it might be the means of building up a very desirable clientele.

In a theater district, snacks served in an attractive atmosphere may bring in patrons during otherwise dull hours. This is particularly true of moving picture theaters. Patrons may be attracted if the exact time when features are scheduled to be shown is publicized on the menus. Theater owners will be glad to cooperate in this idea since it will ease their seating problem in the theater, with fewer patrons arriving in the middle of a picture.

In addition to the general character of the neighborhood, the specific characteristics of the customers should be considered. First, an effort should be made toward determining in what income group the majority belong. This will decide what grade of food will be purchased, the type of preparation, and the menu pricing. Next is an analysis of the average age of the customers. Are they young boys and girls or are they business men and women? The menu in a restaurant catering to college students would be quite different from one in a metropolitan city catering to adults. Third is the sex of the majority of the patrons. Are they largely men? In this case, even for lunch, the menu should carry heavier entrees than would be the case in a restaurant catering largely to women. In the latter case, salads, sandwiches, soufflés and light entrees should be conspicuous. The occupation of the patrons is the fourth consideration and has a decided influence on the menu. Men who do physical labor require very different food from sedentary workers.

The astute operator is ever alert to customers' inclinations as expressed in their complaints and rejects. The customer who takes the pains to complain is, with the exception of the habitual fault-finders, a constructive critic. Careful recording and analysis of their comments will lead to the systematic removal of menu deficiencies.

Any selection that is merely nibbled at by a patron can be considered a rejection, unless a specific comment to the contrary is forthcoming. Inquiry by the service staff should be a fixed policy in such instances. It is always best to know why a particular dish disappointed a patron and to make amends, if possible.

The Kitchen. A menu-writer may observe diligently all of the foregoing points—the refrigerators, the market, the calendar, the clock, and the neighborhood—but fail miserably because he has not taken into account the preparation staff. A great deal of stress has been laid on food cost and certainly it is of primary importance. But of what benefit is a low food cost if the payroll cost runs away with the profits?

In setting up menus, it is important to distribute the work loads in proportion to the capacities of the preparation staff. Therefore, a thorough knowledge of the size and experience of the staff is a vital necessity. Overloading any part of the crew is likely to cause resentment, friction, absenteeism, labor turnover, and excessive overtime. Synchronizing the work of the kitchen staff results in greater efficiency, a smooth flow of work, better service, and a greater potential turnover of patrons in a crowded restaurant. If the work is balanced between the various cooking and preparation stations, the result will automatically provide a better selection for the customer. Too many roasts or fried items please neither the customers nor the cooks.

The equipment in the kitchen must also be taken into consideration. Too many dishes requiring the same method of cooking will overload that particular type of equipment as well as the cooks on that station. Some of the problems of overworking a station due to banquet business will be dealt with in the chapter on banquets.

In the dining room, if the tables are small, side dishes should be few as it means overcrowding and discomfort to the patrons. Also, if there is no space in the dining room for sufficient side tables, certain elaborate dishes that require this type of service should be eliminated.

Appearance of the Food. Menu planning involves a subtle type of merchandising. Eye appeal is tremendously important in any form of merchandising but particularly so in food because of the very personal association between the customer and the product. Let no menu-maker make the mistake of believing in the careless generalization that only female patrons are concerned with the appearance of food as it is served. They may make more comments; they may be more willing to admit they are influenced by appearance; they may be more aware of the reason why a plate of food does not appeal to them. But male customers are just as sensitive although they may not realize it. During the war, there was a great deal of complaint from some of the officers about the food served in their messes. They admitted that the quantity and quality was right but for some reason it didn't appeal to them. Why? Because in most cases it consisted of bowls and platters of food heaped on the table with no thought given to attractive service. There wasn't time for training for this during war, but restaurants must take the time or they will lose their customers—the men right along with the women. In the minds of men, the appearance of food is so bound up with taste, good service, and atmosphere that they do not realize how much they are influenced by appearance.

It is important to remember that in a restaurant each meal is a separate sale. Continuity of patronage is likely to be broken by one unpleasant meal. It may be unfair but it is true that one indigestible meal in a restaurant is, more often than not, the one meal a patron will remember although he may have enjoyed a dozen others. Therefore, it is important to make every meal taste and look good.

The nutritive value of a "chunk" of cucumber is the same as that same "chunk" cut into thin slices, but what a difference in appearance!

Two pieces of bread with slices of turkey between them make a turkey sandwich, but it doesn't take an artist to see how much better the appearance of that sandwich would be if a leaf of lettuce were added and the sandwich cut into three or four sections, topped with an olive garnish.

Color is an important factor in improving the appearance of food. One slice of tomato can enliven an entire plate. A touch of paprika or grated parsley makes a boiled potato look much more appetizing. A sprig of parsley can kill the monotony of an otherwise colorless plate. Mint jellies or cranberry sauce or a square of tomato aspic introduce color to a plate of light-colored meat. A segment of lemon will help brighten a fish platter. Paprika and grated parsley sprinkled over the fish improve its appearance also.

A menu-writer is well advised to become familiar with a dietician's chart in order to avoid overloading any meal with too many starches, proteins, or acids. The sight of starch alongside starch is likely to be quite disturbing to customers with the slightest knowledge of food values. Any colorful food may be served with potatoes—peas, a broiled tomato, or any green vegetable. Carrots and peas or beets and peas harmonize well, while carrots and beets do not. Furthermore, the latter are the same type of vegetable—both grow under the ground and one basic rule of dietetics for a balanced meal is one vegetable that grows below the ground and one that grows above.

Contour is another important factor in the appearance of food. It is poor showmanship to have all of the items on a plate look as though they had passed through a clothes-wringer on the way from the kitchen. Variety in shape helps dress up a plate. Too many creamed or mashed items on a plate are not attractive. Every plate needs to have "body" in at least one item of food. An effort should be made to visualize the items on the menu as they will appear when served. An interesting plate should contain one flat item, one in a mound, and one in strips. A combination of cabbage, spinach, and beet greens would be a plate of one texture. This should be avoided. Potatoes, peas, carrots, and celery have a variety of textures and add to appetite appeal.

The same food should not be served twice in the same meal even though the preparation methods vary. No menu should contain tomato juice, meat with a tomato sauce and lettuce and tomato salad. Every menu should be varied. Too many light-colored sauces in one meal is another thing to avoid. A cream sauce with the fish, a white sauce with a fritter, and custard or tapioca pudding for dessert are monotonous. Variety is the spice of the menu—in the cooking, in the colors of salads and vegetables, and in the garnishes, combinations of foods, and the flavors.

Temperature of food is important also. Even on hot summer days at least one hot dish should be on the menu. Cold dishes should be really cold and hot dishes hot when they are served. A fruit cup, fruit and vegetable juices, as well as fruit and vegetable salads should always be thoroughly chilled. Soups, meat, and fish entrees, in addition to tea and coffee, should always be served hot, unless the menu indicates otherwise.

Price. There are two important points to consider in pricing. Items that are priced too high will drive away customers; items that are priced too low will drive away profits. In either case, the restaurant is the loser. Pricing must be right to meet competition, satisfy the patrons, and afford a reasonable profit. That, after all, is the only reason for remaining in business. Otherwise, the owner is only trading dollars and at the end of the year has nothing to show for his efforts and the headaches which every business is bound to produce.

In a highly competitive location, the margin of profit is often narrow and can easily be wiped out by high food costs, excessive payroll, waste or low volume of business. Keeping the price right for the customer and allowing a satisfactory profit for the owner means exercising extreme economy in the places where economy really counts. Food and labor costs must be kept at the lowest point possible compatible with good quality and service; spoilage and waste must not exist; volume must be increased through alert merchandising. All this requires extreme diligence and imagination.

Adequate food cost records and an analysis of sales are indispensable to proper pricing. Constant experimentation with various types of dishes—blue plates, chef's specials, salad plates—and a careful watch kept on the resulting sales may smooth out some of the food cost troubles through larger volume.

Waste and spoilage are inexcusable. They usually result from laziness or carelessness and should not be tolerated. Merchandising does call for some effort and imagination but good ideas are easily available if one is alert and watchful. The advertising pages of the magazines are full of good ideas. All they need is a little adaptation. The editorial pages of the trade magazines are crammed with good merchandising hints that are being used successfully by others right in the food field. The competitor across the street or down the block or across town or even out on the highway is doing a big business. What kind of merchandising is he using? Effort, research, and experimentation will pay dividends if they are mixed with common sense.

Chapter IV: MENU SUGGESTIONS

THE MENU writer must bear in mind that the appetizers on a menu serve as an introduction to the meal. As such, they should be eye-appealing, appetizing and of the highest quality. Naturally, the cost factor has to be considered and, in line with this, it is well to remember that it is always better to serve smaller portions of the top grade than larger portions of low-priced brands. Third-rate tomato juice, slightly fermented fruit cups, hand-me-down hors d'oeuvres, or weary looking seafood cocktails, served with wilted lettuce and stale cocktail sauce, are worse than nothing at all. Such appetizers may be the result of carelessness or too much sharpening of the pencil but they should not be tolerated. The unpleasant aftertaste of an inferior appetizer may completely spoil the balance of an otherwise well prepared meal.

Every list of appetizers should contain at least two juices—one fruit and one vegetable. Mixed fruit juices may prove very popular. Fresh fruit is far preferable to canned fruit. If the latter must be used, then it should be as a filler with as much fresh fruit as possible. Juices and fruit cups must be served chilled. The fact that they are chilled or iced should be indicated on the menu since these two words, "chilled" and "iced" have a very appetizing sound. Chilled fresh grapefruit or melon in season are also very popular. Celery, olives, or radishes must be absolutely fresh and iced. If hors d'oeuvres, antipasto or canapes cannot be served attractively or if they are not fresh, it is better to omit them.

Shrimp, crabmeat, oysters, clams, lobster, or mixed seafood cocktails, are expensive items and usually it is not possible to serve them on budget-priced meals. If a la carte appetizer sales are substantial or the table d'hote prices permit a selection of six, seven, or eight appetizers, at least one should be seafood, also chilled. However, if the price of the meal is such that it is necessary to scrimp on a seafood cocktail it is better not to have it on the menu. Three small shrimp or two oysters cannot really be called a cocktail. It displeases the patrons even though they know they should not expect more for the price they are paying. They should not be lead to think they are getting a cocktail unless a real cocktail is served. Table d'hote meals offering seafood cocktail should include a minimum of five shrimp or three oysters. When an extra charge is to be made for a *premium* appetizer, the price should be noted clearly on the menu so that no adverse customer reaction will result.

Sliced, chopped or stuffed eggs can help round out an attractive selection. Sliced eggs should be served with some form of dressing; chopped or stuffed eggs should be arranged on a lettuce leaf. They may be combined with deviled ham, chopped liver, olives, mushrooms, herring, or julienned tongue, strips of smoked salmon or sardines, grated beets or avocado segments and other seasonal or regional snacks.

Descriptive adjectives and place names are important on all menu items but particularly so for appetizers since these are the first to get attention. The possibilities are limitless. A few examples are:

Chilled Hawaiian Pineapple Juice
South Sea Island Papaya Juice
Pride-of-New Jersey Tomato Juice
Bouquet of Mixed Vegetable Juice
Louisiana Shrimp Cocktail, Creole Sauce
Cherry Stone Clams on the Half Shell
Fresh Florida Orange Juice
Cape Cod Cranberry Juice
Iced Cherry Juice
Sun Land Prune Juice
Texas Pink Grapefruit
Marinated Herring Canape
Ruby Red Pomegranate Juice
Sun Ripened Apricot Nectar
New Hampshire Apple Juice
Supreme of Melon, Maraschino
Blue Point Oyster Cocktail
Gaspe Coast Smoked Salmon
Chesapeake Crabmeat Cocktail
Filet of Maatjes Herring in Wine Sauce
Eastern Shore Seafood Cocktail
Assorted Antipasto with Pimiento
Chopped Egg and Anchovy Delight
King Olives and Western Celery
Talk-of-the-Town Tomato Surprise
Celery Stuffed with Imported Bleu Cheese

SOUPS

Soups should be listed on the menu to inform rather than confuse. "Consomme Gabriel" doesn't mean anything to the average customer as far as the flavor of the soup is concerned. He either has to pass it by, ask the waiter what it is, or take a gamble that it is something he wants. As a rule, these "blind ads" are just taking up space on the menu as most people simply pass over them. If the customer asks the waiter, even he may not know and will have to take the time to go to the kitchen and learn the nature of the soup. Of course, the waiter should be briefed on every item on the menu but he can easily confuse this with some other item and misinform the customer. If the customer takes a gamble and it is something he likes, well and good. On the other hand, if he doesn't want the soup when it is served, he either returns it and asks for something else, causing loss of time and effort, or he doesn't eat it and is dissatisfied right at the start of the meal.

Unfortunately, soup stock is a neglected item in the kitchen and the result is often a watery or greasy soup. If care is exercised in the preparation of soup, it can be a very profitable item.

If there are only two soups on the menu, one should be clear and the other a thick soup. Clear soups are consomme, broths, and bouillons. Thick soups include chowders, bisques, purees, okras, veloute, pepperpot, minestrone, gumbo, borscht, milligatawny, clam, and vegetable soups. During cold weather, a variety of soups adds particular interest to the menu. A simple description of the contents of a soup can build sales. Most patrons have seen the words, "Printaniere," "Vermicelli," or "Bouquetiere" in conjunction with a consomme. They may have ordered it at some time and forgotten what it contained or whether they liked it. They will appreciate learning exactly what these terms mean. This explanation need take very little space. The following listings are examples:

Consomme Printaniere—with minced vegetables
Consomme Vermicelli—with very fine macaroni
Consomme Bouquetiere—with finely chopped vegetables

Thick Soups. This type of soup has many varieties. Clam chowders alone offer great variety. This is strictly an American dish and is not to be found in French cookbooks. Because it is American, every section of the country has its own favorite recipe, such as Manhattan Clam Chowder, New England Clam Chowder, and Philadelphia Clam Chowder, with variations even on these. There are also various types of fish chowders originating in different parts of the country. New England has some. Various oyster chowders are named for the Chesapeake and Eastern Shore areas. Louisiana and other gulf states have their own rich chowders made from shrimp and other types of fish peculiar to that region.

Bisques are the cream of shellfish soups and they can be made from clams, oysters, shrimp, lobster, scallops, and crabmeat.

Purees are basically creamed vegetable soups, the most popular being green pea, celery, mushroom, cauliflower, lima bean, corn, lentil, and turnip. Farina, tapioca, whipped cream, or milk are used to embellish these soups. It adds a nice touch to serve them with croutons which can be done with little effort—slices of bread toasted and cut in half-inch squares.

Okra and gumbo soups are the same type of purees but it adds a change to use both words in listing them. Chicken gumbo, shrimp gumbo, cabbage gumbo, chicken okra, and okra gumbo are the most frequently used.

Veloute is a chicken, fish, seafood, or veal broth. It is a light colored soup and should not be used with too many light colored vegetables on the menu such as cauliflower, turnips, rice or potatoes.

Pepperpot is a highly seasoned stew type of soup. Philadelphia pepperpot features small cubes of tripe.

Minestrone is a heavy vegetable soup that is gaining in popularity. It usually contains macaroni, and powdered cheese should be served with it. If it is new to the patrons of any region, the menu should indicate that it is an "Italian vegetable soup with grated cheese."

Borscht may be served either hot or cold and an explanation on the menu should state that it is a beet soup. It may be served as a clear soup in which case it is a brilliant ruby red, or may contain raw cucumber slices, boiled potatoes, shredded beets, diced carrots, cabbage strips, sour cream, or any combination of the foregoing. However, a description of the soup should be included on the menu.

Mulligatawny is a curry flavored, heavy soup that had its origin in the lands of southeastern Asia. It contains vegetables, meat, mangos, cocoanut, and rice. The curry, mango, and cocoanut contents should be noted on the menu.

In the summer, jellied consomme, jellied bouillon, cold borscht, jellied madrilene, and cold Swedish fruit soups are popular and good drawing cards. Swedish fruit soups are similar to vegetable soups except fruit is substituted for the vegetables. These soups are gaining in favor.

Onion soup and onion soup au gratin became very popular as our people traveled abroad and tasted this delicious soup as it was originally made in France.

ENTREE SELECTIONS

There are three important considerations in deciding upon the entrees: variety, balance, and merchandising appeal. If a restaurant is serving the best food in town, it should talk about it. Any fourth-rate restaurant may have on its menu "Roast Beef, Lamb Stew, Pork Chops, Liver and Bacon." If these listings are dressed up with appetizing phrases, it will make eating more of an adventure for the patrons and less of an everyday chore. They may not realize why they look forward to having their meal served, but they will certainly remember where they enjoyed it—and that is half the battle.

There are eight basic categories for entree selections: Seafood, Fish, Beef, Veal, Lamb or Mutton, Pork or Ham, Poultry, Game, and Eggs. If eight entrees are necessary, it is well to select one from each of the eight. Otherwise, seafood or fish, veal or lamb, and eggs may be omitted and the menu will still be well balanced providing the methods of preparation are varied. In listing the methods of preparation, they should be simple. Most patrons would be confused if they were confronted with a menu listing "Chicken Domonicaire" or "Sea Scallops Monticello" or "Omelet Chasseur" and settle the whole thing by ordering a sandwich.

Seafood. One primary consideration in offering seafood on the menu is that it be in good condition. It deteriorates rapidly if not properly refrigerated and every precaution should be taken to see that shipping services, prior to arrival, and storage conditions, after the merchandise reaches the storeroom, leave nothing to be desired.

Following are some entree offerings having good sales appeal:

Maryland Crabmeat a la Newburg, Fresh Asparagus, Shoestring Potatoes
Fried Deep Sea Scallops, Tartar Sauce, Parsley Potatoes, Cole Slaw
Deviled Jumbo Clams, Cole Slaw, French Fried Potatoes
Assorted Sea Food en Casserole au Gratin, Bermuda Potatoes
Curry of Maine Lobster with Pearl Rice, Diced Carrots and Green Peas
Chesapeake Crab Flake Salad with Sliced Tomatoes
Broiled Whole Live New England Lobster with Brown Butter
Casserole of Fresh Lobster with Shrimp, Newburg
Grilled Frog Legs, Creole Style, Buttered Potatoes, and Tomato Slices
Baked Oysters au Gratin, Buttered Potatoes, and String Beans
Lobster Thermidor with Carrots, Celery, and Shallots
Jumbo Deviled Crabs, Julienne Potatoes, Cole Slaw

Fish. Because many doctors and diets are increasingly opposed to fried foods, in certain geographical areas it is best to omit the word "fried" from the menu. Fried fish and fried potatoes have been such favorites with many restaurants, particularly in the lower-priced brackets, that this may seem difficult to do, but it is not, as the following listings will prove:

Mountain Brook Rainbow Trout, Saute with Eggplant
Baked Individual Flounder, Drawn Butter, Cole Slaw
Baked Boston Mackerel, Tomatoes, Creamy Whipped Potatoes
Swordfish Steak, Saute, Drawn Butter, au Gratin Potatoes
Breaded Silver Smelts, Chili Sauce, Shoestring Potatoes
Poached Supreme of Lake Trout, Sauce Hollandaise, Parsley Potatoes

Filet of Boston Scrod, Saute, with Julienne of Mushrooms
Creamed Columbia River Salmon Flakes with Mushrooms au Gratin
Baked Florida Shad Roe, Bermuda Potatoes, Leaf Spinach
Planked Lake Erie Whitefish, Bouquet of Fresh Garden Vegetables

Beef. Beef dishes are frequently the most popular ones on the menu because, to many persons, beef is the very backbone of a meal. Since they are so popular, it is reasonable to suppose that customers are familiar with the different cuts of beef. Hence, it is good merchandising to spell out not only the preparation method but also that part of the animal from which the meat comes.

Broiled Chopped Beef Steak, Bordelaise Sauce, French Fried Potatoes
Braised Short Ribs of Beef, Baked Tomato, Rissole Potatoes
American Beef Stew and Fresh Vegetables, Parisienne Potatoes
Medallion of Roast Beef, Madeira Sauce with Mushrooms
Grilled Beef Tenderloin Steak with Mushrooms, Tomato Slices, Minute Potatoes
Braised Beef Tenderloin, Mushroom Sauce, Parslied Potatoes
Roast Top Sirloin of Beef with Natural Gravy and Glazed Onions
Braised Top Sirloin of Beef, Sauerbraten, with Potato Dumpling
Yankee Pot Roast with Fluffy Dumplings, Mushrooms and Onions
Sizzling Hamburger Steak, French Fried Potatoes, Tomatoes and Gherkins
Charcoal Broiled Steak Sandwich with Sliced Tomato and Pepper Rings
Chopped Beef Tenderloin from the Grill, French Fried Potatoes

Veal. Veal is a popular meat, particularly in those regions which were settled by people from western and central Europe, where veal is widely used. Some of the terms associated with the preparation of veal, such as "Scallopine" or "a la Holstein," are widely known in this country. They may be included in practically any menu without risk of causing confusion. Listing of successful veal sellers, including calf's liver, kidney, and sweetbreads, follow:

Baked Breast of Veal, Piquant Mushroom Sauce and Mixed Vegetables
Breaded Veal Chop with Fried Egg and Garden Peas
Veal Fricassee with Mushrooms and Golden Bantam Corn
Broiled Veal Chop, Asparagus Tips, Julienne Potatoes
Veal Cutlet Saute, Fried Egg and String Beans
Roast Stuffed Milkfed Breast of Veal, Pan Gravy, Shoestring Potatoes
Milkfed Veal Steak Saute, New Asparagus, Olivette Potatoes
Braised Loin of Milkfed Veal, Sliced Tomato and Roast Potatoes
Veal Cutlet a la Holstein, New Peas and Lyonnaise Potatoes
Calf's Kidney Saute, Piquant Sauce, Mashed Celery, Garden String Beans
Pan Fried Calf's Liver, Sliced Mushrooms, Buttered Noodles
Veal Scallopine with Marsala Sauce, Mushrooms and Shallots
Scalloped Sweetbread with Ham Slices in Cream au Paprika

Lamb and Mutton. Lamb is popular and much in demand for many reasons in addition to its flavor. It is preferred by light eaters because it does not seem to be as heavy a meat as either beef or pork. Also, many people troubled with high blood pressure have been warned against eating too much beef. As far as pork is concerned, many people do not order it for fear it may not be well cooked. Therefore, well prepared lamb becomes a highly desirable offering. Successful lamb listings are as follows:

Broiled English Mutton Chop with Kidney, New Peas, Steamed Potatoes
French Lamb Stew with New Spring Vegetables
Broiled Loin Lamb Chops, New Peas, Home Fried Potatoes, Mint Jelly
Broiled Lamb Steak, Currant Jelly, O'Brien Potatoes, New Peas
Grilled Deviled Breast of Spring Lamb, Mustard Sauce, Glazed Onions, Tomato Slices
Grilled English Lamb Chop, Mushrooms and Select Bacon
Roast Spring Lamb Shoulder, Mint Jelly, String Beans, Roast Potatoes
Curry of Spring Lamb, Indienne Style, Boiled Rice, String Beans
Spring Lamb Saute in Red Wine Sauce, Minute Onions, Mushrooms, Carrots
Irish Spring Lamb Stew with Dumplings, Mixed Green Vegetables
Baked Leg of Spring Lamb, Mint Jelly, au Gratin Potatoes
Baked Shoulder of Spring Lamb, Buttered Carrots, White Bretonne Beans

Pork and Ham. If, for any reason, beef is unavailable or a change seems desirable, pork or ham may be substituted as they rank with beef as a "heavier" meat. Ham lends itself to auxiliary items that may enliven a jaded menu and appetite. These may be noticed in the following listings:

Baked Maryland Ham, Raisin Sauce, Roast Potatoes and New Peas
Grilled Virginia Ham Steak, Hawaiian Pineapple Slice, Candied Yams
Broiled Pork Tenderloin, Special Crabapple, Julienne Potatoes
Broiled Canadian Bacon with Spinach, Glazed Apples
Smoked Loin of Eastern Pork with Lentils
Breaded Pork Chops with Spanish Sauce, Browned Potatoes, String Beans
Baked Sugar Cured Ham, Champagne Sauce, Idaho Potatoes with Melted Butter
Grilled Canadian Bacon with Country Style Corn Fritters and Sliced Tomato
Roast Fresh Ham, String Beans, O'Brien Potatoes, Baked Apple
Broiled Pork Chops, Brussel Sprouts, Buttery Mashed Potatoes

Poultry and Game. Poultry dishes are very popular with all people and in all sections because they are known and used as food the world over. Turkey is generally served with some form of stuffing which simplifies the problem of portion sizes and aids materially in selling the dish. Some imagination used in flavoring the stuffing plus good menu description helps to stimulate sales. Representative menu listings are as follows:

Roast Young Tom Turkey with Savory Dressing, Cranberries, Giblet Sauce
Scalloped Turkey a la King with Wine Sauce and Steamed Texas Rice
Milk Fed Chicken with Mushrooms, Fried in Butter
Broiled Half Chicken, Fresh Peas, Chateau Potato
Roast Long Island Duckling, Spiced Stuffing, Apple Sauce, Paprika Potatoes
Roast Long Island Duckling with Orange Sauce, Browned Potato, Green Beans
Royal Squab en Casserole, New Peas and Minced Mushrooms, Currant Jelly
Broiled Squab, Guava Jelly, French Fried Potatoes
Casserole of Curried Chicken with Baked White Rice, New Garden Peas
Pressed Mallard Duckling, Wild Rice, Guava Jelly, Brussel Sprouts
Disjointed Milkfed Chicken Saute, Pearl Onions, Pan Gravy
Chestnut Stuffed Roast Turkey, Cranberry Sauce, Candied Yams

Eggs. A menu writer misses a good opportunity for variety if he regards eggs as only a breakfast dish. Many people are not heavy meat eaters and for them eggs, served in the following varieties, make a splendid substitute:

Omelet with Crisp Bacon Slices, Stewed Tomatoes, and French Fried Potatoes
Minced Mushroom Omelet with Garden Broccoli and Browned Potatoes
Scrambled Eggs, Country Style with Link Sausage and New Lima Beans
Shirred Farm Eggs with Canadian Bacon
Cheese Omelet with Olives, Mushrooms and Green Peppers
Poached Eggs on Toast with Asparagus Tips and Paprika Potatoes
Deviled Eggs with Celery, Green Pepper and Creole Sauce
Stuffed Eggs with Capon Liver, Mushrooms and Spanish Sauce
Jelly Omelet with Currant and Apricot Preserves, Diced Celery
Fluffy Omelet with Chicken Livers, Mushrooms and Shallots
Anchovy Omelet with Chicory and Minced Olives
Cheese Souffle with East India Ginger

Miscellaneous Entrees. Such selections as Main Dish Salads, Cold Plates, Spaghetti or Macaroni, and Vegetable Platters, supplement the major categories of entrees. During warm weather, salad bowls are very popular. Fruits, raw vegetables, canned fish, seafood, chicken, grated liver, cottage cheese, chopped or sliced eggs, and diced roast beef, may all serve as the basic structure of a salad.

In salads, the dressing is important. Women are particularly quick to catch a new and unusual seasoning in salad dressing. For this reason, strict standardization in dressings should be avoided. Many restaurants have only two standard recipes, one for French Dressing and one for Mayonnaise. They are missing a great opportunity for merchandising their salads. There are scores of herbs to be had which add a subtle and delightful flavor to salad dressings. There are many good books on the use of herbs and one of them should be in the hands of every chef. It will help sell salads if the menu states that they are served with such dressings as Celery Seed French Dressing, Garlic French Dressing, Horseradish Dressing, or Garden Herb Dressing.

Assorted cuts of cold meats can prove very popular if the plate is garnished attractively. Cold cuts should never be served without a garnish of one or several of the following: green vegetables, rose-bud radishes, pepper rings, shoestring slices of Swiss cheese, or small serving of potato or vegetable salad, or slices of tomato.

Spaghetti and macaroni dishes may be served with a variety of sauces such as meat, mushroom, tomato, butter, lobster, and Marinara.

Vegetable platters are usually made up of four or five of the du jour vegetables. The sales of these platters will be increased by the addition of a stuffed egg, anchovy strips, cheese strips, poached egg, corn fritters, potato pancake, apple turnover or a prune dumpling. In listing a vegetable plate, it is best to list the vegetables which are served. Many people have a liking for certain vegetables which will help sell the plate. On the other hand, they have an aversion to others and it is wise to let them know what they are getting at the outset. It saves a returned plate and avoids a dissatisfied customer.

VEGETABLES

A point the menu maker should keep in mind when considering vegetables, is to keep down his listing. They can easily prove too numerous and result in over-production. When fresh vegetables are on the menu he should, by all means, state this fact. The one common fault in vegetable preparation is over-cooking. It not only takes away their nutritional value but completely ruins their appetite appeal as they lose their color and become drab and tasteless. Fortunately, vegetable cooking appears to be getting more attention in the kitchen in recent years as it is realized that they must be cooked in small batches as the meal progresses. If they are cooked in one large batch and kept in the steam table throughout the meal period they are ruined.

The vegetable offerings should be relatively limited but they should always be of good quality and well prepared. If the variety is limited, much more careful preparation is possible. Menu listings of vegetables are important, as a few appetizing-sounding adjectives will help to increase their sale. There are many ways of preparing Irish potatoes and even more words to enhance their appeal to the appetite. The following list has been taken from menus of successful restaurants:

Whipped
Parsley
Rissole
Browned
Baked
Paprika
Bermuda
Parisienne
Grilled
Shoestring

Long Branch
Minute
Pan Roasted
Duchesse
Riced
Creamy Whipped
Buttered
Roast
Saute
Lyonnaise

Steamed
au Gratin
French Fried
Delmonico
Julienne
O'Brien
Cottage Fried
Snowflake
Fluffy
Chateau

Sweet potatoes may be listed as:

Candied
Baked
Sugared
Pan Fried

Honeyed
Roasted
Glaced
Browned

Saute
Boulangere
Grilled
Whipped

Descriptive words for other vegetables are:

Fresh New Peas
Garden Peas
Baked White Rice
Pearl Rice
Stewed Texas Rice
Pilaf of Rice
Stewed Tomatoes
Grilled Tomatoes
Baked Okra
Asparagus Tips, Butter Sauce
Sunripe Tomatoes
Tomato Wedges
Tomato Slices
Buttered Carrots
Diced Carrots
French Fried Onions
Glazed Onions

Leaf Spinach
Leaf Spinach in Butter
Baked Eggplant
Broiled Eggplant
Baked Squash
Asparagus Spears
Buttery Mashed Celery
Diced Celery
White Bretonne Beans
Golden Bantam Corn
Broccoli Parmesan
Creamed White Turnips
Creamed Parsnips
Cauliflower au Gratin
Cauliflower Hollandaise
French Fried Zucchini
Garden Fresh Kale

SIDE SALADS

Side salads must be simple as to preparation or they will clog the flow of work in the pantry section and hold up service during meal time. They cannot be removed from refrigeration too long before they are served or they will be wilted when placed before the guest. Simplicity is the only answer because the cost of preparation must be taken into account as well as the cost of ingredients. A few side salad listings are:

Combination Salad, Chive Dressing
Mixed Green Salad, Thousand Island Dressing
Waldorf Salad
Leaves of Lettuce and Sliced Cucumber Salad
Cottage Cheese and Lettuce Salad
Romaine and Grapefruit Salad
Mixed Green Salad, Russian Dressing
Tossed Green Salad, French Dressing
Chicory and Beet Salad
Escarole, Endive and Watercress Salad, Chili Dressing
French Endive and Tomato Salad

DESSERTS

There is a good potential profit in the sale of desserts but, to realize an adequate return, proper planning and effective merchandising is required. For many people, the dessert is the best part of the meal. If the menu planner shrugs off the dessert section with indifference, he is very likely shrugging off a great many patrons at the same time. Very few successful restaurants have poor desserts. Good desserts are a great drawing card and many establishments have built up their business by specializing in them.

If the desserts are baked on the premises, that fact should be stated somewhere on the menu as there is magic in the phrase "home-made" or its equivalent. Description is a vital part of selling and this is particularly true of desserts. They should never be listed as "Choice of Pie" "Assorted Ice Cream," "Layer Cake," "Assorted Cookies," "Ice Cream or Sherbet." Such listings excite no interest and give no information. They also take up the time of the waiter or waitress in answering questions. There are eight major types of desserts:

Pie
Pudding
Gelatin
Sherbet

Cake
Fruit
Ice Cream
Cheese

Suggested listing for each of these are:

PIES

Cherry Deep Dish Pie
Lemon Meringue Pie
Strawberry Chiffon Pie
Banana Nesselrode Pie
Deep Dish Rhubarb-Apricot Pie
Blueberry Boston Cream Pie
Tropical Chiffon Pie
Deep Dish Dutch Apple Pie
Chocolate Chip Meringue Pie
Apple Chiffon Pie
Blackberry Meringue Pie
Open Peach Pie
Prune Chiffon Pie
Hot Mince Pie
Mince Pie with Hard Sauce
Orange Cocoanut Chiffon Pie
Old Fashioned Pumpkin Pie
Lattice-Crust Rhubarb Pie
New Orleans Pecan Pie
Macaroon Custard Pie
Chocolate Chiffon Pie
Banana Cream Pie
Holiday Cranberry Pie
Pineapple Chiffon Pie
Deep Dish Peach Pie
Chocolate Bavarian Pie

In the same category as pies belong tarts, turnovers, cream puffs, and eclairs:

Frozen Eclair, Mocha Sauce
Ice Cream Puffs with Chocolate Sauce
Banana and Cherry Tart
Apricot and Fig Tart
Viennese Plum Tart
Apple Turnover, Apricot Sauce
Strawberry Charlotte Russe
Cherry and Mocha Tartlet

CAKE

Orange, Marshmallow Layer Cake
Devil's Food Cake, Mocha Frosting
Apple Crumb Cake with Ginger and Cinnamon
Mint Frosting White Layer Cake
Old Fashioned Spiced Apple Crumb Cake
Frozen Layer Cake, Eggnog Sauce
Spiced Rum Cake, Marshmallow Frosting
Baba au Rhum
Old Fashioned Ginger Cake, Caramel Sauce
Fresh Fruit Peach Pastry
Individual French Pastry
Petit Fours
Rum Ice Cream Cake, Mint Sauce

PUDDING

Cabinet Pudding, Wine Sauce
Creamy Rice Pudding with Raspberries
Snow White Farina Pudding with Fruit Sauce
Tapioca Pudding, Strawberry Sauce
Golden Custard Pudding, Hawaiian Sauce
Chocolate Bavarian Cream, Vanilla Sauce
Strawberry Blanc Mange, Whipped Cream
Caramel Custard Pudding, Raisin Sauce
Orange Chiffon Pudding, Pecan Wafers

Cinnamon Bread Pudding with Fudge Topping
Chocolate Walnut Pudding, Whipped Cream
Apple Brown Betty with Lemon Sauce

FRUIT

Florida Fruit Compote, Whipped Cream
Compote of California Fruit, Crystal Ginger
Chilled Watermelon
Baked Apple with Cream, Marshmallow Topping
Fresh Plums in Champagne Sauce
Frozen Tangerines and Pineapple Sauce
Frozen Pineapple in Raspberry Sauce
Brandied Peaches a la Mode
Strawberry Nuggets a la Mode
Spiced Tropical Fruits with Marshmallow Crescent
Melon Balls in Minted Pomegranate Sauce
Iced Honey Dew Melon, Lemon Sauce
Kadota Figs in Minted Syrup
Cantaloupe a la Mode with Maraschino
Date Nut Slice, Whipped Cream
Minted Fruit Cup a la Mode
Half Cantaloupe filled with Blueberries and Nutmeats

GELATIN

Raspberry Gelatin, Whipped Cream Frosting
Port Wine Gelatin with Fresh Apricots
Black Bing Cherry Gelatin, Cocoanut Topping
Royal Cherry Gelatin, Marshmallow Frosting
Honey Dew Gelatin, Whipped Cream
Wine Jelly, Whipped Cream Crown
Minted Pineapple Gelatin, Butterscotch Sauce
Peach and Tangerine Gelatin, Mocha Sauce
Tart and Tangy Lime Gelatin, Peppermint Sauce
Apricot Gelatin, Whipped Cream and Maraschino
Nectarine Gelatin with Hawaiian Vanilla Sauce
Orange and Walnut Gelatin, Caramel Sauce
Strawberry Gelatin with Cinnamon and Raisin Sauce

ICE CREAM

Vanilla, Peach, Coffee or Chocolate Ice Cream
Venetian Spumoni with Pistachio Topping
Coffee Rum Parfait
Peach Melba with Maraschino
Rum and Raisin Ice Cream Coupe
Roasted Almond Ice Cream, Ginger Sauce
Chocolate Chip Ice Cream Parfait
Peppermint Stick Ice Cream Coupe

Butterscotch and Maple Walnut Sundae
Bisquit Tortoni with Maraschino
Mint Ice Cream with Hot Chocolate Fudge

SHERBET

Minted Pineapple Sherbet
Lemon and Strawberry Sherbet
Raspberry Sherbet, Marshmallow Cream
Peach Sherbet with Whipped Cream
Frozen Raspberry Whip, Cocoanut Topping
Creme de Menthe Ices
Lime Sherbet with Maraschino
Apricot and Mint Sherbet
Root Beer Sherbet with Cream Frosting
Peppermint Sherbet, Maraschino Cherry
Port Wine Sherbet

CHEESE

American
Bel Paese
Bleu
Brie
Camembert
Cheddar
Edam
Gruyere
Liederkranz
Muenster
Philadelphia Cream
Port-du-Salut
Roquefort
Swiss
Wisconsin Brick

Serving toasted crackers rather than plain crackers seems to add a special something to cheese when it is used as a dessert.

"Mystery" listings should generally be avoided. "Coupe Venus" may mean nothing to a large percentage of a restaurant's clientele. Often, however, there are some elaborate desserts that may be made a specialty of the house and offer great merchandising possibilities. In such cases, the listing should carry a complete description of the dessert, and the more extravagant the phraseology used, the better. For example:

Baklave	Honeyed nutmeats from the tropic lands of the Orient baked in wafer-thin crust.
Cherries Jubilee in Flames	A fiery torch of brandied cherries crowning an exotic glace parfait.

BEVERAGES

It takes very little imagination to write the three words "Coffee-Tea-Milk" at the bottom of a menu. To be sure, most customers will order a beverage regardless of how inadequate the listing, but a pleasanter impression is created if beverages are "dressed up" in keeping with the balance of the menu. If coffee or tea are served in a pot, it should be so stated. If whipped cream is served with hot chocolate or cocoa, that fact should also appear on the menu.

Many dinner patrons shun coffee or tea because it keeps them awake —or so they think. They may not care for milk and, since nothing else is offered, they omit their beverage order entirely although their meal seems incomplete. It takes very little effort to cater to their requirements. Some suggested beverage listings follow:

Pot of Coffee
Demi-Tasse
Coffee Expresso
Sanka
Postum
Chocolate or Cocoa with Whipped Cream
Tea with Lemon or Cream
English Breakfast, Oolong, Ceylon or Orange Pekoe Tea
Buttermilk or Yogurt
Individual Bottle of Grade-A Milk
Homogenized Vitamin-A Milk
Malted Milk
Ovaltine
Sweet Cider
Cherry Cider
Gingerale
Cola Beverages

BREAKFAST SUGGESTIONS

Since many patrons exercise a rather narrow choice in their breakfast selections, menu writers are prone to pay little or no attention to this meal and merely repeat the same choices day in and day out the year around.

It is not uncommon to find the following menu, with only the slightest variations, appearing 365 times each year with an extra time at Leap Year:

Breakfast No. 1. Juice, Toast, Coffee or Tea
Breakfast No. 2. Juice or Cereal, Two Eggs, Toast, Rolls or Muffins, Coffee or Tea
Breakfast No. 3. Juice or Cereal, One Egg with Ham, Bacon or Sausage, Toast, Rolls or Muffins, Coffee or Tea
Breakfast No. 4. Juice or Cereal, Two Eggs with Ham, Bacon or Sausage, Toast, Rolls or Muffins, Coffee or Tea
Breakfast No. 5. Juice or Cereal, Hot Cakes or Muffins, Coffee or Tea

The above selections illustrate the saturation point in lack of imagination. It happens all too often. However, a little variation may accomplish a great deal for the volume of sales. French toast lends itself to a variety of treatments and has enough substance to appeal to patrons who do not eat a light breakfast but will welcome a change from their standard breakfast diet. It may be served with syrup, fruit or preserves, or sprinkled with powdered sugar. Giving it a name having some local significance may turn such a dish into a featured seller.

Different types of cheese omelets with an added touch of chopped pimiento, chives, green pepper or olive butter, will make an interesting change.

Fruit topping on cereals is extremely popular. It may be augmented with a bit of honey, shredded cocoanut, or malt powder. It may become a meal in itself and will send the customers away satisfied and ready to try this same dish again. Mixed fruits, fresh or canned, topping graham crackers or muffins are also worth trying. The inevitable toast or sweet rolls may also be varied by serving toasted muffins containing nuts, prunes or blueberries. Fruit fritters such as apple, pineapple, prune, banana, apricot, or pear, with syrup or a sauce of some kind, make a very palatable breakfast dish.

Various kinds of juices may be combined to get interesting flavors. Tart and sweet juices make the best combination as each one is improved by the taste of the other. Such combinations might be cranberry and pineapple; pomegranate and apricot, cherry and papaya.

OFF-HOUR MENUS

Supper. Many restaurants located near evening entertainment facilities, or transportation terminals, can build up a satisfactory supper business with effective menu planning. The supper patron may be in the market for "coffee and . . ." intending to spend fifty cents or less, but may easily finish with a check close to a dollar if the menu selections are persuasive.

It is not necessary to follow a definite format in setting up a supper menu. Often, sales are increased by highlighting one or two featured dishes through a menu tip-on. Some popular items for supper menus are:

Tangy Juices
Highly Flavored Soups
Seafood Platters
Sandwich Specialties
Hamburger Platters
Spaghetti Dishes
Rarebits
Ham and Eggs
Cheese with Toasted Crackers
Waffles and Griddle Cakes

Of the tangy juices, clam juice, sauerkraut juice, and a hot mixed vegetable juice, are suitable. Seafood platters may consist of crabmeat, shrimp, or lobster cocktail, or hot plates of individual or mixed seafood au gratin, a la Newburg, Creole Style, or curried. The most popular supper soups are onion, turtle and minestrone. Sandwich specialties may be extensive or limited but they should include a few of the following:

Grilled Cheese	Smoked Salmon
Cheeseburger	Pastrami
Roast Beef	Lobster Salad
Western	Club Sandwich

Hamburger platters may be made highly salable if they include freshly prepared French fried potatoes, tomato wedges, Bermuda onion slices, gherkins or relish. Baked beans and dill pickles may serve as substitutes for the French fried potatoes and gherkins.

Spaghetti dishes may be served with a variety of sauces or a la Caruso—with chicken livers.

The rarebits most frequently appearing on supper menus are Welsh, Long Island, and Golden Buck.

Ham and eggs may be served in a skillet for added merchandising appeal. The skillet should be provided with a closely fitted wooden base for ease in handling.

There is practically no limit to the types and kinds of cheeses that may be offered but it is confusing and impractical to list too many at one time. Waffles and griddle cakes should be accompanied by butter and syrup or honey—also served with sausages, bacon or ham.

Dessert offerings should be on the simple side except for one or two specialties which should be changed daily.

Brunch. The planning of brunch menus may be simple but this meal affords opportunities to build up enormous sales, particularly over week-ends if it is properly merchandised. The brunch menu need be no more than a reprinting of the breakfast selections on a different card headed by the word "Brunch," and adding a few items from the luncheon menu since brunch is a combination of these two meals. Or it may be treated as a special type of week-end meal.

Brunch serves all manner of appetites. For many people it will be the first food they have had since arising. Others may have had a very light breakfast—coffee and toast perhaps, or a juice—and they are more inclined toward the luncheon dishes.

Suggested brunch main dish listings follow:

Browned Corned Beef Hash with Fried Egg
French Toast with Broiled Deerfoot Sausages
Golden Brown Waffle with Hot Maple Syrup and Canadian Bacon
Scrambled Eggs with Smoked Nova Scotia Salmon

Grilled American Cheese and Pineapple Ring on Pumpernickel
Avocado and Seafood Salad Plate
Minced Ham Omelet with Cheddar Cheese Strips
Cassolette of Crabmeat and Shrimps a la Newburg
Buttered Buckwheat Cakes with Maple Syrup and Red Currant Jelly
Grilled Kippered Herring with Poached Egg and Asparagus Tips
Broiled Calf's Liver on Toast with Crisp Bacon and New Peas
Creamed Turkey on Toasted English Muffin with Garden String Beans

Chapter V: MERCHANDISING THE MENU

A GOOD MENU and a restaurant with the facilities for perfect service are not enough to attract maximum patronage. People still have to be sold. There are many types of selling by means of the printed word, but the menu is the one type that is sure to be read. It will not be tossed into the wastebasket since it reaches the customer when he wants to read it—when he wants what it offers for sale. How many other merchants are in such a favorable position? Not many. It is an advertising man's dream. It is probably the most direct piece of advertising in existence. For that reason, every detail of the menu deserves the closest scrutiny—the paper on which it is printed, the format, the layout, and every item that is listed.

FORMAT

The format of the menu should change with each type of meal served—breakfast, lunch, dinner, and supper, if supper is served—and vary for different types of rooms or restaurants. Easy readability is of prime importance. Patrons have been conditioned through usage to a two-page menu and are likely to be confused when confronted with four pages or an insert. In many instances, the back page can be successfully used for a drink list if attention is called to this fact on the inside pages. When the clientele varies considerably between the noon and evening meal, separate drink lists may be advisable. This is true of the higher priced places. In the latter the drink or wine lists may run to several pages. On many menus, a "clip-on" calling attention to a drink special often increases beverage sales.

At least half of the items on any menu should be double-spaced. Single spacing tends to give a menu the quality of a telephone directory. Clear readability with plenty of white space is essential. Restaurant owners should realize that menus are printed to be read. They should *test* the lighting at *all* tables themselves to see whether they can read their own menus. Customers are annoyed when type on a menu is so indistinct or the light so poor that they cannot read it.

The name and full address of the restaurant should never be omitted from the menu, for there is no telling when this "silent salesman" may take to the road and bring in some customers. Failure to include the local address on the menu is sometimes the result of vanity but it isn't good business.

Printed menus are the most desirable. Typewritten or mimeographed menus should be avoided at all costs. They are invariably carelessly typed with misspelled words and smeared carbon. They are cheap and they look it. If the operation does not warrant the expense of printed menus, a good typist should type one clear, black copy and have it duplicated by the offset process. Most offset houses have their own electric typewriters and will make their own original copy. In this way a very creditable menu may be turned out at relatively small expense. However, before resorting to this, it would be well to get bids from local printers. They will very often make a very fair price for work of this kind of which they are sure every day.

The a la carte items need not be changed daily. Four changes each year are adequate. Therefore, enough of these menu cards could be printed at one time for three months and the *du jour* items printed in each day. The format or layout of the menu should be changed about twice each year. Seasonal changes of cover designs are also a good idea. If the faces of steady customers are watched when they see changes in the menu format, their expressions are enough to prove that the change was worth while.

As the principal internal merchandising medium in the restaurant, the menu should contain information regarding days and hours of operation, banquet and party facilities, if any, take-out and/or office delivery service. Obviously, extreme care must be exercised that the inclusion of such information does not detract from the basic purpose of the menu, that is, the selling of the current day's offerings.

MENU COPY

Menu copy is as varied as the personality of the man who writes it or the operator who dictates the type of menu he wants. Some go to extremes and each dish is described in the manner of a prose poem. This may not find favor with many restaurant managers; nevertheless, using brief descriptions of some of the dishes is good selling technique.

Small items of historic, community or culinary information may be carried on the menu as they add to the interest and customers will soon begin to watch for them. Another way of attracting attention is to have descriptive headings. Instead of merely listing "Appetizers," "Fish," "Entrees," "Salads," "Desserts," try out headings similar to: "From the

Seacoast," "Seacoast Delights," "From the Oyster Bar," "Salad Suggestions," "Salad Bowls," "Chef's Salads," "Broiled to your Order," "From Our Charcoal Broiler," "Sizzling Platters," "Gourmet Selections," "Piping Hot Specials," "Casserole Specials," "Fresh Garden Vegetables," "Cold Buffet Specials," "Dessert Delicacies," "Assorted Cheeses.'

Flavor is added to the menu by using words which describe the method of processing such as "Sugar Cured," "Honey Cured," "Candied," or "Hickory Smoked." Almost all menu readers are hungry and the right words such as "savory" or "flavorsome" can whet an appetite and build sales volume. Often a chef, in describing the dishes he makes will use phrases which, in print, appeal to the appetite. Trade names may have merchandising appeal if they are well known.

In using place names, caution should be exercised to avoid misrepresentation. It may not be of great importance if a Vermont apple is listed as coming from New Hampshire but "Virginia Ham" should only come from Virginia. "Vermont Maple Syrup" is another designation that should not be applied carelessly.

Language Comprehension. The manner in which some dishes are listed on the menu is puzzling to patrons unless they are gourmets. Such terms as "Breast of Capon, Eugenie," "Paupiette of Veal, Toscanini," "Noisette of Lamb, Pollard" do not indicate whether the food is broiled, boiled, braised or fried. There is no way of knowing whether it will arrive on a plate under glass, via a skewer or floating in a casserole dish. Many people will avoid these dishes because they hesitate to ask the waiter what they are (all too often the waiter doesn't know), and be very disappointed when a customer at an adjoining table is served something that looks delicious but which it seems could not be listed in simple English.

It is not belittling the knowledge of the customers to indicate on the menu clearly of what a dish is composed or how it is cooked. People like to know what they are getting. A menu dripping with foreign phrases may heighten a chef's professional self-esteem but it will not sell as much food as will one that includes more home-spun descriptions of the dishes. If a chef insists that he cannot "cook in English," the traditional foreign terms may be used with English descriptions telling the patrons what to expect.

Variety. There is nothing so tiresome to a customer as to be confronted with the same menu day after day until he can recite it from memory. Even when a restaurant is in the highly favorable position of having no direct competitors in the neighborhood, patrons are likely sooner or later, to go elsewhere from sheer boredom. Once they go they may not return. Menu variety is absolutely necessary to maintain maximum patronage. There is no valid reason for menu monotony.

The best way to find out whether or not a menu has variety is to keep a simple tally of the number of times an item appears on the menu during any one month. In doing this, however, it should be remembered that a different method of preparation doesn't mean a different item. Roast beef, beef a la mode, beef pie, beef en casserole, ragout of beef, braised beef, fillet of beef, and beef stew are all beef dishes. A menu overloaded with them will lack variety. The same is true of fish, seafood, lamb or mutton, pork or ham, veal, poultry, egg dishes, spaghetti, and main dish salads.

Occasional menu conferences may help the menu writer and he should not hesitate to suggest this. Several heads are always better than one and many good suggestions may come out of such a conference. Possibly some of the subordinate cooks have been employed in excellent restaurants and they may be gold mines of good suggestions. All they are waiting for, quite often, is an invitation to tell what they know.

Flexibility. It is unwise, merely because a menu format has been established, to adhere to it from week to week and season to season in order to avoid extra printing cost. If a sales analysis proves that the format of the menu is wrong it is far more economical to reprint it. A menu carrying out-of-season items that are not available in the rigidly fixed a la carte section is extremely poor merchandising. It is very annoying to patrons to ask for two or three different items which are plainly printed on the menu and be told they are not available. They are sure to ask, "But why are they on the menu?" There is no satisfactory answer to that question. Restaurant men must remember that outsiders do not understand the problems of the food business. It is not their business. They are offered a menu. Presumably everything on it is available or it wouldn't be there and they get a very poor idea of the business ability of anyone responsible for what appears to them to be sheer foolishness. Format changes need not be made too frequently. Three or four changes each year should suffice.

Limited Menus. There is no reason, except professional vanity, for overloading a menu with ten or fifteen entrees and a proportionate number of surrounding items. It results in so many evils that they are worth enumerating:

(1) It confuses and does not please the customer.

(2) It slows up the service as the waiter must wait at least twice as

long while the customer reads over all the selections and decides what he wants.

(3) It overburdens the preparation and service staffs.

(4) The quality of preparation almost invariably suffers.

(5) Bottlenecks are created or aggravated in the kitchen.

(6) With so many items on the menu, waste is bound to be increased.

(7) The menu writer's burden is increased as he will have many more left-overs to work off the next day.

(8) Buying, receiving, storing, and issuing food are all more difficult.

It is decidedly a better policy to have a few well prepared dishes, well served with a minimum of confusion and friction in the kitchen. In cutting down a menu, if there is any doubt in the mind of the menu writer as to which item he should omit, a tally of sales will show him which dishes sell below average. It will not take long to find out which are the "best sellers."

House Specialties. There is a tremendous merchandising value in having at least one house specialty that is truly outstanding. A single dish of superb quality, such as Veal Scallopine, or Lobster Thermidor, or Southern Fried Chicken, readily re-creates a specific palate-picture that helps stimulate "impulse" patronage. Reawakened taste-memory can be made to do half the job of selling.

REASONS FOR PATRONAGE

Price. It is often of value to the menu writer to know the factors that prompt customers to patronize his restaurant. It may be any one of several—price, quality of food, service, location, and atmosphere. It is a mistaken idea to believe that a low price is the main consideration. Rather, it is good value for the money spent. Poor food is never economical food—to either the customer or the restaurant. Even the most saving office worker will patronize a place where the noon sandwich satisfies hunger, even though it may cost ten cents more. This does not mean that prices can be out of reason and "get by." The public is quick to detect this.

In many restaurants, there is a definite price resistance to club breakfasts that exceed ninety-five cents. A one-dollar charge for breakfast is a sort of "Chinese Wall" to many patrons—a barrier which they will not cross. They prefer smaller portions—less cereal served with "half and half" instead of cream, two slices of toast instead of three, a smaller glass of fruit juice.

For luncheon or dinner, many will choose only an entree and a beverage. They will shun a table d'hote meal since many times the portions are so large they cannot eat as much as is served and they do not want to pay for something they will not touch. Smaller portions and a slightly lower price on table d'hote meals might sell more of them.

Quality. There is no substitute for quality in food. No restaurant can long maintain a maximum patronage if it serves food of poor quality, regardless of its decorative motif, its service or its entertainment. Patrons soon spread abroad the word that food is good or bad—the most favorable kind of advertising on the one hand—the most deadly on the other. Since the overhead expenses are practically the same for preparing and serving food of mediocre quality as that of good quality, it seems strange, with so much to gain, more restaurant operators do not insist upon food of high quality.

Frequently some stations in the kitchen are better equipped or better staffed to serve good food than others. This is something for the restaurant manager to straighten out as it can be a great handicap to the menu maker.

Service. A menu writer should be able to depend upon reasonably good service when he plans the menu. But he must know the capabilities and capacities of the service staff and not expect more than they can do. If the noon hour is an extremely busy one, he should not put items on the menu which require additional time for service. He must also take into account the kitchen crew, the kitchen traffic conditions and other matters mentioned earlier in this chapter. If, for example, ice cream is difficult to obtain in the kitchen, the waiters and waitresses will rarely bother with pie a la mode.

Good service is likely to mean different things to different people. To the man who is in a rush for his breakfast or lunch, speedy service is likely to be considered good service. To the lone diner, a courteous greeting, prompt attention and a few remarks about some of the dishes on the menu may mean good service. The service staff should always be briefed on the menus before a meal. The waiters and waitresses can then ask questions and make suggestions which will be of enormous help to the menu writer, resulting in better menus and improved service.

Atmosphere. The atmosphere of a restaurant or dining room is of importance. The menus must fit the surroundings. Otherwise patrons, expecting a certain type of food and service will be disappointed and not return. A room that has the decorative motif of a business man's club should not provide food that is appropriate for a tea room. Sandwiches and snacks may have great pulling power in a coffee shop or a room gayly decorated, but would be out of place in a formal dining room with French service.

Location. A menu writer should have a detailed map of the surrounding area within five minutes' walking distance of his restaurant. Each building should be properly marked so that the map may serve as a potential guide to potential customers. This map should indicate the nature of all the buildings in the immediate vicinity—office buildings, stores, theatres, railway stations, bus terminals, competitive establishments, schools, churches and all places of amusement. Local bus and street car loading points should also be indicated. This map of the neighborhood will be of tremendous help to any newcomer on the job of menu-writer. It will also facilitate any advertising campaign undertaken to stimulate business.

Table d'Hote, a la Carte or Blue Plate Selections. In most operations it is advantageous to include all three types on the menu—table d'hote, a la carte, and blue plate specials. The sales should be analyzed to learn just what the proper balance between the three should be. Each has advantages and disadvantages. The major advantage of the table d'hote meal is the all-inclusive price. Patrons know at a glance what their final bill will be. The disadvantage is that many patrons do not want full course meals and do not wish to pay the price for them. For such people, an a la carte or blue plate arrangement is the answer.

The a la carte meal is to the advantage of the restaurant as far as the check average is concerned since it is usually higher than for other types of meals. However, if the patron is dissatisfied with the amount of his check, the restaurant suffers. For that reason, it is wise to offer him a choice. If he chooses to order a la carte, the size of the check is not likely to bother him.

The blue plate, which usually includes a beverage, has a low price appeal, but since it is fundamentally a minor variation of the a la carte set-up, the same disadvantage applies as far as the customer is concerned. For the above reasons a combination menu is the most satisfactory to the greatest number of patrons. The number of items which the menu should offer in each section will be determined by an analysis of the sales figures.

Sales Analysis. A tabulation of the number of sales of each of the entrees and whether they were sold on table d'hote, a la carte or blue plate offerings, will reveal the preferences of the patrons. Nothing should be taken for granted in such an analysis since luncheon and dinner may reveal entirely different preferences from a widely varied clientele. In restaurants, the trend of customers' tastes may vary from day to day. Out-of-town visitors, week-end traffic, date of pay day, nearby entertainment features, and many other factors make it vitally necessary to study each day of the week separately. For example, blue plate offerings may seem to be running high on the list. If the menu maker has been offering two of these he might switch to four but it would usually not be advisable to switch from one to five blue plates. That would be overloading the menu with the same type of offering and too many of the others would be crowded out. If the blue plates appear out of favor for a time, the number might be dropped from four to two but they should not be removed from the menu entirely.

Souvenir Menus. In many establishments, the menu itself is hastily thrown into the nearest trash-bin directly after the meal is ended. When this happens, an excellent merchandising opportunity has been lost. A menu that is requested as a souvenir becomes an "outside salesman". It automatically indicates that a favorable impression has been created.

In addition to the name of the restaurant, the full street address, city, and state should be conspicuously apparent on the menu.

If the courtesy of mailing is extended to patrons desiring a souvenir menu, a mailing list based on customer satisfaction may easily be compiled. A knowledge of the geographic origins of patrons can help tremendously in slanting the menu structure. It may also help in selecting advertising media.

Breakfast Menus. An attractive and appealing breakfast menu can provide an excellent inducement to patrons to return for other meals. On the other hand, unimaginative, hopelessly repetitious breakfast menus are the worst possible form of merchandising. They reach the patrons when they are feeling at their worst and only increase their general feeling of disgruntlement.

The menu maker must bear in mind the type of the dining room when planning his breakfast menu. One that would serve admirably in a coffee shop is not the one that will prove effective in a formal dining room. Speed of preparation and service is an important factor in all breakfast operations. Even though a patron may seem buried in his newspaper, he has timed himself through habit for this morning ritual and he will not tolerate delays in service.

A bright, colorful format is a good springboard from which to display a breakfast menu. Soiled or worn menus should be discarded immediately they become unfit for service. Restaurants on the whole seem particularly careless about breakfast menus, probably because they do not have many variations and, therefore, frequent reprinting is not required. They should be checked constantly to see that only fresh ones are used.

A variety of juices, fruits, cereals, egg dishes, hot cakes, waffles, toasts or sweet rolls may serve as a satisfactory base in a coffee shop. In a formal dining room, particularly if patrons tend to drift in until eleven o'clock, additional items may prove to be good sellers. Some people are accustomed to heavy breakfasts if they arise late in the morning and their breakfast serves as lunch also. Chops or small steaks might sell at this hour.

Club Breakfasts. Club breakfasts have become an American institution. Failure to recognize this fact and provide for it will certainly affect business adversely. Four or five breakfasts at different prices, varied from time to time, are all that need be offered.

Luncheon and Dinner Menus. A well-located establishment is at a great advantage as far as customer potential for these two meals is concerned, even though competition is much greater. On the other hand, a location slightly off the main line of traffic may do a very good business with clever, alert, and flexible menu merchandising.

A simplified menu is usually the best menu. One basic rule of selling any type of merchandise is "Don't confuse the customer with too many choices." This certainly holds true with a menu. Patrons have a feeling of urgency when they know that the waitress or waiter is standing by waiting for their order. If they are confronted with a long menu, they may decide hastily and regret their choice later. With good quality food and a streamlined menu, a greater number of patrons will be pleased. Many people know quite a bit about cooking in their own homes. They know it is not possible to have so many prepared dishes ready to serve and have them all fresh and of good quality. Even in a large restaurant with many customers, this is a difficult thing to achieve and since it isn't smart from either the point of view of the management or the customers, why do it?

Each item should have some form of appeal and create a picture for the patron. He is in a receptive frame of mind. All he needs is a little coaxing and the primary function of the menu should be to start the machinery going that will make the patron want to return again and again. It is the repeat business that makes a successful restaurant.

Seasonal Changes. The ideal arrangement is to change the fixed body of the menu four times a year—once for each season. This provides the perfect opportunity to highlight new seasonal dishes and to eliminate any out-of-season deadwood. It makes for a shorter, more vivid menu.

If four changes per year are too burdensome on the budget, at least two changes per year—not less—are an absolute necessity. In such cases, changes should be made approximately May 1 and October 1. Obviously, in certain sections of the country the dates will vary because of particular local or regional conditions.

Price Tag Appeal. Quite frequently establishments of a better type make the mistake of ignoring the magnetic pull of "bargains". It can be a sound instrument for attracting additional patronage for any caliber of restaurant.

The airlines with their ever-increasing usage of travel bargains have demonstrated how new sources of patronage can be created through eye-catching and mind-stirring price tag appeal.

One or two offerings priced at about 25 or 30 per cent less than the prevailing average receipt per cover will often attract patrons for an exploratory initial visit. Once the "ice has been broken," an establishment may prove to be less expensive than had been imagined.

Filling Empty Seats. The need for trying bold new experiments exists in direct proportion to the ratio of empty seats at any given meal. Filling an empty seat means spreading the overhead cost. In many instances 10 per cent added volume can often result in close to 50 per cent gross profit for the increased number of covers, since little more than the cost of food will be involved. Bargains of every type, including blue plate specials, junior-size portions, and open-face sandwiches, should be offered to attract seat fillers. Nothing improves the atmosphere or operating statement of a restaurant like an enlarged stream of customers.

Price Range Patterns. A breakdown and analysis of the percentage of business in the various price brackets may occasion some startling surprises. For example, the matter of patronage for a luncheon may take the following form:

Price Range	*Percentage of Total Covers*
$1.50—$1.70	21%
$1.75—$1.95	17%
$2.00—$2.20	13%
$2.25—$2.45	13%
$2.50—$2.70	16%
$2.75—$2.95	20%

Thus, without realizing it, a restaurant operator might easily be catering simultaneously to both ends of the budget scale. Bargain hunters and self-indulgent customers might be rubbing shoulders without being aware of it. Some customers will tend to spend as little as possible while a percentage will head in the opposite direction. It is wise to cater to a broad segment of the public, and to make certain that there is a sound distribution of offerings at all price ranges.

Chapter VI: FOOD PURCHASING GUIDES

For a food operation to be successful, every phase of it must function efficiently. There can be no weak links in the chain. Tastefully prepared food is wasted effort if it is indifferently served. Large sales volume may not prove profitable if there are consistent cash shortages. All the functions of a food operation are interrelated and interdependent. The success of a food establishment can very well be measured by the degree of coordination of these various functions.

However, since all food operations must necessarily be processing operations before the product can be sold, the base point at which merchandise cost and the character of the product is determined must be the purchasing of the raw materials. Although poor preparation practices may destroy the quality of a product, good preparation practices cannot instill that characteristic where it has never existed. The best menu merchandising policies cannot compensate for unimaginative purchasing that is not alert to new products, new markets, and new trends. Nor can cost controls be wholly effective in production or service if buying is wasteful. Food cost begins at the time of purchase. The lost margin on a light-weight hamper of green beans or a poorly trimmed loin of beef purchased at an uneconomical price can never be recovered.

With the cost of food frequently accounting for the greatest part of the sales dollar, and with these costs so specifically dependent on purchasing practices, it is readily apparent that unless food products are purchased effectively there can be little chance for success in any food operation.

Buying must always be judged by its over-all effectiveness, and never by price comparison alone. The price at which an item is purchased is only as important as the item itself; it may be 5 cents less per pound or 15 per cent cheaper by price, but 30 per cent more expensive in actual yield. The good buyer is interested in the lowest price only when the items are comparable as to quality and yield.

Good buying is that procedure which provides a food operation with the products most suited to its merchandising policy at the most economical price possible.

It is with the elements of this definition that this chapter is concerned. What the best procedures are; what merchandise is best suited and how it can be so determined, and when and how this merchandise can be purchased most economically.

THE FOOD BUYER

While the importance of the purchasing position has long been recognized in general industry, this recognition has come to the food buyer only since the recent progress in the industrialization of the food service business. The food buyer is certainly not merely an order clerk, telephoning requests for purchases of items which he has been asked to buy. This is a key position requiring technical knowledge together with a high level of skill and executive ability.

In order to fill such a position effectively, the food buyer should have long experience in food operations. He must understand the workings of a kitchen and know what happens to food in production. He should be able to tell the meat dealer why the pot roast was poor; he should know that light syrup or water-pack fruits are best for salads and that, when a steam table service is used, the Blue Lake green bean stands up better than the usual refugee bean.

The food buyer should be well trained in the technique of market buying and familiar with market trends. He must be alert to new markets, new products and shifts of market availabilities. He should know how stock prices paid in Chicago today will affect the price of loins in his local market next week; and he should be able to judge if a fair price was quoted on berries by Dealer B, based on current market reports.

Modern communications and transportation have made markets so interdependent and so sensitive that much experience is needed to obtain a real perspective. In addition, local markets are often affected by factors other than supply and demand and require a working knowledge of current market practices if a buyer is to get the best results.

He should have some knowledge of accounting controls, and understand the mechanics of purchase orders, invoicing, receiving sheets, and credit memorandums.

He must be familiar with his products and their mathematics, for not only will he buy them but he will often supervise butchering and yield tests. He must be able to set up standard purchase specifications.

He must have the ability to work with chefs as well as with delivery men. He must be friendly with salesmen, who may be potential customers, yet strict in his business relationships. He must have initiative and the willingness to be thorough. Buying food to serve the public is not a sinecure. The hours cannot always be regulated. They depend largely on the public—not an easy taskmaster.

He must be a good trader but never a chiseler.

It goes without saying that loyalty and honesty must be his in full measure.

These may seem like quite an array of "musts" and much like the qualifications for a general manager rather than merely the food buyer. However, with more and more successful managers coming from the back of the house, these qualifications are well placed.

Manager. While it is not usual in hotels because of the other demands on the manager, in the great majority of restaurant operations where size permits, the manager or restaurant owner himself does the food buying. Where such procedure is possible, it provides the most effective method. The only drawback is the possibility that the press of other duties will prevent the allowance of sufficient time for a regular routine to be followed.

Chef-Steward. In many food operations, the buying of food supplies is done by a chef-steward. This is a hyphenated position and combination of work that is rapidly disappearing since both functions are likely to be full time jobs. In such a case, purchasing never fails to be the collateral duty while acting as chef the primary one. Such a combination usually results in the chef spending most of his time at a desk ordering food over the telephone while one of the cooks takes over his duties as chef, to the detriment of both the purchase and preparation of the food. If the food operation is such as not to afford two men for this work, smart operators have found it advisable to take over the buying themselves and let the chef do the work for which he has been trained.

Food Operations Manager. A relatively new position has developed in large commercial and institutional operations, that of food operations manager. This position usually provides for a food operations expert to administer the food department under the direction of the general manager. In many such cases the food manager does the buying. This has proved successful because experienced personnel, well versed in production methods, and in the problems of the specific operation, do the purchasing.

Steward. In large hotels and restaurants, the buying is usually done by a steward who also is in charge of the food storeroom. Too often, unfortunately, he is also in charge of receiving which should always be an accounting function. If duties must be added it is wiser to put him in charge of warewashing and kitchen sanitation. Frequently these two latter departments have no responsible person over them.

Purchasing Agent. In many large industrial organizations operating food departments, in institutional feeding establishments and in some large hotel and chain operations, the food buying is done by a purchasing agent. In this system practically all purchases are made on a formal, businesslike basis according to strict specifications. Careless, offhand buying is kept at a minimum, and effective control in the receiving department is strengthened, since under this method, receiving is almost always an independent function of the accounting division. Where the food operation is a major activity of the establishment, such an arrangement provides experienced personnel who have had much technical training. However, where the food operation is not the paramount activity, the general purchasing agent may lack special knowledge of food, and is often saddled with so many other duties that he is not able to devote sufficient time to the very necessary butchering and cooking tests, visits to market and other pertinent food department problems.

Dietitian. Although it is customary in the larger schools, hospitals and similar institutions to use a central purchasing agent for the buying of food stuffs, the dietitian usually determines the specifications for the goods to be purchased, and operates in close liaison with the purchasing department. In small institutions the dietitian is directly charged with the purchasing of food stuffs. Since all dietitians have an educational and training background in dietetics and home economics, they are usually well versed in the consumption and dietary values of foods and in the intricacies of institutional menu planning. They are well trained in purchasing routine and have a knack of visualizing entire well-balanced meals when buying a single item. Lack of a thorough knowledge of food costs and experience in competitive market purchasing have been the difficulties most often encountered.

CHOICE OF BUYING PROCEDURE

A buying procedure is a course of action. While the determination of general policy is the responsibility of ownership, the actual mechanics of buying are usually left to the department head responsible. Since no two operations are exactly the same, the buying procedures for each individual establishment must be built to fit the requirements of that particular operation. For example, it might be wise in one operation to take refrigerator inventories after lunch and then order; at another operation, morning ordering may be best. The location of one hotel may permit daily visits to the market; in another hotel, weekly visits with future deliveries may be the most suitable policy. In order to determine the best buying methods the following should always be considered:

Ownership Policy. Does ownership want the greatest portion of purchasing done locally? Are there chain or group commitments? What rate of inventory turnover is desired?

Type of Operation. Is it an all-night restaurant, or is it a specialty house? Is it part of a group or chain? A hotel or restaurant? Luxury or commercial? Does size restrict advantageous purchasing? What is the credit position and the policy regarding discounts?

Storage Space Available and Handling Costs. What size deliveries can be accommodated? Is warehouse space available for profitable "futures" buying or are storage and handling costs prohibitive?

Location and Availability of Markets. How far from the nearest market? Is the operation fortunately located in a truck farming area or will delivery be expensive and difficult? Is it close enough for daily market visits or will the telephone do the buying? What are trucking arrangements? Will wholesale supply houses be the major supply? Will there be sufficient availability for open market bidding?

General Market Conditions. What is the direction of market prices? Does the market trend (and size of the operation) warrant contract purchasing? Or, is movement so rapid that open buying on the daily market is best?

PURCHASING METHODS

Of the many varied procedures the following are those methods most widely used:

Open Market Buying. This method is used by at least 95 per cent of all commercial operations. In this procedure quotations are requested from one or more purveyors and orders are placed where the terms are of best advantage to the buyer, all elements of price, quality, yield, and service having been considered.

Sealed Bid Purchasing. This procedure is used almost exclusively by large hospitals, institutions, schools, and governmental agencies. Wants are advertised in several forms, and sealed formal bids are returned by a stated date. This procedure is almost never used in commercial operations.

Futures and Contract Purchasing. This form of buying consists of contracting for future delivery of food stocks that are now or will be available at a current or future price. Buying in this manner usually augments other buying methods and although it is used by many operators, it is most often employed by large volume purchasing operations in a calculated attempt to insure a supply at a favorable price. At best, this is a speculative operation in any of its forms, whether in futures buying or in overstocking at current prices in anticipation of price rises. This is not recommended for general operations. Buyers and operators might better concentrate on operations than on speculation and leave such practices to the jobbers. Investment charges, storage costs, losses, and balancing trends in price invariably account for such potential profits and emphasize the old axioms that in operational purchasing "there is no future in buying futures" and "there are no bargains in food."

WHERE TO BUY

The major sources of supply usually available to food buyers are as follows:

Wholesale Supply Houses. These constitute the usual purveyors of food to institutional users. They perform a service function as jobbers, accumulating many varieties of merchandise from numerous sources and offering them for demand sale. They buy in quantities which would be uneconomical for operators and utilize outlets for by-products and items not usually used by food service establishments. For example, while restaurants use many more ribs and loins than they do chucks and rounds, the purveyor buying his beef in sides or in quarters will also sell the chucks and rounds. A real service is provided not only in this manner but also in the consistency of quality and in the delivery service available. Often, food operators, where volume is large, have given thought to the possibility of eliminating the middleman and his profit margin. However, the same factors which created the wholesale purveyor—the problems of market availability, use of cuts and items not in similar demand, the consistency and uniformity of quality, storage and delivery costs—have made such action impractical.

Manufacturers and Packers. Such organizations sometimes sell their products directly to the operator or they may sell to the wholesaler or they may do both. Ice cream and condiments are usually sold direct to the users. The major meat packers also make their products directly available; however, in such cases they act as wholesale purveyors and are competitive with them.

Local Farmers and Producers. In some areas this group constitutes the major source of supply for fresh fruits and vegetables, and for farm and dairy products.

Municipal Markets. These markets in the large cities offer many possibilities for good buys, especially in fruits and vegetables. Although these markets are primarily for wholesalers, a keen buyer who knows his operation and his product can obtain excellent values.

Cooperative Associations. Since the war these organizations have become increasingly important in the wholesale field. They consist of many producers (usually of farm products) who combine for the benefits gained through central and large scale distribution and selling. Dairies and fruit growers are the most common example of this type of concern.

Retail Food Stores. Aside from their availability for emergency use, some chains frequently offer advantageous prices to those who buy in good-sized quantities.

RELATIONS WITH PURVEYORS

It is important that the food buyer understands the business and the business problems of those with whom he deals. The buyer should know the dealer's reputation for honesty and for quality. He must know if the dealer is a solid business man or merely a fringe broker, using the buyer's orders to get merchandise. The food buyer must understand the operating difficulties of the purveyor and not spread his orders so thinly that no one will make a profit. He should be fair in his demands for service. In New York an average delivery costs between seven dollars and nine dollars. Too many "emergency orders" are costly and unfair to the dealer. A good dealer knows his products and his business. He is out to make a fair profit. Every customer is an investment in time, service and money, and the dealer will do anything possible to keep good customers. However, the chiseling and over-demanding buyer can never best the purveyor. Sooner or later the purveyor will make up for it. It is only human nature that causes a dealer to take advantage of sloppy buying practices. A good dealer expects to be competitive and respects good buying practice. His knowledge, confidence, and good will are worth much.

THE MARKET

What Markets Have to Offer. This implies more than familiarity with the list of products available in the local market. It requires a full knowledge of products and their markets. The buyer should know all the available varieties, the best brands, where they are grown, and how they are packed. He must know their standards of quality, weight, and grading. It is well to be familiar with the seasonal varieties, when they appear on the market, possible substitutes, the expected supply and the probable price. He should know what comparable varieties and qualities are entering the market and which are "running best." He should know when there are surplus crops or items in "long" supply, and when fruits and vegetables of a russeted appearance or with minor blemishes can be purchased advantageously for his use.

Visiting the Market. The information and perspective required to handle present day market buying in the above manner is not available to the food buyer at his desk or over his telephone. He must visit the market whenever possible since quality and price are most often a matter of availability, and it is only by being at the market frequently and making the true test of comparison that the best value can be obtained. Yet, today, all too few buyers visit the market with any regularity. It is difficult to imagine a department store or a manufacturing concern tolerating a buying procedure where the buyer is not constantly visiting his sources of supply and continuously studying market conditions. However, this tendency toward telephone purchasing is one of the major weaknesses of present day food operations.

Suitability to Particular Needs. In the determination of what is best for use, the following should be considered:

1. Type of operation and clientele.
2. Menu and Price Policy.
3. How and when food is to be used.
4. Desired Quality.
5. Physical conditions of storage.

No matter what the purchase price, unless the product can be profitably sold it should not be purchased. The food business is no less a merchandising operation than a department store or a snow-shoe factory. It would be no more illogical to try to sell snow-shoes at the equator at "bargain" prices than it would be to put caviar on a lunch room menu in a rough-and-ready neighborhood because the food buyer could get a "good buy." Buying must be geared to use. Two-and-one-half pound lobsters should not be purchased where menu and price policy call for pound-and-one-quarter size, notwithstanding a quoted price of ten cents less per pound. While a luxury hotel correctly uses a size 46 grapefruit for an a la carte portion, a commercial restaurant will use a 54 and often a 64 size. Salad oranges should not be bought for orange juice, nor should full loins be purchased where there is no profitable outlet for the loin end. Buying the most suitable size and grade specifications is of great importance in holding the line on food costs. The section on standard purchase specifications will amplify this further.

The principle of buying only for profitable use is illustrated also in the following instance. Since there is a limit to the price customers will pay for a menu item or a meal, there is also a limit to the price which the buyer can pay for the food he buys. If he finds that an item of suitable quality is overpriced for his selling market, he should report this to the chef and unless detrimental to sales policy, that item should be kept off the menu until such time as the price has returned to a profitable level.

QUALITY BUYING

This does not necessarily mean buying the best and most expensive grade of any particular item. It *does* mean the best grade sold to fit the need. The right grade where eye appeal is important, such as in stuffed tomatoes for salads, may well be the highest grade; but certainly such uniformity and expensive quality are not necessary where the tomatoes are to be cooked.

In times when meat prices are high, with the differential between grades of U. S. Good beef and U. S. Choice often approaching 30 cents per pound, it is well for the operator to question buying by grade alone. He will find that a carefully selected U. S. "Top" Good grade rib or loin will very often be a better value as to price, yield and suitable quality. The dividing line of quality between a regular U. S. Choice and a well selected "Top" U. S. Good is much too narrow to be worth any real price differential. The operator who claims he buys nothing but U. S. Choice meats and the most expensive grades of fruits and vegetables may be boasting of wasteful expenditures rather than of good operations.

Quality in food may be defined as the combination of factors in a product which provides the greatest desirability. However, composed of so many varied factors, quality is an elusive thing and difficult to control. Although quality is regulated at the source by prices paid for animals or for crops, this quality control is a matter of comparison—the highest price paid for the "best of the lot." Quality will then flow into a market as long as prices in that market are profitable. In a given market then, price, while influenced by quality, is no true index of that quality. Conditions of supply and demand, shipping and storage, will have affected both the price and condition of the merchandise by the time of sale. The skill of the buyer is then the determining factor in the consistent purchase of quality merchandise as close as possible to a given standard. While Federal grading and standards have provided the greatest advances in the uniformity of grades and qualities, it must be remembered that such grading is done at the source, and often utilizes minimum standards for each grade, allowing for considerable variations within each grade.

SPECIFICATION BUYING

The United States Government defines a specification as a "statement of particulars in specific terms." Specification buying is then merely the utilization of such well defined particulars in the purchasing of merchandise.

A set of specifications by itself does nothing. It is a tool that must be selected with care and then *used*. If used effectively, it will provide suitable buying standards for a particular operation and a common denominator of market bidding for the food buyer and purveyors. It will give a uniformity and consistency to purchasing and receiving that will aid in maintaining a desired food cost.

The specifications currently in effect should be distributed to the various purveyors for their information and use. Such specifications should also include delivery conditions and instructions. A set of specifications must also be available for use by the receiving clerk on inspecting incoming merchandise. Effective specification buying requires receiving by specification as well.

In buying to specification, just as in other procedures, purchases must be made at the most favorable prices obtainable through competitive market quotations. However, unit price is never the paramount consideration. For example, a hamper of green beans quoted at a price 50 cents below the market by Dealer "X" is not cheaper if the hampers from Dealer "X" weigh 5 pounds less than the others. If prices were quoted on a specification which read:

> *"Green Beans—Firm, crisp and stringless, uniform size, no decay, should have a clear green color, 25 lbs. net weight per hamper,"*

and Dealer "X" was still 50 cents below the market, then his beans would actually be cheaper, for then bids would have been received on the same item and prices would be comparable. The preceding example also illustrates the value of buying by weight designation rather than by container name alone.

Specifications must be followed consistently in order for specification buying to achieve results. Where the markets or small volume of purchases make this procedure impractical, the operator should use the specification methods as a guide in order to know the most suitable purchase weights and qualities, proper yields and legitimate trims.

Formulating Standard Purchase Specifications. The value of a set of specifications depends on the manner and accuracy with which they have been developed. In determining these specifications the purchaser should be guided by those principles of effective buying previously discussed and by actual kitchen tests of yields of the products to be purchased. In this manner the determination of what is best for use will be based on need, merchandising suitability, and final portion costs rather than unit prices.

Specifications should be written for all products usually purchased. The information for complete and accurate writing should be based on the aforementioned kitchen tests and trade and government information concerning packs, grades, and varieties.

Following is an example of a well-written, detailed specification for canned sliced beets:

Beets, Sliced:

Fancy Grade. Locality: New York State. Slice Dimensions: 2½" Diam. ⅜" Thick. Dark Red Color. Free from Blemishes, Broken Slices and End Cuts. Texture: Tender and Succulent.

Can Size: No. 10
Drained Weight: 4 lbs. 10 oz.
Net Weight: 6 lbs. 10 oz.

KITCHEN TESTS

Kitchen tests are of the following four types:

Raw Food Tests. These determine the best count and weight for fruits and vegetables; i.e., a case of size 150 California oranges for use in salads should weigh at least 70 pounds net per crate.

Canned Food Tests. These tests are made to check on the yields and actual cost of the different varieties of canned foods. In these tests,

TYPICAL STANDARD PURCHASE SPECIFICATIONS

CLASS A RESTAURANT

ITEM	GRADE	HOW PURCHASED	DESIRED WEIGHT OR COUNT
BEEF:			
Corned Beef Brisket	Steer Brisket	Deckle off - Kosher Style	14-16 lbs.
Chucks - Square Cut	U. S. Choice	Whole Chuck	50-60 lbs.
Shell Strip	U. S. Choice	10 inch Flank Trim	20-22 lbs.
Boneless Strip Loin	U. S. Choice	10 inch Flank Trim	12-16 lbs.
Short Loins	U. S. Choice	10 inch Flank Trim	36-40 lbs.
Filet - Steer	City Dressed	30% or Less Fat by Weight	5½ - 6½ lbs.
Beef Ribs	U. S. Choice	7 Ribs - 10 inch Flank Trim	35-38 lbs.
Oxtails	Steer	Fresh	1½ lbs. each
Beef Rounds	U. S. Choice	New York Cut	80-90 lbs.
Short Hips	U. S. Choice	Short Cut	24-26 lbs.
VEAL:			
Legs	U. S. Choice	Double Legs	45-50 lbs.
Liver	Fancy	Fresh	2½ - 3 lbs.
Sweetbreads	Fancy	Fresh-large size	1 lb. per pair
Loin Saddles	U. S. Choice	Double	14-16 lbs.
Racks	U. S. Choice	Double	10-12 lbs.
LAMB:			
Chucks	U. S. Choice	Double	14-16 lbs.
Racks	U. S. Choice	Double Rack-8 ribs	5½ - 6½ lbs.
Loin Saddles	U. S. Choice	Double	7-8 lbs.
Legs	U. S. Choice	Double	13-15 lbs.
Backs	U. S. Choice	Double	15-17 lbs.
Whole Spring Lamb	U. S. Choice	Whole Carcass	45-50 lbs.
POULTRY:			
Broilers	Grade A	Fresh Killed - N. Y. Dressed	2¼ lbs.
Roasting Chickens	Grade A	Fresh Killed - N. Y. Dressed	3¼ - 3½ lbs.
Fowl	Grade A	Fresh Killed - N. Y. Dressed	5½ - 6 lbs.
Duckling	Grade A	Chilled-Long Island	5 - 5½ lbs.
Turkey-Roasting	Grade A	Young Tom-Fresh if Available	25-28 lbs.
Turkey-Boiling	Grade B	Chilled or Frozen	22-25 lbs.
Turkey-Hen	Grade A	Chilled or Frozen	10-12 lbs.
PROVISIONS:			
Bacon	#1 Fancy	6# Box	20-24 slices to 1 lb.
Ham-Smoked	#1	Skinned Back	14-16 lbs.
Ham-Fresh	#1	Short Hock	12-14 lbs.
Ham-Canned	#1	Boneless	10-12 lbs.
Pork Loins-Fresh	#1	Full Loin	10-12 lbs.
Beef Tongues - Smoked	Fancy	Short Cut	4-5 lbs.
Link Sausages	#1	Fresh	10-12 per lb.
Frankfurters	Fancy	Box	8-10 per lb.
SHELLFISH:			
Little Necks	Fresh	Per Hundred	550-600 per bushel
Cherrystone Clams	Fresh	Per Half Barrel	300-350 per bushel
Oysters-Blue Point	Fresh	Barrel	900-1,000 per barrell
Crabmeat-Back Fin Lump	Fresh	1 lb. can	

ITEM	GRADE	HOW PURCHASED	DESIRED WEIGHT OR COUNT
SHELLFISH: (Cont.)			
Shrimp-Jumbo	Chilled	Per pound	18-20 per lb.
Scallops-Sea	Chilled	Gallon	7 lb. drained weight or 150-180 per gal.
Lobsters	Live	By Weight	1½ lb. average
Soft Shell Crabs-Jumbo	Fresh	Per Dozen	4 inch diameter
FRESH WATER FISH:			
Blue Pike	Fresh	Whole-Individual	3-6 lbs.
Brook Trout	Fresh	Whole-Individual	1/2 - 3/4 lb.
Lake Trout	Fresh	Dressed - Head on	4-8 lbs.
Whitefish	Fresh	Dressed - Head on	2-4 lbs.
Yellow Perch	Fresh	Whole-Individual	3 per lb.
Yellow Pike	Fresh	Dressed - Head on	4-5 lbs.
SALT WATER FISH:			
Bluefish	Fresh	Dressed - Head on	5-6 lbs.
Butterfish	Fresh	Whole-Individual	3/4 lb.
Cod	Fresh	Dressed - Head on	6-8 lbs.
Flounder	Fresh	Whole-Individual	3/4 lb.
Flounder - Sole	Fresh	Dressed - Head on	2-3 lbs.
Flounder - Filets	Chilled	Filets	-
Haddock	Fresh	Dressed - Head on	4-6 lbs.
Haddock - Filets	Chilled	Filets	-
Halibut - Chicken	Fresh	Dressed - Head off	8-10 lbs.
Kingfish	Fresh	Dressed - Head off	6-10
Mackerel	Fresh	Dressed - Head on	1½ - 2 lbs.
Pollock	Fresh	Dressed - Head on	6-10 lbs.
Pollock - Filets	Chilled	Filets	-
Pompano	Fresh	Whole-Individual	1-1/4 - 1-3/4 lbs.
Roe Shad	Fresh	Dressed - Head on	4-5 lbs.
Salmon	Fresh	Dressed - Head off	6-8 lbs.
Sea Bass	Fresh	Whole-Individual	3/4 - 1 lb. each
Sea Bass	Fresh	Dressed- Head off	8-10 lbs.
Smelts, Silver	Fresh	Whole - Entrails in	6-8 per lb.
Sole - Filet	Chilled	Filets	-
Striped Bass	Fresh	Dressed - Head on	4-5 lbs.
Swordfish	Chilled	Center Steak	12-15 inch diameter
White Perch	Fresh	Whole-Individual	½ lb. each
DAIRY PRODUCTS:			
Butter - Table	93 score	Sweet Pats - 32 lb. Box	Cut 60 per lb.
Butter - Cooking	92 score	Salt Print	32 lb. box
Eggs - Boiling	Grade A	Hennery White - 30 doz. crate	60-62 lbs. gross, 55-57 lbs. net
Eggs - Cooking	Grade A	Fresh Westerns - 30 doz. crate	54 lbs. gross 49 lbs. net
Cream	Light	By Quarts	20% minimum butterfat
Cream - Whipping	Heavy	By Quarts	40% minimum butterfat
Ice Cream	DeLuxe	2½ Gallon Tube	18% butterfat
FRESH VEGETABLES:			
Asparagus	Fancy	Crate - 12 bunches	2½ - 3# bunch 32-36 lbs. per crate
Beans-Green String or Wax	Fancy	Hamper	25# net
Beets	Fancy	Crates or Bushel	4 doz. bunches
Broccoli	Fancy	Crates	18-24 bunches-50-60#
Brussels Sprouts	Fancy	Qt. Boxes	1-1¼# per box

ITEM	GRADE	HOW PURCHASED	DESIRED WEIGHT OR COUNT
FRESH VEGETABLES: (Cont.)			
Cabbage - Spring	Fancy	Basket or Hamper	40-50#
Cabbage - Winter	Fancy	Bushel or Bag	50# or 100#
Carrots	Fancy	Bag	50#
Cauliflower	Fancy	Crate	2-2½ per hd; 1-1½ doz.
Celery	Fancy	Crate or doz.	12-15# per doz.
Chard	Fancy	Bushel or doz. bunches	
Corn	Fancy	Dozen Ears	Golden Bantam
Cucumbers	Fancy	Dozen	3/4 lb. each
Egg Plant	Fancy	By the head	1½ - 2# each
Endive	Fancy	Crate	4 - 6 doz.
Endive - Imported	Fancy	Boxes	10 lbs.
Escarole	Fancy	Crate or doz.	4 - 6 doz.
Kale	Fancy	Bushels	
Leeks & Scallions	Fancy	Bunches	
Lettuce - Iceberg	Fancy	Crate - 4 doz.	1½# per head
Lettuce - Boston	Fancy	Crate - 2 doz.	½# - 1# per hd.
Mushrooms	Fancy	Basket	2-3/4 - 3 lbs.
Onions - Yellow	U.S.#1	Bag	50#
Onions - Spanish	U.S.#1	Crate	50#
Parsley	U.S.#1	Bunch	Medium
Parsnips	U.S.#1	Bushel	42-45 lbs.
Peas	U.S.#1	Bushel	25 lb. net
Peppers	U.S.#1	Doz. or Bushel	25-30 lbs.
Potatoes - Irish	U.S.#1	Bags	100 lbs.
Potatoes - Baking	U.S.#1	50 lb. box	Idaho - Russets
Potatoes - Sweet	U.S.#1	Bushel	50 lb.
Radishes	Fancy	By the bunch	
Romaine	Fancy	Dozen	3/4 - 1# per hd.
Spinach	Fancy	Bushel	18-20 lb net
Squash	Fancy	Bushel	40-45 lbs.
Squash	Fancy	Bag or Barrel	
Tomatoes	Fancy	Lug	30 lbs.
Turnips	Fancy	Bushel	55 lbs.
FRESH FRUIT:			
Apples - Baking	Fancy	Roman Beauty) Box-Baldwin)	64 size
Apples - Cooking	#1	Bushel-Greenings	48# per bushel
Apples - Dessert	Fancy	Box	Delicious, McIntosh, Northern Spy-Jonathan
Apricots	Fancy	Lug or Flat Crates	25# net or 4 baskets 5# each
Avocado	Fancy	Flat 16-18	
Bananas	Fancy	Hand	4-5# per hand
Cherries - Sweet	Fancy	Box	16# per box
Cranberries	Fancy	Box	25#, 33# or 50#
Grapes	Fancy	Lug or Pound	25-28# per lug
Grapefruit	Fancy	Crate	54 & 64; 70#-80#
Lemons	Fancy	Box - Red Ball Sunkist	360 (84#)
Melons-Cantaloupe	#1	Crate	45's
Melons-Honey Dews	#1	Crate	6-8 size
Melons - Persian	#1	Crate	6 size
Melons-Watermelons	#1	Each	35-40 lbs.
Oranges - Salad	Fancy	Crate-Cal. Naval Valencia	150 size
Oranges - Juice	Fancy	Crate-Fla. or Cal.	216 size
Peaches	Fancy	Bushel or Lug	48# or 28#
Pears	Fancy	Doz. or Bushel	45# per bushel
Pineapple	Fancy	Dozen	Approximately 3# each
Plums	Fancy	Baskets or Flats	
Rhubarb	Fancy	Box	40 lbs.
Tangerines	Fancy	Crate-Medium	144 size
Strawberries	Fancy	Pts. or Qts.	

drained weight, count, quality, density and clearness of syrup and uniformity of product are taken into consideration.

Butchering Tests. These are cutting tests of the various wholesale units of meat, fish and poultry as received. Tests are made by the butcher or chef under the supervision of the food buyer or food controller. They are made in order to determine the actual portion costs after waste, trim, and by-products have been considered. The items are trimmed and cut as they would regularly be used. Values are assigned the by-products and waste in accordance with use and regular market value.

Cooking Tests. Cooking tests often follow butchering tests since they determine the final portion cost not only after waste and trim have been accounted for but also after cooking, slicing, and service loss has been considered. For example, a loin of pork that was to be used for pork chops would have had a butchering test made to determine the cost of each chop. A test for a roast loin of pork, however, would have had a butchering test to determine the cost of an item as "oven-prepared" and then a cooking test to determine the final cost of each serving. Cooking tests are also used to determine the relative efficiency of the cooking methods.

These tests are illustrated by examples and discussed in detail in the chapter titled "Pre-Cost Pre-Control Procedure."

Kitchen Tests Indicate Proper Trim. Wholesale cuts and trims are based on a mathematical relationship to the dressed carcass. While cutting methods may differ in various parts of the country, these relationships remain constant within each type of cutting method. For example, in the New York style of cutting, with proper trim, a short loin should weigh 12.5 per cent of the dressed carcass, while the tenderloin should be 2 per cent of the carcass, or 16 per cent of the short loin. A wholesaler prices his cuts based on this relationship and his competitive position. With such relationships as a guide, a food buyer, through tests, can determine whether or not the "cheaper" prices are being provided through inadequate trimming or "strong cutting" into cheaper adjoining cuts. For example, with beef ribs selling at 67 cents per pound, and beef chucks at 38 cents, an unscrupulous purveyor may well make up more than the difference he is quoting below the market by cutting the rib "strong" into the chuck, that is, leaving two to three pounds of the cheaper cut on the more expensive rib.

The following test results on Beef Tenderloins of the same grade (City Dressed #1) are a further example of how testing indicates poor trim:

	WEIGHT	PRICE PER POUND	TRIMMED WEIGHT	YIELD	COST PER USABLE POUND
Tenderloin A	7 lb. 4 oz.	$1.60	3 lb. 11 oz.	51%	$3.14
Tenderloin B	7 lb. 6 oz.	$1.55	2 lb. 14 oz.	39%	$3.98

This test indicated that one purveyor, while quoting the lower price for the same grade and weight of tenderloin, more than made up his lower price in the excess suet left on the tenderloin.

On pages 79, 80 and 81 is an example of a typical working set of Standard Purchase Specifications for a Class A restaurant.

FEDERAL GRADING AND STANDARDS

Since 1900 the greatest single influence on the agricultural economy in the United States has been the activity of the Federal government in that field. Specifically, its services in rating and in the standardization of farm products has so advanced uniform standards and uniform application of these standards that the market process, as we know it, could not operate without them. With the great movement and action of today's agricultural markets, and with the fabulous number of products and varieties available all over the country and in all seasons, there must necessarily be an intelligent basis on which the price of meat products, dairy products, processed foods and other items can be compared. Federal standards provide that basis for comparison.

The wise food buyer recognizes the value of Federal standards in obtaining uniform quality and uses them wherever practicable. A buyer will often utilize the same scales of measurement used in Federal grading, in judging quality and usability of ungraded products and in the establishment of specifications. It must be emphasized, however, that Federal grading and standards cannot substitute for a buyer's skill and experience. The variations within grade and particular conditions of local markets require additional factors of judgment.

U. S. MEAT GRADING SERVICE

The government grading service started in 1927 as an experiment and was conducted for one year at the expense of the United States Treasury. It proved so beneficial to everyone connected with the meat industry that it was made a permanent part of the activities of the United States Department of Agriculture. In 1928, to make it self-supporting, it was placed on a fee basis, a charge of 2 dollars per hour being made for the grader's time.

Reports are current that graded meats cost 2 cents or 3 cents per pound more than meats that are not graded. The fact is that the cost for grading is so small that it does not noticeably affect the price per pound. The cost in the entire United States averages less than one-fiftieth of a cent and in Chicago less than one-eightieth of a cent per pound.

Government meat graders are under the United States civil service. The government holds examinations periodically, and the highest qualifying applicant is given the first appointment. The requirements are at least eight years of experience in wholesale buying and selling meats. Chicago has over 20 graders, and the least experience any of them has had is fifteen years, running up to twenty-five years. They are all practical beef men.

Appointments. When the grader is first appointed to this service, he is on probation for one year, training under a competent supervisor. It is weeks before he is ever allowed to grade a piece of meat. After one year, if he proves competent and if his character and integrity are what they should be, he receives a permanent appointment. Only the Secretary of Agriculture can terminate that appointment. This point is important since no amount of political pressure or threats to "get" his job will influence that man in the conduct of his work. He knows, if he does his work as he is told to do it and is honest and fair in his judgment, he has the job for the rest of his life.

Availability of Service. This service is now available in every major meat center in the United States. It is a voluntary service, meat being graded at the request of the buyer or seller. Despite its voluntary aspect, meat is being graded at a rate of almost four billion pounds per year.

Stamping Procedure. The carcass is stamped with the grade stamp by the grader or by someone under his direct supervision. The stamping is done in such a manner that all of the principal cuts will have the grade imprint. The grade stamp should not be confused with the Federal inspection stamp which also appears on the principal cuts.

GRADING

Grading is done by concept. The grader carries a picture in his mind of what constitutes a grade and fits each carcass or cut into the picture. If a part of the carcass does not measure up to his mental picture of the highest grade, then the carcass is graded down one or more points for each deficiency.

Grading meats under Federal standards is based on three fundamental characteristics:

Conformation. Conformation applies to the general form and structure of the carcass, side or cut of meat. It generally indicates the ratio of meat and fat or bone. It might be said that it is based on (a) build; (b) form; (c) shape and (d) outline. In a choice carcass of beef, the ratio of bone to the total weight of the carcass is from 16 to 19 per cent. In a U. S. good carcass this ratio will average 21 to 22 per cent, while in the commercial grades, the ratio will run up as high as 24 to 26 per cent. This difference is balanced somewhat by the fact that the prime carcass may have as high as 36 per cent fat as against approximately 21 per cent in the commercial grade.

Conformation or lack of conformation is very quickly seen when judging the carcass. A prime carcass will be blocky, thick and well rounded with well fleshed ribs and full loins. The lower grades of meat will be thinner, more lengthy, and will not be so well curved, especially around the hip and shoulder joints.

Finish. Finish generally refers to the finish on the outside of a carcass but it must be remembered that it also means the finish on the inside of the carcass as well.

It refers to the amount, color, character and distribution of fat on the outside and on the inside of the carcass in and around exposed bones. The amount of fat that is around the kidney also has a bearing on the grade, and the evenness of the fat over the carcass is considered.

Quality. Quality refers to the factors that have to do with the palatability of the cooked meat and includes any of the elements of conformation and finish. While there is no true scientific basis for any measurement of this quality factor, it is thought that it is related primarily to the texture of the meat, the amount of connective tissue, and the consistency and flavor of the juices set free in the cooking process.

The following is a compilation of the Federal grades for the various kinds of meat:

Beef	*Veal*	*Lamb*	*Mutton*
Prime	Prime	Prime	Choice
Choice	Choice	Choice	Good
Good	Good	Good	Commercial
Commercial	Commercial	Commercial	Utility
Utility	Utility	Utility	Cull
Cutter	Cull	Cull	
Canner			

With the exception of veal which does not have as much fat as the comparable grades of beef, the grading of the above items is based on the same aforementioned fundamentals.

The Department of Agriculture has recently made a change in the grading structure. They have combined the two top grades, *choice* and *prime*, calling it prime, as formerly. What was previously specified as *good* is now the *choice* grade. The former *commercial* grade has been divided, the top half of young commercial beef being classified as the *good* grade and the remainder is now the *commercial* grade.

This has the effect of slightly down-grading the quality and widening the range within each grade. This requires even more skill on the part of the food buyer since the guide of Federal grades is much less specific.

What was formerly classed as *prime* beef has been in such limited supply (less than .5 per cent of the beef available) that it could not be considered for consistent use. Combined with the former *choice* grade, it now becomes the highest grade of beef consistently available throughout the year. It is produced from young animals and has comparatively large amounts of lean and fat, together with a small amount of bone. The amount of fat helps to insure palatability of a high degree. Most of the cuts from the round, loin, rib, and chuck are suitable for roasting and broiling.

That grade now specified as *choice* is the grade most used by the buying public. While it does not have the marbling of the prime in the over-all appearance of that grade, it would be difficult to recognize the very slight difference in eating quality between a good *choice* and *prime*.

Good and *commercial* are the next grades downward. While these grades are not usually suitable for broiling or roasting, they provide a low-cost meat that is very acceptable in dishes that call for slow, long cooking.

Cutter and *Canner* are the lowest grades of meat, and usually not available to the food buyer but are used principally in the manufacture of party and luncheon meats.

"Selected Grades." These refer to packers' brand names which indicate their own grades. These brands usually parallel the government grades. At times, meat which will not be graded *choice* because of a small apparent defect which does not affect its eating quality, will be upgraded by the purveyor. He will do this in order to obtain a price closer to the *choice* grade level rather than have it down-graded as *good* and suffer the full price differential. An experienced buyer will often be able to get good value in ungraded beef by watching for such instances.

GRADES OF PORK

The official grades of pork are

U. S. #1
U. S. #2
U. S. #3
Cull

All of these grades are further divided into Meat Type, Fat Type, Packing or Sow. The same principles of conformation, finish, and quality determine the grading in pork as well as the other meats. While such standards have been developed for pork carcasses and cuts, they are not in as widespread use as other meat grades. Since the variations in market hogs is much less than in market beef, there has not been the same need, and a larger portion of the pork is graded as "Selected," with packers' own grades.

POULTRY

U. S. standards and grades for broilers, fryers, roasters and turkeys are the same and are set forth as follows by the Production and Marketing Administration of the Department of Agriculture:

U. S. Special or U. S. Grade AA. Young, fine-grained, soft-meated birds with broad, full-fleshed breast, the entire carcass fully covered with fat and with skin soft and glossy lying close to the flesh. Must be well bled, well dressed, and free of pinfeathers. No flesh or skin bruises allowed, and only slight skin abrasions, or discolorations permitted, none of which shall be on the breast. No crooked breasts or other deformities allowed. A broken or disjointed wing above the wing tip, or a broken or disjointed leg not permitted. No open tears or torn skin permitted. Must be dry-picked or semi-scalded, and dry packed.

U. S. Prime or U. S. Grade A. Young, soft-meated birds, with well-fleshed breast, the entire carcass well covered with fat, and with soft, glossy skin. Must be well bled, well dressed, and practically free of pin-feathers. No flesh bruises and only very slight skin abrasions, or discolorations permitted, none of which shall be on the breast. No crooked breasts or other deformities allowed. Broken wings above the wing tips or broken legs not permitted. Torn skin not permitted. No sewn skin permitted on the breast or fleshy part of the carcass and only slight sewn tears permitted on the back. Birds with crops properly removed and sewn up may be included in this grade. Must be dry picked or semi-scalded and dry packed.

U. S. Choice or U. S. Grade B. Young, soft-meated birds, with fairly well-fleshed breast, and with carcass fairly well covered with fat. Must be fairly well bled and dressed, and may show few scattered pinfeathers over the entire carcass. Slight flesh or skin bruises, abrasions, or discolorations permitted, but not more than three such defects if on the breast. Abrasions or tears over 2 inches in diameter not allowed unless properly sewn up. Dented or slightly crooked breast bones or other slight deformities permitted. One broken wing or one broken leg in the flesh permitted if bone does not protrude through the flesh and if not showing excessive bruise or blood clot.

U. S. Commercial or U. S. Grade C. Young birds with poorly fleshed breast and with carcass poorly covered with fat. May show evidence of poor bleeding and have numerous pinfeathers over the entire carcass. Abrasions and discolorations permitted and hunchbacks or other deformities allowed if birds are fairly well fleshed. Birds badly bruised so as to make any appreciable part of the carcass inedible or birds emaciated or showing external evidence of disease not permitted.

U. S. Standards for Dressed Ducks are:

U. S. Grade A Young
U. S. Grade B Young
U. S. Grade A Old
U. S. Grade B Old
U. S. Grade C

The boxes in which poultry is packed are stamped with the U. S. Grade of the poultry each contains, whether or not the individual birds have been tagged. Grade names are now printed on tags and attached to each bird by means of a seal which passes through the wing. The seals are so designed that they cannot be used more than once.

EGGS

Since eggs are among those products whose characteristics of quality undergo very rapid changes, it should be kept in mind when buying eggs that the grades indicate the quality at the time of grading. Each grade stamp will indicate the date of grading. The four official grades of quality are: AA, A, B and C. These grades are determined by the size, exterior and interior appearance of the eggs. All grades come in all sizes and the size is an important factor in price.

The size classes of eggs are divided as follows:

SIZE CLASS	MINIMUM NET WEIGHT (IN POUNDS) 30 DOZEN CRATE
Jumbo	52
Extra Large	48-½
Large	45
Medium	40
Small	34

The grading of the egg's quality depends on the clearness of the white, blemishes of yolk, size of the air cell within the egg and the condition of the shell.

BUTTER

Butter is graded in terms of score—100 points being considered a perfect rating. Such a rating is only theoretical since under practical conditions a 93-95 score is the best available. Scoring depends on flavor, color, body, salt content, and freshness with certain degrees of tolerance allowed in each category, the amount of which partly determines the score level. The following summary indicates the grades and several scoring characteristics:

SCORE	U.S. GRADE	DESCRIPTION
93 or above	U.S. Grade AA	Clean, highly pleasing flavor, fresh sweet cream base.
92	U.S. Grade A	Desirable flavor, clean, lacking somewhat in creamy flavor.
89-91½	U.S. Grade B	Fairly pleasing, though may contain slight off-flavor, sour taste.
83-87½	U.S. Grade C	Possesses fishy, stale, rancid, onion flavor.

CANNED FRUITS AND VEGETABLES

Government grading and standards are especially useful to the food buyer in the determination of the quality of processed foods. Without grade labels, and since canned foods are in sealed containers, quality grades are difficult to determine. Prices cannot be considered safe guides nor can superlative brand names as "Superb" or "Superfine."

The government grades are as follows:

CANNED FRUITS	CANNED VEGETABLES
Grade A or Fancy	Grade A or Fancy
Grade B or Choice	Grade B or Extra Standard
Grade C or Standard	Grade C or Standard
Below Standard in Quality	Below Standard in Quality

These grades are determined by a scoring system based on values assigned to the following factors:

Character	Finish	Density
Texture	Flavor	Clearness of Syrup
Firmness	Color	Drained Weight
Tenderness	Appearance	Clearness of Liquor
Cut	Type	
Consistency	Style	

While packers may grade their own products, if terms such as "Grade A," "Grade B" or "Grade C" are used, they are responsible for meeting the requirements of the grade.

No matter what the grade designation, canned foods are wholesome and fit for use otherwise they could not be marketed in interstate commerce.

Continuous inspection of the grading process is also available to packers and any of their products packed in this manner can use the "U. S." prefix before the grade designation:

WEIGHTS AND YIELDS OF CANNED VEGETABLES

ITEM	GRADE	CAN SIZE	*MIN NET WT. PER CAN	*MIN. DRAIN WT. PER CAN
Asparagus-Spears	A-Fancy	No. 2	1 lb. 3 oz.	13½ oz.
Asparagus-Bleached	C-Standard	No. 2½ sq.	1 lb. 15 oz.	22 oz.
Asparagus-Spears	A-Fancy	No. 2	1 lb. 3 oz.	12¼ oz.
Asparagus-All Greens	C-Standard	No. 2½ sq.	1 lb. 15 oz.	20 oz.
Beans, Snap, Green, Whole	A and C	No. 10	6 lbs. 5 oz.	61 oz.
Beans, Wax-Cut	A and C	No. 10	6 lbs. 5 oz.	65 oz.
Beets-Diced	A and C	No. 10	6 lbs. 8 oz.	75 oz.
Beets-Whole & Cut	A and C	No. 10	6 lbs. 8 oz.	73 oz.
Beets-Sliced	A and C	No. 10	6 lbs. 8 oz.	70 oz.
Carrots-Diced	A and C	No. 10	6 lbs. 8 oz.	70 oz.
Carrots-Whole & Cut	A and C	No. 10	6 lbs. 8 oz.	68 oz.
Corn-Cream Style	A and C	No. 10	6 lbs.10 oz.	
Corn-Whole Kernel	A and C	No. 10	6 lbs.10 oz.	72 oz.
Mushrooms, Stems or Pieces	Fancy	No. 1 small	12½ oz.	8 oz.
Okra-Whole & Cut	A and C	No. 2	1 lb. 3 oz.	14 oz.
Okra-Whole & Cut	A and C	No. 10	6 lbs. 3 oz.	80 oz.
Peas	A and C	No. 10	6 lbs. 9 oz.	72 oz.
Sauerkraut	A and C	No. 10	6 lbs. 3 oz.	80 oz.
Spinach	A and C	No. 10	6 lbs. 2 oz.	60 oz.
Squash (Pumpkin)	A and C	No. 10	6 lbs.10 oz.	
Succotash	A and C	No. 10	6 lbs.12 oz.	
Tomatoes	A-Fancy	No. 10	6 lbs. 6 oz.	
Tomatoes	B-Ex Standard	No. 10	6 lbs. 6 oz.	72¼ oz.
Tomatoes	C-Standard	No. 10	6 lbs. 6 oz.	63½ oz.
Tomato Juice	A and C	No. 5	46 oz.	54-3/4 oz.
Tomato Juice	A and C	No. 10	96 oz.	
Tomato Puree	Fancy	No. 10	6 lbs. 9 oz.	

*Weights per unit and drained weights represent in most instances minimum government requirements. In commercial practice both weights will vary and are apt to be higher.

WEIGHTS AND YIELDS OF CANNED FRUITS

ITEM	GRADE	CAN SIZE	*MIN. NET WT. PER CAN	*MIN. DRAIN WT. PER CAN	APPROXIMATE COUNT
Apples-heavy pack	A-Fancy	No. 10	6 lbs.	96 oz.	
Applesauce	A-Fancy	No. 10	6 lbs.11 oz.		
Apricots-halves	A-Fancy	No. 10	6 lbs.14 oz.	66 oz.	(*65 to 86
Apricots-halves	B-Choice	No. 10	6 lbs.12 oz.	66 oz.	(*86 to 108 (*108 to 151
Apricots-halves	F-Solid pack-pie	No. 10	6 lbs.10 oz.	92 oz.	100-110
Blackberries	A-Fancy	No. 10	6 lbs.12 oz.	65 oz.	
Blackberries	B-Choice	No. 10	6 lbs.10 oz.	65 oz.	
Blackberries	F-Heavy pack-Pie	No. 10	6 lbs. 7 oz.	80 oz.	
Cherries, Royal Anne	A-Fancy	No. 10	6 lbs.14 oz.	66 oz.	(*180 to 306
Cherries, Royal Anne	B-Choice	No. 10	6 lbs.12 oz.	68 oz.	(*306 to 378 (*378 to 522

WEIGHTS AND YIELDS OF CANNED FRUITS (Cont'd.)

ITEM	GRADE	CAN SIZE	*MIN. NET WT. PER CAN	*MIN. DRAIN WT. PER CAN	APPROXIMATE COUNT
Cherries, Red Sour	Pitted				
Cherries, Syrup Pack	A-Fancy	No. 10	6 lbs.12 oz.	70¼ oz.	
Cherries, Water Pack	A-Fancy	No. 10	6 lbs. 7 oz.	74 oz.	
Cranberry Sauce		No. 10	7 lbs. 5 oz.		#1
Figs	A-Fancy	No. 10	7 lbs.	66 oz.	(*70 to 90
Figs	B-Choice	No. 10	7 lbs.	66 oz.	(*90 to 110
					(*110 to 130
Fruit Cocktail	A-Fancy	No. 10	6 lbs.14 oz.	71 oz.	
Fruit Cocktail	B-Fancy	No. 10	6 lbs.12 oz.	71 oz.	
Fruits for Salad	A-Fancy	No. 10	6 lbs.14 oz.	64½ oz.	
Fruits for Salad	B-Fancy	No. 10	6 lbs.12 oz.	64½ oz.	
Grapefruit Sections	A-Fancy	No. 5	3 lbs. 2 oz.	29-3/4 oz.	
Grapefruit Sections	B-Choice	No. 5	3 lbs. 2 oz.	27¼ oz.	
Grapefruit Juice	A-Fancy	No. 5	46 oz.		
Grapefruit Juice	A-Fancy	No. 10	96 oz.		
Orange Juice	A-Fancy	No. 5	46 oz.		
Orange Juice	A-Fancy	No. 10	96 oz.		
Peaches, halves	A-Fancy	No. 10	6 lbs.14 oz.	66 oz.	(*40 to 50
Peaches, halves	B-Choice	No. 10	6 lbs.12 oz.	68 oz.	(*30 to 40
					(*40 to 55
Peaches, halves	F-Solid pack-Pie	No. 10	6 lbs.10 oz.	92 oz.	
Pears, halves	A-Fancy	No. 10	6 lbs.12 oz.	64 oz.	(*45-55
Pears, halves	B-Choice	No. 10	6 lbs.10 oz.	65 oz.	(*30 to 40
					(*40 to 55
Pineapple, sliced	A-Fancy	No. 10	6 lbs.12 oz.		(*28 or
Pineapple, sliced	B-Choice	No. 10	6 lbs.12 oz.		(*50
Pineapple, crushed	A-Fancy	No. 10	7 lbs.	76 oz.	
Pineapple, reg. pk.	B-Choice	No. 10	7 lbs.	76 oz.	
Pineapple, crushed	A-Fancy	No. 10	7 lbs.	98 oz.	
Pineapple, heavy pack-Pie	B-Choice	No. 10	7 lbs.	98 oz.	
Pineapple Juice	A-Fancy	No. 5	46 oz.		
Pineapple Juice	A-Fancy	No. 10	96 oz.		
Plums, purple	A-Fancy	No. 10	6 lbs.14 oz.	60 oz.	66 to 70
Plums, purple	B-Choice	No. 10	6 lbs.12 oz.	62 oz.	Over 70
Plums, green gage	A-Fancy	No. 10	6 lbs.14 oz.	60 oz.	60 to 75
Plums, green gage	B-Choice	No. 10	6 lbs.12 oz.	62 oz.	Over 75
Raspberries	A-Fancy	No. 10	6 lbs.14 oz.	63 oz.	
Raspberries	B-Choice	No. 10	6 lbs.12 oz.	63 oz.	
Strawberries	A-Fancy	No. 10	6 lbs.13 oz.	63 oz.	
Strawberries	B-Choice	No. 10	6 lbs.12 oz.	63 oz.	

*Depending upon count specified.
Brackets indicate that counts are applicable to either or both grades.

FRESH FRUITS AND VEGETABLES

Federal standards for fresh fruits and vegetables have not developed as rapidly as other types of grading because it was thought that under past methods of distribution the sale of produce by grades was impractical due to the very rapid changes in quality and the many stages of handling. However, the great advances made in storage, packaging, and transportation methods, together with the need for standards in the great

CALENDAR OF FRESH FRUITS AND VEGETABLES

A – Available B – Low price period

	Jan.	Feb.	Mar.	Apr.	May	June	July	Aug.	Sept.	Oct.	Nov.	Dec.
Apples	A	A	A	A	A	A	A	B	B	B	B	B
Asparagus	A	A	B	B	B	B	B	A	A	A	A	A
Bananas	A	A	A	A	A	B	B	A	A	A	A	A
Beans (Lima)	A	A	A	A	A	A	B	B	B	B	A	A
Beans (Snap)	A	A	A	A	B	B	B	B	A	A	A	A
Beets	A	A	A	A	A	B	B	B	B	A	A	A
Blackberries	..	..	..	..	..	A	B	B	A	A	..	..
Blueberries	..	..	..	..	A	A	B	B	A	..	..	..
Brussel Sprouts	B	A	A	A	A	..	..	..	..	A	B	B
Cabbage	A	A	A	A	A	A	A	B	B	B	B	A
Cantaloupes	..	..	..	..	A	B	B	B	B	B	A	A
Carrots	B	B	A	A	A	A	A	B	B	B	B	B
Cauliflower	B	A	A	A	A	A	A	B	B	B	B	B
Cherries	..	..	..	..	A	B	B	B	A	A	..	..
Cocoanuts	A	A	A	A	A	A	A	A	A	A	A	A
Corn	..	..	..	A	A	A	B	B	B	B	A	..
Cranberries	A	A	A	..	..	..	..	..	..	B	B	B
Cucumbers	A	A	A	A	B	B	B	B	B	B	A	A
Currants	..	..	..	..	..	..	A	A	..	..	..	..
Dewberries	..	..	..	..	A	B	B	A	..	..	..	..
Eggplant	A	A	A	A	A	A	B	B	B	B	A	A
Figs	..	..	..	..	..	A	B	B	B	B	B	..
Gooseberries	..	..	..	..	..	..	A	..	..	..	..	..
Grapefruit	B	B	A	A	A	A	A	A	A	B	B	B
Grapes	A	A	A	A	A	A	A	A	A	B	B	B
Honeydew Melon	A	A	A	A	A	B	B	B	B	B	A	A
Huckleberries	..	..	..	..	..	A	B	B	A	..	..	..
Kale	A	A	A	A	B	B	B	A	A	A	A	A
Lemons	A	A	A	A	A	B	B	B	A	A	A	A
Lettuce	A	A	A	A	B	B	B	B	A	A	A	A
Limes	A	A	A	A	A	B	B	B	B	A	A	A
Loganberries	..	..	..	..	..	A	B	B	..	..	..	..
Nectarines	..	..	..	..	..	A	A	..	..	..	..	..
Onions	A	A	A	A	A	B	B	B	A	A	A	A
Oranges	B	B	B	B	A	A	A	A	A	A	B	B
Parsnips	A	B	B	A	A	A	..	..	A	B	B	B
Peaches	A	A	A	A	A	A	B	B	B	A	A	..
Pears	A	A	A	A	A	A	B	B	B	B	A	A
Peas	A	A	A	A	B	B	B	B	A	A	A	A
Persimmons	..	..	..	..	..	..	..	..	A	A	A	A
Pineapples	A	A	A	A	B	B	B	A	A	A	A	A
Plums	..	..	..	..	..	A	A	B	B	A	A	..
Potatoes	A	A	A	A	A	B	B	B	B	B	A	A
Quinces	..	..	..	..	..	..	..	..	A	A	A	A
Raspberries	..	..	..	..	A	B	B	B	A	A	..	..
Rhubarb	A	A	A	A	B	B	B	A	A	A	A	A
Spinach	A	A	A	A	A	A	A	A	A	A	A	A
Squash	A	A	A	A	B	B	B	B	B	B	A	A
Strawberries	A	A	A	A	A	B	B	B	..	..	..	A
Sweet Potatoes	A	A	A	A	A	A	A	A	B	B	B	B
Tangerines	A	..	..	..	..	..	..	..	..	..	..	A
Tomatoes	A	A	A	A	A	B	B	B	A	A	A	A
Turnips	B	B	B	A	A	A	A	A	A	B	B	B
Watermelons	..	..	..	..	A	A	B	B	B	A	..	..

volume of market trading have stimulated such rapid developments in Federal grading that nearly a million cars of produce shipped by rail annually are traded on the basis of Federal standards.

The number of grades varies with the product. Some U. S. grades are U. S. No. 1, U. S. Combination, U. S. No. 2, Orchard Run, and Cull. Most fruits are graded U. S. Fancy and U. S. No. 1 or U. S. No. 1 and U. S. No. 2. While most vegetables are graded U. S. No. 1, U. S. Fancy is also used as well as several lower grades.

Because of the nature of the merchandise government standards vary with the products, but some common characteristics used in grading all fruits and vegetables are the amount of decay and injury by damage or disease, form of product and degree of maturity.

SOME FACTS ABOUT FISH

Each section of the country has its own seafood; for example, lobsters and oysters come from the Atlantic seaboard and salmon from the Pacific. The Great Lakes abound in whitefish, and Southern waters furnish pompano, Spanish mackerel, shrimp, and red snappers.

Fish may be purchased in many forms, as fresh, frosted, frozen, canned, mild-cured, pickled, dry-salted, and smoked. The first four constitute the bulk of the industry. Quick-freezing and modern refrigeration have made it possible to ship fish to inland markets so that restaurants in the Middle Atlantic States and on the Pacific Coast may serve seafood from the shores of New England or the Gulf of Mexico. Since the freezing is done as soon as the fish is taken from the water, the product retains the qualities of the fresh article and, as a rule, only the highest grades are put through this process, so that the "Quick-frozen fish" may be superior to the so-called "fresh" unless the fresh is carefully handled. Quick-frozen fish need not be thawed before it is cooked, but more time must be allowed for cooking. However, after they have thawed they should be cooked immediately. This process has brought to restaurants in inland cities the fish which were formerly available only at the seashore or nearby markets. By featuring these items on the menus they may come to occupy the place which they deserve and become a source of profit.

There are "fat" fish and "lean" ones. In the first class are salmon, mackerel, shad, butterfish, turbot, lake trout, pompano, whitefish, bluefish, herring, catfish, eels, and halibut; whereas, cod, haddock, flounder, pollock, pickerel, perch, and smelts contain very little fat. It is well to remember these two classes and be guided accordingly in cooking. For example, since mackerel contains considerable fat, it is not necessary to add much fat to it, but baked haddock would be very dry indeed if it were not basted frequently or did not have strips of salt pork laid upon it during cooking.

CHECK LIST ON FISH

GOOD FISH	BAD FISH
Full, clear eyes	Eyes cloudy, wrinkled and sunken
Skin bright	Skin dull, or slimy, color pale
Scales tight	Scales loose
Gills bright red	Gills yellowish, gray or brown
Flesh firm and elastic; does not keep a dent when pressed with the finger	Flesh soft and flabby and fingerprint remains
Smells fresh, both inside and at gills	Smells stale, spoilage first noticed at gills
Body stiff	
Whole fish sinks in water	Whole fish floats in water (when badly decomposed)
Flesh sticks firmly to bones	Flesh separates from bones easily

BUYING ROUTINE

No food purchasing department can operate efficiently unless there is an established routine and system to provide a framework for the mechanics of buying. While the routine will vary to fit the needs of different establishments, it must always insure the coordination of the purchasing, receiving, and preparation departments. The chef must provide the necessary information to the food buyer in sufficient time for effective buying and the buyer must furnish the proper merchandise.

Perishables. Purchases of perishables should be scheduled to meet the requirements of the daily menus and not a par stock. Based on delivery schedules, raw food requirements should not be purchased for more than two to three delivery days hence. Refrigerators should be stocked with *current* menu items *only*. Buying to a hypothetical par stock leads to excessive buying and is costly in the following ways:

(1) It overloads the storage facilities. If storage was built to accommodate such buying practice, unwarranted expenditures have been made for oversized capacities.

(2) It creates larger inventories, necessitating more attention, more handling and, therefore, higher labor costs.

(3) With a larger inventory, the greater the loss from shrinkage, trim, spoilage, and pilferage.

At a fixed time every day, the steward or storeroom man should take an inventory of all perishables in the storeroom, in all the refrigerators, both in the kitchen and storeroom, and in all other locations where they are chargeable against food stores. After the inventory has been completed, the buyer should meet with the chef to discuss the current requirements based on the next three days' menus. The requirements based on the weekly "blocked out menu" and on all other sales projection information are discussed. From this the buyer can anticipate certain necessary purchases and plan accordingly. The food buyer then compares his requirements with what he has on hand and indicates on the market list the quantities of each item it is necessary to buy. He is then ready to obtain his market quotations.

Canned Goods and Grocery Items. The food buyer, in cooperation with the chef, should set up a par stock for every grocery item to be carried in the storeroom. Generally the par stock should provide for about one week's needs plus a 50 per cent safety factor. Each week a list is prepared of replacements for the storeroom in order to keep the stock up to par. The list is then approved and the buying proceeds along regular channels.

This signed and approved list of grocery items becomes a part of the permanent files of the purchasing department, just as the daily market quotation sheet.

Standing Orders. The practice of having standing orders for any food, even for milk, cream, bread or rolls, is unsatisfacaory. Volumes of business for the various days of the week will vary in every establishment and orders should conform to the expected pattern of business for each day of the week, giving consideration to week-ends and holidays.

Total food inventories, while dependent to a degree on local market conditions, deliveries, and the size of the operation, should turn over from 3½ to 4 times each month in dollar value.

Market Quotations. In the larger cities there is no difficulty in obtaining quotations from three or four dealers for every item on the Steward's Market Quotation Sheet. In smaller cities, however, it is often impossible to obtain more than two. Sometimes there is only one dealer in town handling the requested item. Every effort should be made to get at least two quotations on each item, if possible.

A regular routine should be established for receiving price quotations from the various dealers. This routine will depend necessarily upon the location in which the buyer finds himself. In most instances, it is best to call the dealers in the afternoon and tell them what the requirements will

STEWARD'S MARKET QUOTATION LIST

ON HAND	ARTICLE	WANTED	QUOTATIONS T.C.	X.Y.	Z.R.	M.O.
	VEAL					
	Breast					
	Brains					
	Feet					
	Fore Quarters					
	Hind Quarters					
	Head					
	Kidneys					
① 5 lb.	Legs	3	60	62	63	62
2 lb.	Liver U.S. No. 1	10 lb.	118	115	117	117
	Loins					
	Racks					
	Saddles					
	~~Shoulder~~ Chop Conval	1	30	28	30	32
	Sweet Breads					
	LAMB					
	Breast					
① 14 lb.	~~Fore Quarters~~ Chux 14-18#	2	38	40	40	43
	Feet					
	Fries					
	Kidneys					
	Loins					
① 7 lb.	Legs Pr. 16-18#	1 pr.	56	58	57	60
	Lamb, Spring					
	Racks, Double					
	Racks, Spring					
2	Saddles	Conval.	63	64	62	65
	Shoulder					
	PROVISIONS					
	Bacon					
	Bologna					
	Bologna					
	Crepinette					
	Salami					
	Hams, Corned					
	Hams, Fresh					
	Hams, Polish					
1	Hams, Smoked	1	49	48	49	50
	Hams, Virginia					

ON HAND	ARTICLE	WANTED	QUOTATIONS F.G.	K.S.	T.R.	A.B.
	POULTRY					
	Chickens					
	Chickens, Roast					
3	Chickens, Broilers 2½#	24	36	35	37	37
	Chickens, Broilers					
	Chickens, Supreme					
	Cocks					
	Capons					
	Ducks					
	Ducklings					
	Fowl					
	Geese					
	Goslings					
	Guinea Hens					
	Guinea Squabs					
	Pigeons					
	Poussins					
			M.Z.	A.Q.	F.R.	M.M.
	SHELL FISH					
	Clams, Chowder					
30	Clams, Cherrystone	150	200	225	225	250
/	Clams, Little Neck	100	275	250	300	275
	Clams, Soft					
	Crabs, Hard					
	Crabs, Meat					
	Crabs, Oyster					
	Crabs, Soft Shell					
	Crabs, Soft Shell Prime					
	Lobsters, Meat					
	Lobsters, Tails					
	Lobsters, Chicken					
	Lobsters, Medium					
	Lobsters, Large					
	Oysters, Box					
25	Oysters, Blue Points	200	225	200	225	225
	Oysters					
	Scallops					
	Shrimps					
	Turtle					

be. They, in turn, will call back later that afternoon or early the following morning and give their quotations. The buyer then has the option of taking his quotation sheet to the market and picking out the merchandise personally or placing the order by telephone.

The original copy of the completed market quotation sheet is delivered to the accounting department for checking against purchase orders and/or invoice prices. A copy is kept in the purchasing department as part of the permanent records.

PURCHASE ORDERS

While it is usual practice to use purchase orders only for the purchase of supplies, equipment, and food ordered out of town, it is advisable to utilize them in the purchasing routine wherever practical. As a general rule, it is not considered necessary to issue purchase orders for perishables which are purchased locally and delivered on the day purchased.

The purchase order should be prepared in duplicate, listing those items ordered from each purveyor, the accepted price and delivery conditions.

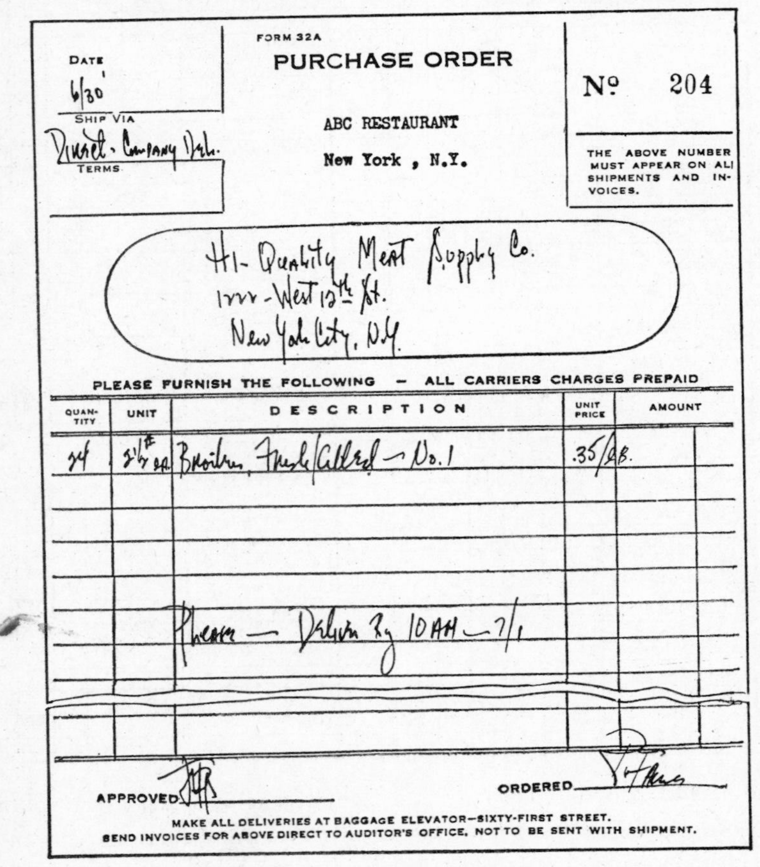

FORM 32A

PURCHASE ORDER

DATE 6/30

SHIP VIA Direct - Company Del.

TERMS

ABC RESTAURANT

New York, N.Y.

№ 204

THE ABOVE NUMBER MUST APPEAR ON ALL SHIPMENTS AND INVOICES.

Hi-Quality Meat Supply Co.
1222 - West 12th St.
New York City, N.Y.

PLEASE FURNISH THE FOLLOWING — ALL CARRIERS CHARGES PREPAID

QUANTITY	UNIT	DESCRIPTION	UNIT PRICE	AMOUNT
24	2½# ea.	Broilers, Fresh/Killed – No. 1	.35/lb.	
		Please — Deliver by 10 AM — 7/1		

APPROVED [illegible] ORDERED [illegible]

MAKE ALL DELIVERIES AT BAGGAGE ELEVATOR—SIXTY-FIRST STREET.
SEND INVOICES FOR ABOVE DIRECT TO AUDITOR'S OFFICE, NOT TO BE SENT WITH SHIPMENT.

The duplicate copy remains in the purchasing department's records; the original is delivered to the receiving clerk. In some cases a third copy is made which is forwarded to the purveyor as a confirmation of the original order.

Some advantages of using the purchase order are:

(1) It provides a complete record of the market order for each purveyor.

(2) It provides a guide for the receiving clerk, allowing time to take action on merchandise late in arriving and immediately indicates overshipment or undershipment of orders.

(3) It provides the receiving clerk with an immediate verification of invoice prices with accepted quotations.

An illustration of a purchase order appears on page 98

DAILY MARKET INFORMATION

In order to supplement the market quotation sheet and to provide a check against quoted prices, the food buyer should make use of other professional sources of market information. Federal and local government releases, with information concerning commodity food prices and other valuable data, appear in daily newspapers and in mailed newsletters. Very often prices for butter, eggs and poultry are based on an agreed mark up over such reported quotations. In addition, there are local trade sheets, radio programs and commercial market reports, which give much useful information.

SALESMEN

Ninety-nine per cent of the salesmen who visit the food buyer are hard-working, honest men, and specialists in their field. It is advisable to have their friendship and cooperation. They generally merit consideration but it should not be carried to extremes. They can do the buyer a great disservice by taking up a great deal of time which he should spend on more important matters. It is well to limit their visits to one day each week. They may grumble about this at first but if it is explained to them that, welcome as their visits are, there just isn't time enough to see them every day, they will cease to grumble, particularly if the food buyer is careful to see that the proper salesmen get credit for purchases.

BUYER AND RECEIVING CLERK

In every food buyer's routine, there should be sufficient time available for him to check the major deliveries. While he should not be responsible for count and weight, he or the chef should make certain that the quality and specifications of the received merchandise are in accordance with that ordered. All the effort put into effective purchasing will be wasted if the receiving procedure does not insure the receipt of commodities commensurate with buying orders.

Chapter VII: RECEIVING PROCEDURES

THE FUNCTION of the receiving department is one of the most important in any food service establishment—and one which is, perhaps, the most often neglected. Unless receipts of food and other supplies are carefully checked, both as to quantity and quality, of what use is careful buying on the part of the steward, purchasing agent or whatever department head functions in this capacity?

It is clear that a restaurant cannot offer for re-sale goods which fail to arrive, even though purchased and paid for. Yet many food establishments fail to realize the extent of the leaks that may occur through failure to provide proper personnel, receiving facilities, and controls.

The essential requirements of an adequate receiving procedure that should serve to provide proper controls are summarized as follows:

(1) Competent receiving personnel.
(2) Adequate facilities and equipment for receiving.
(3) Charts showing specifications for guidance in receiving.
(4) Proper receiving routine.
(5) Periodic independent checks of receiving methods and procedures.

With regard to personnel, the primary qualifications of a receiving clerk are alertness, sound judgment, the ability to organize his routine, and some basic knowledge of food. He should be qualified to inspect food, at least initially, in order to determine that it generally meets the establishment's specification standards. The degree of further inspection required, to be made by a fully qualified person, will depend on the ability of the receiving clerk.

A steward may do the most careful kind of specification buying, but if the receiving clerk does not check the receipts against those same specifications, the establishment loses hundreds, and possibly thousands, of dollars and the operator wonders what has happened to the profits he should be making.

As an example, one grade of peaches may be specified for a certain item on the menu, another grade for a different item. The differential in price may determine profit or loss. To the careless receiving clerk, peaches are peaches. He checks in two cases without noticing grade or price.

He may not watch for damaged cans, shortages in weights or in number. Deliveries are often made up hastily in vendors' establishments and errors are bound to occur. Items may be broken in transit or stolen from an open truck. Sometimes a truck driver does not notice these things but frequently he does. When he sees that a receiving clerk does not do a conscientious job, that particular establishment becomes a disposal center for much damaged or partially spoiled merchandise. Weights and counts will be exaggerated and many items diverted to other destinations.

Selling food to the public is certainly no easy road to riches, but it can be an easy road in the other direction if the food that is paid for is never received or received in such poor condition as to make it unusable.

MECHANICS OF RECEIVING

The receiving department should have adequate facilities and be located between the service entrance and the storeroom so as to control the flow of deliveries coming into the premises. Sufficient space should be provided so that deliveries will not tend to pile up and disrupt the normal receiving routine.

Equipment. No worker can do a thoroughly efficient job unless he has the proper equipment. Since weight is of prime importance in the receipt of food, a suitable set of accurate scales is a necessity. Faulty or inaccurate scales will hamper the work of the most conscientious clerk and result in costly errors, arguments, and loss of payroll time. However, it must be recognized that precision weighing instruments do not automatically insure exact weight. The best scale is only a tool and will never be more accurate than the care exercised by the person who is using it.

There are recording scales which stamp the weight of merchandise on the invoices or receiving tickets. This is labor-saving and eliminates the possibility of clerical errors in jotting down this information by hand. However, a scale weighs anything that is placed on it and extraneous material may easily be added to the legitimate merchandise to give an inflated, false weight.

Platform scales built into the floor are widely used. They minimize the effort of lifting and for this reason are time and labor-saving. Various types of dials are used with this type of scale. The clear-view full-face dial avoids disputes. The magnified dial that is visible to only one person is of dubious value. In the event of a weight shortage, considerable time might be lost in argument between the delivery man and the receiving clerk as to the correct weight. This type of haggling is avoided by use of the open-face dial. The ordinary platform scale is usually a sufficiently satisfactory weighing device when used by a competent and conscientious receiving clerk.

Weighing Each Item. One practice of the receiving clerk, when he is in a rush because of several deliveries received at one time or because he is hurried by delivery men, who usually claim they are double parked, is to weigh an entire shipment of meat in one operation and compare only the total weight with the total of the weights on the invoice. This is a practice which should be prohibited at all costs. Ten pounds of top sirloin lacking in the order will not be counter-balanced in value by ten pounds more of short ribs. Each item must be weighed separately. The receiving clerk should be instructed to tag each incoming meat item as to weight. This will prevent any wholesale weighing and insure accuracy.

Deliverymen will try to speed up the checking of their deliveries. There may be no motive for this except their desire to be on their way. On the other hand, they may know about the shortages and hope that the incorrect weights will remain undiscovered. Traffic tie-ups are an every-day occurrence and may be used as a convenient excuse for hurrying or "rattling" a receiving clerk, particularly one that is inexperienced. Old hands at the job will take frequent admonitions to "step on it" in their stride without allowing it to affect the accuracy of their work. When they are unduly harassed by these demands from delivery men, it may take some of the responsibility off their shoulders if signs are posted by the management, stating that each incoming item *must* be weighed and checked. If the pressure on the receiving clerk continues, the management can post a sign indicating that any delivery man who cannot wait for a delivery to be weighed and checked can take back the merchandise.

Checking for Quality. Specific information is required when it comes to checking the quality of perishable fruits and vegetables. Receiving clerks who very conscientiously check the weight of items received, often neglect the equally important function of checking to see that the grade, or quality of the goods, is in agreement with that shown on the delivery slip or invoice. This occurred on one occasion in a large Eastern hotel where a shipment of meat received was correct in weight but was two grades below the quality specified. The over-charge amounted to more than the day's salary of the receiving clerk.

Heads of lettuce should be chosen at random, cut open and checked for rust. Oranges and grapefruit must be tested for taste and juice content. Fruits and vegetables in the center or bottom of crates must be checked. This can only be done by reaching in and selecting several items or by up-ending the crate to get at those that are buried.

Whenever any doubt arises as to the quality of meat or fish, the receiving clerk will save himself grief by calling on the steward or department head for final judgment.

NO. 101
DATE 2/20
DEALER B + R
CUT CHUCK LAMB
WEIGHT 50½ UNIT PRICE 34
EXTENSION 17.17

NO. 101
DATE 2/20
DEALER B + R
CUT CHUCK LAMB
WEIGHT 50½ UNIT PRICE 34
EXTENSION 17.17

Incoming meats should be tagged by the receiving clerk with their weight at the time of delivery. This practice serves more than one useful purpose:

(1) It facilitates checking on the accuracy of the receiving clerk.
(2) It prevents disputes over the weight when the meat is issued to the kitchen.
(3) It saves a duplication of effort since tagged meat, if it is still in the original package or piece, need not be weighed when it is issued to the kitchen.

STANDARD RECEIVING SPECIFICATIONS

It is obvious that a high quality of food must be purchased if that same quality is to be served to the restaurant patrons. It does not always follow, however, that the standard of the finished product will be the same as that purchased. Food can be, and often is, ruined in preparation, but preparation is the function of the kitchen, not of the receiving department.

However, regardless of how well the kitchen may perform its function, it is *impossible* to serve high quality meals with low quality raw food supplies. With the aid of standard purchasing and receiving specifications, management can more easily trace the guilty party if the finished product is deficient.

Furthermore, these established standards prevent any "buck passing" between the chef, steward, and receiving clerk. Chefs or cooks may be tempted to fall back on the old alibi for a poor meat entree, "but I had only commercial cuts to start with" if they think they can make that alibi stick. They cannot if it is the established practice to buy choice meats. And the receiving clerk can be proved at fault only if substandard meats are found in the ice boxes. Standard receiving specifications remove all guess work for the receiving clerk. They must correspond in every detail with the specifications that have been set up for purchasing and should always be easily available for reference.

The items in the specifications should be classified so that they are easy to locate and, above all, they should be printed legibly. Probably they are most convenient if posted on the wall near the receiving clerk's desk or table, covered with glass or a transparent plastic to prevent soiling since they never seem to be renewed until they are practically unreadable. Since figures are easily mistaken, this is a simple precaution to take and may prevent costly errors. Also, although the regular receiving clerk may know the specifications on most items without referring to the chart, new or substitute employees will not.

A simple specification chart that can be adapted for receiving department use will be found in the chapter on "Purchasing."

A peculiar problem is often posed in the case of fish items, which are heavily iced for delivery. The receiving clerk cannot always unpack a shipment to obtain the net weight. However, particularly in the case of a commodity of high unit value, such as shrimp, he should make an estimate of the tare (container weight) based on the gross weight. A further check of the weight should be made in the kitchen at the time the shipment is de-iced for preparation. To visualize the importance of such a step, the auditor might compile the value of all of the shrimp purchased through the course of a normal month and compute the amount of loss which would accrue if each shipment were five per cent under weight. This same procedure would apply to many other items.

The safest procedure is to check the actual net weight of the merchandise by weighing at least one iced shipment from each purveyor a minimum of once a week.

RESPONSIBILITY OF THE ACCOUNTING DEPARTMENT

Checking the numerical accuracy of food deliveries is primarily the responsibility of the accounting department. In large establishments, the position of receiving clerk is a full-time job under the direct supervision of the auditor. This arrangement should insure the greatest accuracy in receiving food and supplies since the methods of the receiving clerk should be checked frequently by the accounting department.

In smaller places, there is usually not sufficient activity to warrant the employment of a full-time receiving clerk. This has given rise to a combination job of receiving clerk and storeroom man. As receiving clerk, he checks counts and weights but not all quality factors. There are usually forms for him to fill in when shortages occur and when substandard goods are returned. Whenever there is a delivery of meat or any other merchandise that the receiving clerk cannot personally check for quality, he should be under standing instructions to call on the steward, purchasing agent, or chef to pass judgment thereon.

Surprise Receiving Tests. In some establishments, the building is so laid out as to make a combination of jobs inefficient or impossible. In such cases, it is practical to permit the steward to receive food supplies, subject to surprise receiving tests by the auditor. When these surprise tests are made at irregular but frequent intervals, conforming to no fixed pattern as to time, shortages in weights and counts will be much less frequent. Once each week is the absolute minimum for the frequency of these tests by the auditor. As an added safeguard, daily receiving tests should be made by the manager or some other trusted employee in the food department.

These safeguards are necessary where the steward is doubling as receiving clerk because he is checking his own purchases. It is only common sense to stop, before it starts, any opportunity for dishonesty which, in these circumstances, would be great.

If possible, it is advisable to assign the task of checking weight and count to some other employee in the food department but one not connected with the purchasing. Once the verification of weight and count has been completed, the incoming goods may be inspected for quality, price, and trim by the steward or chef.

It may be advisable also, when purchases of linens, detergents and various types of equipment or supplies are made, for the first time, to retain the labels for inspection by the accounting department. On large re-orders, a cross-check with the original labels which can be kept on file, will aid in spot-checking proper quality.

Blind Receiving. In order to compel hasty, careless, or indifferent receiving clerks to weigh and count every incoming item, a system known as "blind" receiving may be instituted. The clerk has no access to any invoice or delivery ticket containing the weight or count of the merchandise ordered. He receives from the steward or purchasing agent a suitable purchase order form stating that certain items have been purchased. The prices and quantities are omitted. There remains no alternative for the receiving clerk but to weigh and count each item. Vendors' invoices are sent by mail to the accounting department where comparisons are made with the receiving data.

DATE 6/1 PURCHASE ORDER S No. 1695

ABC Meat Co

PLEASE FURNISH THE FOLLOWING – ALL CARRIERS CHARGES PREPAID

QUANTITY	UNIT	DESCRIPTION	UNIT PRICE	AMOUNT
		Ribs of Beef		
		Sweetbreads		
		Oxtails		
		Legs of Lamb		

APPROVED [signature] PURCHASING AGENT

INVOICE MUST NOT ACCOMPANY MERCHANDISE

Another form of "blind" receiving is sometimes used by requesting all vendors to omit prices and quantities from their delivery tickets.

These drastic measures are the result of experience with lax or even unscrupulous receiving clerks. All too often they will merely jot down the quantities and weights from the invoice or delivery ticket without any verification. This practice does not go unnoticed by the delivery men.

RECEIVING RECORDS

Suitable receiving records of all incoming shipments must be maintained. The manner of recording is of secondary consequence and may be arranged to suit the accounting methods of any given establishment. The principal media by which such records are maintained are receiving sheets, individual receiving tickets, and receiving stamps.

Receiving Sheets. For large food service establishments, a receiving sheet has the advantage of allowing easy consolidation of each day's purchases. It also facilitates subsequent study and comparison of day-to-day purchases.

Daily merchandise receipts are divided into two major categories, (1) storeroom purchases that are dispatched to the storeroom, and (2) direct purchases that are sent to the kitchen for immediate use.

As will be noted in the illustrated form of the "Receiving Clerk's Daily Report below, the final total in the "Total Amount" column must equal the total of the "Food Direct" column plus the "Food Stores" column.

RECEIVING CLERK'S DAILY REPORT

NO. 157

DATE 2/15

QUAN.	UNIT	DESCRIPTION	√	UNIT PRICE	AMOUNT	TOTAL AMOUNT	PURCHASE JOURNAL DISTRIBUTION		
							FOOD DIRECT	FOOD STORES	SUNDRIES
		Apex							
68	lbs	Filets		165	112 20			112 20	
66	lbs	Chuck Beef		38	25 08	137 28		25 08	
		Jones							
50	lbs	Knackwurst		47		23 50		23 50	
		Winslow							
20	pts	Strawberries		27	5 40		5 40		
1	bag	Yellow Onions			3 75	9 15	3 75		
		American							
30	doz	Doughnuts		30		9 00	9 00		
						178 93	18 15	160 78	

Chas. Press Form 119 2M-5-49

J J Smith SIGNATURE

Receiving sheets are usually made out in duplicate. One copy is retained by the receiving clerk and one is sent to the accounting department for verification of purchase invoices and for use also by the food cost accountant if one is employed.

Individual Receiving Tickets. Individual receiving tickets are used as a direct support for each purchase invoice. They are sent to the accounting department for use by the accounts payable clerk, and are generally attached to the invoice as a permanent record.

Receiving sheets and receiving tickets contain virtually the same information and the use of both entails a duplication of effort. It has, therefore, become fairly common practice for receiving tickets to be used only when merchandise is received without accompanying invoices.

Whenever invoices, invoice duplicates or vendors' delivery tickets accompany a delivery, they should first be stamped with a receiving stamp.

MERCHANDISE RECEIVED WITHOUT BILL
HOTEL ST. MORITZ
50 CENTRAL PARK SOUTH
NEW YORK CITY
2198

FROM XYZ Meat Co DATE 2/20

ADDRESS

QUANTITY	DESCRIPTION	AMOUNT	
72½	Ribs of Beef @ 1.10	79	75

RECEIVED BY MML

Receiving or Invoice Stamp. All incoming invoices should bear an invoice stamp, applied either by the accounting department or the receiving clerk, depending upon the system in use. It should contain four major check points for approval: (1) receiving; (2) accounting; (3) purchasing; (4) payment. Each check point, in the order named, should be initialed by the receiving clerk, accounts payable clerk, department head, and the manager or a delegated authority for payment approved. In format, this receiving stamp will appear as follows:

Received by .... Date ....
Prices & extensions checked by ....
Department head approval ....
Payment approval ....

Returning Unsatisfactory Merchandise. To follow the line of least resistance is a common human failing—one which management must recognize and guard against. It requires far less effort, both mentally and physically, to accept questionable merchandise than to follow through on all the procedures attendant upon returning such a shipment.

The return of merchandise requires at least four separate steps:

(1) An argument with the delivery man who is disinclined to take back a delivery because that means extra work and explanations for him.

(2) The reason for the return of the merchandise must be noted on the invoice or the delivery ticket.

(3) A form requesting a credit memo must be filled out in duplicate and sent to the accounting department for transmittal to the vendor.

(4) Last, but by no means least, the department head must be notified so that plans may be changed and substitutions made in the menu if that should be necessary.

In addition to the above, the return of merchandise is very likely to result in one or more telephone calls at busy moments giving further explanation as to why the return was necessary.

HOTEL LEXINGTON
LEXINGTON AVENUE at 48th ST.
NEW YORK, N. Y.

B 118

REQUEST FOR CREDIT MEMO

TO XYZ Meat Co DATE 1/30 19

GENTLEMEN PLEASE SEND US A CREDIT MEMO FOR THE FOLLOWING:

28 lbs. Breast of Lamb		
Billed as Breast of Veal @ .37	10	36
should be @ .15	4	20
Credit Requested	6	16

REASON: Incorrect billing

RECEIVED ON REC'G RECORD NO 47403

DATE 1/30

BY ORDER OF: JRB DEP'T

HOTEL LEXINGTON
BY J R Brown

Because the acceptance of merchandise as it is delivered is such a simple procedure for the receiving clerk in comparison with the routine he must follow in returning unsatisfactory shipments, it behooves management to see that the receiving clerk understands exactly what the acceptance of poor merchandise involves—a heavy money loss through spoilage, waste, or dissatisfied customers.

Handling Cash. In certain instances, receiving clerks or stewards control a small fund of cash—a "bank" as it is called. This is used in making cash disbursements for truckage fees, cab fares, or similar charges.

Disbursing cash in this manner has only one advantage—it may save some time for the vendors' employees. It has many disadvantages and is, therefore, a practice which should be discouraged. It may lead to faulty approval of vouchers and pilfering when the receiving clerk's attention is distracted. In addition, it is a time-consuming task for the receiving clerk since he must keep his bank in balance. Although this involves only simple arithmetic, he is quite likely, in the rush of other things, to neglect to jot down disbursements. He'll then spend valuable time trying to remember where the money went. It can be seen that the disadvantages of such a practice do not compensate for the one advantage which benefits outsiders only. These disbursements should be handled by the accounting department or the front office cashier.

The receiving clerk—one of the most important links in the chain of internal control.

The proper way to hang fresh meats in refrigerated boxes. This permits the free circulation of air around the meat.

This is a poorly arranged storeroom, lacking in neatness and orderliness. Note overhanging packages. A falling package may cause an accident.

A well-arranged meat box with maximum use of limited space. However, this arrangement is not suggested for lengthy storage as the lack of free air circulation encourages bacterial growth.

This pantry, with modern self-service equipment, reduces delays in service to a minimum.

A dining room service stand such as this helps the staff give quick and efficient service.

The arrangement of this kitchen service bar permits rapid service as the waiters are able to help themselves to glassware.

Bright, gaily colored china for coffee shop and informal service.

Buffet arrangement for small parties. The crowding of equipment mars the appearance of an otherwise attractive table. (Specially posed)

An attractive set-up for six persons, giving a gracious, homelike atmosphere.

Photographs, Courtesy Simtex Mills.

Chapter VIII: STORING FOOD

THE STOREROOM should be one of the show places of any food establishment. Too often it is a hodgepodge of supplies and a convenient place to get rid of obsolete equipment, old menus and other items which will probably never be used and are only taking up valuable space. It behooves a good manager to visit his storeroom once a day to observe first hand how it is being operated.

In any manufacturing industry the tool or supply storeroom is one of the prime points of control. In the business of public feeding this important department has generally received only cursory attention. It is here that the *dollars converted to merchandise* need constant attention and supervision.

The storeroom man should not always be blamed for lack of order, however. The location and layout of the room may be so poor as to make efficient operation almost impossible. Most storerooms seem to be an afterthought on the part of the architect. One wonders if they even appeared on the original blue print—if they were not sliced off the kitchen when the need for them arose, since most of them are far too small, poorly lighted, and ventilated.

The size of a storeroom depends, naturally, upon the volume and nature of the business of the establishment and upon its location. There is no need for excessive size because, except in isolated places, efficient purchasing keeps the stocks down to a minimum. However, it takes careful planning to have a space for everything so arranged that each item is readily available. To reach a can of corn it should not be necessary to pull down a truck load of other items.

There is a definite relationship between inventories and usage. The first thing to do, if space appears to be lacking, is to recheck the inventories. A month-to-month study will reveal the relationship between stock on hand and monthly usage. If the ratio seems too great, the purchasing agent should be reminded that he is not buying for a grocery store. A crowded condition may be partly due to dead stock that has been purchased and forgotten. Every effort should be made to utilize such items. Or it may be due to a crowded menu, over-loaded with slow-moving items. If the menu is thinned down, the condition of the storeroom will improve.

STOREROOM REQUIREMENTS

Location. The ideal location for the storeroom is near, if not immediately adjacent to, the receiving station and the kitchen. Otherwise, there must be payroll cost for a man or men, as well as additional equipment, to haul supplies to and from these posts. If such an arrangement is not possible, conveyors or subveyors will cut down time and effort.

Physical Properties. If spoilage is to be reduced to a minimum, it is imperative that the storeroom be well ventilated and not over-heated. Hot water and steam pipes are a menace and should be heavily insulated. High temperatures play havoc with canned goods. If good ventilation can only be gained by spending some money, the wise operator will spend it. Otherwise, the money will be lost many times over in ruined merchandise.

The floor should be of a material that will take heavy trucking without breaking up. It is well to slant the floor slightly toward a drain to permit frequent flushing. This makes the operation of cleaning the floor a simple one compared with mopping. Strict sanitation is the only way to keep this room (or any room) free from all types of vermin.

Shelving. If possible, the shelving should be of steel with adjustable shelves. If of wood, those shelves for canned goods should be far enough apart to permit the stacking of two No. 10 cans or three No. 2½ cans, and 18 inches deep to permit two or three rows of cans. Greater depth makes it difficult to reach the cans in the back. If more storage space is necessary the shelves lower down—below counter height—may be widened.

Those items most frequently needed by the kitchen should be stored nearest the exit door leading to the kitchen. Also, if the sequence of pages in the inventory books bears a close relationship to the arrangement of items on the shelves, time is saved in locating merchandise and in taking inventories.

To save space, storeroom personnel should realize that only one case of any item need be opened at a time. To conserve shelf space, a convenient way of handling surplus cases is by means of skids which stand on legs six inches above the floor. These cases may then be wheeled in from the receiving room on a "truck-jack" arrangement and remain standing in an out-of-the-way place until needed.

Equipment. A scale which can weigh up to 200 pounds is a necessary piece of equipment. In addition, there should be a small scale with a capacity of 20 pounds for weighing and packaging such items as sugar, beans, split peas, dried fruits and spices. A scoop is extremely handy to assist in this operation.

Additional equipment should include a stout ladder, a hand truck and, if skids are not used, a number of suitable racks for floor storage. These should be on six-inch legs. Nothing should be stored directly on the floor as such storage prevents flushing and cleaning and encourages vermin.

The storeroom needs a heavy work table and, if possible, a "ripening" table. The latter should be equipped with "ripening" lamps which are nothing more than ultra-violet ray lamps mounted on the table underneath the top. These "sun lamps" are controlled by an off-and-on switch which operates five minutes *on* and five minutes *off*. This makes possible the quick ripening of melons, avocados, tomatoes and other fruits and vegetables.

There should be a cabinet suitable for locking up certain small items which are easily concealed and carried away, as well as a cabinet for keeping mops, brooms, and brushes used in cleaning the storeroom. This cabinet should have open vents or ventilation in case any items are put away while they are still damp.

In some storerooms it is customary to store the reserve supplies of linen, china, glass, and silverware. All such supplies should be under lock and key and none should be issued except upon properly authorized requisitions. These reserve supplies are not to be confused with the operating stocks which are not kept in the storeroom but in other storage spaces conveniently adjacent to the departments where they are used.

Storeroom Hours. During the hours the storeroom is scheduled to be open there should *always* be someone on duty. No one should be permitted to enter the storeroom except the people who work there. If there is a locked Dutch (half) door at the entrance, permitting deliveries to be made over a counter, this will go a long way in keeping unauthorized personnel from entering the storeroom.

It is not necessary to have the storeroom open all day and part of the night. This practice breeds carelessness on the part of the kitchen in making their regular requisitions as it is so easy to run to the storeroom for forgotten items, indicating poor planning and resulting in lost payroll time. The number of hours the storeroom must be kept open will depend upon the size and type of the food establishment it serves. However, it should be closed for a portion of the afternoon, say from 1:30 to 4:30, to provide an opportunity for cleaning, restocking shelves and for the maintenance of the records it is necessary to keep each day.

Storeroom Keys. Proper control is necessary in handling storeroom keys to avoid the possibility of losses. One key in active use should be sufficient. An emergency key should be kept in the manager's or auditor's desk in a sealed envelope.

In a hotel restaurant, the control of the storeroom key is quite easy. When the storeroom is closed for the day, the key in use should be placed in a sealed envelope with the storeroom man's signature written across the seal. Stapling the envelope in addition to sealing it gives added security since it prevents tampering with the seal. This envelope should be left with the front office cashier until the storeroom man on the morning shift reports for duty. During each shift that the storeroom is kept open the key should be in the possession of only the man in charge. In a commercial restaurant, two keys—one for each shift—are usually necessary.

When refrigerator equipment is located in the storeroom, the engineer or maintenance man is usually provided with a key to the storeroom in order to attend to this equipment. In such cases, it is well to install a recording time clock on the storeroom door so that entrance during the night may be recorded.

REFRIGERATION

Each storeroom should be equipped with a sufficient amount of refrigerated space. Reserve supplies of meats, fruits and vegetables should be kept here and not in the kitchen where the daily issue of supplies cannot be controlled.

The three types of refrigeration in use for this purpose are the blower, the fin coil and circulating brine.

The blower type employs a high-speed fan to circulate cold air throughout the refrigerated space. While it achieves satisfactory reduction of temperature, it tends to cause considerable dryness in the surface areas of fruits, vegetables, and meats. This type of refrigeration is best suited for beverage storerooms or units containing closed containers of butter, eggs, cheese, or milk.

The most widely used type of refrigeration is the fin coil which provides a slow natural movement of cold air, reducing surface evaporation of foods to a minimum.

Circulating brine in coiled pipes is still very much in evidence in older establishments but it is not as efficient. This method is being re-

REFRIGERATION CHART

All foods in storage, to retain their quality, require varying temperatures. This quality is seriously affected when an attempt is made to keep them all at temperatures of from 40° to 42° F. as is the custom in many food establishments. The following temperatures for various foods are considered ideal:

Item	Temp. in Degrees F.
Apples*	32 - 36
Apricots*	32 - 36
Asparagus*	32 - 36
Avacados**	40 - 45
Beans (Navy)	50 - 60
Beans - Green-Lima*	32 - 36
Bananas	50 - 60
Beets*	32 - 36
Berries*	32 - 36
Berries (Frozen)	0 - 5
Broccoli*	32 - 36
Brussels Sprouts*	32 - 36
Butter	32 - 36
Cabbage*	32 - 36
Canned Fruits	50 - 60
Canned Vegetables	50 - 60
Canned Meats	32 - 36
Cantaloupe*	32 - 36
Carrots*	32 - 36
Cauliflower*	32 - 36
Celery*	32 - 36
Cereals	50 - 60
Cheese*	32 - 36
Cherries*	32 - 36
Coconuts*	32 - 36
Corn (Fresh)*	32 - 36
Cucumbers**	40 - 45
Currants	32 - 36
Dried Fruit	32 - 36
Eggplant**	40 - 45
Eggs*	32 - 36
Figs	32 - 36
Fish (Frozen)	0 - 5
Fish (Fresh)	30 - 34
Flour	50 - 60
Game	32 - 36
Garlic*	32 - 36
Grapefruit*	32 - 36

Item	Temp. in Degrees F
Grapes*	32 - 36
Hams	32 - 36
Kale*	32 - 36
Lard	32 - 36
Lemons	50 - 60
Lettuce*	32 - 36
Limes**	40 - 45
Meats (Fresh)	32 - 36
Meats (Frozen)	0 - 5
Meats (Smoked)	32 - 36
Meats (Pickled)	32 - 36
Mushrooms*	32 -336
Nut Meats	32 - 36
Oleomargarine	32 - 36
Olives (Fresh)**	40 - 45
Onions*	32 - 36
Oranges*	32 - 36
Parsnips*	32 - 36
Peaches*	32 - 36
Peppers*	32 - 36
Pears*	32 - 36
Pineapple**	40 - 45
Plums*	32 - 36
Potatoes (White)**	40 - 45
Potatoes (Sweet)	50 - 60
Poultry (Dressed)	32 - 36
Poultry (Frozen)	0 - 5
Pumpkins	50 - 60
Raisins	50 - 60
Radishes*	32 - 36
Spinach*	32 - 36
Sugar and Syrup	50 - 60
Summer Squash**	40 - 45
Tomatoes**	40 - 45
Turnips*	32 - 36
Watermelon*	32 - 36
Winter Squash	50 - 60

* Should not be kept below 30° F. which is the damaging point for these products.

** Should not be kept below 40° F.

placed by individual refrigerator units of the other two types mentioned.

Ultra Violet Ray Lamps. The use of these lamps in refrigerated storage boxes has resulted in a reduction of mold accumulation in aging meat. The lamps prevent the growth of fungi and diminish odors but in some cases they are too strong and hasten the breakdown of meat fats. Also, it is inadvisable to store fresh or cooked pork in units outfitted with ultra violet ray lamps.

Improvements in these lamps are to be expected and their widespread use will be largely dependent on favorable experimentation.

Refrigeration Temperatures. Refrigerators in food establishments are generally found to have temperatures that hover around 40 to 41 degrees. This is in excess of the proper temperatures for most foods requiring refrigeration. A temperature of 32 to 36 degrees is more nearly correct except for deep freeze or general groceries.

However, when it is possible to achieve proper gradations of temperature, those that are ideal for the various units are as follows:

Deep Freeze Unit	—5 to 0 degrees
Meat Box	32 to 36 degrees
Cheese Box	32 to 36 degrees
Dairy Unit	32 to 36 degrees
Fruit and Vegetable Unit	32 to 36 degrees
Vestibule Box	40 to 50 degrees
Fish Box	30 to 34 degrees

The vestibule box may be used for general groceries and is, in general practice, the section leading to the other units.

Food stored in these refrigerators should be checked over every day to see if there is any spoilage or any food that should be issued to the kitchen and used before losses occur. The same rules apply here as in the storeroom proper as to cleanliness and sanitation. The floors should be kept dry and the shelves and meat hooks free of any spillage or particles of food. No food should be placed on the floor but on low racks so the floor may be easily cleaned.

Butter, milk, and cream should be kept separate from strong-odored foods, especially cheeses and smoked meats and many fruits, such as canteloupe and blueberries.

Egg Storage. There is nothing more distressing to a customer in a restaurant than to be served eggs that are slightly "off color." This does not necessarily mean they are spoiled, for eggs will take on the odors of many foods stored too near them. To the customer, however, any foreign taste means a bad egg and, as a result, the restaurant may suffer far in excess of its deserts. For this reason, it is well to know the peculiar characteristics of eggs and be alerted against their unnecessary spoilage.

Eggshells are not air-tight but quite porous and will readily take on the odors of other foods unless they are stored at a safe distance. The cases should be stacked in a criss-cross fashion with strips of wood separating them to insure the proper circulation of air.

Freezing spoils eggs and they will freeze at 27 to 28 degrees. Close proximity to refrigerated pipes will freeze them. The cases must stand right side up—never on the sides or top since turning the eggs may break the air sack which will cause spoilage.

If eggs get wet or damp because of being delivered while it is raining or for any other reason, they should be changed to dry cases with dry paper separators. Wet eggs will develop mold and turn bad. For just such an emergency, it is well to have on hand a reserve supply of dry cases and separators.

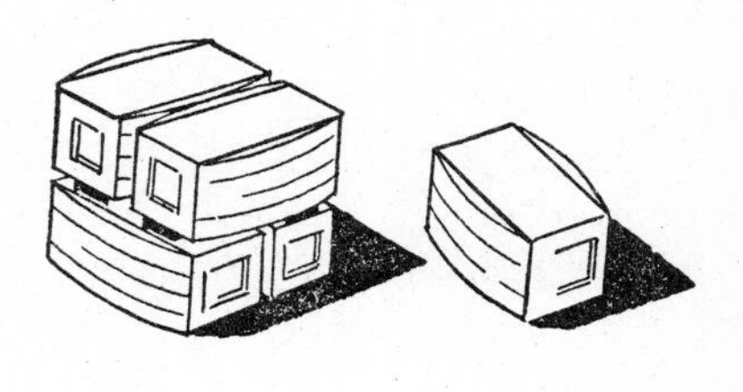

PROPER STACKING OF CITRUS FRUIT (*above*), AND EGGS (*left*).

Excess air flow such as that coming from a fan or blower will dry out the eggs and cause them to deteriorate. If space limitations are such that eggs must be placed in a strong draft, some type of screen should be devised to shield them.

Bearing these characteristics in mind, it saves time as well as eggs if one location is selected, free from the above-mentioned hazards, and the eggs always stored in that place.

Butter Storage. Butter that is exposed to the air will become oxidized and turn rancid. Only the exposed surface will show discoloration but the rancidity will permeate the entire lot. Butter should be carefully wrapped or closely covered. Protected in this way, it will last for several months at a temperature not in excess of 10 degrees.

Lard, shortening and oleomargarine may be kept safely for six or seven months at temperatures from 32 to 36 degrees.

Cheese Storage. Cheese cannot withstand freezing. The taste becomes flat and the texture dry and crumbly. However, if cheese should accidentally be subjected to abnormally low temperature, it may still be used in grated form with spaghetti or similar foods.

Dairy products, although classed under one heading, are, in many cases, poor neighbors. Mild cheeses are the only type that may safely be stored near eggs. By "mild" cheese are meant American, Cottage, Muenster, and Edam varieties. The highly flavored cheeses such as Parmesan, Roquefort, Bleu, Liederkranz, and Gorgonzola should be stored at a considerable distance from eggs.

Fruits and Vegetables. The most commonly used fruits and vegetables have such a tremendously wide range of staying power that each must be considered separately. The strength and weakness as well as the idiosyncrasies of each are noted in the table beginning on page 120.

Because of the possible heavy loss if fruits and vegetables are improperly stored and refrigerated or if they are held too long, all shipments of these foods should be identified in some manner as to the date of arrival. This should be a must in the operation of every food storeroom.

Meats. Fresh lamb, mutton, pork, and veal should be "transients" in the meat box since they deteriorate rapidly and should not be kept more than a few days.

Smoked meats and sausage may develop mold if kept at temperatures above 32 degrees. This may be only a surface condition, however, and if the surface is cut away the remainder of the meat may be edible.

Beef, quite the opposite of other meats, improves in flavor and becomes more tender as a result of ageing. The best temperature for beef is 33 to 35 degrees. In dry air, beef can safely be kept many months at this temperature.

Variety meats, such as sweetbreads, kidney, brain, liver, and tripe should not be kept more than a week.

Fish should be purchased daily and used within 24 hours in communities where fish markets are located. Where such daily purchase is not possible and deliveries are made twice weekly, fish should be stored for no longer than three or four days.

A well-insulated fish box in good repair must be used for fish storage. The fish should be kept in this box surrounded by ice and the temperature should never exceed 34 degrees. These precautions regarding the storage of fish are important since spoiled fish is a great health menace.

If fish is purchased in frozen form it must, of course, be kept in a deep freeze unit. The defrosting process is important and is explained later in this chapter.

Use and Care of Refrigerated Units. Refrigerated food should be stored in the same orderly manner as are the foods in the storeroom proper, not only to make them more readily available but because they must be checked daily to insure their use before excessive losses occur. It is an easy matter for some item of food to be pushed to the rear of the box and not discovered until too late to be used. Such losses will not occur if a daily check is made.

Icebox floors must be kept absolutely dry and no food should be placed directly on the floor but always on low racks to facilitate the cleaning of the floor.

Meat hooks must be kept clean. The smallest particles of meat allowed to accumulate on a meat hook can cause contamination.

Butter, milk, and cream should be kept away from foods with strong odors, especially smoked meats or strong cheeses. Some fruits such as cantaloupe and blueberries will affect butter if stored nearby.

Such delicacies as caviar, anchovies, and imported sardines should be stored in a locked compartment in one of the refrigerators and the key kept by the steward or whoever is in charge of the food supplies. These items are small, expensive, and easily concealed, and might find their way into the possession of unauthorized persons.

Frozen Foods. A minimum of 24 hours should be allowed for thawing out frozen fish, meats, and pie fruits after they have been removed from the deep freeze unit; otherwise, deterioration will result. This thawing-out may take place in the refrigerator or a chill box. Frozen products should never be thawed out in water or by any form of high heat. Hastening the process seriously affects the quality of frozen foods. Once thawed, this food must not be refrozen. Refreezing meats or fish is particularly dangerous.

Defrosting. The refrigerator coils must be defrosted at regular intervals. Otherwise, heavy ice forms on them and greatly increases the cost of maintaining the proper temperatures in the box since the ice acts as an insulator. In establishments where an engineer is available, the defrosting is usually carried out under his supervision.

It is advisable to remove the contents of each unit when defrosting to permit thorough cleaning and to keep the contents dry. Meat may be shifted temporarily to the fruit and vegetable unit since the slight increase in temperature for a short time will not harm the quality of the meat. However, fruits and vegetables should not be transfered to the meat box if the temperature in this box is below 30 degrees which is too low for many of them to withstand. If they cannot be shifted to a unit with suitable temperatures, they should be covered with canvas or sail cloth during the defrosting process.

CANNED GOODS

The storeroom man should check periodically the weights and yields of canned goods. The tables on pages 89 and 90 indicate the minimum net weight, drain weight, and in some instances, the approximate count of the most frequently used canned vegetables and fruits.

INVENTORIES

A physical inventory must be taken, by actual count, once each month as of the close of business of the last day of the month. This should not be left to the storeroom staff as is sometimes done. It should be taken by the food cost accountant, the food controller or a responsible representative of the accounting office.

In addition, periodic mid-month spot-checks of high-priced items are advisable. The opening inventory plus purchases, minus issues, should give the status of the physical inventory at any time during the month for any item.

STORAGE TIME AND TEMPERATURES FOR FRUITS AND VEGETABLES

Apples, Fresh

Store in fruit or vegetable box three weeks to a month. Inspect daily to remove any rotten fruit so that the balance will not be contaminated. Watch for blue mold or black rot.

Apricots

Easily stored for one to two weeks.

Asparagus

Can be kept for two weeks but must be crated with the heels packed in moss.

Avocados

May be kept in the refrigerator one week after ripening.

Bananas

May be kept at 50 to 60 degrees and used within two or three days after ripening. Do not store in the refrigerator at any time.

Beans, String

May be stored for about one week.

Beets

May be stored for two months provided they have been topped.

Berries

All fresh berries can be kept for a week to 10 days.

Broccoli

Can be stored for eight to ten days.

Brussels Sprouts

Will keep in good condition for two weeks.

Cabbage—Early Variety

Will keep for about two weeks.

Cabbage—Late Variety

Much sturdier. Will last for three months.

Canteloupe

Inspect daily for ripeness. When ripe, may be held in the refrigerator for one week.

Carrots

If in good condition, they may be kept in the storeroom for a few days. Under light refrigeration, they will last three months.

Cauliflower

May be kept for two weeks if the leaves are not cut away. After the leaves are removed, cauliflower deteriorates rapidly.

Celery

Should not be kept longer than a few days. If it is wilted, placing it in a jar of water will freshen it.

Corn

Corn is one of the most sensitive of vegetables and should be used within twenty-four hours after arrival.

Cranberries

May be stored in a vegetable box for as long as two months.

Cucumbers

These are not sturdy and should be used within a week.

Egg Plant

Should not remain in storage more than one week.

Garlic

Can be kept for about two months at temperatures from 55 to 65 degrees. In a vegetable cooler at temperatures from 32 to 36 degrees, garlic will last four months.

Grapefruit

Will last six weeks at 32 to 36 degrees.

Grapes

White seedless or red Tokay grapes will keep for four weeks. Red Emperor, obtainable in late fall, for two months.

Kale

In temperatures from 32 to 36 degrees, kale will remain in good condition for three weeks.

Lemons

May be kept from one to two months at 50 to 60 degrees.

Lettuce, Iceberg

If in good condition and inspected regularly, iceberg lettuce may be kept for four weeks. The leaves should not be removed until the lettuce is to be used unless they have begun to rot. However, to obtain maximum quality, lettuce should be used as soon as possible after arrival.

Limes

Will not last in storage over two weeks.

Melons—Honeydew, Casaba and Honeyball

May be stored a maximum of three weeks. Weekly examination is necessary.

Mushrooms, Fresh

Should not be kept more than two or three days.

Onions, Green

If kept under refrigeration, they will last a week or 10 days.

Onions, Yellow

If stored in a cool, dry, but unrefrigerated place, they will last three months.

Oranges

Should be used within a week if possible. If necessary, they may be held in a reasonably good condition for a month or six weeks.

Parsnips

Can be stored two to three months at 32 to 36 degrees.

Parsley

A week is about the time limit for parsley.

Peaches

Most varieties will last about a week, the Yellow Cling variety about two weeks. Peaches must be inspected and sorted each day.

Peas

This vegetable has a tendency to lose its flavor after a few days. However, peas may usually be held in reasonably good condition for ten to twelve days.

Pears—Summer or Bartlett variety

Before ripening, these may be kept three weeks at 65 to 75 degrees. After ripening they must be refrigerated and used within a few days. They require gentle handling to prevent bruising and must be sorted every five days.

Pears—Bosc or Comice variety

May be kept six weeks before ripening if sorted weekly. After ripening, must be used within a few days.

Pears—Winter, Anjou, or Winter Nelis variety

Will keep eight or ten weeks before ripening.

Peppers

May be held for about four weeks.

Pineapple

May be kept as long as two weeks on a ripening table at temperatures from 65 to 75 degrees. Once ripe, they should be used within two or three days.

Plums—Green Gage or Red

Will keep for two weeks but after ripening must be used within a few days.

Potatoes—White

May last four months in a cool, dry well-ventilated place that is refrigerated. New potatoes, however, should not be kept for more than five or six weeks.

Potatoes—Sweet

These do not have the staying power of white potatoes. They require a cool place—about 50 to 60 degrees—and should not be kept for more than a week. They may last for three or four weeks if the air is extremely dry.

Pumpkin

Can last for a month at temperatures from 50 to 60 degrees. However, it is better to buy the canned variety.

Radishes

Should not be kept longer than a week and it is wiser to use them within a few days. The leaves should be removed as soon as possible.

Rhubarb

May be kept for a week but since it loses flavor after a short time it should be used as soon as possible.

Romaine

Will generally last about two weeks.

Spinach

Must be properly iced to last any time at all. Even then, one week is its limit.

Squash—Summer

Will last only two weeks.

Squash—Winter

Can be held at 50 to 60 degrees for three months.

Strawberries

Must not be kept longer than four days and require a temperature from 32 to 36 degrees.

Tomatoes

Should not be kept over a week after ripening. They require daily sorting for ripeness.

Turnips—White

They will keep about 10 days or two weeks without refrigeration. Under light refrigeration, they will last three months.

Watermelon

May be held for a week to 10 days but no longer.

Chapter IX: ISSUING FOOD

In many food service establishments, the responsibility of issuing food from the storeroom is frequently left to the chef or steward. When this is done, the same man often supervises the purchasing, receiving, storing, and issuing. This is a poor plan. It concentrates too much responsibility in one person. With no one to check against him, the possibilities for error are great. Also, this concentration sets up such an ideal opportunity for fraud or dishonesty that it is practically asking for trouble. Many persons might succumb to such an easy opportunity.

Furthermore, it is unfair to place so much responsibility in one person. A strictly honest man runs the chance of being suspected of dishonesty if errors occur, as they will if he is overburdened and has to neglect some of the details of his work. If it is true that too many cooks spoil the broth, it is just as true that too many duties spoil the cook.

Regardless of how small a food service establishment may be, the accounting department (even if this means only one man) should have direct control of food issues. If the size of the operation requires some merging of duties, it is advisable that the job of storeroom man be combined with that of a clerk in the accounting department. Thus, the supervision of food issues is channeled through the proper department. Specific hours for receiving and issuing food will facilitate this type of job merger.

Working with food so constantly, seeing so much of it stacked about, it becomes easy for the people in the storeroom to forget that it all represents money. But money was paid for it and money will accrue to the establishment only through its proper use. No prudent manager would consider allowing cash funds to be handled except under the supervision of the accounting department. The food in his storeroom represents cash just as much as the greenbacks in his safe.

MECHANICS OF ISSUING

The chapters dealing with receiving and storage have made it obvious that if the steps described therein are properly carried out, the issuing of food and the maintenance of inventory records will be greatly facilitated.

A practice of basic importance in food issuing is "first in—first out." Stock must not be buried or forgotten. Naturally, it is easier to place items just received in front of those that are already placed on the back of the shelf. It requires extra exertion to move the old stock to the front of the shelf and place the new stock in the back. But the alternative is spoiled food, resulting in money loss, either through direct waste or through losing good customers.

A lazy man or one who is ignorant of this proper sequence in issuing food, has no place in the storeroom as his failure to observe it will surely result in losses.

Tagging Meat. An unvarying rule in the receipt of meats is that they be tagged with their weight and price. This work must be done by the receiving clerk since it eliminates the cumbersome job of weighing the meat again when it is issued. It also removes the necessity of making adjustments arising from discrepancies in weight caused by evaporation. By using meat tags * the kitchen is more easily charged with the weight of the meat as it is received. This is the only proper method of determining food cost.

Identification of Other Items. A date stamp is a very simple device yet its use on all incoming items provides very valuable information.

(1) It insures greater ease in carrying out the practice of "first in—first out."

(2) It enables a conscientious storeroom man to check the merchandise on his shelves during spare time and keep it stacked in chronological order.

Fruit and vegetable shipments should be tagged with date of receipt since they may lack suitable surfaces for direct stamping.

Unfortunately, it is true that few operators are able to tell the age of most of the items in their storerooms. Suppose their accountants could not tell them how old their accounts receivable were? It is high time operators realize that the food in their storeroom is money.

The cost price of every item should also be placed on every can, jar, bag, box, or other container.

Pre-Packaging. If sugar, spices, nut meats, dried fruits, and similar items are packaged and labeled in the quantities that are usually requisitioned, it will minimize the possibility of short weights to the kitchen and differences in the amount of stocks in the storeroom. It will also save the time of the employee who places the requisition as he need not

* See Illus. Page 103.

wait while the items are being weighed and packaged. It may save time in the kitchen as these requisitions are sometimes made right at the time they are needed. This is a poor practice, however, and should not be encouraged.

Hours for Issuing. Issuing food cannot be done with maximum efficiency unless specific hours are established for filling requisitions. It is practically impossible to keep a storeroom in orderly shape unless it is closed down completely for two or three hours each day. Unless issuing hours are fixed, the backlog of accumulated work will never be properly completed, resulting in lost time and money. Haphazard issuing must mean waste eventually.

Requisitions. These are the equivalent of checks drawn on a bank. Just as checks must carry the proper names and amounts, so must requisitions.

No establishment is careless about the way checks are handled. Cashiers are instructed to pay close attention to the amount of the check, the endorsement, the signature, and to be sure to get proper approval. However, few storeroom men are impressed with the fact that requisitions are checks drawn on a food bank.

In general, there is not the same degree of care used in instructing employees in the proper manner of filling out requisitions. Simply because the requisition is "cashed" within the establishment is no reason for illegibly written requisitions. Payroll checks are often cashed in the same establishment, but these are not "dashed off" as many requisitions are.

Names of items and the grade desired must be very clear on the requisition—not merely in the mind of the employee who has written it. Quantities must be specific. A requisition for "4 cans of peaches" is not sufficient. The size of the can and the grade of peaches should be given.

Sub-department heads filling out requisitions must be trained to obtain the chef's approval. The storeroom man issuing the food must be specifically instructed to insist upon proper approval. Instructions in the methods and requirements for issuing food should be prepared by the accounting department and posted in a conspicuous place, visible both to the storeroom man and to the employee presenting requisitions. The chef and steward should submit a written list of sub-department heads who are permitted to make out requisitions.

When storeroom men make a practice of being careless in the acceptance of unauthorized requisitions, their attention should be called to it by a typed memorandum sent by the accounting office or the management. Verbal admonitions are all too often forgotten. A note is tangible evidence that a remedy has been suggested.

The acceptance of unauthorized requisitions may seem a small offense but one unscrupulous employee, by padding requisitions day in and day out, can do away with a sizeable portion of any potential profit.

Form 118

HOTEL ASTOR
TIMES SQUARE NEW YORK 19

REQUISITION

2/16 19

Bakery DEPARTMENT

Please deliver to bearer

1 Case	Eggs		12.90
10 lbs.	Butter	@ .69	6.90
5 lbs.	Margarine	@ .22	1.10
5 gals.	Cooking Oil	@ 1.40	7.00

Signed JRM

No. 27737 Department Bakery

Pricing the Requisitions. Requisitions must be priced by someone if a daily food cost is to be determined. If this is done by an accounting employee, he will either have to make a guess at the price or embark upon an involved series of calculations with numerous invoices. Therefore, the quickest and most accurate place to price the requisitions is in the storeroom where the price may be entered directly from the merchandise itself. This means that the price must be marked on all incoming merchandise as we have cautioned previously. This may mean extra work for the storeroom man, but it is by far the most satisfactory way of handling the problem.

Forced Issues. Normal requisitions for issues of food originate in the kitchen where the food is processed. Sometimes, however, the origin of requisitions is reversed. Stock that lies forgotten on the shelves must be brought to the attention of someone in authority or it is likely never to be used. Sometimes a change of chef is the cause of certain items falling into disuse.

The storeroom men should have the responsibility of listing all the food in the storeroom that has not been used in a given number of months. Following this, there should be a conference between management and the chef, or the catering manager and the chef or steward, when a definite decision should be made regarding the use or sale of this dead stock. Drastic measures are needed because dead stock does not improve in quality or increase in value.

Spoiling Merchandise. Food that is in the process of spoiling requires quick action to curtail the extent of the loss. A day's delay in using up merchandise that has begun to deteriorate may be too late.

The storeroom man should be able to spot spoilage at the very outset and immediately notify the chef or steward. It may not be possible at the time to add items to the menu. Processing the food for later use may be the best thing to do.

Controls. Food that is in transit from one department of the hotel to another requires control. All food items leaving the kitchen are generally controlled by a food checker functioning under the immediate supervision of the accounting department. All food entering or remaining in the storeroom must also be closely controlled.

The chapters entitled "Food and Beverage Control" will elaborate on the use of inventory records and other control features that can be utilized to keep the storeroom losses at a minimum.

When it is remembered that the value of the food that enters the establishment in bulk form is equal to approximately 40 per cent or more of the gross food sales, it is instantly realized that the necessity for proper control cannot be emphasized too strongly.

Chapter X: FOOD PREPARATION

THE METHODS of preparing food in quantity have changed considerably from what they were two centuries ago. Then the influence of the traditional French kitchen was beginning to spread throughout the world. In modern times cookery is as exact a science as chemistry, and each product has its perfect formula. In America today, only a relatively small percentage of restaurants employ classic French cooking methods. Most food service establishments function on a basis of modified and simplified methods.

For too long a time, food preparation has been shrouded with an aura of mystery. In some operations, top-level executives have avoided direct contact with the kitchen on the basic belief that they were not "food men." Cooking principles are not fundamentally mysterious; they are based on common sense and sound practices.

To obtain the best preparation results, the following four points should be closely observed:

(1) Use of ingredients of good quality.
(2) Minimum lapse of time between preparation and service.
(3) Proper cooking methods.
(4) Proper care of food after preparation.

Not even a magician can cook quality into a product. It must be there at the outset.

Food that is not served as soon after preparation as possible does not improve with age. Even a short lapse of time can ruin some of the best prepared foods. Cooking schedules must be geared to the actual hours of consumption.

Proper cooking methods are of extreme importance. They cannot be quickly mastered. A major portion of this chapter is devoted to a discussion of these methods.

NECESSARY BASIC KNOWLEDGE

The first requisite of good cooking is an accurate knowledge of the items to be prepared. The chef or cook must know the basic characteristics of the food he is to work with. In meats, the cut or quality of the meat will be a determining factor in the cooking, affecting the length of time the item is to be cooked, the temperature at which it is to be cooked, and to a very great degree, the method which is to be used—broiling, roasting, stewing, etc.

In the cooking of vegetables, the age of the vegetables and the necessity of conserving the vitamins present, are to be considered in determining the cooking method. In root vegetables, the cooking time is lengthened in direct ratio to the age of the vegetable, while in green vegetables, palatability, eye-appeal, and nutritional value are all sacrificed by long periods of cooking. The season of the year is also an influencing factor in the cooking of vegetables as, for instance, in the cooking of old and new potatoes. Potatoes are best in the fall, but will keep well throughout the winter. By spring the starch found in potatoes is partially changed to dextrin, which gives the potato a sweetness, and when cooked, a waxiness. This waxiness is also produced by freezing. However, waxiness can also be caused by a larger proportion of proteins. If all food is bought in compliance with standard purchase specifications, much of the guesswork will be eliminated in deciding the proper cooking method to be used.

FISH COOKERY

With the advent of better storing conditions and particularly frozen packaging, the popularity of fish has greatly increased. Fresh, frozen, and smoked fish prepared by broiling, pan-frying, deep-fat frying, baking, steaming, or poaching, and with the great variation permitted in the accompanying sauces, should provide the restaurateur with original, attractive menus at a gratifyingly low food cost. The most popular restaurant fish is broiled or deep-fat fried. In deep-fat frying it is important that the fat used does not smoke at low temperatures. A tasteless, odorless vegetable shortening is good for this purpose. Much can be accomplished in producing uniform products by the use of a deep-fat thermometer. Thermostatically controlled deep-fat fryers are excellent for deep-fat frying of fish as well as meats and vegetables.

As most of the broiled, pan-broiled, and deep-fat fried fish dishes require fairly short cooking periods, it is recommended that these be cooked to order so that they reach the table in the most palatable condition and piping hot. Baked, steamed or poached fish can be cooked in small quantities prior to the service period and kept in the kitchen until ordered.

There are a rich variety of sauces that complement the various types of cooked fish, including curry or mustard mayonnaise, sour cream cucumber sauce, whipped cream horse-radish sauce, anchovy or brown butter, cheese or creamy egg sauce, tartar sauce, fresh dill or goldenrod sauce, onion or garlic butter, mushroom sherry or vinaigrette sauce, herb vinegar sauce or chile-sauce butter.

MEAT COOKERY

It is the usual practice to plan menus around meat. In addition to its nutritive value, meat has an important place in menu planning because of its appetite appeal and its faculty for making the meal interesting. The aroma and appearance of well-cooked, attractively served meat dishes enhance the atmosphere of a restaurant. If the meat dish is different, the entire menu seems to have variety, even though the accompanying dishes are much the same as those served the day before.

Fundamentals of Meat Cookery. The method used in cooking meat depends on the type of cut involved. The tender cuts, with a minimum of connective tissue, are cooked by methods which cannot be used successfully in cooking those cuts which have any considerable amount of connective tissue.

Cooking Principles. Fundamentally, there are only two principles involved in cooking meat: (1) dry heat and (2) moist heat. The tender cuts are cooked by dry heat because they contain little connective tissue, whereas moist heat is required to make tender those cuts which contain much connective tissues. There are a few exceptions to this general rule due to certain inherent characteristics of beef, veal, pork and lamb which makes it necessary to modify the methods in order to get the best results.

Dry and Moist Heat Methods. There are three methods of preparing meat by dry heat: (1) roasting (2) broiling and (3) pan broiling. There are just two methods of cooking meat by moist heat: (1) braising and (2) stewing or cooking in water.

Roasting. To roast is to cook by dry heat before a fire or oven, hot stones or metal. Originally, roasting meant to cook before a hot fire, the meat being on a spit and turned frequently. Now the term roast has come to be applied to meats or poultry cooked by dry heat in the oven.

Broiling and Pan Broiling. Broiling is cooking by direct heat or to grill. It may be done over hot coals, under a gas flame or an electric unit. In pan broiling the heat is transmitted to the meat from the hot metal of the frying-pan rather than directly as in broiling.

The objectives in broiling and pan broiling are the same: to produce steaks or chops with an attractively browned exterior, a plump full appearance and juicy interior of the desired degree of "doneness."

MEAT CUTS FOR ROASTING

BEEF	LAMB	PORK		VEAL	VARIETY MEATS
		FRESH	SMOKED		
Rib	Leg	Ham (Leg)	Ham	Leg	Liver
Sirloin Butt	Loin	Loin	Picnic	Loin	
Loin Strip	Rack	Boston Butt	Shoulder Butt	Rib	
Tenderloin	Rolled Shoulder	Picnic	Canadian Style Bacon	Rolled Shoulder	
Rump Butt	Cushion Shoulder	Rolled Shoulder			
Round-Top-Bottom		Spare Ribs			
Shoulder Chop		Cushion Shoulder			
Inside Chuck					

MEAT CUTS FOR BROILING AND PAN OR GRIDDLE BROILING

BEEF	LAMB	PORK		VEAL	VARIETY MEATS
		FRESH	SMOKED		
Club Steak	Loin Chop	Fresh Pork is not Broiled or Pan or Grill Broiled	Sliced Ham	Veal Chop or steaks are only Broiled when fairly mature and well-fatted	Sliced Veal or Lamb
Rib Steak	Rib Chop		Sliced Bacon		Liver
T-Bone Steak	Leg Steak		Shoulder Butt		Lamb Kidneys
Porterhouse Steak	Shoulder Chop		Sliced Canadian Style Bacon		Brains
Sirloin Steak	Lamb Patties				Sweetbreads
Butt Steak					
Top Round Steak					
Tip Steak (Knuckle)					
Beef Patties					
Flank Steak					

Fry and pan broil frequently are used interchangeably, or at least the distinction is not finely drawn. There is an inclination to say of any meat cooked in a frying pan that it is fried. Yet to fry means to cook in fat, either in a small amount of fat or in a deep layer of fat as in deep-fat frying. Although most cuts of meat are cooked by other methods than frying to produce the best results, there are some cooks who do fry such cuts as veal steak and chops or liver. There is some sacrifice of tenderness to flavor in this method.

Braising. Braising is one of the two methods of cooking by moist heat. It is used in the preparation of those cuts containing considerable connective tissues. To braise means to brown meat in a small amount of added fat, then to cover and cook slowly in juices from the meat, or in a small amount of added liquid.

MEAT CUTS FOR BRAISING

BEEF	LAMB	PORK	VEAL	VARIETY MEATS
Flank	Breast	Chops:	Breast	Liver:
Brisket	Neck	Shoulder	Cutlets	Beef
Plate	Shank	Loin	Neck	Pork
Chuck	Shoulder	Rib	Shoulder	Kidneys
Neck		Feet	Chops:	Heart
Heel of Round		Spareribs	Loin	Tripe
Rump Butt		Tenderloin	Rib	
Short Ribs		Hocks	Shoulder	
Ox Tails			Shank	

MEAT CUTS COOKED IN WATER - STEWING OR SIMMERING

BEEF		LAMB	PORK		VEAL	VARIETY MEATS
FRESH	CORNED		FRESH	SMOKED		
Chuck (All Cuts)	Brisket	Neck	Spareribs	Ham	Neck	Kidney
Rump Butt	Rump	Breast	Backbones	Shoulder	Shank	Heart
Shank	Plate	Flank	Pigs Feet	Picnic	Breast	Tongue
Heel or Round	Round	Shanks	Hocks	Shoulder Butts	Flank	For Pre-Cooking:
Brisket				Hocks		Brains
Plate						Sweetbreads
Flank						
Short Ribs						

Stewing. Stewing, or cooking in liquid, is a moist heat method used in the preparation of the less tender cuts although tender cuts are also cooked in water. Stewing or simmering was used to designate this method of meat cooking; however, the only difference between stewing and simmering is the size of the pieces of meat, and not in the cooking principle.

Meat Shrinkage due to Cooking. The question of shrinkage in meat during cooking is one of considerable practical importance, because shrinkage affects appearance, palatability, nutritive value, and the number of servings. This reduction in the number of servings through excessive shrinkage losses produces higher costs per portion served. It is important, therefore, that shrinkage in cooking be kept as low as is possible with an attractive and palatable product.

Shrinkage is the difference between the weight of meat before it is cooked and its weight after cooking. There are two factors which have been shown to influence this cooking loss. These two factors are (1) temperature of the oven (2) the degree of "doneness" of the meat. Both of these factors may be controlled; therefore, it lies within the power of the cook to hold shrinkage losses to a minimum.

Controlling Meat Shrinkage. The importance of controlling cooking shrinkage may be summarized as follows:

(1) Excessive shrinkage in meat during cooking can be controlled by:
  a) Using low cooking temperatures.
  b) Cooking only to the degree of "doneness" desired without overcooking.
  c) Using the meat thermometer to eliminate guesswork as to the degree of "doneness."

(2) The nutritional value and palatability of meat after cooking is greater when cooked by methods which prevent undue shrinkage.

(3) Minimum shrinkage produces maximum yields.

(4) Meats cooked at high temperatures are difficult to slice, thereby decreasing the available amount of "sliceable" meat.

(5) The use of high temperature in moist heat cooking is as detrimental to the meat cuts as excessive dry heat.

Proper Cooking Temperature Curtails Meat Shrinkage. For many years it was believed that by searing meats at high temperatures prior to actual roasting, the juices and natural flavors of meats were sealed in. The fallacy of this theory has been proven many times over. Cooking meat slowly at temperatures ranging from 250° to 325° has resulted in increasing the number of meat servings obtainable, and also in improving the appearance, palatability and nutritional value. Actual tests have shown that normal cooking losses due to shrinkage are approximately 10 to 15 per cent when an oven temperature of between 250° to 325° is used. However, if the same degree of "doneness" is achieved at an oven temperature of 450° to 500°, the cooking loss through excessive shrinkage increases to 15 to 20 per cent. This additional loss through excessive shrinkage not only lessens the palatability, appearance, and nutritional value of meat but materially contributes to a higher food cost per portion served.

Reducing the degree of "doneness" is another important phase in meat cookery which will influence the loss through shrinkage. Here again palatability, appearance, and nutritional value of meats are affected by overcooking. There are a number of factors which affect the cooking time of meats:

(1) Oven temperatures will affect cooking time inasmuch as higher temperatures will lessen the cooking time necessary, whereas a lower temperature will increase the cooking time necessary in order to achieve the same degree of "doneness."
(2) The size or style of the cut of meat will affect cooking time in that a chunky or rolled cut will require a longer period of time, whereas a flat or standing cut will require fewer minutes per pound. This is due to the varying length of time required for the heat to penetrate from the outside to the center of the meat.
(3) The fat covering of meat will also affect the cooking time necessary. This is particularly true of roast meats, for when they contain a heavier fat covering they will cook faster because melting fat has been found to be a better conductor of heat than lean meat.

Use of Meat Thermometer. The meat thermometer has become a very important aid in eliminating excessive shrinkage by preventing overcooking. However, there are still many persons who believe that by controlling the cooking temperature a meat thermometer is unnecessary or when using a meat thermometer, controlling the oven temperature is eliminated. Both the controlling of the oven temperature and the use of a meat thermometer become a necessity in attaining some degree of perfection in meat cookery. With the use of both controlled oven temperatures and a meat thermometer, it becomes a simple process to eliminate both overcooking, or undercooking.

VEGETABLE COOKERY

Boiling does the most damage to vegetables, yet this method is used most frequently in the preparation of cooked vegetables. When the boiling method is used in the cooking of vegetables, only a very small amount of salted water should be used. It should be boiling vigorously when the vegetables are immersed. They should then be cooked until just tender.

Color can be controlled by slightly undercooking. Green vegetables contain the pigment called chlorophyll which is slightly soluble in water, and which turns brown when heated in the presence of acid. All vegetables contain at least small traces of acid, but fortunately it is in a volatile form so that it escapes with the steam if the cover is removed during cooking. If a pressure cooker is used in cooking a green vegetable, the color can be improved by permitting the steam to escape during the last seconds of the cooking process.

Red vegetables also tend to become a brownish color during the cooking process, but this can be counteracted by the addition of a small amount of vinegar.

White vegetables such as cabbage, cauliflower and onions are strongly flavored due to their special oils. Hard water will change these oils so that the white color will turn either yellow or brown. However, this condition can easily be corrected by the addition of lemon juice or vinegar in small quantities.

Baking is the best method to preserve vitamins and minerals. Dry baking in their skins, generally used for potatoes, squash, turnips, carrots, onions and parsnips, is a simple method whereby they are baked in a hot oven until they are just tender when pierced with a sharp fork. Baking, however, also includes the roasting of whole vegetables with meat, gravy or fat.

Au gratin and scalloping are other forms of baking, especially when vegetables are used with cheese or crumbs. Leftover cooked vegetables may also be prepared by these methods. However, the vitamin and mineral value will be determined by the first cooking. Only baking in the jacket will insure the preservation of the vitamin content of vegetables.

In the preparation of vegetables for restaurant service, it is advisable to cook them in small quantities and at frequent intervals. This method of preparation preserves flavor, nutritional value, and enhances eye-appeal, all of which suffer when cooked vegetables are allowed to stand for any length of time on a steam table. In addition to the greater attraction of freshly cooked vegetables, there is also the distinct advantage derived from keeping leftover vegetables at a minimum since they do not lend themselves easily to re-use. This is particularly true in the case of mashed potatoes, an item which appears almost daily on the average restaurant menu. They are bound to create a poor impression on the guest if they have remained for any time on the steam table or, even worse, when an attempt is made to re-use them from one meal to the next.

With the increasing awareness of the American public to the benefits derived from the eating of a well-balanced diet and the growing popularity of salads, vegetables are coming into greater importance in food preparation. Cooked vegetables make possible a great number of varieties and combinations that round out a menu and produce a good food profit if properly handled. Raw vegetables lend themselves well to salad making in grated, julienne, and curled form, producing large portion yields.

Another low-cost item is the dried vegetable. This item can be an attractive and appetizing menu accompaniment when properly cooked and seasoned. Dried vegetables must be of good quality and should be the produce of the current year. If one must use old or inferior dried vegetables they might be put to soak in bicarbonated water, but only for a minimum time to swell them slightly. Prolonged soaking of dried vegetables may give rise to incipient germination which will depreciate the value of the food.

Potatoes with a starch content of 18 to 20 per cent are usually mealy when cooked. Among the potatoes with a high starch content are, Green Mountain, Norcross, State of Maine or Gold Coin. Certain early varieties such as Bliss Triumph or Early Ohio are also notably high in starch content. Mealy potatoes are desirable for baking, boiling and deep-fat frying. Waxy potatoes are sometimes preferred to mealy ones for salads, scalloping, and creaming because they retain their shape better. A few varieties of waxy potatoes are Sir Walter Raleigh, Heavyweight, Rural New York #2, and Rural Russets.

Potatoes may be prepared in a wide variety of ways and are always popular. They make a pleasing border on casseroles when squeezed through a rose-tube. They can be served as an accompaniment to almost any dish and have the added virtue of producing a very low food cost.

SOUPS

Cooking in water is the method used in making soups or meat stock. The purpose is to obtain a rich broth by extracting as much flavor as possible from the meat and bone. It should be remembered that the meat used in making soup retains much of its food value and may be used as any leftover meat by supplying flavor through the addition of seasonings. The broth contains soluble proteins, fat, minerals, and gelatin. The gelatin gives the broth a jelly-like consistency and adds body and richness. The shank is desirable for soup making because there are more tendons near a joint, and these tendons contain collagen, which is converted into gelatin. Bones also contain collagen, especially those of a young animal, such as veal. Smoked ham shanks are often used to flavor bean or pea soups; otherwise, pork is not used in soup making.

Soup stock is used as the base of many soups, gravies and sauces. Since the object is to make a rich, highly flavored stock, as much meat as possible should be cut from the bones when using meat bones. The actual temperature of the water at the start of the cooking process makes very little difference in the results obtained. However, soup stock should not be permitted to boil. It should be simmered gently throughout the entire cooking process. Vegetables, herbs and spices are used to season soup stocks.

Brown stock is made from beef or other meat which has been browned. This gives color to the stock and helps develop flavor. White stock is made from veal or chicken, or a combination of the two. The meat is not browned and the stock is seasoned delicately.

In making a clear soup the stock should be strained through several thicknesses of cheesecloth. It should then be cooled very rapidly to prevent spoilage. Upon cooling the fat will solidify into a cake on top of the broth at which time it can be easily removed. In making a sparkling soup the stock must be clarified still further with egg whites and egg shells.

Since it is the usual practice to make soup stocks for several meals, care should be taken to keep the remainder from spoiling. After straining, the stock should be cooled quickly in an uncovered container. It should then be covered and stored in a cold place. The cake of fat which forms over the surface will exclude the air and retard spoilage.

The indiscriminate use of one basic gravy for all meats is a poor practice. Sufficient time should be allowed to prepare a suitable gravy to conform with each of the various types of meats appearing on the menu.

Fish should have its own stock which should not be cooked too long or diluted too much. White wine adds flavor and zest to fish stocks.

Glazes are made from stock which have been reduced to a point of glutinous consistency.

Basic brown sauce called Espagnole or Spanish Sauce, and basic white sauce, called Veloute, are made by blending roux with stock. The color of the sauce is determined by the length of time the roux is permitted to cook in order to acquire the desired color, and the color of the stock to be combined with the roux. Roux is made by combining butter and flour which is heated in a sauce pan over a moderate fire. A roux that is properly combined will form a mass capable of absorbing six times its own weight of liquid when cooked. However, when a roux is cooked too rapidly with extremely high heat the binding quality of the starch is destroyed and two or three times the normal amount of roux becomes necessary to obtain the desired consistency of the sauce. Brown roux is considered cooked when a fine nut brown color is obtained. Pale roux is considered cooked as soon as the color begins to change, whereas white roux is cooked only long enough to eliminate the disagreeable taste of uncooked flour.

Brown sauce or Espagnole is prepared by combining brown roux with brown stock to which either fresh tomatoes or tomato juice has been added.

White sauce or Veloute is prepared by combining white roux with veal stock to which nutmeg, salt and white pepper have been added.

Chicken Veloute is prepared by combining chicken stock with white roux.

Fish Veloute is prepared by combining a fish stock with white roux.

The cooking time required for the above sauces, with the exception of fish Veloute, which is cooked only a short time, is between six to eight hours. Careful attention must be given to the skimming and straining operation in order to obtain a clear and brilliant sauce.

Bechamel Sauce is prepared by combining white roux, made from a base of fowl or veal stock, with boiling milk to which salt, pepper, nutmeg and thyme have been added. The cooking time is about 20 minutes.

Hollandaise Sauce is prepared by combining melted butter, egg yolks, pepper, salt and vinegar or lemon juice. The seasoning is combined with lemon juice or vinegar to which the egg yolks have been added and whipped to a creamy consistency over warm water. Care must be taken to add the melted butter gradually while briskly stirring the same. When the butter is completely absorbed the sauce should be thick and firm. The consistency of sauces prepared by the same process as Hollandaise, can be varied at will. The addition of more egg yolks, or the longer cooking of the egg yolks, will produce a very thick sauce, whereas the reverse is true in reducing the number of egg yolks or lessening the cooking time in producing a thin sauce.

The above basic sauces along with tomato offer multitudinous variations for use with meat, fish, fowl and vegetables.

BAKING

In baking, just as in any other phase of food preparation, top-notch products are dependent on ingredients of good quality.

Of all the ingredients employed in baking, flour is used in the greatest amount. Certain flours have characteristics which make them especially suited for the production of specific types of baked goods:

(1) Fancy Patent—bleached or unbleached hard wheat flour is used in bread and roll production. Soft wheat or cake flour can be blended with hard wheat flour when the hard wheat flour is too strong.

(2) Straight flour is frequently preferred for the production of hard rolls and hearth breads. This type of flour is stronger than fancy patent flour and will produce superior results in the production of hard rolls and hearth breads.

(3) Soft winter wheat flour is used in the production of cakes, pastries, cookies and pie crusts. Sometimes a little bread or hard wheat flour will be blended with soft wheat flour in order to give the soft wheat flour additional strength.

(4) Whole wheat or rye flours are blended with clear flour for the production of specialty breads.

If it is impractical to purchase a special type of flour for each class of baking product much care must be exercised in the blending of available flours.

Fats and shortenings are next in importance in baked goods production. This principal function in yeast-raised dough is to facilitate proper dough expansion during fermentation and baking, and to produce a soft velvety crumb. The fats also coat the tiny dough particles and help to prevent the evaporation of moisture. With the exception of Angel Food and some types of sponge cakes in which no fat is used, it aids materially in creating the desired volume, grain and texture in the finished product.

In order to produce quality baked products it is important that the shortenings used be free from foreign odors, and that it is light in color. The consistency or plasticity of shortening is also important. It should be of a consistency that will permit easy mixing without being too soft in hot weather or too hard in cold weather.

Sugar in baked goods adds sweetness, improves keeping quality, produces tenderness, adds food value, and imparts crust color. Sugar should be at least 99 per cent pure, light in color, have no flavor other than sweetness and be free from lumps. Sugar can be replaced by invert syrup, honey, molasses, corn syrup, or malt syrup, all of which will impart characteristic flavor and improve keeping quality by prolonging freshness because of their moisture retaining properties.

Frozen eggs have replaced shell eggs to a very great extent in the production of baked goods. Eggs and egg products containing yolk contribute color, volume, food value, flavor, and improved grain and texture to baked goods. Egg whites will also produce volume, grain, and texture in baked goods.

Milk used in baking products can be whole, skim, evaporated, condensed or dry solids, all of which will lend texture, food value, flavor, and keeping quality to the finished product.

Yeast, through fermentation, produces the gas to raise the dough and mature the gluten. This balanced action of yeast changes the inert, heavy mass of dough into a light, porous, elastic product which, when baked, becomes appetizing, nutritious, and easily digested.

Chemical leaveners such as bicarbonate of soda (baking powder) or ammonium carbonate release carbon dioxide gas that serves as a leavening agent.

Water is the universal wetting agent used in the production of baked goods. Hard waters require increased amounts of yeast, whereas soft waters require an increased percentage of salt.

Salt is important in helping to bring out the flavor of the finished product.

Flavoring material cannot be strictly considered a basic ingredient, yet it is of equal importance in imparting the desired flavor to the finished product. Flavoring materials of inferior quality should be avoided since they will impair the taste and quality of the finished product.

Quality pies are based on two factors—a good filling and a good pie crust. Only top quality pie fillings should be purchased. Fruit fillings for pies are available in four forms: dried, canned, fresh, and frozen. There are differences of opinion as to the one best method in the preparation of pie fillings. Care must be exercised in the proper use of a thickening agent. Starches which are improperly cooked will not jell satisfactorily. They may produce a gumminess and create an undesirable flavor in the finished product. Starches, if used properly, will not discolor the fruit. Pie crust may be either flaky or mealy. Flaky crusts are produced by rubbing the fat and flour together only long enough to produce irregular lumps about the size of a walnut. This produces tender thin layers or flakes in the crust. Mealy crusts are produced by uniform distribution of the fat throughout the flour so that it will coat practically all of the flour particles. Mealy crusts will not normally require as much water as flaky crusts.

During the past few years the freezing of bakery items after baking has proven quite satisfactory. This method of freezing after baking is especially useful for yeast-raised products. These products are usually re-heated after defrosting and before serving. This method of operation permits a more even distribution of work and provides an ample supply of baked goods on exceptionally busy days. The freezing of unbaked products has also proven satisfactory. However, all yeast-raised products must be proofed prior to the baking process.

USE OF LEFTOVERS

Over-production in food preparation is the result of improper planning which, in turn, materially contributes to a high food cost. With proper production planning, only a small quantity of leftovers are available at the close of the service period. However, the proper utilization of all leftovers has become an important phase in food preparation. It should be part of the menu design to permit the use of leftovers in the meal-planning pattern of the day.

Liquids from cooked and canned vegetables contain vitamins and minerals which can be utilized in cocktails, soups and stocks. Leftover vegetables can be reused in salads, added to soups, or used as a garnish. Fruits can be used to brighten aspics, garnish a chop plate or decorate a cake. Meat is no longer only a hash ingredient but an adventure in ingenuity, with a choice of reuses as wide as the imagination. There are any number of attractive and appetizing combinations possible with leftover cooked meats in meat pies, turnovers, or shortcakes.

Poultry leftovers can be utilized in a number of ways. However, it must be remembered that poultry is a very perishable food that spoils easily and should not be permitted to remain in the refrigerator any length of time.

In the preparation of leftover poultry dishes, meat, skin, fat, bones, stuffing, and gravy can be reused. The stewing of bones will produce usable broth. Well flavored skins when ground will serve as a source of fat that can be used in sauces, gravies, and soups. Stuffing and leftover gravy can be used in the preparation of such recipes as chicken loaf. In the preparation of creamed chicken any number of variations becomes possible with the use of hot biscuits, patty shells, spaghetti, noodle nests, whipped potatoes, or rice.

An abundance of sandwich fillings becomes available with the use of leftovers. Plain omelets and scrambled eggs, when combined with fish, ham, chicken, vegetables, or cheese, provide a great variety of profitable luncheon dishes.

SALADS

Salads have shown a tremendous rise in popularity during recent years and, with this increased demand, has come a greatly widened consideration of the basic content of salads. Fresh, crisp greens such as romaine, lettuce, escarole, chicory, and watercress with cabbage, celery, and endive are as popular as ever. With the addition of color from both raw and cooked vegetables, and the wide variety of salad dressings, much has been accomplished to warrant this increased popularity.

Fruit salads that are so American in origin, permit innumerable variations. Almost all fruits grown today find their place somewhere in our salads. Meats, poultry, seafoods, cheese, and eggs combined with vegetables and fruits are popular entrees.

Individual wooden, pottery, china, and glass salad bowls enhance the presentation of all salads.

Care must be taken in the proper planning and preparation of salads. All ingredients must be thoroughly cleaned and properly chilled. If sufficient advance preparation is made, little or no difficulty is encountered in the actual formulation of salad bowls or platters.

Ingredients to be used in the preparation of salad bowls should be arranged in orderly heaps or rows keeping in mind color and contrast. For example, in the preparation of a simple green salad where romaine, lettuce, and chicory are used, the top of the salad could be garnished with overlapping sweet onion rings around a center of watercress. The same salad could be garnished with sliced hard cooked eggs or with tomatoes cut in wedges.

Molded salads, with the innumerable attractive color and taste combinations available in the blending of aspics and gelatins with fruits, poultry, meats, and fish, are fast becoming warm weather favorites. Here again, the vast possibilities of artistic and appetizing presentations is only limited by the imagination of the salad maker.

Chapter XI: EMPLOYEE TRAINING

EMPLOYEE training costs money. Trainer and trainee must take time off from active production if a training program is to fulfill its purpose. That time must be paid for in dollars and cents. However, it is the only effective way to combat the inefficiency that will mount up to ten times what the training costs, to be reflected in wasted food, breakage, damaged equipment, poor service, excessive staffing, and loss of patronage.

ANALYZING TRAINING NEEDS

Initial Interview. Large organizations have a personnel manager who hires new employees. In some places this is left to each department head. In smaller places, the manager is responsible. Whoever does it should have the authority to use his discretion in selecting employees who may be worthy prospects but who require a certain amount of training.

After long experience, interviewers have found that only about 10 per cent of the potential employees exactly fit their ideal of what an employee should be. These are alert and have latent executive ability. Another 10 per cent are completely unemployable. The remaining 80 per cent are those who can learn if exposed to training but who will always need guidance and direction.

Whoever does the hiring should not permit his personal likes and dislikes to sway his judgment of an applicant as this may lose many good employees. For example, a man may intensely dislike colored nail polish. For this reason, 50 per cent of an applicant's chances are cancelled at the start if her nails are colored. Or the interviewer may have had an idea, all his life, that a man whose brows grow together across his nose has a bad temper. We all have these ideas and most of them are completely false. In interviewing an applicant, a man should forget his personal fetishes.

Whether or not an applicant is hired, a record of the interview should be filed. Questions may arise later about certain applicants and it is impossible for anyone to remember all the details.

It is erroneous interviewing to lead an applicant to believe that a job will be his, only if he is exactly fitted for it. This encourages "bluffing" about past experience. Since job requirements vary with regions, an applicant can sometimes keep the exact nature of his past employment a mystery for a time. But it will come to light eventually and the experience will have cost the establishment money.

On the other hand, if the applicant feels that his chance of employment is not based solely on past experience—that native ability with some training will also count—there is a better chance of complete frankness and sounder employer-employee relations. Recommendations for job training made during the initial interview should be kept on file. As training is received, this fact should be added, so that, later, an analysis may be made of actual accomplishment.

It is to be emphasized that the relationship between employer and employee works two ways. With the former supplying the necessary working tools consisting of (1) proper training and instruction, (2) adequate and modern equipment, and (3) sound working conditions, he is entitled to receive from the employee (1) alertness, (2) courtesy, and (3) efficiency, a winning platform for any operation.

On the Job. New employees must be checked for any deficiencies over a period of time before the need for training can be ascertained. Some employees may do a satisfactory job during slack hours but become "flustered" under pressure. Some may know their work up to a point but if they ever had training beyond that point, it has not registered. Others have developed certain short cuts that were acceptable in some establishments where they have worked but are fundamentally wrong where good training is the watchword.

Job deficiencies are present when the following conditions exist:

(1) When work is delayed because the employee becomes confused during peak periods.
(2) When the employee does not know what is expected of him.
(3) When he causes and is responsible for an abnormal amount of breakage and spillage.
(4) When equipment shows unusual wear and repairs are frequent.
(5) When absenteeism is excessive.
(6) When an employee is frequently at fault for accidents, either to himself or his fellow employees.
(7) When peak loads bring with them nervous tension and irritability among the employees.
(8) When food is returned to the kitchen because it is improperly

prepared or because of errors in order taking.

(9) When customers complain of poor service.

(10) When servers show favoritism to some guests and ignore others.

(11) When disputes over checks are frequent.

(12) When courtesy to the patrons is lacking.

(13) When no effort is made to sell the items on the menu.

(14) When patrons are annoyed by the unnecessary clatter of china and silverware.

(15) When complaints about the size of tips are too frequent. A good server usually has no cause for complaint on this score.

TRAINING PROCEDURE

Induction Routine. The department heads should be charged with the responsibility of seeing that each new employee is oriented immediately upon arrival. Either he should do this himself or delegate the work to a subordinate. There is probably no one so thoroughly lost as a new employee. He knows none of his fellow workers as a rule. They are all busy and seem very much at ease while he flounders around not knowing exactly what he is to do or where the things are with which he must work. He may not even know where to put his hat and coat or get his uniform if he is to wear one. He doesn't know where the washroom is, what time he is to go to lunch or how much time he is allowed. Unless these things are explained to him, he may become disgusted and bow out of the picture.

Although a new employee is more or less on trial, the establishment too, has a selling job to do. The better this is done, the lower will be the cost of breaking in a new employee.

Whoever is assigned to this orientation process should see that the employee is thoroughly posted on the following points right at the outset:

(1) He must know the type of establishment with which he is connected and his relationship to it.

(2) He should be informed about the company benefits, if any, such as vacations, bonuses, and sickness and accident benefits.

(3) He must be made to feel a part of the establishment from the first day. He should be introduced to all the people with whom his work will bring him in contact and know what they do. He should be conducted on a tour through those parts of the establishments which concern him and his work. He must be given a key to his locker or told where to keep his street clothes, shown

the location of the washroom and informed as to his lunch hour and his days off. A copy of the house rules and safety rules should be given or explained to him.

(4) As to his own job, he should be shown where the materials he may need can be procured and what disposition to make of any materials he handles.

(5) His work should be checked frequently over a period of time to find out if he is developing as well as it appeared he would at the time of the initial interview. If not, the reasons should be ascertained. Is it his fault or are other factors preventing him from doing a good job? The matter of inducting a new employee into the organization is not a matter for the first day only.

With this careful induction, an employee will very soon start to do the best work of which he is capable. First impressions are lasting. They may be the determining factor in holding an excellent employee and they will smooth the rough edges of many unpleasant little episodes which may come up later.

Refresher Techniques. There will always be some employees who need more training than others. If they alone are singled out, it lowers their self-confidence. Frequently the remaining ones assume a very smug attitude and the morale of the entire staff is affected.

The best way to avoid difficulties with either type of employee is to institute a training program and call it a "refresher" course. This "saves face" for everyone and gives the trainer a chance to spend more time on some than others. Everyone profits, since in this business no one can be overtrained.

Selecting the Trainer. Special aptitudes are necessary in a teacher. Department heads are not necessarily "born teachers." They may know every detail of their departments well but not be able to train others. As a matter of fact, they are inclined to slide over basic points because they know the work so well. They forget to explain *why* things are done in a certain way. An employee may follow a teacher's motions and become quite adept at his job but he will never be as good an employee as the one who understands why he does things in a certain way.

To train employees requires advance preparation of material. This keeps the training running along a straight line and cuts the time needed for training to a minimum. Some department heads may be too busy with their daily duties to prepare advance material. A trainer hired from outside the establishment may prove the better plan. Employees may feel more free to question an outsider than someone who is their superior when they are working.

Training Methods. Training an employee for an entirely new job requires a different method than a so-called "refresher" course. The former should be done in small groups so that personal attention may be given to each trainee. The trainer of this group will usually find his people interested and eager since new work always holds the attention. Retraining can be given in much larger groups but not so large that attention wanders and the trainees become listless.

Four steps are usually necessary in training for new jobs:

(1) *Preparation.* Employees must feel at ease. If the training is such that they must handle equipment manually, they should be able to stand in the correct position to handle it with the proper muscular coordination. For example, if the demonstration is that of table service, the trainee should have ample room to walk around the table in order to demonstrate the service properly.

(2) *Presentation.* The job should be broken down and demonstrated step by step. Patience is necessary. No details can be missed if a thorough job is to be done. The pace must be slow enough so that every employee can follow the demonstration. Next, the trainee must be questioned to be sure the information is absorbed. These review periods should interrupt the demonstration frequently to make sure the pace is not too fast. Slow learners are often thorough learners.

(3) *The Try-Out.* In this step, the trainee is asked to perform the steps himself. Errors are to be expected and should be corrected with tact. The trainee is asked to repeat the demonstration, explaining each step as he goes along. This impresses on his memory what he has learned and continual questioning brings out what is done, how, and why. The try-out should be continued until there is no doubt in the mind of the trainer that the lesson has been well learned.

(4) *The Follow-Up.* This step puts the trainee on his own after he has been told where to go for help or for materials. Errors during the follow-up period should be patiently corrected and further instruction given if it seems necessary.

Re-Training Employees. Diplomacy is needed for re-training employees in jobs which they have held for years. Few employees are willing to acknowledge that they need further instruction. Some preliminary selling is necessary before introducing a re-training program. A frank discussion at a staff meeting where the reasons for the training are explained, is a good approach. All employees are familiar with bottle-necks that cause congestion and slow up service. They do not like these situations any better than the management and will usually be glad to cooperate in helping overcome the conditions that cause them. A safety program is another idea that may be successfully introduced at such a time.

Once employees accept the reasons and the necessity for the re-training, the new method should be introduced rather casually—not as a superior making new rules but as one worker talking over an idea with another. If the new method is good, most of the employees will adopt it readily. On the other hand, some of them may have been thinking along the same lines. They may have developed an even better method or, because they are doing the work themselves, they may be able to point out flaws in the one the trainer has proposed. In either case, they should receive a fair hearing and, if the trainer can see there is merit in the plan they suggest, a test should be made. Once the employees see that their suggestions are welcomed, they may be the source of some excellent changes in the work processes.

Equipment and Materials. It loses time and dissipates interest if the trainer must move about collecting equipment and materials after the training session starts. They should be immediately available and well checked beforehand. Flaws in materials or broken-down equipment can ruin a training session.

JOB BREAKDOWNS

By a "job breakdown" is meant the simple step-by-step description of the way a job is performed. The most reliable way to prepare a job breakdown is to have someone do the job, breaking it down into steps and record the steps, one by one. Once they are down on paper, they may be revised and listed, according to major and minor steps. The job should then be repeated, following the steps as outlined. Flaws will show up immediately and can be corrected before the training session.

There are a few rules to follow in writing a job breakdown which will permit it to last, without changes, as long as that particular job lasts.

(1) The writer should never use pronouns or proper names but always refer to the "trainee" or "employee."

(2) Words which, in themselves, cover a multitude of acts, should not be used. For example: "*Operate* the machine," "*Prepare* the vegetables for slicing," "*Assist* the waiter in removing the dishes." If they are used, they must have clarifying explanations to support them.

(3) If technical terms must be used in describing a job or in describing some piece of machinery or equipment connected with a job, they must be carefully explained.

(4) All the duties that the job calls for must be carefully enumerated. The frequency with which each task is to be performed should be specified, whether weekly, daily, or hourly. This is very helpful to a new department head, since he can readily learn just what each employee is supposed to do. It prevents any shirking or "buck passing" when a new man takes over.

Once a satisfactory job breakdown is made, it can serve as a blueprint for that job. With such a breakdown, the most complicated job becomes simple because each step is simple and recorded in the correct chronological order. There is no opportunity for the trainer to say, "I should have mentioned earlier," or "I forgot to tell you . . ." Another reason for a job breakdown is that it eliminates the chance of important steps being overlooked.

JOB ANALYSIS

A job analysis determines the tasks which comprise the entire job and the skills, knowledge, ability, and responsibilities required of the worker to successfully perform the job. An analysis of each job should be on file in the office of the man who heads the food department. It should also be in the office of the personnel manager, where one is employed.

Supervision. A job analysis gives first, an exact indication of the lines of supervision and authority. Dual supervision should be avoided if possible as it is confusing to the worker and may give him an opportunity for alibis. In addition, it may easily create conflict between superiors. Instructions from sources higher than the department head should be channeled through him and/or the trainer. Otherwise, the workers will have a feeling that there are "too many bosses."

In addition to supervisory details, the analysis should indicate where the employee is to work and with whom he will come in contact. If his work is such that he is part of a team or a group, the analysis should establish this fact. This aids the worker and builds confidence.

Lines of Promotion. The analysis should also list the lines of promotion from jobs of lesser importance to those of greater importance. This is valuable many times when quick substitutions or promotions must be made. It also is an aid in reviewing staff structure and duties.

Sometimes a line of promotion is not a straight line. At a given point, an employee may be promoted in one of several directions. This may depend very much upon his own skill and preference. Such situations should be noted carefully in the job analysis.

Working Conditions. If an honest appraisal of working conditions is given in the analysis, it may be found to be the reason for a high rate of labor turnover.

Special Qualifications. Certain jobs require special technical, physical, educational, or personal qualifications. With these, in some jobs, it is also essential to get along well with other people. This qualification should be added to others and all of them placed in the job analysis.

Relation to Job Breakdown. A job *analysis* is a listing of the work performed by a particular employee such as a waitress, fry cook, bartender, or grade manger. A job *breakdown* is a detailed description of how the various parts of the same job are performed. Hence, the work each employee does has only one job analysis but may have several job breakdowns.

Chapter XII: FOOD AND BEVERAGE SERVICE

THE TYPE OF SERVICE in a restaurant sets the tone for the establishment. Luxurious and leisurely service with elegant appointments is the type one finds in the formal dining room of de luxe hotels or in fashionable restaurants. Speedy and efficient service with more durable china and glassware and possibly with paper place mats, is the pattern for the coffee shop and other table service restaurants. In addition to these, the lunch counter and cafeteria have greater speed in service and less value in appointments. We will consider first the type of restaurant where the standard of service is highest. Other restaurants, with the exception of the lunch counter and cafeteria, differ only in modifications of the service and appointments. The lunch counter and cafeteria will be taken up in another chapter.

TYPES OF DINING ROOM SERVICE

There are three major types of service used in restaurants—the French, Russian, and American. For special occasions or for large parties or banquets, two additional services are sometimes used—the English and the Buffet.

French Service. This signifies luxury and is found only in restaurants catering to a wealthy clientele. It is expensive to maintain and this expense is reflected in the patrons' checks. The food is brought to the table on silver platters, carefully arranged and suitably garnished. The guest is always given an opportunity to view the food before the service starts. Chafing dishes are used to maintain the temperature of hot foods. This type of service requires extreme alertness on the part of the waiter or captain. They must be on hand to serve the patrons at exactly the moment the food is required.

Salads are usually mixed at the table by the captain who makes a ritual of it. He must be practiced in the art of mixing salads with a flourish. Sometimes a choice of salads is offered from a cart or tray. A selection of French pastries is presented on a large tray. Elaborate flaming desserts are also a feature of this type of service.

The cost per cover should be carefully considered, taking into consideration not only the waiters, captains, and bus help needed, but also warewashing and the maintenance of the table appointments. Also, fewer tables can be placed in a given area because of the side tables needed for French service. This type of service should never be attempted unless a restaurant manager knows that his clientele wants it and is willing to pay for it.

Russian Service. In this comparatively simple service, the portions of food are put directly on the plate from the range or steam table in the kitchen, which involves no duplication of work. This type of service is used in most restaurants and for banquets. Great economies have been made in staffing for banquet service by the use of hot and cold storage units. With these units, food may be pre-plated some time in advance of its service.

American Service. This is a combination of both the French and Russian service. Chafing dishes may be used for some foods, with direct plating for others. Soup is sometimes served from a tureen but many times the soup dishes or cups, ready filled, are placed before the patron. Side salads are usually plated in the pantry. In some places, however, salad and relish trays are used. Hot rolls are offered from a cart or a large basket, or they may be placed on the table on a bread plate. A roast beef wagon with carving and service at the table is another choice in this type of service. With some ingenuity, operators can adopt some features of French service to tone up a restaurant at very slight additional cost.

English Service. Sometimes known as "host" or "holiday" service, this type is usually requested at special functions or on holidays. The carving and service is the responsibility of the host. Sometimes he serves the vegetables or they may be passed in serving dishes by the waiter and each guest serves himself. A waiter always stands at the left of the host and takes the plate, as it is filled, to each guest in turn. He is usually instructed in advance which person is the hostess (if one is present) and which the guest of honor so that they may be served in their proper order. Birthday cakes or elaborate desserts are often served in this manner even though the service of the meal, up to that time, has been of a different type.

Buffet Service. Buffet service involves the placing of substantial quantities of food on platters on a large table, usually arranged in courses. Plates, silverware, and linen are conveniently arranged and the guests serve themselves. Sometimes table napkins are placed on the tables in advance. This type of service is occasionally used at banquet functions. Swedish restaurants feature this type of service as the Smorgasbord forms the buffet.

Although buffet service may be handled by a smaller crew of employees, there is no really effective method of portion control, so that any waste of food may cancel the payroll saving.

SCOPE OF DUTIES

Since the duties of employees in a dining room are found to overlap at times, it is advisable to make up a chart of the day-to-day tasks of each employee. This work chart should be supplemented by a list of occasions when duties must overlap. The weekly work schedule of each waiter or waitress and of each bus boy should be conspicuously posted. Special assignments should be listed at least a week in advance. Rotation of stations should be followed unless a seniority preferential system is in effect.

On page 156 will be found a sample work chart involving eight waitresses working six stations on a five-day week, with one station closed down twice a week due to lower business volume.

In organizing a rotating work schedule, two important principles merit close attention; (1) consecutive days off, and (2) rotating days off. If employees, on a five-day week, are obliged to have disconnected days off rather than consecutive days off, employee morale is likely to suffer. Also, if employees are obliged to have the same days off each week, without equitable rotation, those who have week days off are likely to become disgruntled.

There is no valid reason why employees should not be satisfied in this respect. A useful hint in setting up such a schedule, is to establish the days off first; then, shift these days off as has been done in the illustrated sample schedule. In the course of a number of weeks, equal to the number of employees, a complete rotation of stations and days off should be possible. In the event it is not easily possible to rotate all work stations on an absolutely perfect basis, the choice can be given to the staff between perfect station rotation or consecutive days off. The choice will almost invariably be the latter.

In all of the foregoing it should be borne in mind that intelligently planned work schedules make for better employee morale with the much-desired result of improved customer relations.

	STATION A WAITRESS	STATION B WAITRESS	STATION C WAITRESS	STATION D WAITRESS	STATION E WAITRESS	STATION F WAITRESS	OFF WAITRESS
SUNDAY OCTOBER 1	#3	#4	#5	#6	#7	#8	#1, #2
MONDAY OCTOBER 2	#4	#5	#6	#7	#8	Closed	#1, #2, #3
TUESDAY OCTOBER 3	#5	#6	#7	#8	#1	#2	#3, #4
WEDNESDAY OCTOBER 4	#6	#7	#8	#1	#2	#3	#4, #5
THURSDAY OCTOBER 5	#7	#8	#1	#2	#3	#4	#5, #6
FRIDAY OCTOBER 6	#1	#2	#3	#4	#5	Closed	#6, #7 #8
SATURDAY OCTOBER 7	#2	#3	#4	#5	#6	#1	#7, #8
SUNDAY OCTOBER 8	#4	#5	#6	#7	#8	#1	#2, #3
MONDAY OCTOBER 9	#5	#6	#7	#8	#1	Closed	#2, #3 #4
TUESDAY OCTOBER 10	#6	#7	#8	#1	#2	#3	#4, #5
WEDNESDAY OCTOBER 11	#7	#8	#1	#2	#3	#4	#5, #6
THURSDAY OCTOBER 12	#8	#1	#2	#3	#4	#5	#6, #7
FRIDAY OCTOBER 13	#2	#3	#4	#5	#6	Closed	#7, #8, #1
SATURDAY OCTOBER 14	#3	#4	#5	#6	#7	#2	#8, #1
SUNDAY OCTOBER 15	#5	#6	#7	#8	#1	#2	#3, #4
MONDAY OCTOBER 16	#6	#7	#8	#1	#2	Closed	#3, #4 #5
TUESDAY OCTOBER 17	#7	#8	#1	#2	#3	#4	#5, #6
WEDNESDAY OCTOBER 18	#8	#1	#2	#3	#4	#5	#6, #7
THURSDAY OCTOBER 19	#1	#2	#3	#4	#5	#6	#7, #8
FRIDAY OCTOBER 20	#3	#4	#5	#6	#7	Closed	#8, #1, #2
SATURDAY OCTOBER 21	#4	#5	#6	#7	#8	#3	#1, #2

Head Waiter or Hostess. The head waiter is responsible for all phases of service, including the appearance of the room and the staff, and for the seating of patrons. The duties of the hostess are the same, although in a room employing a head waiter, the type of service is likely to be more elaborate, the beverage service more extensive, and advance reservations more numerous.

In some restaurants, the hostess is little more than an usher and does not function as the floor supervisor. This means that someone else must assume that responsibility or supervision is neglected. However, a competent hostess can effect considerable savings for the restaurant in combating waste and inefficiency.

The appearance of the dining room and the staff can be checked only by actual inspection. Sufficient time should be allowed for this before the opening of the dining room. If a standard check list is used, anyone substituting in the job may have a precise blueprint of the inspection routine. Check lists will vary, depending on the type of place, its equipment and certain architectural details. The major items to be checked in most restaurants are:

Doors
Cashier's station
Floors
Walls
Windows
Curtains, shades, and drapes
Mirrors and pictures
Table linen
Chairs, including reserve high chairs
Table settings
Ash trays
Menus
Lamps and lamp shades
Condiment containers
Table legs for steadiness
Table cloths for even hanging
Both table legs and chair legs for splinters

In addition, the light, heat, and ventilation should be checked.

At least once a month, on different days, a surprise inspection should be conducted by the maitre d'hotel, the catering manager, or the manager, and deficiencies noted for future reference so that corrective measures may be taken.

Every waiter or waitress should report to the head waiter or hostess before each meal, ready for duty, subject to inspection for neatness of dress and cleanliness of person. This inspection also insures proper coverage of each table at a station. When absenteeism occurs, the head waiter or hostess must make re-assignments so that every table is covered. At this time, the service staff can be briefed on the menu. Every waiter or waitress should be required to know:

(1) Prices of all entrees;

(2) Made-to-order and prepared entrees;

(3) Approximate time required to wait for entrees cooked to order;

(4) Entrees and desserts that should be "pushed."

In dining rooms where there is no entertainment, the problem of choice table locations is not great. In such a room, the head waiter or hostess should endeavor to divide the patrons as equally as possible among the various servers. In large rooms of this kind, some find it best to keep an actual tally card of the number of patrons assigned to each server. This not only divides the work load but enables each server to share equally in the gratuities.

In dining rooms where entertainment is provided, the seating of patrons is much more difficult. In these cases, the head waiter may need some supervision since his opportunity for gratuities is great. Some very worth-while patrons may be shunted into a far corner because they have not handed the head waiter a tip upon entering the room or because he does not know from experience that a tip will be forthcoming. Entertainment costs money, and it may well be wasted because of the rude actions of a "tip hungry" waiter. People who are shown to poor locations once may not complain, but after a second time they will not return, especially if they notice that tables in better locations remain empty because the head waiter has set aside too many for good "tippers" who did not materialize.

On the other hand, in a place where reservations are numerous, a clever head waiter can make his establishment very popular. Reservations give him a chance to learn the patrons' names. Many people consider it a great distinction to be recognized by the head waiter—particularly in fashionable restaurants.

Courtesy and alertness should be the rule in seating patrons. They should be greeted pleasantly, led to a table, chairs pulled out and, after they are seated, a menu placed in front of each guest. No guest should be seated long before a glass of water is placed before him. This is the duty of either the bus boy or the waiter, depending upon the size of the room and the number of employees.

A real effort should be made by the head waiter to extend some parting word to every guest or group as they leave. As a rule, he is near the door and should be able to comply with this rule easily. If he feels this simple courtesy is too burdensome, he is in the wrong job.

Supervision of Service. One thing a head waiter or hostess must watch is the length of time a patron is seated before he places his order—also, the length of time between courses. This duty may be delegated to the captains or assistant hostesses but it must not be neglected.

The distance from the kitchen to the dining room is one factor causing delay. When the kitchen is far removed from the dining room, it is well to have the waiters work in teams. One member of the team is in the dining room taking an order while the other is in the kitchen picking up the previous order.

Another cause for delay may be indifference on the part of the service staff. Sometimes a waiter will delay making a trip to the kitchen until he has two or three orders to fill. At other times, he becomes so interested in a conversation with a fellow worker that he seems to have forgotten his surroundings. Such lapses in service should not be tolerated. If they are, the head waiter is at fault.

A third cause of delay may be bottle necks or confusion in the kitchen. These are often beyond the control of the service staff. The steam table or pantry section may be understaffed; the layout may be such as to make the smooth flow of work impossible; the supply of clean dishes or silverware may be inadequate; the supply of coffee, cream, or incidentals may be delayed. These are all matters which the manager must discover and correct.

In some cases, both serving staff and kitchen employees are at fault for slow service. The waiters may call out their orders indistinctly or they may have their checks so poorly organized as to cause confusion among the kitchen staff. It is impossible for the head waiter or hostess to visit the kitchen to learn the cause of delay. They are too busy supervising the service and seating patrons in the dining room. The only answer is a weekly staff meeting where the situation is explained and where all concerned have a chance to iron out the difficulties. Almost all congestion in the kitchen can be overcome. Sometimes it takes only minor changes. At other times, it may mean a general re-arrangement of the equipment and the hiring of additional employees. In such cases, outside consultants are valuable since they are accustomed to these situations and can often put their finger on the trouble immediately. In one case, a badly congested kitchen was greatly improved by moving the coffee service into the dining room. It happened that the coffee urns were in a bad location in the kitchen and when three or four waitresses were waiting for coffee, the entire kitchen was thrown off balance. After the remedy was suggested, the manager could not understand why he had not been able to see the solution himself. His failure is best explained by a trite but very apt expression—he was "too close to the forest to see the trees."

One source of annoyance to patrons is the failure to receive their checks promptly when their meal is finished. The problem of presenting the check is not always a simple one. In formal dining rooms, guests may not be ready to leave and if they are presented with their check, they feel the waiter is rushing them. On the other hand, when they are ready, they want the check immediately. In such places, the captain should be charged with the responsibility of seeing that the checks are given to the patrons when they are preparing to leave. At lunch or in less formal dining rooms, few patrons will be offended if the check is placed on the table after the dessert has been served.

Some head waiters, when business is heavy, become very dictatorial, ordering the captains and waiters about in loud and haughty tones. No employee should ever be reprimanded in the presence of the patrons. It makes the guests uncomfortable and humiliates and antagonizes the waiters. If there are lapses in service, the head waiter or hostess should keep a pad or card on which notes will recall to mind the items to speak about in private. The head waiter or hostess is completely responsible for training the service staff. Lapses in service by the people under them, if repeated continually, are a reflection on the ability of the man or woman in charge of them.

Captains. In dining rooms where captains are employed, they are assigned to specific sections that are under their immediate supervision. Each section is made up of several stations and each captain should remain in the immediate neighborhood of his section. The assistance which the captains give the head waiter in seating patrons depends upon the head waiter's preference, and also upon the rate at which incoming patrons arrive. During the early part of the meal period, when the rate of arrival is slow, the head waiter may escort a group of patrons to a captain's section and the captain will do the actual seating. On the other hand, some head waiters will not leave the door for even a brief interval. They will either beckon for a captain or arrange for at least one captain to be at the door to escort guests to their proper tables. The head waiter decides on the system to be used.

Some captains seat patrons with too great a flourish in the expectation of receiving a tip. Others make a point of appearing somewhere along the patron's route of exit to inquire if everything has been satisfactory. This may appear to be a subtle hint for a tip. When head waiters at the door make the same inquiry with the same subtle suggestion, patrons begin to feel that they are required to run a gauntlet of outstretched palms. This can easily discourage their desire to return.

At the table, the captain should make sure that the glass of water is placed on the table and the order taken without delay. The water glasses must be refilled and dishes removed promptly after each course. It is the captain's duty to see that checks are placed on the table when the guests appear ready to leave.

A "scrub" captain is an assistant to the captain. He may serve as captain on the latter's day off and possibly as a waiter the balance of the week. Sometimes he may act in the partial capacity of a waiter and take the order. Even the captain sometimes does this when the waiter is busy.

Waiters and Waitresses. Courtesy and alertness are the two important factors for this job. Courtesy is natural to some people; others have to be trained in the small ways that typify courtesy. If, after training, waiters or waitresses still remain rude and unpleasant, they are not qualified for the job. Alertness in taking orders creates a good impression, helps improve the rate of turnover, and results in increased volume of business. Since this improves the earning power of the service personnel, it should be explained to them that alertness is a habit that pays.

When an order is being taken, symbols should be used on the checks to designate various preferences such as meat rare or well done, toast dry or buttered, coffee served with the meal or later, tea with lemon or cream. This will cut down the number of trips to the kitchen to rectify errors.

When a group of people are at one table and no one is acting as host, it is best to take the orders around the table in order, left to right or right to left. In this way, no order is overlooked and when the waiter returns with the orders it is easier to place the correct order before each person. When a patron insists that he is not being served what he ordered, it is best to make the exchange cheerfully. The waiter may prove that the guest is wrong, but the restaurant may lose a customer.

In many restaurants, the patron never sees the manager, the chef, or any other employee except the waiter or waitress who, therefore, represents the restaurant. This is one reason why his, or her, manner and appearance are important. Another reason is that food will not be appetizing if served by a person who is in any way objectionable as to personal appearance or cleanliness. Uniforms must be clean and well pressed. Lightweight uniforms should be changed daily. If food is spilled on uniforms, some provision should be made for quick changes. Hands and nails should always be clean and well groomed. The same applies to hair. Long, loose hair arrangements have no place in a restaurant. If bobbed, the hair should be very short. Otherwise, any arrangement is satisfactory as long as the hair is kept in place. If this seems difficult, a net or attractive cap should be worn. If the latter, it should be an integral part of the uniform and standard for all waitresses. Daily baths are necessary and the use of a deodorant for both waiters and waitresses cannot be stressed too firmly. These are the things which the head waiter and hostess must insist upon.

Bus Help. The bus help assists the waiters and waitresses. Occasionally their work will overlap that of the dining room porters. This occurs generally when a cleaning-up job is necessary during meal service or when dust blows in through an open window and accumulates on the sill. In hiring them, the manager should keep in mind their eventual promotion to members of the serving staff. If they realize this, they will assist more cheerfully with less grumbling. Bus help takes a little closer supervision than the service staff. When the latter is slow or inefficient, it is reflected in tips, and for personal gain, if nothing else, they will do better work. Bus help, on the other hand, can do unsatisfactory work in a number of ways that cannot be detected except by the closest scrutiny. They can be noisy; their trays badly stacked, causing spillage and breakage; food spilled during meal service only partially cleaned up; food scraped from the plates at the table while the guests are seated there; carelessness in changing table cloths, flicking crumbs over the floor and adjoining tables —all of these bad habits of the bus help can be discerned only by close inspection of the head waiter or hostess and overcome by proper initial training.

Bus help assists in setting up the tables. They fill and refill water glasses and pitchers, remove all the tableware after a meal, keep side stands supplied with linen and silverware, replenish supplies for a coffee station (if there is one in the dining room), and reset the tables after each patron or group has left. In various establishments, they may perform any of the tasks assigned to waiters, except taking, processing, and serving the orders.

When captains are used in a dining room, they are in the best position to supervise the activities of the bus help. In a dining room supervised by a hostess, the seating of patrons is likely to keep her occupied and control of the bus help is difficult. In such cases, a head bus boy may be able to assume supervision. It is not wise to permit the service staff (waiters or waitresses) to "boss" the bus help. It is always resented and is reflected in their standard of work. It is a case of "too many bosses" and even though the criticism may be deserved, the bus help do not appreciate receiving it from members of the service staff.

TECHNIQUES OF SERVICE

Although good service is unobtrusive, it is not always simple or easily mastered by the beginner. The first thing to learn is the proper way to set the table. If table cloths are used, the table pad should be centered on the table. The table cloth should be centered also, so that the over-hang is the same length all around. Table cloths that are stained, torn, or badly wrinkled should not be used. It is not the fault of the service staff if various sized table cloths are used. However, if this is the case, the manager should look at his own dining room when it is partly empty to see the haphazard effect this gives. Some cloths nearly touch the floor and others barely cover the table.

The folded napkin should be placed between the silver service with the open edge to the right. If a service plate is part of the setting, the napkin may be placed on it or at the left of the forks. When a table cloth requires changing during the meal service, every effort should be made to make the change before the table is occupied by a new patron. This is the joint responsibility of the head waiter or hostess, and the waiter or waitress serving the station. Sometimes, however, when the pressure of business is heavy, patrons are seated before the cloth is changed. In this case, the changes should be made as quietly as possible, without waving of arms or flicking of crumbs.

About nine inches in the center of each service setting should be allowed for the plate. The handles of the silverware should be about two inches from the edge of the table. The forks are placed at the left of the cover with the tines up, the salad fork the furthest to the left. Knives belong on the right of the cover with the cutting edge turned toward the plate. Spoons are placed to the right of the knives with the bowls up. Silverware is always placed in the order of usage, with first course equipment furthest from the plate. Sugar bowls as well as salt and pepper shakers are placed in the center of the table that seats four; along one side of tables for two. If the table for two is a wall table, the side toward the wall is the one to use; if not a wall table, the side away from the broader aisle should be used for this purpose.

Ash trays stocked with matches belong alongside the sugar bowls. After the departure of each set of patrons, the ash trays should be cleaned and restocked with matches whenever necessary. During the meal, if the trays are used, they must be emptied as often as necessary and replaced with clean trays.

Before each meal, sugar bowls, salt and pepper shakers, syrup jugs, catsup and sauce bottles, oil and vinegar containers are checked and filled when necessary. This is known as "side work" generally performed on a rotation basis according to a prearranged schedule. These condiment containers should not be on the table unless applicable to the meal being served.

Food should never be picked up with the fingers by the waiters or waitresses. Forks or spoons must always be used in handling food in the dining room. Cups are picked up by the handles and glasses by the base; knives, forks, and spoons by the handles. When silverware falls on the floor, it is placed with the soiled ware and a clean utensil given the guest. There must be no deviation from this practice. If bottle tops have an accumulation of catsup or sauce on them, they are wiped clean with a napkin before being placed on the table. When dishes require wiping, this should be done at a side table.

An adequate number of side-towels must be procured before a meal and kept conveniently near. This is particularly true in restaurants using composition table tops that require frequent wiping.

Waiters and waitresses should make a practice of checking all the items on the menu to be sure they have all the extra equipment that may be needed. They must never leave the table after serving food without being sure that all the necessary silverware is on the table. It is particularly exasperating for a hungry guest to gaze upon a plate of food and have no utensils with which to eat it.

Coffee and other beverages are served on the right side of the cover. Unless black coffee is ordered, the waiter should be sure that a creamer accompanies all coffee service.

When boiled eggs are served, the length of time for boiling must be learned when the order is taken. When the eggs are ready, the patron is asked if he would prefer them to be opened. If so, they are opened at the side table.

When a refill of coffee is requested, the waiter either refills the cup at the table, if facilities permit, or he brings in the second cup at the same time the first is removed, preventing any question about a mix-up in cups in the kitchen.

Insufficient side tables and overloaded trays are the two things responsible for most of the spillage and breakage. Service is greatly speeded up if there are enough side tables. Overloaded or improperly loaded trays are common failings. It is done with the mistaken notion that time is saved. In reality, it takes longer to negotiate the route between dining room and kitchen and to disentangle the crowded dishes. Quick trips to and from the kitchen help the flow of work and save money through less breakage and spillage.

In the kitchen, cold foods should be picked up first, hot foods last. Sometimes the kitchen layout makes this difficult. If this is the case, changes are worth while.

Checks should always be placed face down to the left of the host, if there is one. If two men, two women, or two couples are at the table, it is best to make separate checks unless advised otherwise by the patrons. The checks should be placed on the table between the guests. Before placing the checks, an inquiry should always be made as to whether anything else is desired. Change should be returned to a guest on a plate or small tray, in places where the waiter or waitress collects the payment. In a hotel, when a guest signs a check, it is the duty of the waiter or waitress to make certain that the room number is included. Failure to do this will cause a prolonged search by the accounting department if the signature is illegible or if there are other charge accounts under a similar name. The total loss of the amount of the check may be incurred if the right name is not found or if the guest checks out before the correction is made.

If the waiter or waitress takes payment for the check and returns with the change, there is no reason why he cannot thank the patron pleasantly for the tip. If the tip is left at the table and the patrons pay the cashier, the waiter should make an effort to say "thank you" before patrons have left the table.

Care should be taken by the waiter or waitress when signing for a book of blank restaurant checks. The responsibility for lost checks is theirs. Unused checks should be returned to the person in charge of issuing them. A misplaced blank check can easily be a source of temptation.

Coordination. The duties of the waiters and waitresses will vary, depending upon the type of dining room, the size of the station, the bussing arrangements, the layout of the kitchen, and the set-up of the service bar. Provision should be made for the service staff at the stations nearest the entrance to fill in when the hostess is momentarily called away and indicate to arriving patrons that she will return shortly to seat them. Patrons are often embarrassed if they must stand at the door for some time without receiving any attention.

There are times when the waiter or waitress may be delayed in the kitchen. The hostess should keep an eye on patrons for about five minutes after seating them. If, by that time, the order has not been taken, an inquiry by the hostess will serve to relieve the patron's mind.

If the bus help are assigned to filling water glasses, the waiters or waitresses may help out when the bus boy is rushed. If this results in his shirking, a report of this should be made at a weekly staff meeting.

The clearing of the tables is sometimes so neglected that patrons entering a dining room cannot be seated at a cleared table. The hostess is to blame for allowing such a situation to develop. When bus help is available, the waiters and waitresses will often stand idle because they feel this is not part of their work. If the bus help is neglectful, the matter should be reported to the manager by the hostess or head waiter.

The relationship between the serving staff and the kitchen staff is often very difficult to control. The work activities overlap and there is usually no supervisory dining room employee present to act as arbitrator. When waiters or waitresses have been abused by customers, there is always the danger that they may try to "take it out" on the kitchen crew. Perhaps not consciously, but because they are angry, they shout their orders in an unpleasant voice and generally act disagreeably. If friction develops, it may be advisable to have a coordinator on hand during meal times and rush periods, who is directly responsible to the head of the dining room—the catering manager or manager.

Waiters and waitresses will find that the time spent at the checker's stand will be greatly reduced if they will systematically lift the covers from all covered dishes.

Equipment. One unfailing mark of food service is that food be served in the proper dishes. The following list will serve as a general guide:

Juices—3 or 4-ounce glass, paper underliner on 3-inch plate.
Grapefruit—5-inch cereal plate, paper underliner.
Cantaloupe—5-inch cereal plate, paper underliner.
Melons—5-inch cereal plate, paper underliner.
Fruit, Sliced—3 or 4-inch fruit plate, paper underliner on 5 or 6-inch plate.
Berries—3 or 4-inch fruit plate, paper underliner on 5 or 6-inch plate; 2 or 3-ounce creamer.
Apple, Baked—4 or 5-inch cereal plate, underliner on 6-inch plate.
Cereals, Cooked—3 or 4-inch cereal plate, underliner on 5 or 6-inch plate; 3 or 4-ounce creamer.
Cereals, Raw—3 or 4-inch cereal plate, underliner on 5 or 6-inch plate; 3 or 4-ounce creamer.
Eggs, Fried or Scrambled—7-inch plate.
Eggs, with Bacon or Ham—7-inch plate.

Eggs, Poached—4 or 5-inch cereal plate, underliner on 6 or 7-inch plate.
Jams—paper cups on 3-inch plate or on entree dish.
Toast—5-inch plate.
Side Orders—5-inch plate.
Side Salads—4 or 5-inch plate.
Toast, French—7-inch plate.
Waffles—7-inch plate.
Milk—8 or 10 ounce glass, bottle on 3-inch plate.
Tea, Iced—10 or 12-ounce glass, with straw.
Coffee, Iced—10 or 12 ounce glass, with straw.
Coffee, Cup—3 or 4-inch saucer.
Tea, Cup—3 or 4-inch saucer.
Coffee, Pot—3 or 4-inch plate, paper underliner.
Tea, Pot—3 or 4-inch plate, paper underliner.
Soup—5 or 6-inch soup plate or bouillon cup on 3 or 4-inch saucer, paper underliner.
Main Dish Salads—7-inch plate.
Fish Entrees—7-inch plate.
Meat Entrees—7-inch plate.
Vegetables—3-inch plate.
Pie—4 or 5-inch plate.
Cake—4 or 5-inch plate.
Pudding—3-inch fruit or cereal plate, underliner, 5-inch plate.
Fruit Cocktail—supreme bowl or fruit cup on 5-inch plate, paper underliner.
Cheese—5-inch plate.

Controlling Waste. Waiters and waitresses, in their zeal to increase their personal remuneration, frequently confuse good service with excessively generous service. Extra rolls, butter, coffee, cream, jams, jellies, and other food accessories cost them nothing but they materially increase the restaurant's food costs. The service staff should be cautioned against the needless waste of food. Sometimes guests request extra portions but often the waiter or waitress voluntarily serves it, thinking it may increase the size of their tip. By checking the soiled dishes returned to the kitchen, the manager may be able to tell, by the amount of wasted food, whether this habit is practiced by certain waiters. There should be a house policy on the serving of extras. If they are to be served, a note to this effect might be placed on the menu. However, before making this policy, it is prudent to measure the cost of food against any possible customer good will that may result.

Closing Duties. These duties vary according to the equipment available. In general, the common practice is to strip the room of china, glassware, silver, linen, etc., so that the cleaners may do their job speedily, without damage to furnishings or equipment. The stripping of the room is performed very quickly as the service staff leaves after this work is completed. It should follow a fixed routine so that no part of the task is overlooked. In their haste, employees will frequently toss fresh, unused linen in with soiled linen to save time. They will not use care in seeing that all the articles are removed from the table before gathering up the table cloths. This means breakage, badly damaged silverware and linen stained or cut beyond repair. Flowers should be removed from their vases, placed in suitable containers and stored in the refrigerator overnight.

It is important that every waiter or waitress be told the exact locations for storing china, glass, and silverware. Breakfast can sometimes be unduly delayed because of carelessness in this respect on the part of the night crew. Before leaving for the night, the head waiter or hostess should check the kitchen locations of all equipment to see that everything has been properly replaced. If not, instructions should be given the next day. Often, too much reliance is placed on the staff in the matter of showing a new employee where materials belong. This responsibility should rest upon the shoulders of the head waiter or hostess.

HARMONY WITH THE KITCHEN

Knowledge of Preparation Time. To avoid friction, slow-downs of service, or reheating of dishes, it is of utmost importance that the entire dining room staff be briefed on the preparation time required for each entree selection. The simplest and most certain method of achieving this result is to have a short meeting before each meal. The dining room supervisor should obtain accurate information from the chef regarding preparation time and relay this data to the entire service staff. This can be accomplished in a very brief time, simultaneously with the last-minute inspection of the personal appearance of the dining room staff.

Layout Problems. Many dining room establishments function with kitchens that are not systematically designed. Much of the basic equipment is arranged in haphazard fashion. This causes waste motion as well as loss of time and tempers. Quite often a redesigning of the kitchen layout, although it seemingly involves an expenditure of money merely to move equipment around, will improve the flow of service to the point where it will considerably curtail labor turnover.

A definite pattern to assure the soundest flow of traffic is necessary. Many kitchens have satisfactorily arranged their equipment to conform to the general sequence of the meal.

Where kitchen space is at a premium, the service of some items, such as coffee, juices, soups, and salads can be handled in the dining room itself adjacent to the kitchen entrance. This area is usually considered an undesirable location for patrons and quite frequently goes to waste through disuse.

Traffic Control. The flow of traffic in the kitchen must be definitely controlled or at peak periods near-chaos will result.

The stream of traffic should move in a generally circular pattern to avoid criss-crossing. Since the entrance to the kitchen is usually made by keeping to the right, the general tendency is to continue traffic in a counter-clockwise direction. Where congestion is likely to occur, brilliantly painted arrow markers on the floor will aid in directional control, especially in large kitchens. All kitchen stations should be clearly marked as to which items are available from each. This will minimize the creation of bottlenecks by new employees, emergency substitutes, or casual banquet help.

The dish-drop area should be a suitable distance from the swing of the door in order to avoid collisions.

Placing Orders. One of the most disturbing elements in the work-day of the kitchen personnel is the "hash-house" practice by service employees of shouting orders at a considerable distance. This is confusing and nerve-wracking. The dubious saving of a few steps or a few seconds is usually more than lost in the lengthy delays caused by errors and disputes.

The use of an expediter eliminates this evil and also results in the removal of friction in getting orders. Without an expediter, the scramble for orders is likely to resemble the mad dash for a bus during rush hours. With an expediter, the placing and getting of orders take on the orderly procession of a lineup of customers buying seats at a baseball park. An expediter usually makes up in savings for the cost of the added salary, especially in a large kitchen. Order-snatching, arguments, and running feuds are eliminated.

Even if there is no expediter, there should be a house rule prohibiting order-shouting. Where long distances are involved, a mechanical communicating system may provide a feasible solution.

Checker-Station Bottlenecks. A great cause of aggravation in the kitchen is the disorderly bottleneck that frequently develops at the checker's station. There must be ample shelf space to accommodate at least four trays. If this space is lacking an added burden is unnecessarily imposed upon the service staff. They become irritated and nag the checker into hurrying. Arguments ensue and the quality of work that the checker can perform under these difficult conditions suffers, with possible loss of revenue to the house. Adequate tray-storage space at the checker's station is an absolute necessity. As an added measure to insure the sound flow of work at this station, the authority of the checker to fulfill his duties properly should be signed by top management and conspicuously posted.

ROOM SERVICE

This type of service is found in hotels and has proved to be one of the most difficult of the various food and beverages services to control. This is true because the service is scattered throughout the entire hotel and because the *actual* service takes place without supervision. It is difficult from the human angle also, as guests may act quite differently in their own rooms than in a public dining room. Situations are constantly arising which are difficult for the staff to handle, regardless of how well trained they may be. Consequently, only the most competent waiters should be used for room service.

Order-Taking. Correct order-taking is even more important for room service than in the dining room. In the latter case, errors in orders may be corrected with comparative ease and speed. In room service, it is another matter. It is sometimes a very long journey back to the kitchen and guests are annoyed by the lapse of time. This is particularly true in the morning when tempers are not always well controlled. Because of the noise in the kitchen, the order-taker finds it doubly difficult to avoid errors. The construction of a sound-proof booth for the order clerk will probably pay for itself in a short time in reduced waste and more accurate service.

The order clerk must have a pleasant voice and be familiar with food and beverage terms. After taking the order over the telephone, he verifies it and re-checks the room number. It is necessary that he, or she, be able to write rapidly and legibly. All orders must be time-stamped when the order is taken and when it is delivered.

Speed of Serving. Many guests use room service because they think it will save time. Unless the service is slow, they are correct. If it is slow, a great deal of good will is lost. Room service can bog down all along the line unless good training prevails—at the point of origin, in transit, and in the final service to the guest.

An efficient telephone order clerk and a simplified system of order recording and check writing will help achieve speed at the point of origin. During rush periods, orders will arrive as rapidly as the order clerk can take them. He may not have the time to take the order in the book and write up the check for the waiter. It may help if the order book is printed in duplicate, one copy remaining in the book and the other given to the waiter who can write up his own check. The order clerk has then only to tear out the order for the waiter and shift the carbon paper.

The waiter, or, in large hotels, the room service captain, should see to it that there is a continuous supply of food and equipment ready for room service orders.

Service elevators are frequently responsible for the orders being slow in transit. If complaints of slow service are prevalent, this is one place for a check to be made. It is not always the fault of the operator. In the morning the chambermaids and housemen may be using the service elevators as they are starting their day's work just about the time breakfast orders are pouring into the room service order desk. Since guests usually do not want their room put in order before they have their breakfast, it may be advisable to change the work schedules of the housekeeping staff in order to ease the pressure on the service cars. A staggered arrival schedule may be one way of working it out.

The use of service tables on wheels will tend to reduce the total time needed for meal service in the guest rooms. Such accessories should be stored in a convenient location.

Courtesy. Courtesy and tact are of first importance in serving food and beverages to guests in their own rooms. Because the law makes a hotel responsible for the conduct of its own employees during the course of their work, the slightest indiscretion on their part may form the basis for a lawsuit. Careful instruction in all house rules, particularly in regard to serving women who are alone, should be given to each waiter. Some hotels require the waiters to leave the door ajar in such cases. They should never linger in the guest's room or display interest in anything in the room. Conversation should be confined to the business of service.

Room service waiters should be equipped with a corkscrew, bottle opener, matches, pencil, a supply of change, and extra napkins. If it is the policy of the hotel to place a newspaper on the breakfast tray, the waiter should be careful to see that this rule is followed.

Dish Removal. The removal of soiled dishes can be a problem unless it is properly organized. Frequently guests may require very late service and will not want the equipment removed from their room at the time the room service department closes for the night. This means the maid is confronted with this equipment the next morning. Since this removal is not part of her assigned duties, she is inclined to handle it in an unsatisfactory manner. She either leaves it in the room, which annoys the guest, or she puts it out into the corridor which certainly does not improve the appearance of the corridor and invites pilferage and breakage.

The only solution to the problem is the preparation of a list by the room service department of rooms where equipment remained over night. Each chambermaid should then telephone room service as soon as she enters a room and sees the equipment. The person in charge of room service must then send an employee to remove it. Since the average maid generally requires a minimum of twenty minutes to make up a room, this should permit ample time for the dish removal while she is still there.

At other times, the man in charge of room service makes up a list of room numbers and the time the orders were stamped by the order-taker. This serves as his guide for subsequent dish removal. When guests do not state when they want the dishes removed, an hour for breakfast and an hour and a half for dinner should be allowed. Such entries should have a question mark beside them, and when the time is up, an inquiry can be made by telephone before an employee is sent for the dishes. If this record—known as an equipment control sheet—is carefully maintained, the overnight list can be prepared from it. Frequently, the guests themselves will place a tray or room service table in the corridor. All employees—maids, housemen, bellmen, and porters—should notify the room service department when they see this.

No waiter should enter a room during a guest's absence unless another employee accompanies him. This extra employee serves as a witness, if necessary, that nothing was disturbed by the waiter. His full name and time-card number should be entered by the waiter, with his own initial, on the equipment control sheet.

Checks and Payment. In the dining room the check is not presented until after the last course is served. In room service, it is necessary for the waiter to present the check before the guest begins the meal. Otherwise, the guest may have left his room and checked out of the hotel before the waiter returns for the dishes. Every waiter should be instructed to turn over payment of checks to the cashier immediately upon receipt. All checks should be time-stamped twice—at the check's station and again when presented to the cashier. A periodic check should be made of the time lapses between the taking of the order, the checker's stamp, and the cashier's stamp. If there are complaints of unreasonable slowness in service, a check of these lapses will show where the time is spent and further study will indicate the causes for delay.

BEVERAGE SERVICE

Duties. In the small hotel as well as the average size restaurant, the service and control of beverages rests between the steward and head-waiter, and do not present the problems found in the larger establishments.

In the more extensive operations the wine steward is responsible for supervision of the beverage department under the guidance of the catering manager.

The head bartender is in charge of the bars and bartenders. Usually the scheduling of employees' shifts, the appearance and stocking of the bars, the standards of service, and the selection of bar personnel are also under his supervision. It is his duty to check the qualifications of newly-engaged or extra bartenders. He should check all equipment periodically and make sure that all beer is stocked at the bar for a minimum of 24 hours before usage, and maintained at a temperature varying from 42 to 45 degrees, if possible. The absolute limits of temperature range should be 40 to 50 degrees.

The bartenders mix and serve all drinks ordered by customers or waiters. Regional differences in taste will account for certain deviations in the method of preparing many drinks. There are certain rules, however, that are the same throughout the country. Ice should never be placed in any kind of wine unless specifically requested by a patron. When beer is drawn, the first few drops should be allowed to run down the drain. This clears out the slight amount that has settled in the faucet and is warm. If beer is in almost constant demand during rush hours, the beer in the faucet will not have time enough to get warm and this draining is not necessary. When two or more glasses are filled at a time, the faucet need not be shut off between glasses. All bartenders should become acquainted with the full details of proper wine service by reading the four booklets available without charge issued by the Wine Institute.*

Waiters in a cocktail lounge or dining room are responsible for beverage service and should be properly informed on all correct methods of bottled service—red wines in a wine basket; champagne carried in a silver ice bucket and wrapped in a napkin when served.

Bar boys are general utility men at the bar. They prepare fruits,

* 717 Market Street, San Francisco 3, California

juices, and sundry accessories. They assist in obtaining stock from the cellar, and in such cleaning up as is necessary during the operation of the bar.

Bar porters usually are assigned to the heavy duty cleaning, after the bar closes or before it is opened for business. In smaller establishments, they may have other cleaning duties. In a hotel they may be part of the housekeeping staff or employees of an independent cleaning contractor.

Standards. The stand-up bar is an exacting beverage service station. The bartenders are confined to a limited working area that is constantly within sight of the customers. Because of this close scrutiny by the patrons, high standards are extremely important. Personal neatness and cleanliness, efficiency and orderliness are necessary.

At this type of bar, a customer is afforded a view "behind the scenes" and is able to see how an order is prepared. Any flare for showmanship which a bartender has is desirable, but it is not a substitute for competence. Accuracy is also essential, since patrons appear to enjoy seeing a drink "come out even," signifying the absence of waste or short measure. All guesswork is eliminated when proper jiggers are used to measure the ingredients.

At some stand-up bars, due to local regulations or preference, a row of stools is added. This encourages lounging by the customers. Excessive conversation from some customers is inevitable and must be regarded as an "occupational hazard." The best policy for bartenders is to be friendly but not familiar.

Stations should be checked carefully when the bar is opened because shortages during rush periods can be extremely awkward. All bottles and supplies should be returned to their proper places immediately after using. Failure to observe this simple rule causes untold confusion. There is usually a peak of activity in the late afternoon that extends to the pre-dinner hour and again before midnight. It is not wise to change shifts or work short-handed during these peak periods.

Cocktail Lounge. Service in a cocktail lounge is under less pressure than in a stand-up bar since a more leisurely atmosphere prevails. Food accessories, such as peanuts, popcorn, and pretzel sticks should be kept in proper supply on the tables. In some cocktail lounges, hors d'oeuvres and hot canapes are served. It tends to stamp an establishment in a patron's mind if this service is deficient.

Beverage service for a cocktail lounge is obtained by waiters or waitresses from either a service bar or a designated section of the stand-up bar. In a lounge where a section of a stand-up bar is used, the standard of service will suffer considerably if waiters are delayed unduly in serving drinks. Bartenders may ignore waiters to serve bar customers because of the expected tip. In smaller lounges where there is no hostess, captain, or head waiter, the waiters or waitresses are likely to try to persuade patrons to take a table in preference to a place at the bar. The bartenders will resent this competition. A tip pool may be the only equitable solution to this problem if a feasible formula can be established.

Service Bar. Drink measurements for a service bar require proper attention to avoid spillage. The most skilled waiters cannot avoid spillage if glasses are filled too full. The waste of ingredients, general messiness, and need for constant mopping can be eliminated by the use of miniature decanters. The latter method permits pre-stocking of individual portions of Scotch, Rye, and Bourbon, which can be quickly picked up by the waiters, provided such pre-pouring is permitted under the applicable government regulations.

It is extremely important that house rules be established by the men in charge of this part of the service—catering manager, maitre d'hotel, or head bartender—regarding the division of tasks between the waiters and bartenders. The waiters must know what equipment they should pick up and set up for service. Clearly defined house rules will eliminate disputes, delays, and grudges. If these rules are posted, service should be speeded up since all shifts of both groups of employees would know exactly what is expected of them.

When a customer makes no attempt to leave after his first order, the waiter should inquire as to whether he wishes to re-order. Waiters must watch their own customers. During dull periods, they often wander off and forget about them. Bartenders too, are likely to get involved in a conversation at the other end of the bar and overlook empty glasses.

In any establishment open to the public, there are bound to be situations arising from time to time that must be handled tactfully if the reputation of the establishment is to remain unimpaired. Many times, patrons become belligerent or offensive. An employee, in the midst of working at a station cannot be expected to handle a difficult customer properly. However, rules should be established whereby the person in charge of the room or the house officer or an assistant manager can be summoned quickly. These people have a certain degree of authority in the eyes of the patron which will make it easier for them to handle him.

Minors. The problem of minors seeking to be served beverages can be embarrassing and costly because heavy fines and loss of license may be involved. Law enforcement officers have an obligation to the community to enforce existing regulations and are likely to scrutinize service at any time. Often, it is impossible to tell the exact age of a prospective patron or demand a birth certificate. There is always the problem, also, of older people who bring minors with them. The greatest caution and tact are necessary in serving patrons whose age may be near the legal limits.

Check Disputes. It is inevitable that some patrons will feel that a mistake has been made in their checks. They may wish to discuss the matter with a waiter, bartender, cashier, or head waiter. The bartender is responsible to the beverage department and will expect disputes to be ironed out in accordance with instructions he has received. The cashier or checker is answerable to the accounting department and may see things differently from a bartender or a waiter who is answerable to the head waiter and the maitre d'hotel. An inter-departmental dispute among the personnel of all these departments becomes very awkward. It should be the fixed policy of the establishment to permit the employee in charge of a room to settle all disputes if he signs or initials the disputed check. The beverage department and accounting department employees should be instructed to abide by this decision, even though they may disagree. If the amount of the check is large enough to make it worth while, these other employees should be requested to submit the facts as they see them, in writing to their superiors.

Glassware. The proper selection of glassware can help tone up beverage service and, at the same time, aid in effecting economies. Glasses should be as thin as practicable, particularly in the better grade establishments. Clear crystal is best. A well-equipped bar should have the following kinds of glasses:

- Absinthe Drip Glass
- Beer Glass
- Brandy Inhaler
- Brandy Liner Glass
- California Cocktail Glass
- Large Decanter
- Old-Fashioned Glass
- Pousse Cafe Glass
- Punch Glass
- Rhine Wine Glass
- Sherry or Port Glass
- Small Decanter
- Champagne Cut-Down Coupe
- Claret or Red Wine Glass
- Cordial or Pony Glass
- Delmonico Glass
- Highball Glass
- Standard Champagne Coupe
- Tom and Jerry Mug
- Tom Collins Glass
- Water Goblet
- Whiskey Glass
- White Wine Glass
- Zombie Glass

All glasses should be kept spotlessly clean. Waiters and bartenders should make it a habit to check every glass for lipstick stains before serving.

An effective use of tiers and banquettes for formal dining rooms.

A coffee shop may be very attractive and profitable without excessive decorating costs.

An attractive counter service arrangement. Quick turnover produces more profits.

A commercial cafeteria must be attractive, air-conditioned, neat and clean if it is to be profitable.

In an industrial cafeteria such as this, proper design and choice of equipment keeps down maintenance costs.

Small warewashing unit—outmoded and obsolete. Time to change.

Small warewashing unit—latest type of equipment with pre-wash machine attached.

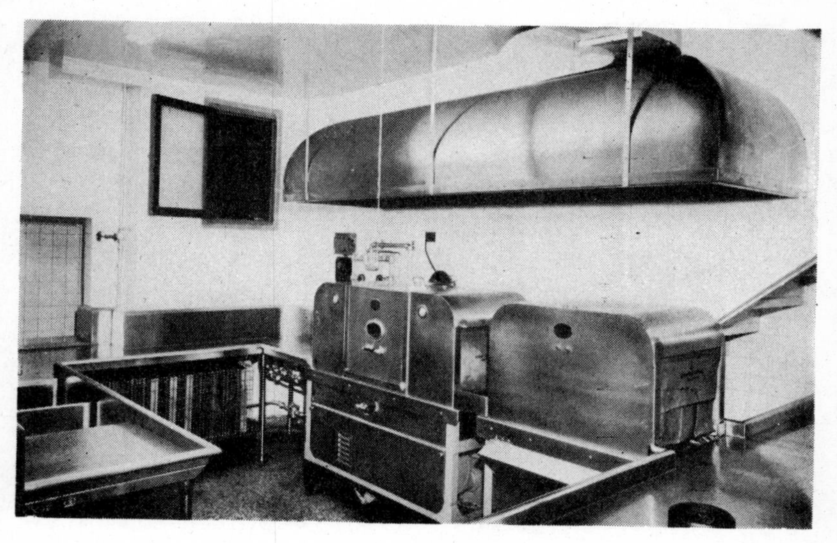

One way to improve wine sales. The proper use of the wine basket prevents unnecessary agitation of aged wines while serving.

A neat and orderly beverage storeroom, showing the use of bin cards.

Beer glasses should not be washed with soap but with a compound especially recommended for this purpose. They should be scalded and allowed to drain, but not toweled. Beer goes "flat" if any foreign substance gets into it. Beer glasses should not be used for any other drink and should be wet before they are filled with beer. When bottled beer is served, the guest does the pouring.

MERCHANDISING WINE

An efficient wine service is a desirable, almost essential part of the dining room operation of any really good hotel or fine restaurant. It can be a profitable element in the overall operation. There is a substantial number of hotels, clubs and restaurants where wine is sold in large volume easily and profitably.

The formula of establishments that have succeeded with wine sales is no secret, nor are their customers unusual. They are ordinary, everyday Americans, a cross section of the patrons of public dining rooms everywhere. Yet there is a formula for successful wine selling based on the experience of hotels and restaurants which have succeeded, consisting of a few essentials that must all be present if wine is to be sold successfully:

1. Palatable wine.
2. Satisfactory quantity at a reasonable price.
3. Prompt wine service.
4. Service of white wines cold.
5. Suggestions to the diner.

Every restaurant that has supplied all five of these essentials has succeeded in selling wine in profitable volume. Supplying one or two or even three does not do the job, but when all five are present, wine sales mount to a satisfactory level.

Stated another way, these essentials mean: A good buying policy so that a representative list of wines will be in stock at all times; pricing these wines realistically in terms of the patronage enjoyed; trained personnel that knows enough of the ABC's of wine and wine service to make it easy for patrons to order and obtain wine; and, finally, calling the attention of patrons to the wines that are available.

The absence of a well-rounded wine program in the great majority of American hotels and restaurants is the only explanation for the great lag in sales of wine with meals evident during the last fifteen years when home consumption of wine has been climbing rapidly.

In most public dining rooms it is difficult for a guest to order wine because waiters and waitresses are not acquainted with the five classes of wine, the few most popular wine types or the stocks available in the establishments where they work. In such places the guest has a difficult time obtaining a wine he will enjoy and, by the time he gets it, his disposition often is frayed, the waiter is unhappy, and what should have been an enjoyable dinner proves to be just the opposite.

In the occasional dining room where a well-rounded wine program has been installed, the ordering and service of wine is practically effortless. The guest is given quick access to a wine list he can understand; the waiter is familiar with the wines listed and can take an order without making the guest feel he is talking a foreign language; the order is filled promptly and both waiter and guest are in good spirits. The essentials of efficient wine service are very simple and involve only the same kind of management attention to wine that is given to virtually every other aspect of dining room operations, for example, attractive table settings or the service of coffee.

Once a suitable wine stock has been acquired, it is necessary to provide physical handling facilities that make it easy for a waiter to fill an order without interrupting his table schedule. This often may be achieved through the establishment of a wine service cupboard or counter between the kitchen and the dining room, plus suitable provision for wine stemware and a corkscrew that will work for each waiter. The next step involves personnel training, which is not a complicated matter. A few brief instruction periods will serve to acquaint the average waiter with all he needs to know about wine in order to sell and serve it easily. It takes no longer to become familiar with the five wine classes and the principal wine types than it does to learn the names of a comparable number of entrees or desserts. A part of the training of personnel should stress the importance of prompt wine service. It is just as important to deliver the wine to the table promptly with the food as it is to deliver the bacon with the eggs or the cream with the strawberries. Patrons must have their wine served in time to enjoy it with the main course of the meal. If the wine arrives late, they will not enjoy it and they may not order wine again in that particular restaurant; in fact, they may not return again to that particular dining room.

The ideal time to begin serving table wine is immediately after the salad. However, some successful dining rooms have found it better to deliver the wine to the table immediately after it is ordered, permitting the patrons to enjoy it when they are ready. Good dining rooms are distinguished by the care with which they serve hot foods hot and cold foods cold. Just as soup and coffee need to be piping hot and salads well chilled, white wines should be served cold. Chilling is necessary to bring out the pleasing qualities of these wines. This ranks as one of the five essentials of successful wine selling and it is often neglected—often enough to spoil an otherwise excellent dining room wine sales program. Chilling is necessary for all white table wines such as Sauterne, Riesling, Rhine Wine, Chablis; pink table wines such as Rose; all sparkling wines; the appetizer wines such as Sherry and Vermouth; and the white dessert wines like Angelica and Muscatel. The red table wines, on the other hand, are normally preferred at or slightly below room temperature.

The next step is merchandising or selling the wine. There is no point in purchasing and stocking an assortment of wines unless attention is given to selling those wines. Patrons may order wine without its being suggested to them. Most of them, however, have to be told about it, just as they need to be told what food is available before they will buy. Wine is still new to most Americans. It is easy and natural to sell wine with meals, but, like any other "new" items on the menu, it needs to be specifically suggested to the diner. Patrons don't need any special reminder to order soup, meat, salad, coffee or dessert, yet most restaurants suggest these items to their patrons, both on menus and through personal suggestion by waiters and waitresses.

All wine needs is the same kind of suggestion which can be made in a variety of ways. One of the simplest, most effective ways to sell wine is by listing it prominently on the menu. An adequate menu listing is the backbone of a continuously successful wine selling program. The menu is to the restaurant what an advertisement is to a department store. It sells the things the dining room wishes to sell. It is read by every patron, whereas very few patrons ever see a special wine list, particularly the elaborate leather bound type that is guarded by a Maitre D' and a captain or two. Menu boxes and special lines featuring wine—the same as are used to call attention to specific foods—can help to sell wine. Such messages on menus cost the restaurant nothing extra and yet are productive and reliable silent salesmen.

Another way of suggesting wine is through a miniature wine list that may be a part of the menu or may be a separate abbreviated list placed on every table for the patrons to examine while waiting for the food order. Unless the diner has some familiarity with wine already, he is unlikely to ask for a wine list because of fear of appearing ignorant.

Other ways of suggesting wine to patrons include dining room displays of wine with cards calling attention to the availability of certain wine types and the very effective practice of setting the tables with wine glasses. Every hotel dining room in America makes it a practice to set its tables with water goblets and to promptly fill them with ice and water when the patrons are seated. Even less effort by the waiter is required to also set the tables with wine glasses. If the patrons do not order wine, the glasses may be removed, but they are powerful merchandisers, particularly when supplemented by oral suggestion by the waiter.

The latter is the strongest wine selling method in any restaurant, from the most elaborate to the family type establishment. Tests have shown that sales of wine can be made to 45 per cent of the patrons to whom it is suggested orally. This method supplements and reinforces all other methods of promoting wine.

One other method of suggesting wine is the wine service itself. There is showmanship in opening a bottle of wine and pouring it. Many an extra wine sale is made when a patron sees wine being served at a neighboring table. The pop of a single cork, the appearance of one bottle in a table cooler, often starts a series of wine sales in that section of the dining room.

Together, the five essentials of dining room wine selling are easier and simpler to supply than any comparable set of essentials that might be necessary for the sale of most other items served. If they are all present, a profitable wine operation should result—profitable to the house which sells the wine in addition to the meal and makes a satisfied customer, and profitable to the staff.

Great care must be taken, however, to avoid having customers order wines that are out of stock. It is irritating for any patron to be obliged to wait several minutes for an order to arrive only to hear, "Sorry, we don't have it."

All that is required is a daily reference to the perpetual inventory to determine which items are no longer in stock and a standard policy of making this up-to-date information easily available. This can take the form of immediate deletions on the wine card of unavailable listings or of appropriate briefings of the service staff each day regarding exhausted stock. Either procedure will eliminate lost motion and lost sales.

Chapter XIII: CAFETERIA AND COUNTER SERVICE

PROBLEMS FOR CAFETERIAS and counter service restaurants are basically the same as for other feeding establishments. However, these restaurants do have certain problems common to no others which this chapter will discuss.

The primary advantages that patrons generally seek in a cafeteria are speedier service and a lower price range. The more rapid pace of service is made possible by the self-service arrangement. This eliminates service personnel and the consequent wait for orders to be filled, resulting in a lower price range due to decreased payroll and a higher rate of seat turnover.

PATRON APPEAL

Cafeterias have the added opportunity of permitting people to see in advance the food they are buying. Display of merchandise is a time-tested technique in merchandising. The ability to "shop around" rejecting items that lack appeal and selecting those that do is an added point of appeal for some patrons.

Two things that bear close watching in a cafeteria are the quality of the food and the manner of service. The idea that a cafeteria is expected to have a lower price range than other commercial restaurants can easily lead to carelessness in maintaining standards. Since cafeteria personnel are seldom tipped by the patrons, there is the likelihood of indifferent attitudes toward the customers.

In those communities where the standards of food and service have been maintained on a high level, the cafeterias are regarded by the local populace as "show places" and their respect for these establishments is reflected in the large volume of business.

TYPES OF CAFETERIAS

There are two major types of cafeteria. In the Line Cafeteria, patrons form a line, select their desired foods, and show their trays of food to a checker, who calculates the amount of their checks. In the "island" or "spot service" cafeteria, patrons do not form a line but proceed to whatever food station they wish, make their selections and present a check, obtained on entering the cafeteria, to a counter attendant who punches the amount of purchase on the check.

The "spot service" type of cafeteria has the advantage of speedier service since patrons need not wait in line. However, since counter attendants must punch the patrons' checks, often a larger staff is required.

Arrangement of Silverware. A teaspoon, fork and knife may be prewrapped in a napkin which the customer picks up at the time he takes his tray or holders may be used for each type of silverware. The first method takes additional time of employees to wrap the silverware and to wash that picked up by patrons and not used. However, it is more sanitary and often pays for itself in customer satisfaction.

Arrangement of Food Stations. In some cafeterias the food is arranged in the general sequence of a menu with the juices and appetizers nearest the entrance, followed by the soups, meats and fish dishes, vegetables, salads, breads, and beverages. Under this type of set-up it is advisable to have the various categories clearly marked with easy-to-read signs to speed the making of selections by patrons.

It is also helpful if there are signs to direct patrons to pass by stations where they do not wish to make a selection and go directly to the next station. One continuous line delays service unnecessarily and makes a return to an overlooked station all but impossible.

Other cafeterias arrange the food to make maximum use of merchandising techniques. Attractive displays of desserts are near the entrance, with hot foods at the end of the line. This usually results in patrons selecting a dessert and then their main dish, thereby spending a little more than if they selected their entree first. Another point in favor of this arrangement is that hot foods are carried lesser distances and remain more palatable.

Display of Foods. There should be a certain uniformity in the display of salads, desserts, and other pre-plated items. It is confusing to the customers when pie-cut points or cake-frostings face in every direction of the compass. Parallel arrangements of these items, and similarity of position for salad plates, help make the display of foods look neater. All too often, the reason why the patrons hesitate at a station and fail to buy is the unappetizing arrangement and appearance of the food. There is one cardinal principle that must be observed in making food displays in a cafeteria. The food must be arranged—not merely deposited.

Portion Sizes. Portion size control is admittedly more difficult in a cafeteria, since the food server is in direct contact with the customers. If the servers are prone to show favoritism, portion sizes can get completely out of hand.

The use of a multi-counter at the checker's or cashier's station is one practical device by which an accurate count can be made of the major items served. Without this tabulating device, it is difficult to determine correctly the number of portions sold and to ascertain whether the portion sizes conform to standards set by management.

The use of dippers assures greater accuracy in controlling portion sizes but tends to give food the appearance of a factory mold. Personnel can quickly learn to gauge the approximate contents of any dipper size and measure virtually the same amount "by eye" with a serving spoon.

Bus Help. The most serious breakdown of service is the failure of bus-help to remove soiled dishes promptly. These soiled dishes offend patrons and seriously retard seat turnover. Assignment of stations, adequate dish-drop facilities, and the employment of a head bus-man or head bus-girl to supervise removal of dishes can go a long way toward solving this problem. In some cafeterias too much time is spent in the kitchen by the bus-help sorting soiled tableware.

With the absence of the equivalent of a head waiter or head hostess, there is likely to be no supervision of the bus-help unless someone is charged with the specific responsibility of seeing to it that the soiled dishes are removed quickly.

If an adequate supply of tableware is available, the bus-help can move in and out of the kitchen quickly. It is false economy to skimp on the supply of tableware. It slows down the bus-help and seriously lessens seat turnover.

Soiled Trays. Trays used by the customers easily become soiled by spilled foods. In some establishments, the trays are not washed often enough. Since the trays are generally used by the bus-help to carry soiled dishes to the warewashing station, it seems practical to wash the trays at that time. If a head bus-man or head bus-girl is employed, it can easily be made the responsibility of that employee to ascertain whether trays that do not go to the kitchen require washing.

If certain types of trays are washed in water that it too hot, they develop welts and begin to warp. Washing trays in a separate machine where the temperature of the water is not permitted to rise above 130 degrees F. will considerably prolong the life of trays, providing a mild powdered hand soap, not a detergent, is used.

Tray Removal. It is a universal tendency for patrons to remove the dishes from their trays and place the individual dishes on the table. This leaves them with an empty tray on their hands. Very few patrons will walk back to the original location of the stacked trays. If there is no room under the seats for the trays or no convenient side-table or shelf that is free of soiled dishes, the trays will often be propped up on the floor against the table or chair legs, a common cause of accidents or food spillage. This seemingly small problem cannot be overcome by being ignored. Space must be provided for the easy disposal of trays by the customers if accidents and spillage are to be kept at a minimum.

COUNTER SERVICE

The counter type of restaurant service enjoys a nation-wide popularity. In many metropolitan areas most of the new restaurants feature counter service. They have sprung up in department stores, railway stations, airline terminals and wherever it is important to save time.

Many counter restaurants feature soups, sandwiches, 3 hot dishes, desserts, and excellent coffee. The food is reasonably priced. People like to watch things being done; they enjoy seeing their food being prepared. Seeing is selling! Patrons have greater confidence in the food they eat when they witness its preparation. Watching the process makes the waiting time seem shorter, especially to patrons who come in alone.

This type of service must be geared for rapid turnover. The time of the average patron is generally limited. Although the service must be quick, the quality of food and the manner of service must be good. Proper counter service can make possible an excellent volume of business because of the rapid turnover, even though the average check is less than in the dining room.

Order of Service. The work space behind the counter is limited, but unless the layout has been improperly designed, compactness is an advantage since it saves steps. Each waitress can take care of eight stools, ten at the most.

Following are the eight steps necessary in serving the customers:

(1) Presenting the menu
(2) Placing a glass of water at the right hand side of the cover
(3) Taking the order
(4) Setting up the cover
(5) Getting the order from the kitchen

(6) Serving the order
(7) Presenting the check
(8) Clearing away the soiled dishes and tableware

Special facilities may change the order but each step is always present. An ample supply of menus should be on hand. Soiled menus must be discarded. Unsightly menus are unforgivable. At a busy station, it requires good timing to know when to take an order. Some people are surprisingly slow in making up their minds, but a glance at the position of the menu will generally give the waitress a clue. If the customer is holding the menu, a decision has probably not yet been made. If the menu has been placed on the counter, it can be taken to mean the customer is ready to give his order.

Orders should be written rapidly. At the time they are taken, beverage preference should be ascertained as well as when it is to be served; the way the order is to be cooked, and the type of bread preferred. The procedure for obtaining orders in the kitchen will vary according to the facilities and their location. A microphone has certain advantages if the kitchen is not near the counter, or if a conveyor or subveyor is used for the delivery of food. An open-face kitchen near the counter makes order-taking easier and speeds up service.

If time is required to have an order prepared, this may be used in setting up the necessary tableware. If the order is ready and can be picked up without waiting, it is advisable to set up the tableware before obtaining the food in the kitchen.

In serving the order, the butter, salt, pepper, sugar, cream, and catsup should be within easy reach of the patron. Checks should be made out and placed on the counter immediately after the last item has been served. The used tableware should be cleared away as soon as possible. Soiled dishes are unpleasant for other customers to see, particularly for those who must take the vacant seats. Furthermore, the waitress may become confused as to whether the person seated at the place has been served.

Counter Negligence. One of the most irritating practices that customers complain of is the seemingly deliberate manner in which some counter personnel clean equipment for several minutes while a customer is waiting to place an order. When a counter worker continues with a cleaning task, or shifts from one cleaning task to another without paying the slightest attention to a customer, that patron is likely to feel that there is no excuse for this type of needless delay.

Another annoyance is the constant "gabber." It is extremely disconcerting for a patron to be kept waiting while the counter worker, who should be rendering service, is engaged in conversation with another employee or patron. All conversation should be cut short when customers are waiting for service.

GRATUITY PROBLEMS

Food checking in a fast-moving counter restaurant is extremely difficult. In an open-face kitchen arrangement, there is no suitable location for a checker. In a kitchen separated from the coffee shop by swinging doors, a checker's station is likely to create a bottleneck that would slow up service to the point of cutting down the turnover and the total volume of business. For these reasons, as a rule, it is necessary to rely on the integrity of the serving personnel and eliminate the checker. Under these conditions, some waiters and waitresses may be tempted to favor certain customers with larger portions or with items that may be omitted from the check, hoping to receive a larger tip.

There are ways of combatting this situation, none of them too satisfactory. Spot checking by an outside agency is frequently employed; a service charge based on a fixed percentage is sometimes added to the checks for tips; or the service personnel is paid higher salaries in lieu of gratuities. These have all been tried, and, in some locations, have proved satisfactory. Test checking depends on the law of averages catching up with any "over-generous" waiter or waitress. The imposed service charge, particularly when it is a switch-over from another system, annoys some of the patrons. In the case of the increased salaries, such added costs would have to be passed on to the customers in the form of higher prices, which might create a competitive problem. The only really satisfactory answer is to choose lunch counter waiters and waitresses with care, and depend upon their integrity.

TAKE-OUT SERVICE

Many counter service restaurants that are severely cramped for space in a high rental location, augment their revenue by featuring "take-out" service to nearby offices, stores, and apartments.

One of the primary difficulties in this type of off-premises service is the necessity for serving beverages in paper containers. If there is any delay in delivering these containers, the hot beverages become lukewarm and the cold beverages turn tepid. An innovation that aimed at solving this problem has been the featuring of thermos bottle service that preserves proper temperatures for all beverages. Coffee delivered ice-cold during sweltering weather or hot on chilly days can "add" many "office chairs" to the seating capacity of any counter restaurant.

Whether a deposit is required to insure proper return of the thermos bottles, or whether this extra service is provided without a deposit, is strictly a matter of managerial policy. The extent of neighborhood competition will generally provide the answer to this question.

Since busy people dislike the bother of battling their way through crowded restaurants, "take-out" service that provides some degree of meal-enjoyment is the solution for them, and also for restaurant operators who find it difficult to pay high rentals for spacious street-level quarters that remain virtually idle many hours each day between meals.

PAYROLL

The counter type of operation is often quite profitable because the payroll problem is streamlined. The preparation employees are also servers, and they participate in the receiving of tips. A counterman's wages plus tips will often exceed a cook's wages. This arrangement makes it advantageous for the preparation staff to speed the seat turnover. Volume is no longer a matter of added burdens only, but of added remuneration.

The counter type of food service may seem less pretentious, but it exists and enjoys a wide popularity because the public likes it. In the long run, the general public will always determine the nature of service that is desired. American eating tastes lean toward simplicity for many reasons. When simplicity is accompanied by quality, the combination often results in a profitable food operation.

Chapter XIV: INDUSTRIAL, HOSPITAL, INSTITUTIONAL, SCHOOL, AND CLUB FOOD SERVICE

IT IS THE PURPOSE of this chapter to deal briefly with several types of food service which do not necessarily or wholly fit into the classification of the commercial food service establishment. In the latter category we find the hotel and commercial restaurants of all types, the operations and problems of which are discussed in detail throughout this book. Industrial, hospital, institutional, school, and club food service involves many practices and procedures common to all other public and quasi-public feeding establishments. Here, however, there will be reviewed the special characteristics and particular problems encountered that are not generally found in commercial restaurants.

INDUSTRIAL FEEDING

For many years industrial establishments found that in-plant feeding helped to ease employee traffic and tardiness problems. However, before World War II, food service of this type was primarily regarded as a facility of convenience. During the war years, the need for maximum efficiency led to many new side lights and points of emphasis in industrial feeding.

Nutrition, improved health, and increased industrial efficiency were woven into the fabric of in-plant feeding and superseded the consideration of convenience alone. The easy-to-handle, over-worked frankfurter stand gave way to the service of well-planned, balanced meals. In many industrial plants food service has taken its place alongside safety and medical programs to help preserve the employees' well-being. The value of proper diet in maintaining high levels of efficiency under various working conditions has become quite universally understood and respected.

Types of Service. There are many variations in the type of service to be found in industrial establishments. They may include dining rooms, soda fountains, canteens, lunch stands, mobile units, and cafeterias. By far, the greatest amount of industrial feeding centers around the cafeteria, to the point where other types of service can be considered incidental additions.

Management Responsibility. There are two types of industrial feeding establishments: the management-controlled and operated, and the contractor-operated. Those that are under the supervision of management have one major disadvantage. They require policy-making decisions by executives not acquainted with the restaurant business. In later years, however, there has been a definite trend toward engaging competent restaurant managers and workers, which move has virtually eliminated this disadvantage. In the contractor-operated establishments, it has been found frequently that the contractor is primarily concerned with profit to himself, and secondarily with those aspects of food service that are most likely to benefit the employees and management.

In establishments that are company-operated it is necessary and advisable to treat the service of food as a direct accommodation to the employees. These operations sometimes can function at cost, but more frequently require a subsidy. In such instances, it behooves management to include an Employees' Committee to aid in making decisions affecting the manner in which the service of food is handled. Under this plan there is not only a greater sense of direct participation by the employees, but also the opportunity of providing a suitable channel for submitting suggestions by the employees.

In certain heavily-industrialized areas, it may be possible for an outside contractor to operate a commissary that services several plants. Where such an arrangement is possible, the contractor can usually function on a much more economical basis and thus offer excellent values with a reasonable profit return to himself.

The main reason why management takes the pains to provide food service to employees is the desire to maintain sound personnel relationships. However, if the quality of food is deficient because of management's lack of food service knowledge, or because of a contractor's preoccupation with financial return, the entire purpose behind industrial feeding is defeated. If the food is good, it does not matter so much whether the final supervision is a part of management or by an outside contractor.

Balanced Meals. Attractive color posters furnished by the United States Department of Agriculture have been used widely in industrial food service establishments to stress the need for balanced diets. Eating places are the ideal location for promoting interest in balanced diets.

The basic varieties of foods are:

(1) Vegetables
(2) Fruits
(3) Milk, butter, and cheese
(4) Meat, poultry, fish, and eggs
(5) Bread and cereal

Sound nutrition reduces fatigue. Good health means greater efficiency and less absenteeism.

Menu Planning. Planning menus for industrial workers presents as many, if not more problems than for commercial cafeterias. In addition to nutritional considerations, there is the added burden of feeding the same persons day after day. Few commercial establishments, if any, have the same repeated consistency of patronage that prevails in industrial food service. The dangers of menu monotony become all the greater. The strain of providing a sufficient number of calories, adequate diet balance and menu variety can be extremely great. New dishes must be constantly introduced as well as new methods of serving the same foods.

Between Meal Snacks. The institution of the between-meal rest period and snack has been found a boon in many industrial plants. It also helps to distribute the work-loads for an industrial-feeding establishment.

Under the old system of serving food only at meal-times, there was a tendency on the part of some employees to overeat because of the long stretch of time between meals. With the serving of snacks during rest periods mid-way between meal times, there is a marked tendency by many employees to spread their consumption of food. Drowsiness, indigestion and fatigue have been reduced by the service of snacks.

Research in some industries has revealed that a change from three large meals a day to five smaller ones, that provided the same total amount of food, resulted in the elimination of a dip in production during the late hours of the morning and afternoon.

Staggered Schedules. It is of utmost importance that the schedule of meal service be properly staggered. It is not enough to have a plant schedule staggered on the basis of 2, 3 or 4 lunch periods a half-hour apart. Wherever it is feasible, lunch periods for approximately one-sixth of the total number of employees to be served at one sitting should be staggered every five minutes. Thus, if 2,400 employees are to be served on a 4-sitting basis, 600 will be served during each sitting. Of the 600 one-sixth or approximately 100 should start their lunch-period at five minute intervals. This will avoid serious bottlenecks at the beginning of each meal.

In some establishments, such as newspaper plants, a fixed schedule is not easily possible. Employees have to be allowed to obtain a light lunch whenever their work-load permits. Some organizations serve a light breakfast which is not always susceptible to a stagger schedule unless the starting time for the day's work can also be satisfactorily staggered.

The need for speedy service is a constant problem. Space and time must be conserved to keep the over-all costs within reason. Cafeterias have become the universal solution to this problem. In many industrial cafeterias, one relatively simple time-and-labor-saving procedure is usually required. Employees are expected to return their trays and soiled dishes to a dish-drop station. This reduces the need for bus-help and makes empty seats instantly available for the next customer.

Mobile Units. Where industrial plants cover considerable acreage, it has been found extremely useful to employ mobile units. It is virtually a case of "the mountain going to Mahomet," but this reversal of the usual procedure relieves bottlenecks and reduces cross-traffic in the plant. Bringing the food to the workers can be arranged on a well-timed stagger basis. Compactness and easy mobility are the prime requisites for mobile units. Equipment manufacturers are constantly improving the available models.

Foods prepared for service by mobile units must be susceptible to easy handling. In addition to sandwiches and wrapped snacks, the hot dishes served will generally include soups, stews, baked beans, and scalloped dishes. Foods that are easily poured or spooned out will generally fit into compact containers, from which many servings can be made.

Plant physicians have commented most favorably on the improvement in health when hot dishes replaced the old-fashioned lunch-box that kept foods at room temperatures for hours.

The two types of mobile units most widely used are the combination trucks, that transport hot and cold foods, and the snack trucks that are used for sandwiches, ice cream, fruit, candy, and pastry. The principal advantage of mobile truck service is the flexibility that permits easy expansion or contraction to meet the varying demands. The major problems resulting from mobile truck service are sanitation, lack of time control, and traffic hazards.

Food Purchasing. Purchasing food for industrial feeding is not quite the same as for commercial establishments. While it is true that most industrial cafeterias operate on the basis of cash payments by the employees for the food consumed, the atmosphere is not strictly commercial. The industrial food service establishment is operated for the *benefit of the employees*—and they know it—or they should. Competition from other establishments is quite often not a pressing factor. Disapproval is more likely to be expressed in direct comment by the employees rather than in a withdrawal of trade. The number of choices can easily be much less than in a commercial establishment without evoking unfavorable comment. As long as the quality of the food is good, a narrower selection of items is not likely to prove objectionable. This relieves the food buyer of some of the pressure burden of purchasing. Fewer purchases make for greater concentration on each purchase. Quantity purchasing will generally make many more "good buys" possible.

Advertising and Promotion. Various forms of advertising and promotion have been adopted to popularize the use of industrial feeding facilities. Where geographical considerations eliminate the competitive commercial restaurants from the picture, there is a tendency to be lax about advertising and promotion. However, the employees' lunch-boxes taken from home remain a constant competitor if quality deteriorates. Good value still remains the best form of advertising.

Where there are competitive establishments within relatively short distances, it becomes necessary to maintain quality and value. Copies of the day's menu conspicuously posted or inserts in the house organ have been used to stimulate interest in the feeding facilities.

Basic Control. Regardless of the type of subsidy involved, control is as necessary as in commercial restaurants. Some industrial food service establishments are budgeted to break even, while others are subsidized in varying degrees.

In many instances, covering the cost of food and labor is the target of management so that the necessary subsidy can be kept to a minimum. Reports from various industrial food service establishments indicate an annual subsidy ranging from $4.00 to $40.00 per employee. Inadequate basic controls can easily result in unnecessarily high subsidies.

Daily controls of food issued and served must be maintained. This is particularly necessary where mobile units are used. Attendants are usually charged with the sales value of the food items that leave the kitchen. When the mobile unit attendant returns, he must bring back cash or merchandise to equal the full sales value. This is a simple procedure but is generally very effective.

In canteens, where food is not returned daily, it is advisable to have daily or weekly inventories taken to insure adequate controls.

Centralized and Decentralized Kitchens. Where an industrial plant, department store, insurance company or any other mercantile establishment is housed within one building and the elevator facilities can handle the meal-time rush of traffic, the advantages of a centralized kitchen are likely to outweigh the disadvantages. If the distances to be covered by the employees to reach one central feeding area are excessive, or if elevator facilities cannot adequately handle the peak of traffic, decentralized kitchen facilities will in all probability prove advisable.

The advantages accruing from a centralized kitchen are:

(1) Elimination of duplicated jobs.
(2) Easier supervision.
(3) Concentrated storage.
(4) Simplified control.
(5) Minimal transportation of food.
(6) Standardization of quality food preparation.

The principal disadvantages that may arise in a centralized kitchen are:

(1) Greater bottlenecks in the kitchen.
(2) More crowded conditions in the dining area.
(3) Added traveling time to reach dining room and return to work location.

It is obvious that the advantages and disadvantages must be carefully weighed. If possible, they should be resolved before the feeding facilities are put into original operation.

Internal Inventories. In operations having small service units scattered throughout a building, daily, as well as monthly inventories, are necessary. The function of inventorying falls broadly into two categories.

(1) Inventories taken daily or periodically at various units for sales control purposes.
(2) Monthly inventories taken for the purpose of the financial statements.

HOSPITALS

Hospital feeding must fulfill an extremely important purpose that has no similar counterpart in other food service establishments.

Health Factors. The restoration of the health of patients necessitates the assumption of trying burdens. Meals must be of the precisely proper nutritive value as well as tasty. Patients do not have the option of making a selection from a wide variety of dishes or of taking meals in a competitive establishment. However, patients are in a tense state of mind as well as in a distressed physical state. The sight of food, even though dietetically sound and technically well-prepared, can have a discomforting effect on patients if the appearance is unappetizing.

The dietitians' responsibilities in a hospital are, therefore, far greater than in any other type of food service establishment.

Basic Procedures. The basic procedures for purchasing, receiving, storing, and issuing of food should be identical with those used in commercial establishments. Detailed information regarding these phases of operation will be found in other chapters of this book bearing the appropriate titles.

Types of Service. One of the major problems of hospital feeding is the distribution and service of the prepared food. Unlike most commercial restaurants and cafeterias which usually have only one type of service, hospitals, which must feed patients, employees, nurses and the professional staff, usually have three or four different types of service and, in many instances, require a totally or partially different menu for each. These foods services are as follows:

(1) *Tray service* for patient feeding from a central kitchen or from floor pantries. The various methods of tray service will be discussed in greater detail in another part of this section.
(2) *Cafeteria service* for employees, nurses and the professional staff, if a private dining room is not provided for the latter.
(3) *Table service* in separate dining rooms for physicians and visitors
(4) *Snack bars* or *canteens* for nurses and visitors. These usually are also equipped for complete fountain service.

With such diversified feeding operations it is most important that there be good internal control of the food distributed; that costs are known of every item served, and that standard portions are served in all these service units. This requires close supervision and continuous training of the employees.

The aforementioned points—internal control, portion costs, and standardization of portions are all discussed in various chapters throughout this book.

Since the food served plays such an important part in the patients' stay in the hospital and must contribute toward ultimate recuperation the distribution of food becomes one of the most important services in the hospital.

There are generally two methods of transporting patients' meals from the kitchen to the bedside. In most instances, only one type of service is used but in very large hospitals it is sometimes necessary to employ both methods. There are advantages to both systems and a hospital should adopt the one most practical for its needs.

Methods of Service. The methods of service are:

(1) *Central* service, in which all trays of food are prepared in a central kitchen and sent to the various floors by (a) vertical tray conveyors or dumbwaiters, or (b) on food carts or trucks via an elevator.

(2) *Decentralized* service, in which the food is prepared in a central kitchen and sent in bulk in hot food trucks via elevators to service pantries on each floor where the trays are then prepared and distributed.

Central service is more suitable for smaller hospitals or for special service to private patients. Food carts will hold as many as 25 trays, and the trays can be served to the patients as the cart is wheeled down the corridor. Since the elevator service available is usually limited, the setting up of the trays and carts should not be attempted at the same time but so regulated that there will be a minimum of waiting for the elevators.

When dumbwaiters and tray conveyors are used, the control and signal system on each floor must be in perfect working condition. In order to maintain a continuous flow of trays a well organized schedule must be followed and sufficient handling personnel available in the kitchen and on each floor to unload the trays.

In either method used in centralized service, the element of timing to regulate the rate of flow at a constant pace in each phase of the operation, s of utmost importance. All dishes and covers used for hot food should be thoroughly preheated and the food itself must be very hot so that t will not cool during the transportation period. A general complaint of open dumbwaiters and tray conveyors is that the food is cooled off too quickly by the cold air in the shaft, particularly during the winter months. Although this has been somewhat overcome with installations of thermal heated dumbwaiters, there are a number of hospitals where dumbwaiters or tray conveyors have been abandoned and the truck method of tray transportation has been resumed.

Decentralized service, or some form of combination with one of the methods of central service, is most commonly used in the larger hospitals. In the decentralized service, trays are prepared in the kitchen or the serving pantries and the food is transported from the central kitchen to the pantries in bulk in heated food trucks, then placed on the trays and taken to the patients.

When electrically heated food trucks are used, timing, to the extent described in the centralized system, is not as important and hot food trucks are usually filled with all the food at one time. Invariably, however, it has been observed that where this system is in use, there is a tendency to prepare food too far in advance of service and place it in the heated food trucks as early as 10 A.M. for the noon meal.

When decentralized service is used, great care must be taken in apportioning the correct quantities of food for each truck. Pantry servers must receive accurate instructions regarding the sizes of the portions to be served. Supervision of the serving pantries at meal times to make certain that food is served properly is another problem that stems from the use of decentralized service.

Menu Planning. In planning menus for patients, the dietitian must exercise greater care in the proper selection and combination of foods to see that they are dietetically well-balanced, than a person planning menus for a commercial food operation. Furthermore, one menu will not suffice for the entire hospital feeding since there are such diversified groups to be fed. The various types of service have already been discussed in another part of this section. The following is a list of the groups usually found in hospitals for whom menus must be planned:

Ward Patients—Set menu.
Semi-private patients—For this group either a modification of the private patient menu is made or additions to the ward menu are made.
Private patients—Usually have a choice.
Employee cafeteria menu—Usually a limited menu.
Nurses' cafeteria menu—Usually limited selections.
Physicians' dining room menu—Limited selections.
Guests' dining room menu—Often same as physicians.
Snack bar or canteen—Very simple type of menu. Mostly sandwiches, salads desserts and, perhaps, one hot dish and beverage.

Although dietitians have this greater problem of varied menus, on the other hand, this operation is simpler than a commercial food operation since they practically know the exact number of persons to be served in each group for each meal. With a knowledge of the quantities of food to prepare for a given number of persons, and the use of standard portion sizes, leftovers should be at a minimum. However, only too often in hospital operations, costs, quantities, and portion sizes have not been predetermined, resulting in refrigerators filled with leftovers. Consequently, the cost per meal is often excessive.

Payroll. Another problem confronting the dietitian is the generally lower wage scale for employees in this department, as compared with wage scales in commercial feeding operations. This situation makes it extremely difficult to obtain well-trained personnel. Consequently, the dietitian is called upon to train the workers on the job when and if she has available time. Hospital payroll studies indicate that in many instances the operations could be conducted with fewer employees, if efficient employees were attracted to hospital service. The inescapable question arises whether true economy is achieved through the prevailing lower wage rates.

Food Costs. All too often, dietitians are not kept fully informed as to the food cost figures. Many of them are forced to operate in the hope that they are keeping within their budgets.

As a rule, dietitians are not provided with monthly cost figures. Many dietitians are informed of food costs on a quarterly or annual basis. As in other food service operations, accurate food cost information is needed in order to control costs.

SOCIAL AND PHILANTHROPIC INSTITUTIONS

The one outstanding characteristic of food service in social and philanthropic institutions is the requirement of operating on a fixed budget. All practices are set out to conform to this consideration.

These food operations are usually under the supervision of a dietitian or food director. The operations vary in size from the service of less than one hundred covers daily to as many as several thousand daily. They are all usually 3-meal-a-day, 7-day-a-week operations with a fixed menu generally offering no choice to the diner.

The major problems are the maintenance of a nutritionally balanced diet and the adherence to a fixed budget that often proves quite restrictive. Apart from these two problems that can impose severe limitations as to the caliber of personnel that can be attracted and the variety of foods that can be purchased within the framework of the budget, the operation of this type of food service is much simpler than in commercial restaurants. A limited menu and a standard number of persons to be served should make the problem of leftovers virtually nonexistent. Variations in the number to be served are generally known in advance of preparations for any specific meal.

The type service in these groups will vary. In some institutions they are cafeterias; in others table service or home style service with food placed on the table in large serving dishes. In a few specially endowed institutions, there is table service with uniformed waitresses.

Table appointments range from the simplest, with chipped dishes, to well appointed dining rooms with white linen and quality tableware.

Menus are simple and the greatest problem of the dietitian is to have variety in the menus. Too often dietitians have a series of weekly menus that are repeated from week to week. With a limited budget for food and labor, which often prohibits the hiring of capable cooks who could prepare tasty dishes, the menu often becomes dull and uninteresting.

Purchasing holds the key to the success of this type operation. Every dollar saved through careful purchasing, according to specifications, means an extra dollar that is available for menu improvement. The total outlay will remain the same under alert purchasing as under ineffective purchasing, but the quality of the food will be quite different—better.

There is always the likelihood that when a food director has a fixed amount of money to spend for food, that the line of least resistance may be followed. Effective purchasing may seem like harder work, but once the specifications are established, much of the burden of purchasing becomes simple. With the availability of better food through sounder purchasing, the opportunities for providing variety are greater and the causes for complaints are lessened.

SCHOOLS

In school feeding, certain factors appear that normally do not have an exact counterpart in other types of food service. These factors are:

(1) Simplicity of preparation.
(2) Supervision by Home Economics Department.
(3) Student help.
(4) Parental cooperation.
(5) Part-time community help.
(6) Inadequate facilities.

Simplicity of Preparation. Simplicity of preparation is the backbone of all school feeding. Since most of the work is done by non-professionals, namely, student help and part-time workers, who are primarily housewives, simplicity becomes a necessity.

Menus of school lunchrooms usually assume the following pattern:

Beverages—Milk, cocoa, or chocolate milk.

Sandwiches—Egg, cheese, meat, fish, and raw vegetables on whole wheat, rye, white, or raisin bread.

Soups—Substantial soups, such as cream and vegetable soups or chowders.

Main Dish—Meats, fish or meat substitutes, served with at least one vegetable.

Salads—Fruit, raw or cooked vegetables, egg, fish, or meat.

Desserts—Fresh, stewed or canned fruits. Puddings, pies, cakes, cookies, and ice cream.

Home Economics Department Supervision. The Home Economics Department in larger schools, or the Home Economics teacher in smaller schools, is generally responsible for the operation of the school cafeteria, unless the full time services of a dietitian are employed.

Students studying Home Economics use the cafeteria as a laboratory for their food classes.

One of the major problems in school feeding is the planning of menus to provide sufficient growth-promoting foods for the children. School lunches are expected to provide one-third of the daily nutritional needs of the pupils.

Student Help. Management of luncheon service by the pupils, under faculty guidance, is generally quite popular in certain regions.

The pupils usually form committees to take care of the various phases of the work. These committees most frequently are composed of the following:

(1) Planning and preparing.
(2) Serving.
(3) Dishwashing and clean-up.
(4) Financial record keeping.

Rotation of assignments is generally advisable to distribute the work on an equitable basis and to prevent loss of interest in the work.

Parental Cooperation. School feeding is quite often on a supplementary basis, wherein the students bring part of their lunch from home and supplement it with a hot dish. In such situations, the common practice is to plan meals a week in advance and to publish the planned offerings in the newspapers, or to furnish the students with a weekly list in advance. By this method, together with suggestions for suitable items to be brought from home, a well-balanced diet can easily be achieved through proper parental cooperation.

Part-Time Community Help. Local housewives are usually engaged for such phases of the preparation as are too difficult for students to handle. This generally presents no serious problem, since the supply of applicants for a part-time 5-day, 9 or 10 month, work program is usually more than ample. These working hours are considered ideal for women who have children at school during the regular school hours.

The Home Economics Department usually has, or can easily obtain a satisfactory accumulation of practical recipes for quantity preparation. All that remains is adequate supervision.

Inadequate Facilities. Many schools, particularly in the older sections of the various communities, were built and equipped solely for classroom study long before school feeding became popular and widespread. With the awakening interest in the advantages of planned school feeding, many cafeterias were put into operation in whatever space that could be made available. All too often the entire layout has proven inadequate. Major architectural revisions are often necessary. The newer schools do not have this problem as provision is made for necessary feeding facilities.

Purchasing. The purchasing practices in school cafeterias of perishable commodities are generally geared to direct consumption needs. However, in some operations, the purchasing of canned goods is confined to one or two orders per year. Since budget adherence is a primary necessity, the annual or semi-annual purchase of canned goods is usually done with an eye toward achieving budgetary stability and avoiding repetition of the same task more often than appears essential. With records of past consumption and the exact size of the student body easily available, estimates of needs may prove to be fairly close, but there often remain unused quantities of canned goods at the end of the school year.

There is also a marked tendency toward buying the same brand year after year, without making tests to determine comparative yields of new brands that make their appearance on the market. Each year many excellent canned products become available. It behooves every buyer of canned goods for school consumption to keep abreast of comparative yields.

Schedule of Hours. Schedules in schools are very often difficult to arrange. However, if the entire student body has the same luncheon period, the eating facilities are likely to be overtaxed. Any excessive crowding by the students will result in unduly hurried meals. Violently disturbing habits can result from meals that are eaten hurriedly under extremely crowded conditions. Every effort should be made to induce school authorities to split the luncheon period into two sections. Smaller facilities can thus be made to handle the students with much less crowding.

Where there are two luncheon shifts, the clean-up problem is greater, since it must be accomplished in a limited time to make the facilities freshly available for the second group. Having the clean-up arrangements well-organized and geared to function quickly can make the lunchroom available for study purposes during the remaining hours.

Colleges. College feeding is one of the oldest types of group food service known. Students have been fed at colleges for several centuries. As is usual with many establishments that have their roots reaching far back into time, a wide diversity of practices has resulted.

In the main, there are two major types of college feeding; residence halls that serve 21 meals a week, paid for in advance, and cash-basis establishments that service students, faculty members, and visitors. The cash-payment establishments take various forms, such as, cafeterias, soda fountains, snack bars, and formal dining rooms.

Laboratory Classes. Food service establishments are generally utilized as laboratories for classwork dealing with this subject. As a consequence of the close scrutiny that necessarily evolves from pointing out the reasons for doing things in a particular manner, high standards of operation have usually resulted. Defects become readily apparent and are subject to thorough questioning by the students who are interested in making this field of work their ultimate careers.

Quite frequently some of the personnel used to staff the various work-stations come from the ranks of students enrolled in the food service courses. These students may lack certain technical proficiencies at the outset of their training periods, but they are subject to a more thorough discipline because of their need to receive suitable grades, as well as compensation, for their work.

Nutritional Factors. The general age level for college students is between 18 and 22 years. This means that a considerable number of college students are still in the growing stage. The basic nutritional requirements of this age group necessitates more careful planning than for a group of adults.

Many college students engage in strenuous athletic activities, but this special problem is frequently handled by means of a "training table." This assures a proper grouping of students requiring more than average calorie intake.

COUNTRY CLUBS

Many country clubs are primarily seasonal operations having all the disadvantages of a short term operation plus the added difficulty of maintaining only skeletal activities during the remainder of the year.

The seasonal aspects of a country club food service operation present greater difficulties than a resort hotel operation, where the establishment is usually closed down between seasons. Operating in high gear for a small part of the year and in extremely low gear the balance of the time imposes many problems. The entire structure of the operation has to be revamped at least twice a year.

It is always easier to provide topnotch service when the volume is brisk. During the off season it is extremely difficult to pare down the service structure without deteriorating the caliber of service. The members who do patronize the clubs' feeding facilities during the off season, usually expect superior service and treatment simply because it is off-season, and they feel there is less work for the staff. They are not satisfied with meal service that has been reduced to virtually a "short-order" basis.

Weather. Not only do most country clubs have seasonal peaks of activity, but the week-end operational structure is often in the nature of a super-peak. To make advance planning even more difficult, is the effect of adverse weather conditions. A torrential downpour on a Saturday or Sunday is likely to find the club manager with a heavy supply of prepared food untouched. All week-end menu-planning must be geared to sudden weather changes. Rain has a more pronounced effect on food consumption than in a city commercial restaurant, and yet a sudden clearing shortly before a meal hour is likely to find a throng of guests seeking food service. Reservations become virtually meaningless in the face of sudden weather changes. The menus on the week-ends must be built around semi-prepared and prepared-to-order offerings, together with such prepared items as can easily be worked off at a later date. The ratio of the average week-end volume to the average week-day volume must be borne in mind, lest it be necessary to work off certain leftovers for five consecutive days.

Purchasing. Purchasing food for a country club presents two major problems that do not confront city clubs. The distance from large city markets and the limited number of food deliveries weekly by vendors adds difficulties to the purchasing practices. In some cases these difficulties require close evaluation between local purchases and long-distance, big-city purchases. The solution to these problems, in some instances, is the use of a truck to pick up certain foodstuffs. This requires close integration of personnel and equipment to make these pick-ups when needed.

Even though purchases may be made both locally and from distant sources, it is absolutely necessary to have buying specifications. The use of these standards will automatically facilitate sound receiving—one of the weakest links in the operational structure of some country club food establishments.

Receiving. Receiving must be made rigid, to insure effective purchasing. It is a sounder policy to reject sub-standard merchandise and make appropriate menu changes than to accept and serve inferior quality food.

There is a tendency in some of the smaller clubs to have the receiving handled by any one of several persons—usually not qualified for the task. This is an unsound practice. One person should be designated as the receiving clerk and held responsible for proper receiving, even though it is necessary for this employee to double in another capacity, because of the relatively limited amount of receiving to be done.

Storerooms. Due to the spasmodic fluctuations in the volume of covers served and the necessity for having sufficient food on hand to handle these fluctuations, it is extremely important that refrigerators be checked daily so that leftovers can be used without delay. There is no other method that is as satisfactory in minimizing food spoilage.

Great care must be exercised in the storage and handling of fresh produce, particularly since deliveries are infrequent, to prevent undue loss through spoilage.

Menus. Menus generally present a difficult problem to club managers. There is greater danger of offering menus that seem monotonous in a country club than in commercial restaurants, simply because the clientele is generally composed of a closed membership list. To relieve this situation, it is important that a complete change in the menu layout be made every season. In addition, new dishes must be added to the menu from time to time. A continuing feeling of change and variety must be created and sustained.

The general age level of the membership will indicate the type of menu listings that should be used. If the younger set predominates, gay and unusual wording will be more in order. However, if the patronage is composed of mature members, simpler wording is advisable.

Younger members usually will eat "almost anything." Exotic or unusual dishes are a reasonable risk. Mature members have a greater variety of ailments and indispositions to be concerned about and will tend to be more conservative in their menu selections.

If a club offers vigorous forms of sport, in-between-meal snacks should be available.

Advance Reservations. It is important that the membership be urged to make reservations for holidays, parties, or any other special functions at which food is to be served. There is no reason why complete frankness should not be used. Lack of reservations presents purchasing problems that in turn will cost the club money. The club manager can state quite candidly that his position is similar to that of the housewife whose husband fails to tell her he is bringing four people home to dinner. It is extremely difficult always to have enough for six when only two are expected. Conversely, if ten guests are expected and no cancellation comes through, the arrival of only four guests creates a problem in left-overs. Stated simply and clearly in terms of every day living, the problems of reservations and reservation cancellations can be presented without embarrassment to the members. Most club members are likely to respond favorably when the situation is presented in an honest and straight-forward manner that makes them understand the importance of reservations.

Personnel. Since country club operations are primarily seasonal, obtaining experienced personnel for a short-term operation is difficult. It is almost inevitable that a certain number of inexperienced employees must be recruited. High school and college students form a substantial part of the reservoir of supply for this type of personnel placement.

It is essential, therefore, that a specific training program, with follow-up written instructions on how-to-do-the-job, be instituted. A definite period of time must be allotted for this purpose.

Transportation. The problem of transporting employees to and from a bus stop or railway station does not exist for commercial restaurants, but is often of prime importance in the securing of competent help for country clubs.

Work schedules must be coordinated not only for the food service operation but also for the entire working staff. It cannot be solved by half-way measures. Improper resolution of this irksome problem can easily result in a tremendous loss of work-productivity.

Fountains and Snack Bars. Soda fountains and snack bars are extremely popular, relatively easy to operate and generally quite profitable. A properly equipped operation of this type can ease the pressure on the formal dining room and can often allow for dovetailing of station coverage. Its possibilities should be thoroughly explored by any club when the food cost is excessive, staffing problems are acute, or the speed of service is found to be inadequate.

Business Approach. Generally, there has been too much reliance on the dues income to support the entire country club operations. This is a fallacious approach, and it is incumbent upon managers to view each income-producing department with its profit-making possibilities consistent with the club policies.

CITY CLUBS

City club food service operations generally bear a pronounced resemblance to residential hotel food operations. Their problems are quite similar, with one major exception. Residential hotels are quite often located in neighborhoods where commercial restaurant competition is not intense. However, city clubs are usually located in or near commercial neighborhoods where the competition from commercial restaurants is likely to be extremely keen.

Club members may be acutely aware of the fact that a commercial restaurant around the corner features a virtually identical dish for fifty cents less, but are likely to be oblivious to the fact that any establishment with a restricted clientele cannot possibly match the economic structure of a restaurant with an unlimited volume potential.

Personalized Service. While it is impossible for city clubs to compete on a dollars and cents basis with commercial restaurants, club operations should provide a personal touch that commercial restaurants cannot easily duplicate. Personal likes and dislikes of the various members should be learned, and become a matter of common knowledge to the service staff. In the more exclusive clubs, an analysis of past orders can be reduced to a personal basis, if the membership is not too large.

It may even be possible to have a card index file of previous orders by the club members. A glance at this file by the waiter after a member has arrived will go a long way toward providing a highly personalized service.

Conservative eaters will be repeaters. Their favorite dishes can be suggested to them again and again. The members with esoteric tastes should have each new dish immediately called to their attention. The ratio of the members with a flair for something different will indicate quite readily how often new dishes must be introduced.

Personnel Problems. In some clubs, the methods of hiring personnel do not parallel the procedures that are prevalent in commercial restaurants. Influential members are sometimes inclined to exert pressure to secure a placement for a personal acquaintance. Such influences are difficult to deny and can easily result in substandard work performance.

The entire problem of favoritism can become quite acute, unless it is recognized as such and treated accordingly. Petty politics and good service are often mutually exclusive.

A Home Away from Home. Most members of outstanding clubs have come to expect a "home away from home" at their clubs. This is no catch-phrase, or cliche to them. They expect a home-like atmosphere; they are entitled to it and they should get it.

The criterion of measurement of this type of service can be made quite simple. Each and every employee can be asked quite frankly whether they would treat a guest in their own home in the manner accorded a club member. If the answer is in the negative, the deduction is obvious. Something has gone amiss in the training of the employees. A home-touch connotes cordiality and pleasant treatment. The desire to provide a home-touch must be instilled in all the employees.

Private Dining Rooms. Private dining rooms, seating large or small groups, are quite common in most clubs. The physical condition of the furniture, draperies, and lighting fixtures requires inspection by a responsible employee before and after each function.

In many instances, names are applied to some of the rooms without the slightest tie-in with the predominating decorative motif. One or more carefully selected photo-murals will often serve to enliven the appearance of a private dining room and justify its particular name.

Menu Flexibility. In some clubs there is a rigid adherence to an a la carte menu to the exclusion of any form of table d'hote service. There is a mistaken belief in some club circles that a la carte menus automatically produce a greater average receipt per cover. In actual practice this has not always proven to be a fact.

In many instances, the introduction of a table d'hote menu at a fixed price for the entire meal has actually increased rather than decreased the average receipt per cover. Some members who would have ordered only an entree and a beverage, order an entire meal at a higher price. The table d'hote menu immediately informs the diner of the total price for the meal. Many people are reluctant to go into extensive arithmetic to determine what the cost of an entire meal is likely to be.

Menu pricing should always reflect trends in market prices. It is an unwise practice to maintain menu prices at a constant level even though market prices have declined sharply. Members are likely to resent deeply the need for paying the same price for an item month after month, when it is a matter of common knowledge that outside market prices have experienced sharp fluctuations.

Chapter XV: AMERICAN PLAN FOOD SERVICE IN HOTELS

AT THE PRESENT TIME American Plan food service is limited almost exclusively to resort areas, where two or three meals a day, room accommodations and some sport facilities are sold as a "package."

There are special problems, distinct advantages and certain disadvantages in this type of food operation. Many profitable opportunities unquestionably are being overlooked, because to some operators, the disadvantages seem to outweigh the positive factors.

SPECIAL MENU STRUCTURE

Since the preparation staff is burdened with the necessity of preparing 14 to 21 meals each week, there is an understandable tendency to follow the line of least resistance and to simplify preparation problems as much as possible. When this is overdone the guests are likely to feel that, once on the premises the hotel gives as little as it can "get away with." If such an attitude becomes prevalent, there will be little, if any, favorable comments and business volume is likely to suffer.

Guests are not surprised when menus are shorter than in commercial restaurants. They generally do not resent a narrower choice of dishes, providing the offerings are sufficiently varied, appetizing and interesting. The tendency toward a home-style menu can be extremely helpful and add rather than detract interest. There should be a minimum of three appetizers, two soups, four entrees, four desserts, and three beverages.

This basic minimum provides sufficient opportunity for flexibility of offerings without overburdening the preparation and service staffs.

There is a surprising reluctance on the part of many resort operators to include attractive salad and sandwich selections as entree offerings. Some operators feel that this would be regarded as "skimping." Apart from consideration of guests who may be diet-minded, younger guests, may be contemplating a tennis match or long swim after luncheon. Lighter luncheons will prove more desirable to some guests and less expensive to the operator. The quality and attractiveness of these lighter offerings, and the extent of the guest demand for these items, will decide their desirability.

Vegetable plates are also variations that should be included from time to time, depending on the guests' response. Resorts featuring four freshly cooked vegetables, other than potatoes, for luncheon and dinner, have been known to maintain a high level of business even when competitors, not offering properly prepared vegetables, felt the pinch of slackened volume.

There should be a leading dish at each luncheon and dinner that is likely to absorb about 60 per cent of all the orders of that meal. This permits gearing the kitchen for a rapid flow of service.

Variety in menu structure is a necessity, but there should also be considerable variety in the type of service. When guests have 21 meals a week served at the same table in the self-same manner, the entire process of eating may appear to become monotonous even though the menu-writer has exercised exceptional ingenuity in varying the offerings.

Providing the guests with an opportunity to eat their meals in different ways and under different circumstances can often be the keynote to the success of an American Plan operation.

Additional American Plan Service Features. The additional features embracing different forms of service will require extra work in certain directions, but will also permit some of the staff to have a little extra time off under certain conditions. Some of the features that can be offered are:

Buffet Luncheons
Garden Luncheons
Beach Luncheons
Picnic Box Luncheons
Brunch
Wiener Roasts
Clam Bakes
Barbecues
Campfire Snacks

Buffet luncheons will permit some of the service staff to skip a meal. These luncheons encourage guests to "mix." Some guests at a resort have such a marked degree of reserve that they speak only to the people seated at their tables. Limited conversation for some guests can easily mean an unfavorable reaction toward their entire stay.

Garden and beach luncheons, if such facilities exist, are merely transported buffet luncheons. They require adequate equipment, but they have the advantage of providing a different background for a meal.

Picnic Box Luncheons require advance notice from the guests and an appropriate cutting back of preparation for the guests who remain to eat in the dining room. They require additional preparation but also afford a possibility for thinning down preparation activities for meal service in the dining room. These luncheons are usually doubly appreciated by a considerable number of the guests. They constitute an extra accommodation and provide a change of scene. There can easily be an over-all saving in food cost if handled properly.

Sunday Brunch has taken a firm hold in many large cities. In resorts it is also extremely popular with late risers. There are generally two types of brunch that are served; light or substantial. Where a light brunch is served, usually from 10:00 A.M. to 11:00 A.M., it is primarily a late riser's breakfast and the general practice is to serve dinner from 2:00 P.M. to 8:00 P.M. Where a substantial brunch is served, then dinner becomes an evening meal, served from 6:00 P.M. to 8:00 P.M. Light brunch is usually dramatized by service in a location other than the dining room, such as a lounge or a porch. Where brunch is offered, quite a number of guests confine themselves to two meals on a Sunday instead of three.

Wiener Roasts, Clam Bakes, Barbecues and Campfire Snacks are an excellent means of getting guests outdoors and in new dining patterns. Most guests relish this type of change. Establishments offering these features have received many commendations. With the portable equipment available on the market, the serving of this type of meal or snack is not too burdensome.

Home Style Service. The American Plan type of food service did not grow out of thin air. Its roots go back deeply in American history. All too often American Plan meals are permitted to become fundamentally European Plan meals with the prices omitted from the menu. American Plan originally meant home-style service. Vegetables in large dishes, platters of roast chicken and tureens of soup are all hallmarks of the home style of the American Plan. Wherever this custom has been preserved in the midst of all the niceties of top-notch service, guests have expressed marked appreciation. Wherever the quality of service has been permitted to deteriorate, the establishment has begun to resemble a boarding-house.

Many resort operators have added a certain suavity to the service by offering selections from well-laden relish trays and portable roll warmers. The featuring of vegetable choices from heated trays containing 3 or 4 varieties also adds color to the service.

Salad and juice bars in the dining room speed the service considerably and contribute a distinct display value.

Sample Menus. Sample menus of resort operations that have been experiencing a substantial repeat trade follow:

LOW PRICE LUNCHEON MENU

APPETIZERS:

Chilled Grapefruit Iced V-8 Cocktail
Melon Fruit Cup

SOUPS:

Cream of Pea Soup
Consomme with Egg Barley

ENTREES:

Boiled Fresh Boneless Codfish with Egg and Chive Sauce
Irish Lamb Stew, Fresh Garden Vegetables
Wheat Cakes, Pure Maple Syrup, Homemade Sausages
Roast Leg of Veal with Currant Jelly and Fresh Vegetable Salad
Cold: Triple Decker Tuna Fish Salad Sandwich on Toast, Pimiento Olives

VEGETABLES:

Mashed Summer Squash Parsley Potatoes
Harvard Beets Cabbage and Carrot Slaw

DESSERTS:

Apricot and Raisin Pie
Peach Ice Cream
Compote of Stewed Fresh Fruit
Apple Dumpling
Bowl of Tangerines and Plums

BEVERAGES:

Homogenized Milk
Oolong Tea
Iced or Hot Coffee

LOW PRICE DINNER MENU

APPETIZERS:

Minted Fruit Cup Apricot Nectar
Chilled Cantaloupe

SOUPS:

Consomme Julienne Jellied Madrilene

ENTREES:

Broiled Chicken Halibut, Maitre d'Hotel
Roast Leg of Spring Lamb, Mint Jelly
Shirred Eggs with Chicken Livers
Cold: Roast Top Sirloin of Beef, Potato Salad, Mustard Pickle
Seafood Platter with Crabmeat and Shrimp

VEGETABLES:

Fresh Green Peas
Succotash
Buttered New Potatoes
Mixed Green Salad

DESSERTS:

Fresh Strawberry Tart
Old Fashioned Rice Pudding
Bartlett Pears in Syrup
Open Face Dutch Apple Pie
Bowl of Oranges, Bananas, and Apples

BEVERAGES:

Grade-A Milk
Iced Tea
Postum
Iced or Hot Coffee

HIGH PRICE LUNCHEON MENU

APPETIZERS:

Fresh Seafood on Tomato Slice, Russian Dressing
Orange and Grapefruit Cup, Maraschino
Imported Sardines on Toasted Triangles
Pineapple Juice Frappe with Lime Sherbet

SOUPS:

New England Fish Chowder
Chicken Broth with Rice

ENTREES:

Baked Lake Trout, Melted Butter, Lemon Wedge
Chinese Peppersteak, Rice and Noodles
Roast Loin of Pork, Sage Dressing, Pan Gravy
Poached Kennebec Salmon, Mayonnaise, Shredded Vegetable Greens
Cold: Open Face Chicken Salad Sandwich, Tomato Slice, Celery Curls

VEGETABLES:

Buttered Baby Carrots
Fresh Peas
Cauliflower au Gratin
Roasted Potatoes
Mixed Green Vegetable Salad

DESSERTS:

Deep Dish Cherry Pie
Strawberry Bavarian, Fresh Fruit Sauce
Lime and Pineapple Sherbet
Chilled Cantaloupe a la Mode
Bowl of Tangerines, Peaches, and Grapes

BEVERAGES:

Homogenized Grade-A Milk
Cultured Buttermilk
Iced Ceylon Tea
Iced Coffee
Demi-Tasse

HIGH PRICE DINNER MENU

APPETIZERS:

Supreme of Fresh Fruit
Cherrystone Clams
Canape of Pate Foie Gras
Petite Tomato Stuffed with Crabmeat

SOUPS:

Manhattan Clam Chowder
Vichysoisse
Consomme Celestine

ENTREES:

Broiled Filet of Flounder, Hoteliere
Baked Maine Lobster, Thermidor
Loin Lamb Chop, Mixed Grill
Roast Half Stuffed Spring Chicken, Natural Gravy
Sliced Fresh Brisket of Beef, Potato Salad
Cold: Sliced Breast of Turkey, Ham, Julienne of Fresh Vegetables

VEGETABLES:

New Lima Beans
Brussels Sprouts
Creamed Onions
Whipped or French Fried Potatoes
Hearts of Lettuce with Roquefort Cheese Dressing

DESSERTS:

Boston Cream Pie
Butter Pecan Parfait
Chilled Watermelon
Fresh Apple Pie with Cheese
Bowl of Nectarines, Plums, and Cherries

BEVERAGES:

Homogenized Grade-A Milk
Cultured Buttermilk
Iced Pekoe Tea
Iced Coffee
Demi-Tasse

CONTROLS

Portion Sizes. Portion sizes can generally be smaller than in commercial restaurants, if the entire meal is dressed up to look generous. If a substantial appetizer is served, followed by a soup, an entree with a small side salad, dessert and a bowl of fresh fruits, very few guests are likely to feel undernourished. For those who do, a second helping should prove quite adequate. The additional ounces of all the second helpings will generally add up to less than an extra ounce or two for every guest on the regular menu.

Fresh fruit served in a bowl at every meal is the easiest type of food to prepare, and it gives any luncheon or dinner that extra quality of eye and appetite appeal that makes the entire meal more substantial.

Food Cost Percentages. There are two distinct lines of thinking in regard to calculating and controlling food cost percentages.

One presupposes that a set value for meals alone can and should be established. The other involves a joint account for room and board and the calculation of food costs as a fractional portion of the entire expense structure.

If the former method is used, there is likely to be a rigid adherence to the policy of considering three meals a day to be worth for example $6.00 per guest per day, and a determined insistence upon a flat 40 per cent, or any other arbitrary food cost percentage. It may be possible to keep the desired food cost, but not the guests. A percentage of an arbitrarily allotted sales value figure can often mean little or nothing. Any change in the allocation for food sales automatically produces a change in the food cost percentage.

A sounder approach is to consider income for room and board as part of the same operating structure, and to budget all expenses, including salaries and wages and other expenses, in terms of cost per guest day. Thus, a $15.00 rate for room and board for one guest day might indicate that 20 per cent or a $3.00 allotment per day, for the cost of food, is sound and desirable.

To determine whether this allotment is sound, it is necessary to decide what the general level of the menu offerings would be, and what the cost of these offerings amount to. When the reasonable cost has been determined, a fair "sales value" could then be assigned to the meal's portion of the guests' room and lodgings expense.

Once this procedure has been adopted by management and a fair "mark-up" has been established for meals served, deviations from this norm could be easily determined, and management would know whether the food cost expenses were in line with the budgeted costs. Comparisons could easily be made between budget figures for food cost and actual results.

A realistic attitude toward food cost percentages is advisable. The rate structure, the percentage of former guests returning, the type and location of competitive establishments, the extra avenues of revenue, and the facilities offered, must all be taken into careful consideration.

Sound food control revolves around measuring, *not guessing,* what food costs ought to be, and a comparison with what they are, in order to determine what appropriate corrective action should be taken.

STAFF STRUCTURE

If a flexible, sufficiently varied menu structure, based on a fourteen-day rotation is in effect, it should be possible to operate satisfactorily with a smaller preparation and service staff than would be required for a European Plan menu.

A narrower range of selections is the accustomed practice in American Plan operations. Hence, the possibilities for a smaller staff. The hours of operation are also more easily controlled. Where necessary, two sittings, timed an hour apart, will serve to keep the flow of work at a steadier pace than is likely to prevail in any establishment featuring the European Plan.

Under a European Plan arrangement, guests tend to eat at odd hours, since they are completely "on their own," and they usually insist on complete service at all hours.

SPECIAL FEATURES

Writing Guest Orders. An extremely handy arrangement is the writing of meal orders by the guests themselves. This serves many purposes. It provides control of portion service; eliminates errors in the method of preparation desired; speeds up service, and affords an exact count of the number of second helpings actually ordered.

American and European Plans in the Same Establishment. In some resorts, particularly those located within a relatively short distance of large cities, there are many guest-stays of short duration. In such establishments, the co-existence of the American and European Plans may be desirable and advantageous.

To facilitate the seating, and to insure proper control of guest charges, it is advisable to issue an American Plan Introductory Card to each guest desiring this type of service. When this card is presented to the headwaiter, he can concentrate the seating of American Plan guests at the same service stations. As a cross-check to insure adequate control, the food checkers should be furnished a list by the front office of all guests entitled to American Plan meals.

Table Capacities. The seating arrangements for American Plan food service requires considerable thought and planning. Tables seating six, eight or ten guests are generally the rule. However, where both European and American Plans are in force, some tables seating two or four will be needed for European plan guests. In emergencies these could be pressed into service for American Plan service.

Large tables can present timing problems in the food service. There will usually be some stragglers who will keep the other guests at the table waiting. They cause the service staff to make extra trips to the kitchen to obtain food service.

Late Breakfasts. The scheduling of breakfast service will generally entail certain problems. While most guests will be fairly punctual for a 1:00 P.M. luncheon or 7:00 P.M. dinner, breakfast is a stragglers' meal. Whether service is from 7:00 to 9:00 or 7:30 to 9:30, or even 8:00 to 10:00, there will always be a certain number of guests who will prefer to sleep late and come bouncing in at the last minute. Having reached the dining room on time, they generally tend to order more breakfast than they really want in order to justify the effort of getting there on time. The amount of food left on their plates is proof of this.

Special service of juice, rolls and coffee for late risers is not a great burden to the service or preparation staffs. The saving in food cost, plus the added goodwill of making late breakfasts available, will more than compensate for the effort it requires.

The general practice in many resorts is to have waiters or waitresses work in teams of two. Since breakfast is served over a more protracted period of time than the other meals, a waiter or waitress will be assigned to cover for both members of the team for breakfast service. This provides a morning off every other day for each member of the service staff.

However, there are some resorts where breakfast is not served to the guests in their regular dining room seats. The tables are filled in chronological sequence of the guests' arrivals. The service personnel, under such a setup, generally reports for breakfast service on a rotation stagger basis. The service of light breakfasts for late risers would merely entail further staggering of breakfast service for a longer period of time. This would mean a little extra sleep for some of the staff each day.

Employees' Attitudes. It must be stated frankly that many employees do not like or approve of the American Plan. Their objections, and the reasons behind these objections, must be understood.

Most of the best chefs and other preparation employees are European trained. They never encountered the American Plan in their own countries. It is new and also foreign to them. Some have adjusted to the newness and unfamiliarity of the American Plan, but others have not and prefer not to adjust to it.

Many waiters and waitresses abhor the American Plan because they feel that tips are likely to be less. An average tip of 25 or 35 cents per person per meal is not uncommon in some European Plan establishments but the same guests who are in the habit of leaving either of the foregoing amounts, are not likely to multiply their usual tip by 42 for a two week stay and leave $10.50 or $14.70 in a lump sum. Some of the service personnel have, therefore, been quite emphatic in their denunciation of the American Plan type of food service.

Headwaiters, in many instances, dislike the prospect of an American Plan assignment. Once a guest is seated at a table, he or she will expect to remain for their entire stay at the same table. When seats are subject to change for each meal, as is universally the practice under the European Plan, the tips for favorable locations are likely to add up to a greater total.

Some chefs have an adverse attitude toward the American Plan because they feel that there is greater difficulty in controlling food costs since "guests eat too much." It is unquestionably true that some guests really do gorge themselves under the American Plan, but the great majority do not overeat simply because there is no additional charge for extra helpings.

There is no doubt that setting up a desirable American Plan menu has definite complexities. Variety is expected and demanded. There are fewer opportunities for elaborate showmanship or house specialties. In a European Plan restaurant, house specialties can appear every day, but no dish can be permitted to appear every day on an American Plan menu.

Profit Factors. American Plan food service, properly handled, can be more profitable for a resort operation than the European Plan. It consolidates all phases of restaurant operation, including purchasing, preparation and service. It lends itself to the fullest use of the "Pre-Cost Pre-Control" procedures. The number of guests to be served is subject to relatively few variations. The guests generally make reservations days or months in advance. Therefore, the forecast of the sales expectancy becomes quite simple—much simpler than in commercial restaurants. The number of menu offerings is always less than under European Plan operation, thereby simplifying still further the task of planned production.

The constant effort required under the European Plan for keeping the prices of all items within attractive limits is not so important under the

American Plan. Merchandising techniques to persuade guests to order more items are also not necessary.

Sales analysis figures allow for an immediate evaluation of the likes and dislikes of the guests. A fairly stable guest structure from weekend to weekend is usually the rule, thereby simplifying the task of serving the guests what they want.

One of the basic principles of "Pre-Cost Pre-Control" is the setting of standards for quality and quantity by management. It is, therefore, relatively simple for management to keep direct control of all the subsidiary steps of food service.

With the establishment of Standard Purchase Specifications, all suppliers of foodstuffs will be on an equal footing. Each dealer will prefer to quote on a pure competitive basis without feeling that some other dealer might obtain an order by underbidding and supplying inferior products.

Proper receiving procedures will generally ease the burdens of the chef. In smaller establishments there is a tendency to feel that a receiving clerk is not necessary since the chef checks all incoming goods. Checking for quality is one thing, but a good chef should not be spending his time weighing or counting merchandise and checking invoices.

With proper receiving procedures, dealers will soon learn the exact requirements of an establishment and eventually there will be less likelihood of returned merchandise.

Buying for planned production eliminates the temptation to speculate in tricky food markets. Overstocked storerooms cause waste and tie up capital.

Portion costs can be computed as a result of butchering and cooking tests. Cost factors per portion served can be set up to determine quickly the advisability of including or eliminating certain items on the basis of the prevailing market prices.

Actual sales analysis permit the featuring of dishes of proven popularity and the elimination of unpopular offerings.

The potential savings figures, which constitute the difference between the actual and potential costs, directly indicate to management the degree of efficiency that prevails in the kitchen.

FOOD CHECKING FOR AMERICAN PLAN OPERATIONS

In recent years operators of American Plan Hotels have become increasingly cognizant of the importance of including in their system of accounting and financial control an adequate method of checking meals served to resident and transient dining room guests. It can be said that, in general, American Plan Hotels employ food checkers and a food checking system. However, it can be equally said that a large number of progressive hotelmen have either overlooked or doubted the wisdom of providing for this element of inexpensive yet highly productive control.

Here are some of the more important advantages resultant from the employment of an adequate food checking system for American Plan Hotels:

(1) The operation of a hotel will be assured of receiving all revenue that the hotel is entitled to from the service of food.
(2) Over-service resulting in the waste of food and subsequent higher food costs will be minimized through the diligence of the food checker.
(3) A more accurate and readily obtainable count of the meals served can be made.

In addition to the foregoing, the food checker will be of assistance to the kitchen steward in maintaining a proper degree of decorum and efficiency in the kitchen. He will record and report directly to the management all complaints relative to food returned to the kitchen as being over or undercooked or otherwise unpalatable. He will also watch, in the service of food to guests, that:

(1) Dishes are properly garnished so as to present a pleasing and appetizing appearance.
(2) Proper portion sizes, in accordance with the standards established by the hotel, are served.
(3) Chipped china and glassware never reach a guest's table.

Fundamental Requirements of the System. In order for an American Plan Food Checking System to function with the greatest ease and efficiency, it is desirable to provide the forms illustrated on the following pages in addition to an experienced, reliable food checker and the same type of cashier (if extra and transient meals served are voluminous).

It is mentioned, however, that the design of the form for the "Introduction to Dining Room Card" is shown attached to the "Guest Registration" card, bearing the same number, and is also shown as a separate and distinct record from the "Guest Registration" card. The use of either is optional although many hotels have adopted the combination card feature.

Procedure Under the System For Normal Food Service. 1. Each night after the night audit has been completed, the night auditor prepares the "Meal Checking Sheet" for the food checker, who secures it before the breakfast hour on the following day. The preparation consists of record-

1	PERS	PL.	B	L	D	2	PERS	PL.	B	L	D	3	PERS	PL.	B	L	D	4	PERS	PL.	B
101						201						301						401			
102						202						302						402			
103						203						303						403			
104						204						304						404			
105						205						305						405			
106						206						306						406			
107						207						307						407			
108						208						308						408			
109						209						309						409			
110						210						310						410			
111						211						311						411			
112						212						312						412			
113						213						313						413			
114						214						314						414			
TOTAL						TOTAL						TOTAL						TOTAL			

DATE ______ ______ (CHECKER) ______ (CHECKER)

ing opposite the room number, in the "persons" column, the number of people in the guest's room and recording in the "plan" column the abbreviation for the type plan the guest has registered for such as "A" for American, "M" for Modified and "E" for European.

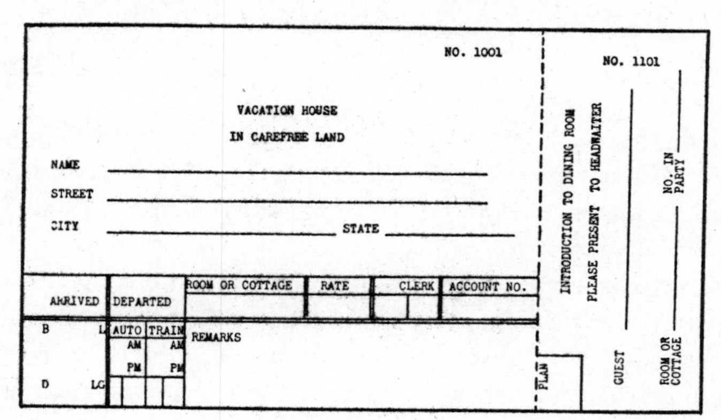
NO. 1001

VACATION HOUSE
IN CAREFREE LAND

NAME ______
STREET ______
CITY ______ STATE ______

ARRIVED	DEPARTED	ROOM OR COTTAGE	RATE	CLERK	ACCOUNT NO.

B L | AUTO AM PM | TRAIN AM PM | REMARKS
D LG

NO. 1101

INTRODUCTION TO DINING ROOM
PLEASE PRESENT TO HEADWAITER

PLAN
GUEST ______
NO. IN PARTY ______
ROOM OR COTTAGE ______

2. After the completion of one meal, but before the start of the next meal, the current day's "Meal Checking Sheet" should be returned to the front office, where corrections are made for arrivals and departures. Arrivals between meals should be recorded in the "persons" column, using different colored pencils in order to distinguish them from the guests who were in the house overnight.

3. As each guest registers at the front desk, he is given the "Introduction to Dining Room" card. The guest presents this card to the head waiter in the dining room who, after extracting any information he may require for his records, sends the card to the food checker stationed in the kitchen. The food checker immediately compares the information as shown on the "Introduction to Dining Room" card with the "Meal Checking Sheet," and if the persons as shown by the card are not recorded on the "Meal Checking Sheet," he makes the necessary entry opposite the correct room number. The food checker will undoubtedly find that, in the majority of cases, the information has already been recorded on the "Meal Checking Sheet" by the front office and it will only be necessary for him to make an entry if a guest should arrive at the hotel while a meal is in progress.

PLAN

NO. 1001

VACATION HOUSE
IN CAREFREE LAND

INTRODUCTION TO DINING ROOM

PLEASE PRESENT TO HEADWAITER

GUEST ______________ ______________

ROOM OR COTTAGE ______________ NO. IN PARTY ______________

4. The dining room guest writes out his meal order on the numerically controlled "Guest Order Check." When the waitress receives it (usually after the first course is served) she should immediately present it to the checker, who compares the information shown thereon with his checking record, records in the proper meal column the number of meals being served, stamps the meal order and returns it to the waitress for her reference and continued service of the meal. If the number of meals being served is more than the checking sheet calls for, the checker should circle the number he has recorded in the designated meal column in order that it may be readily discerned. The proper handling of excess or extra meals by the food checker is explained in subsequent paragraphs.

5. The actual checking of meals served by the waitresses may be accomplished by the checker through the use of the two methods which are universally adhered to in hotels. The first method dictates that the checker should scrutinize each course served, as the waitress pauses by

his desk, and check the items as shown on the tray against the "Guest Order Check," using for this purpose a colored pencil. By the second method, the checker scrutinizes the courses on the tray as the waitress passes the desk, and checks in colored pencil against the "Guest Order Check" one selected course, usually the entree. Under the first method, usually more than one checker is necessary to handle the volume without slowing service. Under the second method, usually only one checker is necessary and service is not retarded to any appreciable extent. While the first method is more exacting, the use of the second method generally suffices for control purposes.

NO. 1001

GUEST ORDER CHECK

GUESTS ARE REQUESTED TO WRITE THEIR ORDER

NAME ____________ ROOM OR COTTAGE ________

DATE ____________ WAITRESS ________

PORTIONS	

(SIGNATURE)

Regardless of which of the aforementioned procedures is used, it is evident that a diligent food checker will accomplish certain things, namely:

(a) That only the number of meals as shown on the "Guest Order Check" will be taken from the kitchen.
(b) That the proper garniture of dishes will be followed.
(c) That proper portion sizes, in accordance with the standards established by the hotel, will be served.
(d) That food or beverages will not be served to guests in chipped china or glassware.

6. After the waitress has served the last course, she gives the "Guest Order Checks" to the checker, who holds them until the end of the day,

and then forwards them to the accounting department for audit purposes.

7. At the close of the last meal for the day, the checker totals the various meal columns on the "Meal Checking Sheet," and summarizes these totals, by meals, to obtain the grand total of all meals, and type meals, served during the day. This constitutes an accurate record of the meals served in a given day.

Procedure Under the System For Extra Meal Service. The service of extra meals to guests occurs when friends or visitors have joined a registered guest's table. It might also be that registered guests in the hotel have joined the table of another registered guest. In this latter instance, it is imperative that the waitress secure all room numbers, else one guest might be charged for extra meals thereby causing a dispute upon payment of the bill.

The function which a food checking system performs in the accounting for and proper charging of extra meals may best be demonstrated by the following hypothetical situation:

Problem. On the evening of December 16th the "Guest Order Check" for Room 264 requests the service of four dinners. The checker upon comparing the order against his "Meal Checking Sheet" ascertains that only two people are registered in Room 264. No other room number appears on the order.

DATE____________ NO. 1001

EXTRA MEAL CHARGE

NAME________________________________ ROOM OR COTTAGE____________

EXPLANATION____

____

____
(CHECKER OR CASHIER SIGNATURE)

Procedure. Although no other room number appears on the "Guest Order Check," the checker verifies with the waitress that she has ascertained that no registered guest has joined another registered guest's table. The checker then proceeds to record opposite Room 264 on the "Meal Checking Sheet," the figure 4 under the "D" column and circles the figure with colored pencil. The checker then makes out a charge for two dinners against the account of the guests in Room 264.

If it is determined that two persons registered in Room 443 have joined the table of the persons registered in Room 264, the extra room number and guest's name is recorded on the "Guest Order Check" and the checker records opposite room numbers 443 and 264 shown on the "Meal Checking Sheet," the figure 2 in the "D" column. No extra charge is necessitated.

There are two methods of charging for extra meals of this type prevalent in hotel accounting. The first is of a regular "Restaurant Check," which is presented to the guest for signature. The second is through the use of an "Extra Meal Charge" voucher, which is not presented to the guest for signature. The use of either method depends upon the policy of management.

If the guest is not to be presented with a "Restaurant Check" showing the extra meal charge thereon for signature, the checker proceeds to prepare an "Extra Meal Charge" voucher, record the data on the "Dining Room Cash and Charge Record" and forward the charge to the front office for entry on the guest's account. The night auditor checks these charges as he would any other departmental charges and agrees the total of the extra meals as shown on the transcript for the day with the total as shown on the "Dining Room Cash and Charge Record."

If the management desires the guest to be presented with a "Restaurant Check" for signature, the checker and night auditor proceed as above mentioned, except that the checker prepares a "Restaurant Check" for presentation to the guest rather than preparing an "Extra Meal Charge" voucher, which the guest does not receive.

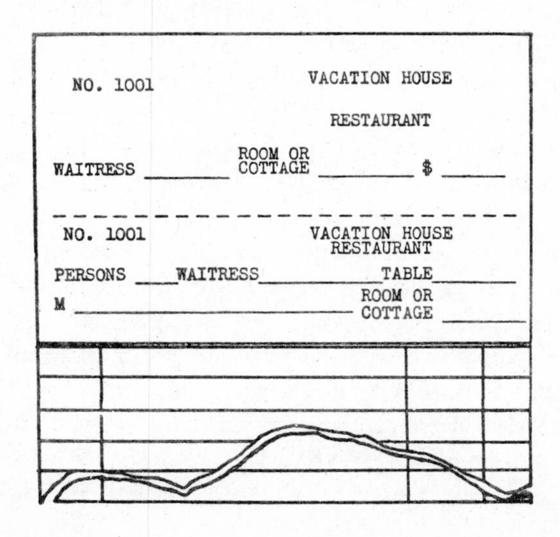
NO. 1001 VACATION HOUSE

RESTAURANT

WAITRESS ______ ROOM OR COTTAGE ______ $ ______

NO. 1001 VACATION HOUSE RESTAURANT

PERSONS ____ WAITRESS __________ TABLE ______

M ______________________ ROOM OR COTTAGE ______

For Transient Meal Service. It is always desirable to have transient guests who arrive for a meal purchase "Meal Tickets" at the front desk. However, this is not entirely practical, as many guests go directly to the dining room without purchasing tickets, and it is not considered good policy for the head waiter to request the guest to obtain a "Meal Ticket" in order to be admitted to the room. One of the desirable procedures adhered to in the accounting for and controlling of the service of meals of this type can best be outlined as follows:

(1) Meal tickets sold at the front desk should be stamped either "charge" or "cash," whichever the case may be, and the cash retained and recorded in the cashier's sheet by the front office cashier. If the meal is to be charged, the front office cashier should note on the ticket the person's name and address.

VACATION HOUSE NO. 1001
IN CAREFREE LAND

____

M ______________________

IS ENTITLED TO ______________

DAY ____________ DATE ______________

PLEASE PRESENT THIS CARD TO
HEADWAITER UPON ENTERING
DINING ROOM
______________ (CLERK)

(2) The guest presents the "Meal Ticket" to the head waiter upon arrival at the dining room and after having been assigned a table proceeds to write the regular "Guest Order Check."

(3) The waitress and checker follows the usual routine with respect to the "Guest Order Check" but in addition thereto, the waitress obtains the purchased "Meal Ticket" from the head waiter and presents it to the checker. The checker records the details of the ticket on the "Dining Room Cash and Charge Record" and cancels the ticket in such manner that it cannot be used again. The checker, in accordance with the policy adopted by the management, either prepares a "Restaurant Check" or "Extra Meal Charge" voucher for those meals to be charged and follow the procedure as outlined under "Extra Meals."

(4) When "Meal Tickets" are not purchased at the front office, the usual routine with respect to the "Guest's Order Check" is adhered to by the guest, waitress and checker. In addition thereto,

the checker gives the waitress a regular "Restaurant Check" when the last course is being served and this check is submitted to the guest for payment by the head waiter or captain. If the check is paid, the check and cash is taken to the front office where the check is stamped paid and the cash retained and recorded on the front office cash sheet. The check is then returned to the checker for proper entry on his record. If the check is to be charged to the account of a guest, the guest should sign it and the check should then be returned to the checker for entry on his record and then forwarded to the front office for charge against the guest's account.

In no instance does the checker handle cash, yet he does enter the detail of cash checks on his "Dining Room Cash and Charge Record." This procedure is followed in order that the accounting department may have an independent check on the total dining room cash business, as reported by the front office cashier.

The question relative to the desirability of employing the services of a dining room cashier who will be stationed at the entrance to the dining room is dependent upon the volume of transient meals served and the convenience of the location of the dining room to the front office. This is an individual problem and should be given careful study by the management in cooperation with the hotel's chief accountant. If it is decided that the employment of a cashier is necessary at certain periods, the procedure as outlined herein need be only slightly revised as the cashier will intercept the natural flow of cash and charge business until such time as the details of it can be taken in bulk to the front office for purposes of recording.

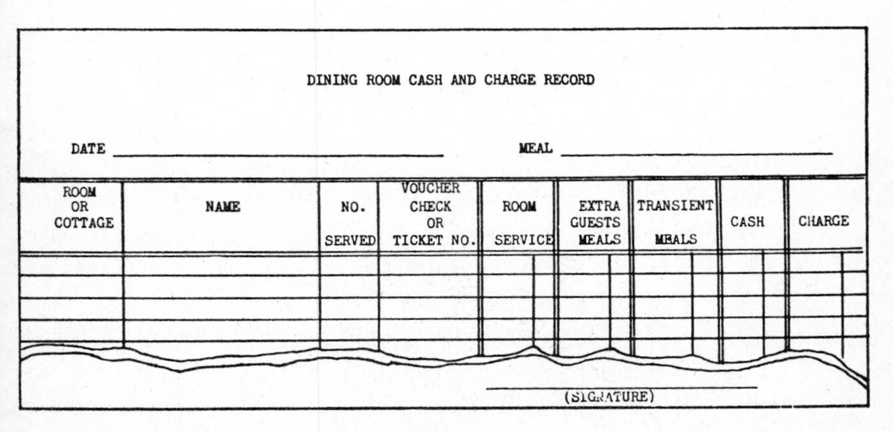

DINING ROOM CASH AND CHARGE RECORD

DATE ____________ MEAL ____________

ROOM OR COTTAGE	NAME	NO. SERVED	VOUCHER CHECK OR TICKET NO.	ROOM SERVICE	EXTRA GUESTS MEALS	TRANSIENT MEALS	CASH	CHARGE

(SIGNATURE)

With respect to the duties of the night auditor, he should check al transient meal charges in the same manner as other departmental charges These charges should be placed on the transcript under "Extra Meals' and the total as shown by the transcript agreed to the total as showr under the charge column on the "Dining Room Cash and Charge Record."

For Room Service and Room Service Charges. Room service order should be checked from the kitchen in the same manner as for dining room service. If the hotel has a room service charge in effect the checke should prepare a "Room Service Charge" voucher, record the details or the "Dining Room Cash and Charge Record" and forward the vouche to the front office for entry on the guest's account. Income from roon service charges should be credited to a separate account in the ledge rather than include it in the food sales account.

DATE____________________ NO. 1001

ROOM SERVICE CHARGE

NAME________________________ ROOM OR COTTAGE__________

EXPLANATION______________________________

____

____
(CASHIER OR CHECKER SIGNATURE)

Distribution of Food Checker's Records. After the last meal for the day has been served, the food checker should do the following:

(1) Send to the Front Office:
- (a) All charge vouchers and checks still on hand in order that they may be posted to the guest's account.
- (b) "Dining Room Cash and Charge Record" (To facilitate night audit).

(2) Send Directly to Accounting Department:
- (a) "Meal Checking Sheet"
- (b) Paid "Restaurant Checks"
- (c) Cancelled cash and charge "Meal Tickets"
- (d) "Introduction to Dining Room Cards" (after guest has checked out)
- (e) "Guest Order Checks"

Internal Control. The food checker is considered a member of the accounting department staff and is, therefore, subject to the control and supervision of the treasurer or chief accountant of the hotel. Periodic consultations should be held with the checker, and he should be visited occasionally in the kitchen when the service of meals is in progress to make sure that he is functioning in his true capacity. Such visits by a responsible member of the accounting department tends to inject a psychological effect in the control process which keeps the checker always on the alert in the performance of his duties.

In general, a responsible clerk in the accounting department should perform the following daily:

(1) Issue all numbered checks and vouchers to the checker, keeping a record of all numbers issued.

(2) Issue all numbered "Meal Tickets" to the front office cashier, keeping a record of the numbers issued.

(3) Account for all numbered checks, vouchers and "Meal Tickets" as to their return or the fact that they are still outstanding. The daily accounting for all numbered "Guest Order Checks" may prove burdensome in some fair sized hotels where hundreds of meals are served each day. If the management feels that such a control is more expensive than productive, it is suggested that periodic spot checks be introduced in place of the daily control in order to forestall any possible collusion.

(4) Agree total of "Meal Tickets" sold at front office with totals as shown on the "Dining Room Cash and Charge Record," "Transcript" and "Front Office Cash Sheet."

(5) Ascertain that charges have been made to a guest's account for extra meals as shown on the "Meal Checking Sheet" and that the total of extra meals shown thereon agrees with the totals as shown on the "Dining Room Cash and Charge Record" and "Transcript."

(6) Check "Meal Checking Sheet" against the "Transcript" to ascertain that guest's accounts have been charged for room and board when the "Meal Checking Sheet" discloses that persons are registered in a room.

Chapter XVI: ADVERTISING AND PROMOTION

THERE IS *no magic formula for successful advertising* and promotion of a food and beverage establishment. In many cases several different methods have been successful and often the best methods are a matter of personal opinion.

No two restaurants are alike—each presents an individual problem. They may be different in character and clientele, size, equipment, service, and prices. Certainly, they are different in location. In addition, each proprietor feels that his restaurant is distinctively different and, therefore, presents an individual problem.

However, there is one basic and very important premise for successful advertising and promotion and that is, to have *a good product.* This means not only good food, attractively served, but also other factors such as cheerful atmosphere, smart uniforms, well-trained staff, and good equipment. Of equal importance, also, is that your product represents *good value for the price.*

EIGHT KEYS TO SUCCESSFUL ADVERTISING

Although each restaurant operation, whether it be located in a hotel, in a club, in an office building, in the city or the country, presents an individual problem, there are certain fundamental principles which are helpful in getting and maintaining good business for your operation. Taken together, all of these emanate from the basic principle of advertising, namely, "The repetition of advantageous mental impressions to bring about the desired action." And in many fewer words, is a slogan taken from the writings of Arthur Brisbane, "Repetition builds Reputation."

In planning your advertising and promotion, the following eight steps are recommended:

(1) Study your restaurant and its services to determine its inherent advantages as well as its disadvantages in relation to others.

(2) Analyze your potential market.

(3) Study all available methods and media to reach this market.
(4) Formulate a definite plan for advertising.
(5) Coordinate all advertising and promotion material.
(6) Set up a budget for advertising and business promotion.
(7) Carry out the program.
(8) Keep the program in force.

Each of these steps will now be taken up in greater detail.

Study Your Restaurant. It is easy to sell a good restaurant but it is very difficult to promote a poor restaurant continuously. Be honest in your self-appraisal, especially with regard to your competition. If you find that your appointments, service, and food are not as good as your competitors', you should first make the necessary changes and improvements before planning an extensive advertising program. In other words, *get your own house in order* before selling it to the public.

If, in your self-appraisal, you find you have certain advantages due to location, equipment, service, food, etc., be sure to capitalize on them. However, it must be kept in mind that it is much more difficult to sell atmosphere than it is to merchandise special dishes and other services.

Analyze Your Potential Market. The food and beverage business in a public eating establishment originates from three sources:

(1) the immediate vicinity and neighborhood;
(2) group business, meaning weddings, banquets, luncheons, and parties;
(3) transients—out-of-town visitors, people from distant parts of the same town, and casual passers-by.

All advertising and promotion efforts should be directed toward these groups. To them, the hotels can add a fourth group—the guest in the house.

The analysis of these three markets is extremely important because experience overwhelmingly indicates that it is easier to increase the flow of business from areas where it naturally originates than to exploit other markets. In other words, it is much simpler for a restaurant operator to increase the number of diners from the type of clientele catered to than to attempt to draw other classes of people to his establishment. This fact is also true of persons residing in various areas. Therefore, it is well for the restaurant operator to be well informed as to where most of his patrons come from and what type they are, and then go out and get more of them.

In this respect, it is wise to check the types of business on various days of the week, holiday periods, and seasonal trends. By keeping abreast of these facts, advertising can be more intelligently placed to reach the proper market at the proper time.

It is crucially important to establish and maintain a continuing study of the type of offerings, price range, and business volume of all competitive establishments (restaurants, hotels, clubs, drive-ins, and highway stands). This will require an outlay of money and time. However, it is only on the basis of minutely accurate information regarding the fundamental elements contributing to the success or lack of success of competitive establishments, that a true picture of the range and scope of customers' likes and dislikes can be ascertained.

A close and repeated study must be made of the appropriateness of the existing hours of operation. Where potential business warrants it, an extension of the operating schedule can frequently induce an additional volume of patronage with relatively little added expense.

A review of most 3-meal operations, involving the service of breakfast, luncheon, and dinner will reveal that staffing can be achieved for supper trade with little extra payroll expenditure. A minimum of two separate shifts are generally needed to service three meals between the hours of 6:30 A. M. and 9:30 P. M. This fifteen-hour span can usually be stretched to cover two or more additional hours by the proper scheduling of a 30 or 40-minute mealtime pause for each shift.

Stimulating supper trade involves three major factors:

(1) potential business volume;
(2) imaginative offerings;
(3) the creation of some semblance of a relaxing atmosphere.

Many customers who may balk at paying over a dollar for luncheon, as a matter of budgetary caution, will frequently spend fifty cents more for virtually the same dish at supper, with only minor trimmings added, simply, because a supper snack is more of a social occasion than luncheon.

In some cities there simply is no potential supper trade worth seeking during the early part of the week. However, in many such instances, there is a considerable area of exploitation during Friday, Saturday, and Sunday. Scheduled variations, geared to such considerations, can often mean added lucrative volume. Only a comprehensive study of the market —plus astute experimentation—will reveal the true potentialities in this direction.

Study All Available Methods and Media to Reach This Market. In considering advertising in newspapers, magazines, outdoor advertising, and other forms, it is well to *eliminate all but recognized and proven media.* Too much money can be wasted by advertising in programs, leaflets, social publications, etc. If you feel it advisable to contribute to certain charities by advertising in their programs, set up a special fund for gifts and contributions instead of considering it an advertising expense.

It is best, of course, to study all of the media which are available to you to reach your market. No one medium is best for all but each one has its place in certain types of operation.

(1) Newspapers

Newspapers are, of course, best for local readership. It is highly desirable for a local restaurant or hotel to be represented regularly in the columns of the local newspapers. It not only helps to sell the operation to readers but builds prestige as well. In larger cities where there is more than one newspaper, the morning editions are usually better for reaching business men and women while the evening editions are carried home and read by all members of the family. Sunday newspapers usually have a wider circulation and very often have a scope far beyond their own trading area.

When advertising in newspapers, it is highly advisable to run regularly. Most daily newspapers have special days for restaurant and hotel advertising, usually twice a week. In addition, they have special editions for dining out during holidays which have proved very profitable.

When placing advertisements in the local newspapers, the restaurant should preferably merchandise certain special dishes for luncheon, dinner, etc. It is well to include a price in the advertisements as well as a brief description of the dish. Of course, well written copy and attractive art work help to make these advertisements productive. Restaurants or hotels which have dancing, entertainment, or accommodations for private functions should include a line to this effect in all advertisements, and occasionally run special advertisements featuring their facilities for banquets, parties, weddings, and other group functions. Naturally, large operations which employ big name bands and expensive entertainment must feature these in their copy.

(2) Magazines

Magazines, as well as newspapers, charge for advertising, as a rule, on the basis of circulation. This circulation may be based on quantity of readers, quality, or both. Are there enough potential customers among the readers of a given periodical to make the advertising pay? An advertiser, as we have said, must be certain that his message is reaching a type of clientele in keeping with the character of the establishment. Otherwise, he is paying for waste circulation. For example, the advertising manager of a large metropolitan hotel located in a city visited by thousands of people each month, may feel justified in advertising in a national magazine. The advertisement will be read or noticed by thousands of potential guests. But an advertisement for a commercial hotel in the average small city has no place in that same magazine. Regardless of the copy appeal of the advertisement, it would not be read by one person in ten thousand who had the slightest reason to go to that city or stop at that hotel. That is an extreme example but it points out the value of studying the media before placing advertising.

Some cities have attractive local magazines which may be used in conjunction with the newspapers with good results. Advertising in magazines definitely establishes prestige but is usually more costly than newspaper space.

(3) Neighborhood Advertising

For the restaurant, the people who work or live in the immediate neighborhood of the establishment form the most productive source of patronage. Even for hotels, this class of people come only second to the guests in the house.

If a restaurant is surrounded by business offices, much of its luncheon business may be turned into dinner business as well. When people are going out for the evening to the theater or some sports event they will seldom go home, but will eat their dinner out. Some restaurants have a special "Theater Dinner", which includes cocktails and assures guests of a leisurely dinner but with alert service which will get them to the theater or stadium in ample time.

Office parties given by firms in the neighborhood offer a splendid opportunity to handle group business. These parties may bring into the restaurant many new patrons who will continue to come. They may also be the source of engagement parties, showers, and weddings.

Many of these neighborhood business firms have small printed or mimeographed house organs which are distributed only to members of the organizations, a few employees who have left, and to some friends or customers outside the organizations. These are made up of small items of news about the various workers and have about as great a reader interest as it is possible for a publication to have. If such a publication would accept a small paid advertisement from a nearby restaurant, this would be an excellent way of building goodwill as well as sales volume. The returns would more than make up for the small investment.

Many people will not enter a restaurant unless they can first look over the menu on the door or window. They want to know what is available and the prices they will have to pay. Many of them feel that if the menu is not displayed, the price of the meal is beyond their means. If a restaurant or hotel wishes to attract the casual passerby, this outside menu display, neatly framed, is the most direct and informative way of accomplishing this result.

(4) Telephone Directories

The classified pages of a telephone directory provide an excellent opportunity to attract prospects who are seeking specialized information. The advertising message can be changed slightly with each new issue of the directory.

In addition, it is possible to rent a special telephone directory which contains names and addresses of telephone subscribers grouped according to their addresses. A list of prospects in the immediate neighborhood or in selected residential areas thus can be easily compiled.

(5) Billboards, Signs, and Poster Bulletins

Judging from the looks of the highways, this would seem to be a widely used means of advertising. For large city hotels or for restaurants that are show places, these large billboards serve the purpose of keeping the names of the establishments they advertise constantly before the public. The expense is high, however, since no more than the name, location of the city, and the minimum rates can be read by the swiftly passing motorist or rail passenger.

A billboard is no place for detailed information and a lone billboard has little value. A series of billboards on one main highway, each featuring the name and location of the hotel and one feature, such as "Coffee Shop," may have value. Here the cost is something to consider as well as the fact that even a series of billboards advertising a hotel or restaurant will be seen by the people traveling on only one highway. If four major highways enter a community, four sets of billboards will be needed to cover all incoming visitors. A billboard near a stop light can often do the work of three or four on the open road.

Before billboards are decided upon as a medium, the location of the hotel or restaurant should be considered. If it is on the same highway that is an advantage. Many people do not want to leave a main automobile route. Also, parking facilities are necessary when advertising to motorists. This fact should certainly be mentioned on the billboard. Lighting is an additional necessary billboard expense unless one wishes to average, over a year, the loss of at least 10 per cent of the value of billboard advertising.

In some larger cities, restaurants and hotels have employed poster bulletins to good advantage. These can usually be bought on a monthly basis while painted billboards along the highways are contracted for on a yearly basis. In considering poster bulletins, it must be kept in mind that the advertiser must pay for the production of the paper posters in addition to the rental of the locations. In the case of the highway billboards, however, the cost of the painting, usually twice a year, is included in the contract.

Compared to billboard advertising, electric signs on or near the premises have become almost a "must" for both hotels and restaurants unless they wish to miss a great deal of business. A suitable electric sign, visible for at least two hundred feet, is a necessary form of on-the-spot advertising. These signs, where city ordinances permit, should extend several feet beyond the building line. A very large electric sign on top of the building which can be seen for many blocks is a welcome sight to the tired motorist entering the city. Chances are that such a sign will result in the immediate selection of that spot for accommodations.

(6) Car and Bus Cards

These cards can carry much more detailed information than billboards since passengers have ample time for reading them. They may prove excellent media for many restaurants and for some hotels that have moderate rates. These cards should always emphasize low prices for accommodations and meals.

(7) Direct Mail

This form of advertising has been extensively used with considerable success by many restaurants throughout the country. It is one method of getting selected coverage providing a good mailing list is used. Many restaurants ask their guests to sign a register which, in turn, becomes an excellent list of names for direct mail purposes. Other restaurants set up credit cards or city ledger accounts for a large number of their regular patrons. This also gives the restaurant an opportunity to use the list for promotion purposes. The most important factor in direct mail, however, is to keep your mailing lists accurate and up-to-date. It often takes years of hard work to compile a good list and it is worth checking regularly to maintain it with active names and accurate addresses.

Direct mail to restaurant guests need not be expensive. Many operators have used the system of sending unused menus to various residents or offices in the neighborhood. The list to be used can be taken from directory boards in building lobbies. In residential neighborhoods, the names may be taken from mail boxes in apartment houses.

In mailing unused menus, those which are left over may be folded, addressed by hand by the waitresses during slack periods, fastened with a clip or red sticker, and mailed regularly. This procedure has produced excellent results in many instances.

Other restaurants send out letters or special mailing pieces for the various holiday seasons. Still others notify those on their mailing lists of the various special dishes they are featuring each week or each month. Still others send out direct mail literature regarding their entertainment, dance band, or private function facilities.

In hotels, a great deal of goodwill may be gained by direct mail if guest histories are well organized. Guests may be in the hotel to celebrate a wedding anniversary, or a birthday, or some other important date in their lives. A letter of good wishes a year later shows thoughtfulness and courtesy. Regular guests who have not returned for quite a period of time should get a letter asking if something was wrong with the service. The daily papers yield many leads for business. For example, when parents announce the engagement of their daughter, they might be interested in a letter describing the facilities of a hotel for a wedding party.

A permanent file containing the dates of all birthday parties, wedding receptions, and anniversaries makes an excellent "reminder" mailing list. Most people like to be remembered on days that are of special significance to them. The personal touch in any form of advertising is subtly flattering and effective.

(8) *Visitors' Guides*

These can be very effective promotion for restaurants and hotels if they are adequately distributed, since they are closely consulted by travelers. They should be placed in railroad, plane, and bus terminals, garages, gas stations, and hotel lobbies located within the city and on its approaches. Motor courts and tourist cabins that do not serve meals are also excellent locations for them.

(9) *Radio*

Most hotels and restaurants cannot afford radio advertising but some of the larger ones have found it very profitable. Restaurants which employ orchestras can benefit by arranging to have their music broadcast on a sustaining basis. By this method the name of the restaurant and the band are broadcast although it is not permissible to include an extensive commercial announcement for the establishment. On this basis, the restaurant pays only for the wire charges which vary considerably with the size and importance of the radio station, but are still much less than the cost of purchasing time.

Another type of radio advertising, which has been employed successfully by hotels and restaurants, is the use of station breaks or one-minute spot announcements. Those located in the smaller cities where a radio station is located can get good results by using either of these forms of local radio advertising. Most station breaks are twenty seconds, which is usually not enough time to tell a good story about a hotel or restaurant unless it is exceptionally well known. One-minute spot announcements, however, allow approximately 120 words, which is ample time to do a good selling job. In such cases, an announcement about dinner or Sunday Brunch or a Smorgasbord Buffet might prove very effective if the cost is not prohibitive. This medium might be employed profitably for the promotion of parties, banquets, and weddings in the smaller communities and particularly in the surburban areas surrounding such communities.

Generally, "disk jockeys" are delighted to broadcast newsworthy bits. Care must be taken not to deluge them with run-of-the-mill items that are basically of limited interest. Arranging interviews with prominent personalities almost invariably will result in a "plug".

In a few of the larger cities, there are cooperative radio

programs which include a large number of restaurants and other eating places. Some of these programs have been very successful and are worth investigating.

(10) Television

Although television is by far the most active and productive medium at the present time, the cost is just about prohibitive for all but the very largest operations. The expenditure for time, as well as for production items such as announcers, film, props, etc., runs into many thousands of dollars so it would be well to explore other media thoroughly before considering television.

(11) Internal Merchandising

Probably because their opportunities are greatest, hotels are the worse offenders in overlooking the value of internal merchandising. Large hotels do a better job than the smaller ones. They realize that a guest who registers and goes to his room, is not able to see all the facilities the hotel has to offer. By means of room cards, he is told about the dining room, cocktail lounge, laundry, and other revenue-producing departments.

Because a hotel has only 50 or 100 rooms does not mean that a stranger entering the lobby to register is necessarily aware of a coffee shop or cocktail lounge. There may be a most attractive cocktail lounge tucked away, but unless the guest is told about it, he goes outside for a cocktail and stays out for his dinner. That revenue is lost as far as the hotel is concerned.

Every hotel has at least five opportunities to remind guests of available facilities by means of cards or posters—in the rooms; in the elevator vestibules on the floors; in the elevators themselves; in the lobby; and on the tables in the dining rooms.

Room Cards

The merchandising value of room cards is great enough to permit some expenditure in their production. Many hotels content themselves with sliding a menu under the glass top on the dresser where it often remains for a year or more without being changed. Certainly a December menu does not sound inviting on a sizzling July afternoon. Often, when guests are leaving and looking through the drawers to see that they have packed everything, they will find the room cards in the back of the top dresser drawer or in the desk drawer under the stationery. "Oh," they say, "they have a cocktail lounge here. Too bad I didn't know about it!" Yes, too bad for the hotel, also.

Room cards should be attractively printed and indicate clearly where the food and beverage facilities are in relation to the elevators. The coffee shop should not be overlooked and the price ranges for all dining rooms should be given. If a guest cannot afford the prices, he will not be lured into a formal dining room merely because there is no card advertising the coffee shop. He will go elsewhere.

The location of the cards is important. If they are lodged in the frame of the mirror they detract from the neatness of the room. Also, they are likely to be used by the guest for memoranda and not replaced. If set under the glass top of the dresser, they may be covered up by the guest's belongings and overlooked. Many hotels have found it desirable to put all the information on one card and have it neatly framed, placing it on the door or over the desk. It should be so arranged that new cards may be slipped in if new rooms or facilities are added or if prices change. The latter is most important, particularly if prices *increase*.

Elevator Vestibule Posters

The elevator vestibule on the various floors is an ideal spot for the day's menus. These posters, neatly framed, are almost sure to catch the eyes of guests waiting for elevators. The poster should give directions for reaching the various rooms mentioned and the menus must be changed for each meal.

Elevator Cards

A framed menu or card inviting the guest to visit the various food and beverage rooms will claim some attention in the elevator if it is placed just over the head of the operator on the front of the car, or at an angle on the side wall. Also, appropriately worded oral announcements by the elevator operators frequently helps to direct patrons to the various dining rooms.

Lobby Posters

The location of a lobby poster will depend upon the floor plan of each hotel lobby. It should be located somewhere between the elevators and the main entrance where it will not form a bottleneck for traffic, but will be seen by the greatest number of people. These posters must be attractively laid out and printed, in keeping with the dignity of the lobby. They may be used effectively to advertise special entertainment or events in the hotel since they should be made large enough to accommodate photographs. The printed matter should be easily readable by people passing by.

Table Cards

Table tent cards are excellent advertising media since people usually have time to read them while waiting to be served. These could announce some special feature of a lunch or dinner menu, a room that is open for late supper service, or a cocktail lounge. Menu tip-on cards are widely used for advertising featured dishes or cocktails. These must be used with discretion so as not to "clutter up" the main menu.

Many hotels and restaurants offer picture postal cards at the table to which they will add the postage and mail for guests who wish to drop a line to distant friends. This is an excellent means of promotion for those operations that have a large number of transient patrons from other cities.

The menu itself is a fine advertising medium. For further information on this, the reader is referred to the three chapters on the subject in this book and to ideas under "Direct Mail."

Garage Posters

If an establishment has an attached garage or parking lot, the wall space near the exit and any adjacent corridors afford excellent opportunity for suitable posters proclaiming any special features. These will easily capture the attention of the patrons at a time when they are likely to be in a receptive frame of mind and interested in the establishment's offerings.

All internal promotion should be completely coordinated in design, color, and copy. In large hotels where there are a number of restaurants, each one will have its own particular logotype and color combination in keeping with the character and decoration of the room. In smaller hotels, one motif is sufficient for the entire food operation.

Restaurants which are not located in hotels must necessarily confine their internal promotion to their own premises. They can use many of the ideas previously suggested as well as those following.

First of all, an attractive entrance is always a great asset. Menus placed in attractive frames or on posters at the entrance, as mentioned before in this chapter, give patrons an opportunity to look over food items and prices before they come in. Stickers or streamers on the windows, particularly those advertising special lunches or dinners, have been found to be very effective in the more moderate priced restaurants. Signs of various kinds in the windows of restaurants are also productive. These may be in the form of show cards placed on easels, indirectly illuminated electric displays, or Neon signs. In most cases these messages include some idea of the price and the size of the meal which is being served. For instance, one sign may read:

Club Breakfast Now Being Served
Fruit or Juice, Cereal or Eggs
Toast or Muffins, Coffee—75¢

After the diner enters the restaurant there are additional opportunities for promoting a larger sale. In addition to the usual featured dishes, chef's specials, etc., menus for dinner should include suggestions for cocktails, wines, champagne, etc. Then there are also opportunities to use the table tent cards to "push" certain items, postal cards to be mailed to friends, and other ideas previously mentioned.

Formulate a Definite Plan for Advertising. The plan for advertising a restaurant operation should be set up as part of a long-range program. The actual schedule or campaign might be limited to a period of six months or one year but it should be a part of an over-all program extending from three to five years. The principal reason for this is that *advertising is cumulative in effect.* You cannot build a good name, or a following, or a reputation in a few weeks, or a few months, or even in a few years.

Most restaurant operators are too impatient with the results of advertising and expect to see business increase immediately by leaps and bounds. Usually, this does not happen, but a steady constant growth can be achieved by continued advertising on a long-range basis.

Coordinate All Advertising and Promotion Material. As stated previously, a vital part of the principle of repetition is that the motif, design, and color of all advertising and promotion material be closely coördinated. This should be in keeping with the character and decor of your restaurant. This is one of the most important steps in successful promoting and merchandising of a restaurant.

To begin this program, it is well to have your advertising agency, or a creative printer, design a distinctive logotype for the name of your establishment. At the same time, a pleasing color combination which harmonizes with the furniture, drapes, and walls of your restaurant should be selected. Then, each of the various tools of advertising and business promotion, including menu covers, waiters' checks, beverage lists, letterheads, advertisements, folders, leaflets, outdoor bulletins, posters, etc., should be designed using this logotype and the color scheme and motif selected. *This is not only good taste but it is good business as well.*

To produce such a program of coordinated material costs no more, and very often less, than when the various pieces are designed and produced individually. Many times it is possible to print several printed pieces such as menus, beverage covers, tent cards, etc., in combination, which saves on production costs.

All restaurants, regardless of size, can use coordinated promotion material to some extent. Even the smallest restaurant can use the same logotype for its name on the sign outside, and on its menus. Larger restaurants extend this to paper napkins, match covers, coasters, place mats, and many other items which are used by the public. When a coordinated program is established in a restaurant it has an immediate desirable effect on the public.

Set Up a Budget for Advertising and Business Promotion. The amount of money spent by restaurants in advertising and business promotion varies between two per cent and four per cent of the total sales. It is usually true that the restaurants with high prices spend a larger percentage of their sales for advertising. The proper amount to spend depends upon a great many factors which make each case an individual decision. It cannot be emphasized too strongly that such decision should be based on careful study and research.

However, if you have formulated a good constructive program, it is important to spend the amount of money *necessary to do the job.* In some cases, especially when opening, restaurants have spent much more than four per cent of their sales, and then later have been able to reduce the amount considerably. It must be kept in mind, however, that except for food cost, there is very little additional overhead expense in feeding a limited number of additional guests which may greatly increase the margin of profit.

Carry Out the Program. Your advertising agency, with your cooperation, should then put this program into effect by creating a logotype and other coordinated material, conceiving a copy theme, working out advertising schedules, and creating direct mail and internal promotion material.

In most cases, this will take several weeks, or even months, before the program is well under way. It is well to be patient and remember that the effect of good advertising is cumulative and not immediate.

Keep the Program in Force. Constant effort is absolutely essential to maintain the progress of an advertising program. The basic principle of successful advertising is repetition. In the case of restaurants, this means repetition of the name over and over again so that the prospects in your market are constantly reminded of your operation. Successful advertising gathers momentum day by day and requires continued attention.

SUGGESTIONS FOR PUBLICITY

Restaurants and hotels can secure publicity in local newspapers if they are alert to the opportunities to recognize information which will be of interest to the newspapers. Although small individual restaurants are limited in their ability to produce newsworthy items, they can occasionally supply facts and information which may be acceptable. For instance, a story on food trends is always interesting. The ratings of the most popular meat dishes, vegetables, and desserts, for example, are something a restaurant operator can compile very easily. Also, prominent guests are always a source of good publicity and an occasional tip-off of the presence of a prominent person might result in a favorable interview.

Other opportunities for publicity include trips through the kitchens by the members of women's clubs, school groups, etc. Various charitable activities, such as supplying Thanksgiving dinners to poor families, entertaining orphan children, or feeding homeless people in cases of emergency, are usually acceptable in print. Such acts often bring more credit to a restaurant than a simple cash donation.

In hotel restaurants, the opportunity for publicity is almost unlimited. Restaurants in large hotels make a practice of regularly sending photographs of prominent persons to newspapers and magazines. Extensive publicity coverage is also given to social and charitable private functions, as well as to certain group meetings, conferences, and conventions. A great deal of publicity is also given to prominent dance orchestras and outstanding entertainers. In fact, it is important that such publicity appear regularly in order to make the restaurant operation successful. However, it must be kept in mind that every effort should be made to have the name of the restaurant and the hotel prominently mentioned in the releases.

In large hotels, publicity is usually handled by a publicity director who may have several assistants. In small establishments, it may be directed by a free lance publicity writer who has other accounts and devotes only part time to each one. In very small organizations, publicity can be handled by the manager's secretary or someone who has a flair for news. In any case, it is advisable to become well acquainted with the staff of the local newspapers, magazines, and radio stations and cooperate with them in every possible way. This does not necessarily mean constant handouts of food and drinks but full cooperation in helping them to get the news they want quickly and effectively.

Newspaper columnists, who must constantly unearth readable material, are happy to receive items that have genuine reader interest. Planning events that have a definite newsworthy slant has often resulted in obtaining mention for a full paragraph in a columnist's allotted space —and in some truly outstanding instances, a complete column.

THE ADVERTISING MANAGER OR AGENCY

As can be seen from the foregoing, advertising is a complicated business. It is necessary and can bring excellent results. It can also run up the cost of an operation without adequate returns unless the advertiser knows what he is doing.

As has been mentioned, the advertising budget for a large establishment may run as high as four per cent of sales. This gets down to about two per cent for the smaller places. In any event, the amount is too large to be wasted on poorly planned and haphazard advertising. Even in the small hotel or restaurant, one person should be assigned the work of handling the advertising under the supervision of the manager. If no employee in the establishment has the ability or the time, a young man or woman can be hired, part time, to undertake the work.

Almost every town has young people who are interested in advertising and who have taken an advertising course in college. Under the supervision of the manager, their work would adhere to the policies set by him, and he, in turn, might learn a great deal from them. They could prepare the publicity stories and take the advertising details off his hands. He might even be able to engage a young person, part time, who is employed on the local newspaper. Unless the work is definitely assigned to someone, it will be a hit-or-miss affair and money will be wasted, to say nothing of the time and effort.

The Advertising Agency. In all large cities and in most communities, advertising agency services are available. The larger hotels and restaurants can and do employ these services with profit to themselves because the professional counsel and skill have made the advertising much more effective.

The principal compensation of the advertising agency is derived from the commission allowed them by the various media. However, the cost of art work, mechanical production, etc., of advertisements, plus a service fee (usually 15%), is paid to agents for producing advertisements, direct mail, and promotion material.

Even in cases where an advertising agency is used, the management should appoint one person in the organization as a contact between the restaurant and the agency. In smaller places this could be the manager; in larger ones, perhaps his secretary; in very large organizations, an advertising manager should be engaged.

THE IMPORTANCE OF ADVERTISING

The advertising, business promotion, and publicity of hotels and restaurants is a very important job. The day of the legend of the better mouse trap is gone forever. Today, you must keep the public continuously informed of your operation by constant repetition of your name. The cumulative effect of good advertising, business promotion, and publicity will continue as long as it is intelligently and steadily maintained. In both hotel and restaurant operation, there is probably nothing quite so important as building a good reputation and the axiom of successful advertising and business promotion is "Repetition builds Reputation."

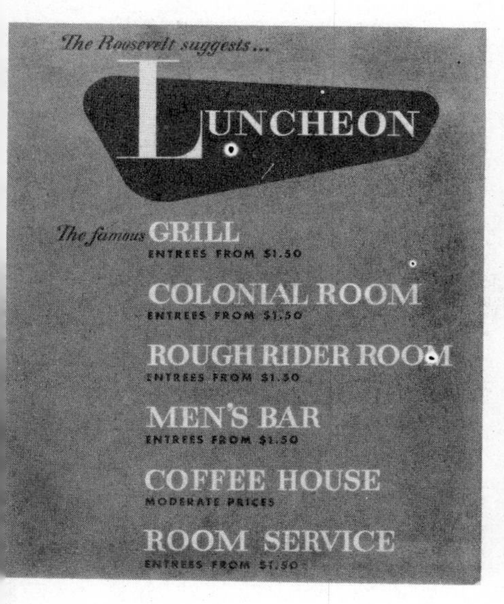

Samples of coordinated advertising and promotion material are shown on the four pages of this insert. On this page there are four examples of cards used in hotel elevators, indicating the various restaurants and including prices for the meal which is being served at the time each card is on display. It is advisable to store one of each of the cards in the frames and merely rotate them at the proper time.

This page illustrates a completely coordinated promotion for a new restaurant. In this display are advertisements, menus, napkins, coasters, match covers, and business cards. This program was reproduced in black and red on a buff colored stock of coarse texture, symbolic of the gas-light era.

e material on this page illustrates a coordinated program for entertainment in otel dining room. It consists of advertisements, lobby posters, elevator cards, cards, direct mail announcements and bill stuffers. Note the logotype and delabra of the Empire Room which is used throughout.

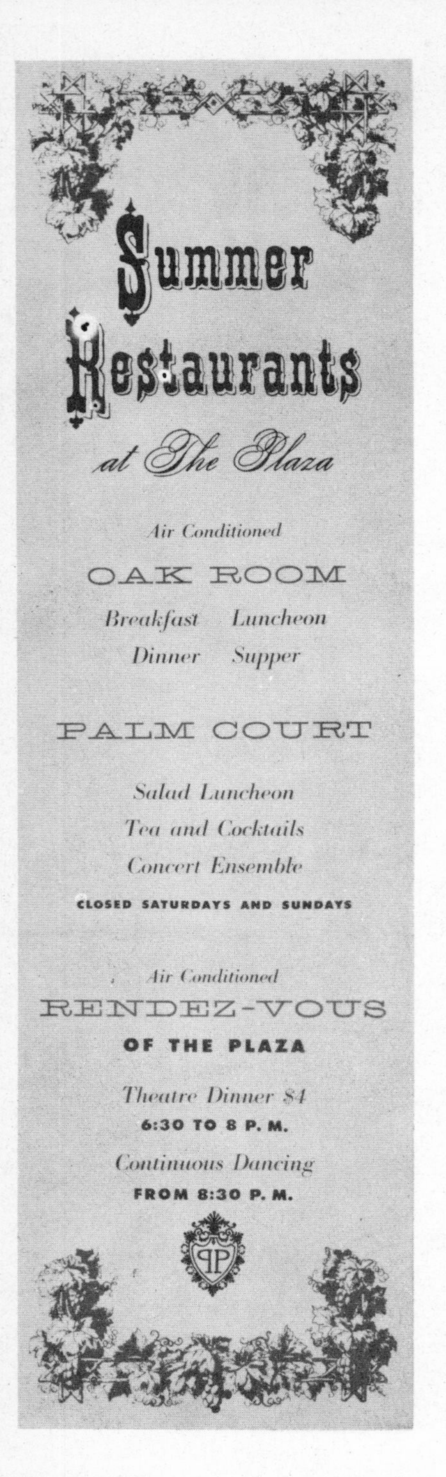

This page illustrates three types of internal promotion displays used at the elevato floor landings in hotels. These cards portray a complete listing of the restauran facilities available to the guest.

Chapter XVII: SANITATION AND HYGIENE

THERE IS AT LEAST one encouraging thing to be said about an unsanitary restaurant—the condition can be cured. It takes constant vigilance to bring about the cure, from the time the food is received at the back door until it is served to the guest. But good sanitation depends solely on the personnel in the restaurant. It cannot be destroyed by a strike of railroad workers or truckers, by snow drifts, shortages or high prices, or any other event over which restaurant workers have no control.

Contamination of food occurs almost invariably after the food gets into the establishment. Government inspection, city ordinances, and health departments are very strict about how food is prepared, stored, and the containers in which it is delivered. Even the methods of delivery, the temperature of the carriers, and their dryness or humidity are matters for careful inspection. What remains, therefore, is to keep all of the rooms where food is stored, prepared, or served, all of the equipment used for these purposes, and the employees that work with food, free from contamination. There will then be no worries about food poisoning. Not an easy job, but a possible one, with care and training.

HEALTH AND HYGIENE OF EMPLOYEES

The health, work habits, and personal hygiene of employees are a major source of food poisoning and unsanitary conditions in public eating establishments. This is not necessarily the fault of the employees. They may never have been taught proper sanitary habits, or the establishment may not provide adequate facilities that permit sanitary conditions.

Health. Most of the larger cities and many smaller ones have made great strides in raising the health requirements for food handlers. Whether or not it is a legal requirement, the management of all food service establishments should, for its own protection, insist upon medical certificates issued by approved physicians. Such certificates should be a requirement of every cook, waiter, waitress, bus boy, dishwasher, or any handler of food in the storeroom, kitchen, or dining room.

These certificates should show that the employee is free from tuberculosis, venereal diseases, skin disease, amoebic dysentery, bacillary dysentery, and typhoid; that he is not a carrier and that he has no transmissible disease. Medical examinations should be given to all food handlers once each year, more often if the Health Department so decrees. If, at any time, it is discovered that an employee has a transmissible disease, he must be dismissed immediately with specific recommendations for treatment.

Temporary ailments, such as a cold, are easily communicated to guests and co-workers. The establishment of a sick leave or sick benefit policy will serve to keep such illness in check. The maintenance of first aid equipment is necessary. Cuts, scratches, and burns occur frequently. A cook's infected finger can cause dysentery among many guests.

Personal Hygiene. Personal cleanliness among workers is possible only when the facilities that make it possible are available. Every restaurant should be provided with adequate and convenient toilet facilities. These toilet rooms must not open directly into any room in which food, drink or utensils are handled or stored. The doors of all such rooms must be self-closing. The floors and walls should be of some light-colored, easily-cleaned material. The room should be well ventilated and used by employees only. Under no circumstances should they be shared by restaurant patrons.

A wash room, either combined with the toilet room or convenient to it, should be provided with soap, preferably in a dispenser, and running water. Individual paper towels for single use and a receptacle for their disposal should be provided. A notice, conspicuously posted, should be in the toilet room or washroom, directing all employees to wash their hands before leaving the room and immediately before beginning work. The use of a common towel should be prohibited.

Toilets, wash rooms, and locker rooms should receive a thorough cleaning with a disinfectant type of solution at least once daily. It is essential that these rooms be kept clean, sanitary at all times, and must also be well-lighted. Light shows up the dirty corners.

Employees ought to have individual lockers and be responsible for their sanitary condition. Under no circumstances should they be permitted to have food in their lockers at any time. If this happens, employees should be penalized. Food attracts rats, mice, and vermin.

These rooms should be inspected daily by a supervisory employee. A definitely specified employee must be responsible for locker-room upkeep.

In a hotel this might be a maid or houseman. In a restaurant it should not be a food handler, dishwasher, or other kitchen employee.

There should be at least one toilet, one urinal, and one wash-stand for each 15 men employed; one toilet and one wash stand for each 10 women.

Each group of rooms in which food is stored, prepared or served, or where utensils are washed, should have a supply of pure drinking water for employees. If any impure water is piped through the building, the pipes should be marked with a distinctive color. In each room concerned with food there should be a wash sink with running water, a soap dispenser, and individual paper towels with a receptacle for their disposal. This is one of the best ways to encourage kitchen employees to wash their hands frequently.

The outer garments of all persons handling food or utensils, including dishwashers, should be clean and made of a washable fabric. The supply of uniforms should be sufficient for daily changes, or more often if food or drink is spilled on uniforms or aprons. Hair bands, hair nets or caps are recommended for all kitchen employees and service staff. Hands and finger nails must be clean at all times. Employees must never run their hands over their faces or through their hair while on duty. Kitchen towels should never be used by employees to wipe sweat off their faces or blow their noses. Sneezes should be caught in a handkerchief or tissue and directed away from food.

Containers or utensils should never be handled by the surface which comes in contact with food or drink. There should be no evidence of spitting or the use of any form of tobacco by employees in rooms in which food is prepared.

All of these rules can be enforced by strict surveillance but the task will be easier if the employees understand the dangers of food contamination. They must be made to realize how great the risk is if the slightest bit of contamination is under the nails, on the face, or any part of the body or clothing. Possibly, periodic talks by a doctor attached to the Health Department may prove convincing and prevent any back-sliding.

SANITATION IN FOOD STORAGE AND PREPARATION

In addition to careless personal habits of employees, improper care of food and utensils are major sources of contamination. The chapters on receiving and storage give complete details on handling, storage, and temperature information.

The following contaminated items should be detected in the receiving room and discarded immediately: swollen cans; insect-infected flour, corn meal, raisins, nuts, and cereals; meat or fish that is mouldy or slimy; green-struck poultry; over-age milk; rancid butter; shellfish that is not tagged; decaying or spoiled vegetables and fruits.

Covered storage boxes should be employed for ice used in fountain drinks, iced water, tea, and coffee, or in connection with the chilling or serving of salads, vegetables, seafood, or cocktails. These storage compartments ought to be located away from sources of contamination, maintained in good repair and kept clean. Ice grinders, pans, and buckets used in preparing chipped or crushed ice should be thoroughly cleaned after each using. Fountain ice compartments, bowls, buckets or other containers should be washed frequently and kept free of scum or rust and protected from drip, dust, cleaning operations, and other sources of pollution. Ice should always come from a source approved by the Health Department and be received only when it is handled and transported in a sanitary manner.

Only pasteurized milk should be used. When served to the patron, it should be in the original container or from a dispenser approved by the local Health Department. The same is true of cream. These containers are all for single service. No milk should be served that is older than 48 hours.

The pouring lips of bottles containing milk or other beverages in non-leak-proof containers should not be submerged in water for cooling.

The following temperatures for refrigerated foods should be closely observed:

Frozen foods	Zero or under
Seafood	30-34 degrees
Meats	32-36 degrees or under
Dairy Products	32-36 degrees
Fruits and vegetables	32-36 degrees
Others	40-50 degrees
Ice Cream	Held at 8 degrees

If several boxes are not available to provide varied temperatures, as indicated, the lowest temperature should prevail in the one box used.

Shellfish spoil the most readily of any food. Next come milk, cream, and egg products followed by meats of which chicken, veal, and pork are the first to deteriorate.

Sugar should be served only in covered containers or in wrapped packages for individual service. If granulated sugar is not wrapped, it should be in the type of container that will not admit a spoon.

Care of Food Prior to Cooking. Fresh fruits and vegetables must be washed before using, even though they are to be cooked. They might be infected by chemical sprays or by handling although in appearance, smell, and taste, they seem perfect.

Ground or diced meat should never be kept in the refrigerator longer than 24 hours before using. Meat in small pieces spoils much more rapidly than large pieces. Variety meats such as liver, brains, and sweetbreads, should be used as soon as possible after purchase. Spoilage may be somewhat delayed by parboiling upon arrival, followed immediately by refrigerated storage.

Among the foods that contain the most active poisoning agents, if improperly handled, are custards, cream-filled pastries and puddings, chicken and seafood salad, particularly those containing mayonnaise or Russian dressing, sardines and anchovies.

Care of Food During Cooking. Contrary to popular opinion, many types of bacteria prove impervious to brief cooking. Home-canned green vegetables are an example of this. They should be cooked for a minimum of 20 minutes to rid them of the sturdiest germs. Commercially canned goods are subjected to sterilization before canning and do not require the same safety margin of 20 minutes cooking time.

Some meats may be safely cooked and served rare since bacteria formed on the outside will be killed by heat. Pork is an outstanding exception. In all pork products, trichina bacteria are apt to be present and pork should be cooked until no trace of pink color remains.

Fats used for frying are frequently carelessly handled. If fat is three or four days old, it becomes dangerously rancid, and if used for cooking it will ruin the food. To prevent the use of rancid fat, a pan of clean fat should be placed on the cook's table each morning, emptied after each day's use and the pan washed thoroughly.

Hollandaise sauce should be freshly prepared and kept no longer than two hours.

Care of Food After Cooking. Food that has been cooked requires careful storing. Hot food, after removal from the steam table, should be reduced to room temperature and placed in the refrigerator. Unless it is allowed to cool first, it will raise the temperature of the refrigerator so high that the other food will deteriorate. Once the food is cool, however, it should be refrigerated, as it will spoil if allowed to remain at room temperature for four or five hours. This happens frequently because steam table attendants vacate the working area as soon as the meal service is completed, to work in another part of the kitchen. The food left to cool is forgotten. Some employee should be assigned the specific task of placing the cooled food in the refrigerator at a pre-arranged time.

Foods that are cooling should be placed in shallow pans about five or six inches deep. In the refrigerator, food should be left partly uncovered to allow steam to escape. The only exception is soup stock which should be completely covered.

Frequently, food is kept on the steam table for excessive lengths of time. Tests have proven that many foods will spoil within two or three hours if temperatures drop below 125 degrees. Foods should be cooked in small batches to prevent their being left too long on the steam table. No hot food should be left at temperatures between 70 and 170 degrees longer than four hours.

Hash spoils very easily. It should be served when originally heated and any remainder discarded. Re-heated hash can be extremely dangerous.

Custard filling for pastry should be chilled rapidly after preparation. All custard-filled and cream-filled pastries must be re-baked, after filling, at an oven temperature of at least 425 degrees for 20 minutes, then cooled to 50 degrees or less within one hour after re-baking. Or, the filling must be heated before the pastry shells are filled so that every particle of the mix is held at a temperature of at least 190 degrees for 10 minutes, then cooled to 50 degrees, either before or after filling the pastry shells. This cooling to 50 degrees or less must be done within one hour after heating. Custard food must be served within 24 hours after cooking. Every effort should be made to use it the same day. It can, and has, caused fatal poisoning.

All foods and drinks must be stored, displayed or served in a manner that is protected from dust, flies, vermin, contamination and pollution by rodents, unnecessary handling, droplet infection and overhead leakage.

When left-over foods are re-heated, the temperature must be brought up quickly and maintained at a high level for five minutes. The food is then transferred to the steam table. Oven heat may be used for foods likely to scorch on top of the range.

No cooked food should be used if it has remained in the refrigerator longer than 48 hours.

SANITATION AND EQUIPMENT

Following are some of the necessary points about the most important items of kitchen equipment as regards sanitation:

Work Tables

(1) Hard, smooth surface; no seams in body, corners, or edges.
(2) Shelves below, at least 12 inches above the floor.
(3) No closed dish-warming cabinets below work tables.
(4) All tables and shelves free of cracks, where food might lodge or roaches hide.
(5) Wooden table-tops must be doweled together to form tight joints.
(6) All tables, cabinets, and sinks should have metal supports.

Sinks

(1) Must be of a hard material (preferably stainless steel) that will not chip or crack.
(2) The overflow should be four inches below the drainboard to allow for displacement of large pots.
(3) Grease traps in the floor for all sinks.
(4) Two-compartment pot-washing sinks—for washing and rinsing. Three-compartment sinks are preferable to permit a primary rinse and a final rinse.
(5) Separate mop sink. *This is imperative.*

Utensils

(1) Pots, pans, small cooking utensils, after washing and rinsing, should be placed in an inverted position on slatted shelves at least 12 inches above the floor.
(2) Grinders, cutters, slicers, mixers and beaters must be cleaned at the end of each day's work.
(3) Ice cream scoops should remain in clear running water or in water of 170 degrees during periods of service.
(4) Kitchen knives, forks, ladles, and beaters must be kept clean and free of corrosion.

Ranges

(1) Stoves, griddles, broilers, and fryers must be free of grease and soot and properly hooded and vented to the open air.

(2) Spreader plates should be placed between ranges or deep fat fryers, when they are assembled in a line. This arrangement eliminates an unsanitary crevice.

(3) Ranges and ovens should be set 12 inches out from the wall to permit easier cleaning.

Cadmium, Lead and Copper

(1) No utensils containing or plated with cadmium or lead should be used. (Solder containing lead may be used for jointing.) If copper utensils are used, they should be lined with tin or stainless steel.

GENERAL KITCHEN MAINTENANCE

Floors

(1) Mopped at least once daily with clear water and disinfectant; more often if it seems necessary.

(2) No rough places or cracks or crevices should be allowed to remain in the floors.

(3) No spaces allowed around pipes or cables.

(4) Grease traps should be provided for all floor drains.

(5) No dry-sweeping of floors to be permitted in the kitchen or dining room.

Walls and Ceilings

(1) Walls should be painted white and be free of cracks or crevices.

(2) Walls should be of an easily washable surface up to 5 or 6 feet.

(3) The ceiling should be painted in a suitable color so as to reflect light.

(4) When walls and ceilings are washed, all utensils and food should be covered or removed.

DISHWASHING

This is one of the most important jobs in the kitchen and also one of the greatest sources of contamination, if carelessly done. Hand dishwashing has no place in a modern kitchen. Any standard dishwashing machine will do a good job providing adequate rinsing facilities, a good detergent, and thermostatic controls in good working order are available.

In dishwashing machines, wash-water temperatures should range between 130 and 140 degrees. The dishes should remain in the wash tank for two minutes with water at 140 degrees and in rinse water at 170 degrees for 60 seconds.

Care should be taken in loading the racks of the dish machines. They must not be overloaded and containers must be placed in such a position that water will reach all parts of them. Silverware racks should not be overloaded or the silver in the center will never be reached by the cleaning processes. Dish machines that are not automatic, but that permit the operators to push the rack through manually, are fast becoming outmoded. Operators sometimes hurry this work and do not permit the proper time required for the rinse.

Dishwashing machines must be kept clean or their purpose is defeated. Nozzles, if not regularly cleaned, often become clogged with food. When hard water is used, lime deposits can easily reduce nozzle efficiency. Periodic inspection and cleaning of wash and rinse sprays are essential for continued satisfactory operation. These parts of the machine must be easily accessible for inspection and cleaning.

The wash-tank water should be changed during operation as often as is found necessary to keep it clean. An effective concentration of detergent should be maintained during the washing operation. Adequate hot water can always be supplied by booster heaters.

No article, polish, or other substance containing any cyanide preparation or other poisonous material should be used for the cleaning or polishing of utensils.

Equipment that is too large to immerse may be treated: (1) with live steam from a hose, in the case of equipment in which steam can be confined; or (2) by a boiling water rinse; or (3) by a spraying or swabbing with a chlorine solution of approved strength.

HANDLING AND STORAGE

All containers and utensils should be stored 12 inches or more above the floor in a clean, dry place protected from flies, splash, dust, overhead leakage, and condensation. Wherever practical, containers and utensils should be covered or inverted. Fingers should not touch the bowls of spoons, the tines of forks, the blades of knives, or the inside surfaces of glasses, cups, and dishes.

Paper cups, plates, straws, spoons, forks, and other single-service containers and utensils should be purchased in sanitary cartons and stored in a clean, dry place until used.

Satisfactory pot washing requires a three-section sink, the first section for hot, soapy water, the second for a primary rinse and the third for a clear water rinse with the temperature at 180 degrees.

DISPOSAL OF WASTE

All liquid wastes from cleaning and rinsing utensils and floors, and from flush toilets and lavatories, should be disposed of in a public sewer or by a method approved by the Board of Health. The plumbing should be so installed as to prevent contamination of the water supply.

Garbage should be kept in tight, non-absorbent, and easily washable receptacles which are covered with close-fitting lids while awaiting removal. The cans must be scalded and washed daily and treated with a disinfectant. The garbage storage area should have a cement floor which is easily flushed out with water each day at the time the cans are washed. If the garbage area is enclosed, it should be well ventilated and lighted.

If possible, garbage should be kept in a refrigerated room until it is removed from the premises. This is the cleanest and most efficient way of handling it.

On pages 264 to 268 is a check list for the method and detergent to be used in cleaning the principal pieces of equipment in the restaurant kitchen.

FLIES, VERMIN, AND RODENTS

These pests are guilty of contributing heavily to food contamination. For this reason, the fact has been stressed that no open cracks or crevices should be allowed to remain in any kitchen or storeroom surfaces, either in work tables, shelves, sinks, floors, walls, or ceilings. Also, there should be no spaces around pipes or cables. These are the favorite haunts and means of entrance of such pests. When a problem becomes serious, professional exterminators should be engaged. Kitchen employees are amateurs and should not be entrusted with the job. They can easily do more harm than good.

IMPURE WATER

Periodic laboratory tests are the surest way of tracing contaminated water. If impurities are revealed, further checks of the water at the point of entry into the building will indicate whether the plumbing within the building is spreading contamination. If the water is impure before entering the building, it is a community problem and should be brought to the attention of the authorities immediately.

STANDARDS OF SANITATION

It can be seen that constant vigilance is necessary to maintain perfectly sanitary conditions. This extends to every worker in the kitchen and dining room. This does not mean that every employee must run about with a microscope like a Sherlock Holmes, spying out dirt and filth. It is just a matter of good training, with each worker knowing his or her job and doing it thoroughly.

A written manual of instructions for each worker or each station is the best way to insure the carrying out of such instructions. Verbal orders are forgotten or misinterpreted when they are passed from one worker to another. Also, they require a "watch-dog" type of supervision.

Instruction Manuals. Written or printed instructions should be available to each employee whose job includes any type of cleaning, detailing each step of the operation and how frequently it should be done. There should be instructions for the cleaning of each piece of kitchen equipment—of the "What-to-do" and "How-to-do-it" type, with distinction made between daily and periodic cleaning.

These same instruction charts should be available for mopping floors, cleaning walls and windows, handling garbage and sterilizing the cans.

Once these charts are established, the whole matter of sanitation becomes greatly simplified. They are not a substitute for supervision but the supervisor will find his job much less worrisome.

Time for Cleaning. During the working day, any major cleaning job will interfere with other workers. After-hours cleaning, on the other hand, does not have the advantage of close supervision. However, if the work is planned and written instructions are available, the head night cleaner and his crew will be able to accomplish more. If arrangements can be made for one supervisory employee to come on duty in the early morning before the night cleaning crew leaves, he or she can easily determine whether the job has been done properly.

Each instruction chart should contain the approximate length of time required for each job. Man hours cost money—the same as a case of eggs or any other commodity. Therefore, it is important to know the cost of a cleaning operation.

Top-Management Supervision. Once each week, the manager or his representative should make an inspection of the sanitary condition of the kitchen. There is no substitute for this high-level supervision. It indicates to the lowliest worker that his tasks do not go unnoticed. It is bound to result in higher standards of work.

Sanitation Check Lists. As an aid in making inspections, the check lists on pages 258 to 264 will insure complete coverage of every detail. After each inspection is made, the list should be dated and initialed. Dating the list enables the person who next inspects the same locations to see what changes have been made since the date of the last inspection. Initialing the list fixes responsibility.

THE FALSE ECONOMY OF FILTH

It should not be necessary to comment upon the value of a clean kitchen and dining room. Unfortunately, however, many managers look askance at the man-hours consumed in cleaning since the costs appear on the financial statement. Some managers are tempted to consider only how much better that statement might look if the money devoted to cleaning should be sliced by 50 per cent or more. The reason they give is that the patrons never see the kitchen and will never know of its unsanitary condition.

Such reasoning will make sadder but wiser men of these managers when they find, a few weeks later, that their business has melted away. There are scores of ways that a dirty kitchen manifests itself to patrons even though they never pass the kitchen door.

Dirty Dishes, Glasses, and Silver. If standards of cleanliness are lowered in the kitchen, every employee gets careless. Dishes are not washed clean. Thermostatic controls are not watched and, consequently, food is baked on the plates, pieces of egg remain on the forks, and lipstick on the drinking glasses.

Unclean Food. It is impossible to serve clean food of good flavor from a dirty kitchen. The very odor of the kitchen will affect the food. Rancid grease and decaying food particles left in the cracks and crevices of work tables will raise a disgusting stench. This might eventually reach the dining room and even travel to the outside air to repel any passersby who might be inclined to enter.

Careless Service Staff. The waiters, waitresses, and bus boys cannot be expected to go in and out of a dirty kitchen and not get into careless habits. Table cloths will not be changed when they become soiled. Service will become sloppy and inefficient. Dirty uniforms will go unnoticed—except by the patrons. No self-respecting waiter or waitress will remain in such a place. Their places will be filled by workers with lower standards if, by this time, there is enough business remaining to warrant filling the vacancies.

Vermin. Roaches and flies are quick to find such a "happy hunting ground." They swarm in and take over. The kitchen door means nothing to them and in no time roaches will be crawling up the dining room walls and flies buzzing about and settling on the food.

Food Poisoning. It is only luck if severe and even fatal cases of ptomaine poisoning do not result from a dirty kitchen. Stomach disorders are bound to be frequent among patrons and they will never return to a place where a meal resulted in illness. A serious case of food poisoning may cause the death of one or more persons, which could result in the closing of an establishment.

Labor Turnover. Just as in the case of the service staff, competent kitchen workers who take pride in their jobs, will not remain in a dirty kitchen. The standard of work of kitchen employees is noticeably higher in a clean kitchen. Good employees know their work suffers since they cannot possibly turn out good food—so they quit. High labor turnover is a hidden cost but it eventually shows up in many increased costs in the financial statement.

If there are not sufficient cleaning men employed, cooks will, for a time, do some of the cleaning tasks, but the scale of cooks' wages at straight or overtime rates is rather extravagant for doing the work of kitchen cleaners.

Before eyeing with a calculating look the money spent to maintain a sanitary kitchen, a manager should think about the cost of empty seats in his dining room, to say nothing of the cost of possible damage suits. Civil damage suits by patrons indicate that the courts are placing the burden of proof for kitchen conditions squarely on the shoulders of the management of hotels and restaurants.

A clean kitchen brings its rewards in increased business. People like clean food and news of a clean restaurant travels fast. One owner of a moderate-priced counter restaurant located in a highly competitive neighborhood paid his head dishwasher as much as his short-order cook. His explanation was simple. "Customers," he says, "notice dirty tableware much more quickly than hasty preparation methods." This is a definite current trend, and it behooves all operators to give careful and constant attention to this all-important problem. Positive action in this regard may be the factor that will counteract any wholesale drastic move by local health departments toward rigid inspection standards and eventual grading and classification as is now found in some states and cities.

SANITATION CHECK LIST

PERISHABLE FOODS

	Yes	No
PERISHABLE FOODS—are they refrigerated between processing or arrival, and time of service?	____	____
PERISHABLE FOODS—are they inspected daily for spoilage?	____	____
CUSTARD PRODUCTS—are they chilled after preparation and kept properly refrigerated?	____	____
HOLLANDAISE SAUCE—is it prepared fresh for each meal and discarded two hours after preparation?	____	____
PORK and PORK PRODUCTS—are they thorough cooked until there is no trace of pink color?	____	____
MILK—is it dispensed from either single service containers or from an approved dispenser	____	____
MILK—is that on hand within the 48-hour age limit?	____	____
MILK AND CREAM CAN TAGS—are they filed for 60 days?	____	____
SHELLFISH—it is received from approved sources?	____	____
SHELLFISH TAGS—are they filed for 60 days?	____	____
UNWRAPPED CAKES, PIES, and BREADSTUFFS—are they kept in a clean show case or covered tray, protected from dust, flies, and handling?	____	____

CHEMICALS

	Yes	No
SILVER POLISHES or DIPS—are those containing cyanide forbidden?	____	____
BLUE or GREEN FLUORIDE—is this the only poisonous insecticide used?	____	____
BLUE or GREEN FLUORIDE or FLUORIDE MIXTURE—is this applied carefully to prevent contamination of food and utensils?	____	____

GENERAL EQUIPMENT

	Yes	No
METAL SLICERS, MIXERS, GRINDERS, FRUIT JUICERS, PEELERS, CREAM URNS, COFFEE URNS, PUMPS, and FILLERS—are they taken apart, washed, and cleaned daily?	____	____
CAN OPENERS—are they clean?	____	____
BINS, SHELVING, and CONTAINERS—are they cleaned before being re-filled?	____	____
KITCHEN KNIVES, FORKS, LADLES, and HEATERS—are they clean and free of corrosion?	____	____
STOVES, GRIDDLES, BROILERS, and FRYERS—are they free of grease and soot?	____	____

	Yes	No
HOODS AND VENTS—are those for stoves and ranges properly arranged?	____	____
FANS, HOODS, AND DUCTS—are they clean and in good repair?	____	____
STEAM TABLES—are they clean and in good repair?	____	____
PROPER TEMPERATURES—are these maintained in the steam tables?	____	____
SPACES—are those between fixtures or counters, behind slicers, tables or shelving, under fixtures and cutting boards, clean and free of food particles or scraps?	____	____
UNUSED EQUIPMENT—it is kept clean?	____	____
BROOMS, MOPS, BRUSHES, PAILS, SOAPS, and DETERGENTS—are these in sufficient supply and properly stored?	____	____
WORK TABLE TOPS—are these smooth and free of cracks?	____	____
FIXED EQUIPMENT—is it so installed as to permit cleaning of the surrounding area?	____	____
KITCHEN EQUIPMENT—is it in good repair and free of rust, corrosion, or defects?	____	____
BAKE OVEN—are the top, front, and shelves clean?	____	____
POT SINK—is it clean?	____	____
VEGETABLE SINK—is it clean?	____	____
JANITOR'S SINK—is it clean?	____	____

WAREWASHING

	Yes	No
DISHWASHING MACHINE—is it clean, free of corrosion, and in good repair?	____	____
THERMOMETERS—are they available on wash and rinse lines?	____	____
TABLEWARE—is it thoroughly washed and rinsed after each use?	____	____
TABLEWARE—is it washed with detergent or compound, rinsed, and then sterilized in water at 170 degrees?	____	____
TABLEWARE—is it air dried and use of towels prohibited?	____	____
CLEAN TABLEWARE—is it properly stored to protect it from dust, dirt, insects, and rodents?	____	____
CHIPPED OR CRACKED TABLEWARE—is it discarded?	____	____
TABLEWARE—is it available in sufficient supply for peak periods?	____	____
RUNNING HOT WATER—is it available in sufficient supply for peak periods?	____	____

	Yes	No
BOOSTER HEATER—is one available to raise temperature of water to 170 degrees or over?	____	____
WAREWASHING BASKETS or RACKS—are they available in sufficient supply to prevent over-loading during peak periods?	____	____
TABLEWARE SURFACES—are they adequately sprayed under pressure during washing?	____	____
TABLEWARE—is it exposed for sufficient time in washing and sterilizing processes?	____	____
SPRAY OPENINGS—are they free of clogging?	____	____
TABLEWARE—is it properly racked when washed sterilized?	____	____
WASHWATER—is it changed frequently?	____	____
DETERGENT or WASHING COMPOUNDS—are they added frequently?	____	____
AUTOMATIC FEEDER—is it in good repair?	____	____
SCRAP TRAYS or STRAINERS—are they cleaned frequently?	____	____
AIR CIRCULATION—is it sufficient for quick drying?	____	____
SPRAY OPENINGS—are they washed and rinsed clean?	____	____
DISH MACHINE PIPES—are they clear?	____	____

WALLS, FLOORS, AND CEILING

	Yes	No
WALLS—are they clean?	____	____
FLOOR—is it clean?	____	____
WALLS, FLOORS, and CEILINGS—are they free of holes, cracks, and crevices?	____	____
WALLS and CEILINGS—are they free of scaling, peeling, and chipping?	____	____
WALLS, FLOORS, and CEILINGS—are they free of spaces around pipes, cables, and doors?	____	____
FLOOR DRAINS—are they in good working order?	____	____

LIGHTING AND VENTILATION

	Yes	No
LIGHTING FIXTURES—are they in good repair?	____	____
BULBS and GLOBES—are they free of grease, grime, and dust?	____	____
GLASS FIXTURES—are those over exposed food protected from breakage?	____	____
LIGHTING—is it adequate throughout the kitchen and storage areas?	____	____
SKYLIGHTS—are they clean and in good repair?	____	____
SKYLIGHTS—are they protected against rodent invasion?	____	____

	Yes	No
VENTILATION IN WINTER—is it satisfactory?	____	____
WINDOWS—are they clean?	____	____

CLEANING

DRY-SWEEPING OF FLOORS—is this forbidden?	____	____
PLANNED CLEANING SCHEDULE—is this in daily use?	____	____
RODENTS—have they been eliminated?	____	____
FLIES—have they been eliminated?	____	____
VERMIN—have they been eliminated?	____	____

GARBAGE

GARBAGE—is it kept in metal receptables only?	____	____
GARBAGE CAN COVERS—are they tight-fitting?	____	____
GARBAGE CANS—are they emptied and cleaned daily?	____	____
GARBAGE CANS—are they scalded when cleaned?	____	____
GARBAGE CANS—are they free from leaks or breaks?	____	____
GARBAGE CANS—are they stored away from foods?	____	____
GARBAGE CANS—are they available in sufficient supply?	____	____
GARBAGE STATION—is it clean?	____	____
GARBAGE STATION—is it free of flies?	____	____
GARBAGE STATION—is it ratproof?	____	____
GARBAGE STATION—is it free of odor?	____	____

CELLAR

CELLAR—is it free of rubbish, ashes, and useless material?	____	____
STORED MATERIALS—are they arranged in an orderly manner?	____	____
STORED MATERIALS—are they moved away from walls and off the floor?	____	____
GRATINGS, LOUVERS, WINDOWS, DOORS, DUCTS, and OPENINGS TO OUTSIDE—are they ratproof?	____	____
SEWER TRAP and CLEAN-OUT PIT COVERS—are they tight and in place?	____	____

REAR YARD

REAR YARD—is it free of refuse, debris, loose garbage, and stagnant water?	____	____
PREPARATION and STORAGE OF FOODS—is the rear yard, alleyway, or public space forbidden for this purpose?	____	____

REFRIGERATION

	Yes	No
REFRIGERATOR FLOORS—are they clean?	____	____
REFRIGERATOR SHELVES—are they clean?	____	____
LEFT-OVER FOOD CONTAINERS—are they covered?	____	____
MEAT HOOKS—are they clean?	____	____
SIDES OF REFRIGERATORS—are they clean?	____	____
REFRIGERATORS—are they free of odor?	____	____
REFRIGERATOR TEMPERATURES—are they properly maintained below 50 degrees?	____	____

LOCKER ROOMS

LOCKER ROOMS—are they clean?	____	____
LOCKER ROOMS—are they properly lighted and ventilated?	____	____
LOCKER ROOMS—are they adequately supplied with receptacles for refuse?	____	____
LOCKER ROOMS—are they free of soiled uniforms and clothing?	____	____
LOCKERS—are they clean and in good repair?	____	____
LOCKERS—are they ratproof?	____	____
LOCKERS—are they inspected daily for food?	____	____
LOCKERS—are they free of any stored materials on top or underneath?	____	____
LOCKERS—are they supplied in adequate number?	____	____
LOCKER ROOMS—are they completely separated from food storage or preparation rooms?	____	____

WASHROOMS

WASHROOMS—are they properly lighted?		
WASHROOM WINDOWS—are they in good repair?	____	____
WASHROOM FAN OR DUCT—is it in good working order and unobstructed?	____	____
TOILET SEATS—are they clean?	____	____
BOWLS and URINALS—are they clean and in good working order?	____	____
BOWLS and TOILET SEATS—are they tight and secure at the base?	____	____
WASHROOM DOORS—are they self-closing?	____	____
WASH BASINS—are they adequately supplied with hot and cold running water?	____	____
SOAP, TOWELS, and TISSUE—are they in adequate supply?	____	____

	Yes	No
SOAP, TOWELS, and TISSUE—are they maintained in reserve supply immediately at hand to prevent shortage?	____	____
SIGN—is one posted indicating that hands must be washed before leaving the washroom?	____	____

STOREROOM

BINS, SHELVES, and CONTAINERS—are they clean?	____	____
PIPES—are they inspected to detect drip?	____	____
FLOOR RACKS or PLATFORMS—are they removable and at least 10 inches above the floor?	____	____
STOREROOMS—are they free of rodents and insects?	____	____
FOODSTUFFS—are they stored in an orderly manner?	____	____
FOODSTUFFS—are they stored on racks above the floor?	____	____
FOODSTUFFS—are they free from rodents and insect infestation?	____	____
FOODSTUFFS—are they free from spoilage or other contamination?	____	____
FOODSTUFFS—are they kept away from pipes?	____	____
LOOSE AND UNWRAPPED FOODS—are they stored in ratproof and insect-proof containers?	____	____
FOODS—are they inspected at least once a week for spoilage or other contamination?	____	____
CONTAMINATED FOODS—are they denatured and marked "Condemned"?	____	____
CONTAMINATED FOODS—are they promptly removed after being marked "Condemned"?	____	____
STOREROOM FLOOR—is it clean and dry?	____	____
UNIFORMS—are they stacked neatly?	____	____
INSPECTION—is this made to check rat runways and to eliminate rat harborages?	____	____
SOILED CLOTHES and UNIFORMS—are these kept in a hamper?	____	____
STOREROOM TEMPERATURES—are they satisfactory?	____	____
STOREROOM—is it free from mustiness and odor?	____	____
STOREROOM—is it well ventilated?	____	____

DINING ROOM

TABLES—are they clean?	____	____
WINDOWS—are they clean?	____	____
PASTRY DISH TRAYS—are they covered?	____	____

	Yes	No
FLOORS—are they clean?	____	____
SILVERWARE HOLDERS—are they clean?	____	____
SIDE TABLES—are they clean?	____	____

COUNTER SERVICE

COUNTER TOPS—are they clean?	____	____
BREAKFAST MENUS—are they clean?	____	____
GLASS SHELVES—are they clean?	____	____
FLOOR BEHIND COUNTER—is it clean and dry?	____	____
COUNTER REFRIGERATOR—is it clean?	____	____
HOT TABLE OPENINGS—are they clean?	____	____
HOT TABLE PANS—are they clean?	____	____

METHODS OF CLEANING

Equipment	Method of Cleaning	Cleaning Compound
Range	1. Remove all burnt sediment and wipe grease from top of range after each using.	
	2. Scrape grease from cracks and openings.	
	3. When cool, wash top of range. Dry well.	Hot water. Mild soap. Fine abrasive powder. Water containing washing soda.
	4. Run oiled cloth over top of range.	
	5. Clean oven by removing grates, scraping off food deposits, washing and drying.	
	6. Keep burners clean. If removable, soak, boil, scrub with stiff brush, rinse and dry.	
	7. Before replacing burners, rub with oiled cloth.	Kerosene.
Bake Oven	1. When cool clean outside. 2. Clean steel shelves. 3. Wipe heat control with damp cloth. Do not loosen dials. 4. Clean thermometers.	For outside, light oil or damp cloth. For shelves: an abrasive and dry cloth mop. For thermometers: soft brush and fine abrasive powder.
Broiler	1. Remove grid and drain pans. Clean, wash, rinse thoroughly, and dry after each use.	Hot water, mild soap and steel wool or abrasive powder.

Equipment	Method of Cleaning	Cleaning Compound
	2. Wash outside, rinse, and dry. 3. Wipe with oiled cloth. 4. Clean grease pan. Wash and dry.	
Coffee Urn	1. Drain after each meal. 2. Rinse thoroughly. 3. Wash bag, if used, in cold water after each use. 4. Clean gauges and faucets daily. 5. Wipe outside surfaces. 6. Clean urn bottom frequently.	Clear, hot water. If discolored inside, use fine abrasive powder or baking soda.
Fryer, Deep Fat	1. Drain off fat and strain off sediment. 2. Fill with water and detergent and boil. Drain. 3. Fill with water and one cup of vinegar and boil. 4. Rinse. Dry. Wipe off outside of fryer.	Detergent: Vinegar. For outside: grease solvent or mild soap.
Steamer	1. Remove racks or shelves and clean drains. 2. Wash inside of cooker daily. 3. Wash outside regularly. 4. Blow out mud leg several times daily during operation. Clean strainer as required.	Water and fine abrasive powder.
Toaster	1. Wipe off all crumbs around toaster after each use. 2. Clean crumb tray after each use.	Soft brush.
	3. Brush operating parts. 4. Wipe outside with damp cloth.	Water.
Waffle Iron	1. Wipe baking surfaces frequently during use. 2. Brush out grids.	Brush recommended by manufacturer.
	3. Place damp cloth between grids over night. 4. Brush grids, re-season by brushing waffle iron with oil, closing and heating for 5 minutes.	Dampen cloth with ammonia.

Equipment	Method of Cleaning	Cleaning Compound
Mixer	1. Use rubber scraper if necessary and wash bowl and beaters immediately after using.	
	2. After mashed potatoes, egg mixtures or flour batters, rinse bowl and whips with cold water before washing with warm water.	Warm water and mild soap.
	3. Dry beaters and bowls thoroughly and hang up.	
	4. Wipe machine, including shaft and cloth.	
Grinder and other attachments	1. Remove disc and nut.	
	2. Remove grinding and cutting part.	
	3. Wash.	Warm water and mild soap or other detergent.
	4. Rinse.	
	5. Dry thoroughly.	
Meat Delicator	1. Remove slide and protector and wash thoroughly after each use.	Hot water and mild soap.
	2. Remove and wash stainless steel blades under running water, using brush to remove all soil between knife-like prongs immediately after using.	
	3. Wash outside of machine after each using.	
	4. Weekly or as required, remove entire casing of machine and brush off parts enclosed.	
* Meat Cuber	1. Clean knife blade thoroughly with tool provided, immediately after use.	
	2. Wash all used surfaces thoroughly with brush.	Hot water and mild soap.
	3. Wash outside of machine.	
Peeler	1. Flush out inside of peeler each time after use.	Water.

* Purchase only machines which have parts easily removed or accessible for thorough cleaning.

Equipment	Method of Cleaning	Cleaning Compound
	2. Remove disc, scrub disc and sides with stiff brush. Rinse base thoroughly.	
	3. Empty and clean the peel trap after each use.	
	4. Wipe outside of machine with damp cloth.	
Slicer	1. Clean immediately after slicing vegetables and fruits.	
	2. Remove all parts to clean.	
	3. Clean knife with damp cloth, dry. Cover with oil.	Tasteless, colorless oil.
	4. Wash carriage slides thoroughly.	Hot water and mild soap.
	5. Wipe outside with cloth.	
	6. Clean table or pedestal under slicer.	
	7. Replace guard after cleaning.	
Dishwashing Machine	1. Remove strainer and trays and wash.	Non-suds detergent suited to water hardness.
	2. Add compound to clean water in empty machine, run for five minutes. Rinse.	
	3. Scrub inside with stiff brush.	
	4. Be sure jets and sprays are removed and cleaned often and are operating at full force.	
	5. Wash outside of machine.	Water and mild soap.
	6. Special periodic cleaning in hard water area.	Recommendation of manufacturer.
Ice Cream Cabinet	1. Place towel in bottom of well.	
	2. Loosen ice by tapping gently with wooden mallet.	
	3. Lift out towel containing broken ice.	
	4. If ice cream has melted into the well, wipe inside with damp cloth.	Cold water and ammonia.
	5. Dry thoroughly.	
Sinks and Drains	1. Keep outlets screened at all times.	
	2. Daily: flush with one gallon of solution.	Boiling, strong solution of sal soda (4 oz. to 2 gals.)

Equipment	Method of Cleaning	Cleaning Compound
	3. Weekly: (or as required) (a) Clean grease traps. (b) Replace all units tightly. 4. Use force pump if drain is slow. 5. Replace washers immediately on leaking faucets. To replace: close the water shut-off valve: loosen the hexagonal nut on the faucet, permitting water in the pipe to drain out; remove interior screw, replace washer; reassemble in same manner.	
Tables	1. Stainless steel: wipe with damp cloth.	Warm water and mild soap.
	Wood top: 1. Scrub with heavy brush. 2. Rinse.	Warm water and mild soap. Clean water.
	Meat Block: 1. Scrape with steel scraper or heavy steel brush. 2. Wipe. Do not use water on top surface.	May use chlorine solution, 100 p.p.m.
	3. Wipe outside of block with damp cloth.	Warm water and mild soap.
Refrigerator—"Reach-In"	1. Wipe up spilled food immediately. 2. Wash inside, shelves and trays at least twice a week. 3. Rinse and dry thoroughly. 4. Flush drains weekly. 5. Put in order daily.	Water and tri-sodium phosphate (½ oz. to 2 gallons of water). Weak solution of baking soda (½ oz. to 2 gallons of water). To flush: boiling strong solution of sal soda (4 oz. to 2 gallons).
"Walk-In"	1. In addition to above, mop floor daily.	
Washroom	1. Clean all washrooms at frequent intervals each day. Current practice is a check for cleaning at two-hour intervals, oftener in busy periods.	Warm water, mild soap, mild abrasive.

Chapter XVIII: BEVERAGE PURCHASING GUIDES

SINCE THERE IS A GOOD margin of profit in the sale of beverages, even when quality products are handled, any compromise with quality is unnecessary and certainly inadvisable. It will result in the loss of repeat business with a consequent heavy loss in volume. No operation can remain successful very long unless it is based on the sale of first class products. This has been proved over and over again in all lines of merchandise and it is particularly true of items as susceptible to personal likes and dislikes as food and drink.

BASIC INGREDIENTS

There is a mistaken idea on the part of some beverage purchasers that the average patron does not know quality, especially in mixed drinks. These purchasers could not be more mistaken. For possibly a few years following the repeal of the prohibition amendment, the tastes of the public may have been less acute, but this situation has not existed for many years, except for a relatively small percentage of patrons. A policy which risks the displeasure of patrons and the loss of their business to make two or three cents more on each drink served is foolish!

Mixes. Quality is necessary for basic ingredients and it is doubly necessary for mixes since an inferior mix can make a quality liquor taste and look decidedly sub-standard. This is particularly true of ginger ale, which must have an excellent quality of ginger flavoring and a high concentration of carbonation to make it taste right as a mix. All high quality carbonated drinks have more effervescence, a factor which allows an opened bottle to remain alive for a few hours, if capped, while inferior carbonated mixes often go flat 15 minutes after they are opened. A large saving in such merchandise necessarily means a cut in the flavoring or the carbonation since the bottling expense is the same, whether the quality is high or low.

The use of small splits of soda, ginger ale, and other mixers is highly advantageous. It assures individuality of service plus perfect carbonation for each drink. It is unwise in the extreme to ruin high-quality alcoholic drinks with inert or dissipated mixers.

Fruit Mixes. In busy bars, bartenders often request the purchase of prepared fruit mixes since they save the time it takes the bar boy to squeeze lemons or cut up fresh fruit. Tests should be made of drinks containing these prepared fruit mixes because the quality of a drink can easily be lowered by the use of inferior fruit mixes.

Customers with sensitive palates are likely to insist that there is no suitable substitute for fresh fruit. If the clientele of a particular establishment is inclined to be composed largely of connoisseurs, consideration might be given to the advisability of adjusting bar procedures to conform to their basic tastes.

Unchanging Overhead. An operator fools himself in two ways when he thinks he is saving money by selling beverages or mixes of poor quality. In the first place, his establishment soon becomes known for cheap drinks and he loses his customers. He must then either go back to quality merchandise and spend time and money to gain back a good reputation or he must lower the price of his drinks and be content with a lower class clientele.

In the second place, he is fooling himself when he thinks he is making any great saving by buying cheaper merchandise at a 10 per cent saving. If that 10 per cent could follow all the way from the purchase to the customer, it might mean something. But the bartender's salary remains the same as do the salaries of bar boys, waiters, bus boys, checkers, and cashiers. His electric meters spin around just the same and there is no change in his bills for fuel, air conditioning, rent, taxes, or insurance. All those fixed expenses continue, so that the little 10 per cent he saved gets lost in the shuffle and dwindles away to almost nothing.

INVENTORIES

The nightmare of any beverage purchaser is that sales may be lost because a certain brand or type of liquor is out of stock. Some may feel that it is practically a matter of honor that no customer should ask for a particular brand and be told it is not available. To be sure, one should endeavor to meet the demands of customers but this practice should not be carried to such extremes as to overload inventories with unusual brands or types of liquor that will never move. There is no profit in stocks that merely gather dust in the wine cellar or on the back-bar.

Some people may be impressed by a vast array of brands but the majority will only be confused. Large and unsold stocks of liquor do not increase prestige to the point where they are worth the loss of interest on the money buried in their investment. Adequate inventories are necessary certainly, but like food, liquor stocks must move if one is to have a successful operation.

Ratio of Inventory Sales to Monthly Sales. Unless an establishment has an exceptional clientele that demands the finest of wine and liquor stocks, a sound policy indicates a total beverage inventory with a value about equal to one month's sales. If the beverage cost is 33⅓ per cent of sales, this will mean the beverage inventory is turned over about once every three months in an average first-class restaurant. Where a wide discrepancy is not justified by a special type of patronage, an effort should be made to reduce the inventory figure each month until it is down to a satisfactory level. The person in charge of the operation, whether the head barman, the manager, catering manager, or wine steward, should review the inventory and sales figures monthly to see that they are kept in line.

Analysis of Sales. One way to avoid an inventory considerably in excess of monthly sales requirements is to analyze the daily requisitions for a period of a month. If this practice is repeated frequently, the reason for an excessive inventory will soon come to light. A certain brand may be very popular for several months and the beverage purchaser automatically orders a supply each month. Public tastes change and that brand may lose some of its popularity but the automatic order still continues. Very soon the inventory is overloaded with that brand. A study of the requisitions will easily reveal this point. A periodic analysis of this type is necessary in any event, so that the beverage purchaser may know what stock is moving and in what quantities.

Bin Cards. Many beverage purchasers, particularly those in large establishments, prefer the use of bin cards for reference in making up their purchase orders. These cards permit direct and easy access to information regarding the movement of stock. The same information is available from the perpetual inventory record which is usually kept in the accounting office. The use of bin cards is really a duplication of effort and whether this takes less time and effort than to get the information from the perpetual inventory is a matter of individual policy. An illustration of a bin card may be found on page 399 in the chapter on wine and liquor control.

Perpetual Inventory. All additions to stock through purchase and all reductions of stock through requisitions by duly authorized employees make up the perpetual inventory. The monthly physical inventory taken by actual count of the stock in the wine cellar should agree with the perpetual inventory. When a difference occurs it should be investigated. These perpetual inventory records are very useful guides in purchasing as they form, in a way, an analysis of sales and are an effective means of maintaining the proper balance between stock on hand and monthly sales.

CATEGORIES OF ALCOHOLIC BEVERAGES

It has long been the popular belief that alcoholic beverages fall into two major categories, distilled and fermented. Technically, this is incorrect—all alcoholic beverages are fermented and certain liquors such as whiskey, rum, brandy, gin, etc. are distilled in order to concentrate the alcohol accumulated by the fermentation process. It is preferable that alcoholic beverages be classified in three categories; wines, which are the product of natural fermentation; fermented malt liquors, such as beer and ale; and distilled spirits, which include whiskey, rum, brandy, gin, etc.

The Wine List. The wine list is to beverage service what the menu is to food service and the same rules apply. It should have variety, an attractive and easily read format and, to a certain extent, be limited in the choices it offers. These are the factors which the beverage purchaser must keep in mind.

The variety offered should be sufficient to please the majority of customers but overloaded wine lists and wine cellars are to be avoided. A record should be kept of requests that could not be filled from the available stocks since a study of this record will indicate the extent and direction any expansion of the wine inventory should take. If a waiter or captain has a sufficient knowledge of wines to suggest a suitable substitute to a guest, the latter will very often be content with the substitution and pleased that his wants and knowledge of wines were so well understood.

When a new wine is being considered for purchase, it is advisable to have it sampled not only by the purchaser but by various members of the staff. If the wine passes this impartial test, it is reasonable to suppose it will appeal to the patrons.

Wine Classifications. Wine is the fermented juice of grapes. In addition, elderberry, blackberry, peach, apricot, cherry, and dandelion juices are sometimes fermented to make wine. It is an "alive" beverage—never inert or dead. It is, therefore, susceptible to change. The rate of change and the causes vary. Some are brought about by temperature, others by light.

In late years wine authorities have come to place all wines in five main classifications designated by the principal uses to which an individual wine is put. These classes are: Appetizer Wines, White Table Wines, Red Table Wines, Sweet Dessert Wines and Sparkling Wines. As a matter of practicality, we shall list and explain in each classification the wines most generally found on sale in the United States, avoiding those of interest primarily in the countries of origin or of interest to a very limited segment of American consumers.

1. *Appetizer Wines,* so called because they are favored for before-meal use and hence are suitable for appetizer-time serving. Sherry, the most popular, is characterized by its "nutty" flavor. Most Sherries have an alcoholic content of 17 to 20 per cent by volume. Vermouth is an aromatically flavored wine, the flavoring having been accomplished by steeping herbs and other aromatic substances in the wine, or by adding an infusion of herbs. Dubonnet is also an aromatized wine. These aromatic wines are most frequently used as mixers. Dry and pale Vermouth (French type) is used extensively for Martini Cocktails; sweet and dark-amber (Italian type) for Manhattans, and Dubonnet for Dubonnet Cocktails. These wines have from 15 per cent to 20 per cent alcohol.
2. *White Table Wines* vary from extremely dry and tart to sweet and mellow, with delicate flavors that blend best at table with white meats, fowl, and seafoods. In color they range from pale straw to deep gold, and in alcohol content from 10 per cent to 14 per cent. The principal white wines are Graves and Sauternes (Bordeaux), White Burgundy and Alsatian among the French wines; Rhine and Moselle among the German; and California Whites and Eastern U. S. Whites among the American wines.
3. *Red Table Wines* are usually, though not always, dry. Rich, sometimes tart and even astringent in flavor, they are preferred, as a rule, with red meats, pastes, and highly seasoned foods. Their alcohol content ordinarily runs from 10 per cent to 14 per cent by volume. (Pink or rose wines are produced, normally, by leaving grape skins with the juice for only a fraction of the fermentation period.) The principal red wines are Bordeaux, Burgundy, Italian, and Californian.

4. *Dessert Wines* get their class name from the fact that they are chiefly used after meals. They are still wines containing generally over 14 per cent and less than 21 per cent alcohol. The name has legal significance also: in many countries all still wines of more than 14 per cent alcohol are grouped together for taxation purposes, usually as "dessert wines;" the "table wines," or wines not over 14 per cent, receive lower tax rates. For legal purposes, and to some extent in use as well, appetizer wines like Sherries and Vermouths come under the dessert wine heading. More typical of the class are Ports, both red and white, Madeira, Marsala and Muscatel, which generally contain around 20 per cent alcohol.
5. *Sparkling Wines* are table wines that have been made naturally effervescent by a second fermentation, conducted in closed containers. They are white, pink, or red, and they have a wide range of flavor characteristics and varying degrees of dryness or sweetness. Their usual alcohol content is 10 per cent to 14 per cent by volume, like that of still table wines; Champagne is the most widely known, then Sparkling Burgundy or Sparkling Moselle.

For some strange reason, the art of advertising comes to a dead stop on most wine lists. Wine is not so familiar to the people of this country as to Europeans because it is not as old an industry here. Therefore, the enjoyment of wine with food takes a bit of selling. It behooves management to acquaint the patrons with the increased enjoyment of a meal when wine is served; and good merchandising on the wine list can do much toward this end.

EUROPEAN WINES

French Wines. Many of the French wines lend themselves to good menu merchandising because they have interesting backgrounds. There is no reason why the wine list should not carry brief facts about the history of the brand names or of the district from which the wine comes. Such items stimulate patron interest.

The wines of France have nine classifications, depending on the district in which they are produced. Three of them, Bordeaux, Burgundy, and Champagne, are the best known and the most extensively used of the French wines in this country. Alsatian and Rhone wines appear on some wine lists in America, but four of them—Loire Valley, Roussilon, Bearne, Jura—are consumed in France and are practically unknown here.

Bordeaux Wines. Red Bordeaux Wines are known as Clarets. Those best known and accepted by the American people are St. Julien, Margaux and St. Estèphe. The names are those of the "commune" or parish (county) which produces each type. In addition, each "commune" may produce several clarets, each one bearing the brand name of its own producer.

White Bordeaux Wines are Graves and Sauternes, grown south of Bordeaux.

Labeling of Bordeaux Wines. There are four different methods of labeling Bordeaux wines:

(1) *Chateau Bottled Wine* is produced, bottled, and labeled at the vineyard and distributed to the shipper. The word "Chateau" and the name of the vineyard appear on the label thus, "Mis en Bouteilles au Chateau." A label reading, "Mis en Bouteilles Par" is not to be mistaken for the same thing as this means the wine has been bottled by the establishment whose name appears below the legend. Chateau-bottled Bordeaux wines are, as a rule, the finest obtainable. Price differentials for wine so labeled do not mean a difference in quality. Here is one place where it is safe to shop around and take the merchandise with the lowest price.

(2) *Chateau Wine* bottled by a merchant is Chateau Wine produced in quantity beyond the means of the vineyard for bottling. It is sold to a merchant who is permitted to bottle it under the name of the Chateau providing the bottler's name appears on the label —"Bottled by Blank & Co." In this case, also, price is no indication of quality.

(3) *Trade mark Bordeaux Wine* is bought by a shipper, labeled, and shipped under his name. The word "Chateau" does not appear on the label. Each shipper establishes his own standard which will vary only slightly from year to year.

(4) *Parish or District Bordeaux Wine* is the collective product of the parish or district named on the label, similar to our farm cooperatives. All wines from a particular district are labeled under the parish label. Quality and price on these wines may vary considerably.

The Graves (pronounced to rhyme with "suave") Wines are clear and tart with a pleasant flavor. Most of these wines are marketed under mercantile labels. Each firm may have several different brands representing a range of flavor and quality. Generally speaking, the lighter the color of a Graves wine, the more tart the taste.

The Sauternes are sweet wines produced from slightly over-ripe grapes. These wines are also Chateau-labeled as are the Clarets. "Haut Sauternes"—of high quality—are generally sweeter and more expensive than the others, and "Chateau Yquem" is the undisputed top quality among Sauternes.

Burgundy. Burgundy Wine is labeled with the name of the vineyard, parish or district where it is produced if these are well known. "Pommard" is perhaps the best known in this country, although "Chambertin" is also widely accepted. They are both red wines. Among the white Burgundies, Montrachet and Chablis have a prominent place on the wine lists of many of the well-known establishments. Probably the finest red Burgundy and also the most costly is "Romance-Conti."

Burgundies are both "still" and "sparkling" wines and many people prefer Sparkling Burgundy to Champagne. They are naturally fermented and have a heavier body and a sweeter taste than Champagne.

Champagnes. Champagne is a naturally fermented, sparkling, white wine. It is a blended wine, produced from the growths of several vineyards. For that reason, no vineyard name ever appears on a Champagne label. The firm name of the bottler is the criterion of quality. Champagne is labeled as to flavor: Brut or Nature, Extra Sec or Extra Dry, Sec or Dry, Demi Sec, Doux. Brut or Nature is extremely tart and the flavor goes through diminishing degrees of dryness (or tartness) to Demi Sec, which is sweet, and Doux, which is very sweet.

Champagne is shipped in bottles of various sizes to avoid waste, since it must be consumed at one sitting. A bottle cannot be re-capped as the carbonic gas escapes rapidly and the wine becomes flat. The most commonly used sizes of bottles in this country are:

Splits	— 6½	ounces	
Half-Bottles	—13	"	
Bottles	—26	"	(fifths)
Magnum	—52	"	(two fifths)

Occasionally a Jeroboam of 104 ounces, or four fifths, is used but this is quite rare. The Rehoboam of 156 ounces, or one gallon and a fifth, is practically unknown in this country. Larger sizes than this are usually not shipped here.

Alsatian Wines. These wines are known as French Rhine Wines and labeled according to the type of grape used. They are all white wines and seldom listed in smaller places. The best known in this country is Riesling. Some of the larger hotels and restaurants also list Traminer.

German Wines. German Wines are classified under three major types:

(1) Rhine Wines
- (a) Rheingau
- (b) Rheinhesse
- (c) Rheinfalz

(2) Moselle Wines
(3) Steinwein

In English-speaking countries, Rhine wines are quite commonly called "Hocks" and "Sparkling Hocks."

The three major types of German wines are easily distinguished by their bottles as well as their labels. Rhine wines are always bottled in tall, flute-shaped, dark-brown bottles. Moselle wine bottles are the same except that the color is dark-green. Steinwein has a squat bottle known as a "bocksbeutel."

German wines have essentially the same labeling as the French Bordeaux wines. The classifications are: (1) Estate bottled; (2) Estate wine, bottled by a shipper; (3) Trademark brand; and (4) District or Township.

It is a legal requirement that the bottle labels of all wines produced and bottled in Germany contain the vintage year, the township or district where the grapes were grown and the name of the shipper.

Of the Rhine wines, the best known of the Rheingau type are Rudesheimer Schlossberg and Schloss Johannisberg. The best known of the Rheinhesse wines is the Niersteiner. Trockenbeeren wine is the most highly prized among the Rheinfalz. Of the Moselle wines, the most famous is the legendary Bernkasteler Doktor.

"Auslese" and "Spatlese" are terms that find their way into some hotel wine lists. The former means selected picking of the grapes; the latter specifies late picking. "Trockenbeeren Auslese" means selected, over-ripe, semi-dried grapes which yield a relatively small quantity of wine. This accounts for the high cost of this type of sweet white wine.

Labels on German wine bottles are likely to appear confusing since they carry a great deal of information. In addition to the required vintage date, township or district designation and shipper's name, quite frequently the type of grape and manner of picking will be specified. The terms "Original Abzug" or "Original Abfullung," indicating original bottling at the estate, are usually found in abbreviated form as "Orig. Abz" or "Orig. Abf."

Hungarian Wines. Of the Hungarian wines, the most notable is Tokay, a very sweet wine usually served with the dessert or immediately following. Wine fanciers consider it one of the truly great white wines. Since it takes several years to develop, it is more costly than some others. For that reason, in purchasing Tokay, the age of the wine is something to watch. It is always shipped in long-necked bottles which add distinction to any beverage display. There is virtually no Hungarian wine sold in the United States.

Spanish and Portuguese Wines. There are many wines produced in Spain but the one with which we are most familiar is Sherry, an Anglicized version of the Spanish name, "Jerez." Sherry was extremely popular in England before the days of the Pilgrims and is one of the best known and most widely used imported wines in all English-speaking countries, including our own.

In addition to being an excellent straight wine drink, Sherry is also a splendid mix and "Sherry Flips" and "Cobblers" are very popular. The tart or dry Sherries should be slightly chilled for serving but the rich, sweet Sherries should be served at room temperature. A tart Sherry is most generally served as an aperitif, while sweet Sherries are after-dinner favorites.

Sherries are classified as to varying degrees of tartness or sweetness, the very tart or dry Sherry being Manzanilla. Next is Pino, still very dry, followed by Vino de Pasto and Amontillado. Amoroso is a medium dry Sherry. Oloroso is a rich, sweet Sherry, and Brown, the richest and sweetest, is dark-brown in color. Of these types, Amontillado is the best known and the most frequently ordered in this country, perhaps because it has been mentioned most often in the writings of many authors.

Of the Portuguese wines, by far the most famous are the Port wines. These wines are medium sweet, full-bodied and have a very fine bouquet. There are both red and white Port wines, but in this country we know best the Ruby and Tawny Ports. Ruby Port is ruddy in color, as the name implies, and is generally a younger wine than Tawny Port, which is lighter in color and more tart in taste.

As a note of interest, it is illegal to call any wine "Port" unless it has been produced in the upper Douro region of Portugal and, although wines of the "Port" type are made in other parts of the world, they must be labeled in such a manner as to show their origin. They cannot be labeled as true "Port" as this comes only from Portugal.

Madeira wines produced on the island of Madeira, over 600 miles from the Spanish peninsula, are generally very sweet wines developed mostly from a mixture of several grape varieties. Some, however, are the product of a single type of grape. The best known of the latter type is Malmsey. These wines are popular as aperitifs or as dessert wines.

Italian Wines. These wines are not as extensively known in this country as the French and German wines. The most frequently used are Chianti, Asti Spumante, Moscato, Marzala, and Vermouth.

Chianti is extremely tart, red in color and is usually consumed with spaghetti, macaroni, and highly seasoned foods. It is supposed to aid the digestion of this type of food.

Asti Spumante is a sparkling wine, sweet in taste. It is produced in much the same manner as Champagne.

Moscato wines are made from the famous Muscat grape. They are usually dark-brown, sweet, and rather mellow in taste.

Marsala wines are fortified wines, also dark-brown and bear a general resemblance to Sherry. They are used quite extensively in cooking, one famous dish being "Scalopine alla Marsala."

Italian Vermouths are used throughout the world as aperitifs, mixers, and after-dinner beverages. They are actually white wines to which some brandy has been added to bring the alcohol to between 17 per cent and 20 per cent and then have been mixed and blended with a number of herbs and other flavoring agents. It takes several years to make a good Vermouth.

Vermouths are made wherever wines are produced, but those most extensively used are French, Italian, South American, and American (Eastern States and California). All of these countries produce both sweet and dry Vermouths, but France is better known for its dry Vermouth and Italy for its sweet Vermouth.

In the United States, American Vermouth is now out-selling foreign Vermouth. Before World War II, the United States produced comparatively little Vermouth; the average for the years 1936-1940 represented only about one-sixth of the total Vermouth consumed in the U. S. However, in 1941, due to war conditions, imports were greatly restricted, so that producers in the United States began to make great strides in Vermouth production. As a consequence, present Vermouth production in this country is over eight times pre-war production. United States Vermouth now represents 70 per cent of total sales in this country.

WINES OF THE UNITED STATES

Wines of the United States have made great strides since 1936, their sales having just doubled, though little progress has been made in the sale of wines, either foreign or domestic, in restaurants and hotels. Sale of wine in these outlets, Champagne excepted, is in small volume.

Wines from the United States can be divided into two distinct classifications: California wines and "American" wines. California is the source of 85 per cent to 90 per cent of the nation's wine; European grape (vitis vinifera) varieties flourish there, and the state has such a range of climate, soil, and topography throughout its length that it possesses eight distinct viti-cultural districts, each capable of yielding good wines.

East of the Rockies the European grapes as a rule do not thrive, but numerous native varieties, principally of the "labrusca" family, have been domesticated and crossbred to provide distinctive wines, into which California wines are often blended. Although dessert and appetizer wines form a large part of United States production, the amounts of red and white table wines and sparkling wines sold are gradually increasing due to educational programs established by the wine industry.

American Wines. Outside of California, the most important wine growing regions are the Finger Lakes district of New York State (noted especially for excellent Champagne, as well as for the production of table and dessert wines), and the Sandusky-Lake Erie Islands region of northern Ohio, also a Champagne and table wine producing area. Wines are also produced in considerable quantities in New Jersey, Michigan, Missouri, Iowa and in restricted areas in Virginia, North Carolina, South Carolina, Georgia, Washington, and Oregon. Eastern wine producers market their still wines under such names as Claret, Sauterne, Burgundy, Rhine, Sherry, and Port, qualified by the word "American" or by the name of the state where produced, if at least 75 per cent of the volume is derived from fruit grown and juice fermented in the state indicated, and if it has been fully produced and finished within that state. The white wines from the East are generally better than the red wines. But their Champagnes are especially well known and appreciated. Though the Eastern grape used is different from the French, having a distinctive flavor, the manner of Champagne production is the traditional French method, "bottle fermentation," and in many cases the Champagnes compare favorably with the finest vintages shipped from France. American-type Champagne from the Finger Lakes district of New York State and from certain sections of the Lake Erie district are considered the best in that type.

As a matter of record, any sparkling wine made in this country cannot be called "Champagne" unqualified, but must be identified as to place of origin, e.g., California Champagne, New York State Champagne, etc. In the case of sparkling wines in which the secondary fermentation has taken place in bulk containers, the wine must be labeled "sparkling wine" and may, in addition to but not in lieu of the class designation "sparkling wine," be further designated as "Champagne style" or "Champagne type" or "American (or New York State, California, etc.) Champagne bulk process."

There is also "Carbonated Wine." This wine is made effervescent by the addition of carbon dioxide rather than through secondary fermentation of the wine within a closed container, tank, or bottle. The sale of carbonated wine is negligible compared to sales of naturally fermented sparkling wines, and seldom finds a place on hotel wine lists.

In the United States, just as in the case of American Vermouths, American sparkling wines are far outselling foreign Champagnes, and a big potential market exists for them. Before World War II, the United States produced less than half of the sparkling wines consumed here. However, during the war years, imports were greatly restricted, so that American sparkling wine production increased greatly. In 1949, sales of U. S. sparkling wines were 2½ times the pre-war amount, and constituted 70 per cent of all sparkling wines sold, of which one third bore a California label.

California Wines. Reference has already been made to the large production and sale of United States Vermouths. Most of the wine used in making this product originates in California, whether for dry Vermouth or sweet Vermouth. Seven out of every ten gallons of Vermouth sold in this country is United States Vermouth.

One third of the Sparkling wines made in the United States is produced in California.

The most widely used wine type names in California (as well as in many other countries) have geographic origin, from the regions in which the types originated. Many others are varietal, representing the principal grape varieties employed. Others are proprietary, some being the names of their producers and others being fanciful titles adopted by individual vintners. Thus, such universally familiar type names as Claret, Burgundy, Sauterne, Rhine wine, Port, Sherry, all having geographic significance, in modern times came to be used in many countries to designate any wines possessing the characteristics generally attributed to the original products.

At various times in the 19th and 20th centuries attempts have been made in France and some other nations to restrain producers of other countries in the use of generic wine type names of European geographic origin. International agreements and many national wine laws and regulations have reflected such efforts. In most countries, including the United States, generic names of geographic origin may be used only when the actual place of origin is stated in direct conjunction with the type name, e.g., Australian Burgundy, Argentine Champagne, California Sherry, American Claret, etc.

California sells most of its table and dessert wines under such generic names. Hence, among red table wines will be found California Claret, Burgundy, Chianti; among white table wines will be found California Rhine, Sauterne, Haut Sauterne; among dessert wines, California Port, Sherry, Marsala, all of which bear a general resemblance to their namesakes.

Recently, however, in the United States, more and more attention is being given to production of high-class "varietal" table wines. In California, among the whites, will be found the Riesling, a Rhine wine type produced from one or more of the Riesling grape varieties; other outstanding whites are White Pinot, Semillon and Sauvignon Blanc (the latter two being the traditional grapes of the Sauterne district) and Traminer. Among the red "varietals" are Zinfandel (exclusively a California grape), and particularly Cabernets and Pinots, the latter two being respectively the traditional grapes of the Bordeaux and Burgundy districts of France. Other well-known red "varietals" are Gamay and Barbera.

Among the white table wines of the Eastern States, we find Elvira, Delaware and Catawba, all of the Labrusca variety of grapes.

Grapes are a primary factor in the production of quality wines. In California growing conditions are a less important factor, so that vintage dates on a bottle are not important as they are on European wines, for in Europe, years vary widely, so that it is necessary to know the vintage dates of the wines of each district, in order to obtain the quality sought. Vintage charts are absolutely required. In California the seasons are uniform so wines do not vary from year to year if properly made.

"Varietals" in California have been produced by small growers of premium wines for many decades. Hotel and restaurant buyers should be conversant with the fact that some of the large California producers now have premium wines of varietally designated wines that are worthy of consideration and placement.

In the merchandising of our own wines on our wine lists, we have not done an outstanding job—in fact, a barely passable one. In the first place, it is poor showmanship to use the term, "Domestic Wines." The use of place names, such as New York State Wines, or California Wines, lends dignity to the wine list and commands greater respect from the buying public. Customer education may be necessary to get across the fact that many of our Champagnes are on a par with the finest vintages shipped from France.

The Treasury Department in Washington, D. C. issues a set of regulations governing the labeling of wines in this country, which they will send upon request. Familiarity with these regulations will prevent the wine buyer from making a dubious purchase.

BEER, ALE, PORTER, AND STOUT

History tells us that wine was the first alcoholic beverage made and, from available records, it appears that beer was the second, as it was first produced by the Egyptians. Our own history tells us that a brewery was operating near Philadelphia as early as 1637, and a few years later a brewery was opened on what is now Wall Street on lower Manhattan Island.

These malt beverages are fermented cereals and malt, or malt alone, flavored with hops.

Beer. This is an all-embracing term signifying all malt beverages, but used in the commercial sense it refers to light-colored brews, generally lagers, which are bright, clear, and efferverscent with an alcoholic content of about four per cent by volume. Imported beers are usually labeled "Lager" or "Pilsner." The latter is a very light-colored brew.

Ale. Ale is dark, heavy, and slightly bitter, containing about six per cent alcohol.

Porter and Stout. These are English brews. They are very dark and have a sweet taste. Stout has a pronounced hop taste that is not present in Porter. They are both rich and heavy, having a decided malt flavor and containing about six per cent of alcohol by volume.

Bock Beer. This beer is especially brewed and is heavier, darker, and sweeter than regular beer. It is made during the winter and is generally offered for sale in the early spring, being sold for a period of about six weeks.

Domestic beer is prepared in two different types as a rule—the full brew and the check brew. These distinctions should be kept in mind in purchasing. Full brew beer permits the malt and cereals to develop to their full alcoholic content which may run up to 14 per cent by volume. It is then reduced to the desired strength and aged. Check brew beer is drawn off and processed, once the desired alcoholic content is reached. This eliminates one step in the process and for this reason, check brews are usually cheaper beers.

Brands. Brands of beer vary from region to region since many of them are sold practically on a local basis. However, as a result of intensive advertising and promotion over a period of years, there are a few nationally known brands of beers and ales, as well as some imported, that are popular everywhere.

Water Content. In purchasing beer, it is extremely important to remember that water constitutes approximately seven-eighths of the total volume. The quality of the water is of the greatest importance. Water that is suitable for beer does not tend to make good ale. This fact should be borne in mind when purchases are made. Since beer is generally sold in greater quantities than ale, first consideration should be given to the water source of the beer. Once satisfactory arrangements have been made, shopping for ale can be made the next order of business. Mountain water is very advantageous for brewing beer.

Packaging. Beer is packaged in three forms—kegs or barrels, bottles, and cans. Bottled and canned beer is pasteurized. This puts an end to any further yeast action but this does not mean that these products may be mishandled or improperly stored. Beer cannot be stored in wooden containers or it will take on the flavor of the wood. Hence, wooden barrels used for beer are lined with pitch which will not dissolve in beer. Aluminum is one metal container which does not affect the flavor of beer but other metal containers are also lined with pitch. Beer in kegs is not pasteurized and is, therefore, still active. Strong odors, warm temperatures, bacteria and light can each, in turn, ruin beer. Therefore, before the beer is purchased, ample storage must be provided where those factors do not exist.

THE PURCHASE OF DISTILLED SPIRITS

Distilled spirits are classified as whiskies, rums, brandies, gins, liqueurs and miscellaneous spirits, which include a large group of unusual products such as Vodka and Tequila.

It is necessary for the beverage purchaser to know the terms used in distillation processes since they decidedly affect the quality of the product. The term "proof" is used to indicate the alcoholic content. Each degree of proof is equal to one-half of one per cent of alcohol. Hence, a spirit of 90 proof contains 45 per cent of alcohol by volume; a spirit of 100 proof contains 50 per cent of alcohol by volume. Any spirit which contains over 100 proof is considered an "over-proofed" spirit.

A rectified spirit is one which has been altered in some way from the original state after distillation. The best illustration of this is the blended whiskies.

Whiskies. Whiskey is a potable spirit obtained from the distillation of a fermented mash of grain, suitably aged in wood. The spelling of the word "whiskey" may be puzzling. It is always spelled with an "e" except in reference to Scotch Whisky, when the "e" is omitted.

For all practical purposes, there are three classifications of whiskey in the world today—Scotch, Irish, and American.

American Whiskies. There are thirteen types of whiskey permitted by federal regulations under this classification:

(1) Whiskey. An alcoholic distillate of fermented grain mash with no specification of any standards.
(2) Straight Whiskey. An alcoholic distillation of fermented grain mash, not blended with other distillations.
(3) Straight Rye Whiskey. Straight whiskey distilled from grain containing not less than 51 per cent rye.
(4) Straight Bourbon Whiskey. Straight whiskey distilled from grain containing not less than 51 per cent corn.
(5) Straight Wheat Whiskey. Straight whiskey distilled from grain containing not less than 51 per cent wheat.
(6) Straight Malt Whiskey. Straight whiskey distilled from grain containing not less than 51 per cent malted barley.
(7) Blended Whiskey. A blend of whiskies and neutral spirits, bottled at a minimum of 80 proof and containing at least 20 per cent of 100 proof straight whiskey. May be labeled, "Whiskey—a Blend."
(8) Blended Rye Whiskey. A blended whiskey containing not less than 50 per cent straight rye whiskey. May be labeled "Rye Whiskey—a Blend." Blended Bourbon whiskey contains a minimum of 50 per cent straight Bourbon whiskey.
(9) Blended Straight Whiskey. A mixture of straight whiskies only, without any other ingredients. May be labeled "A Blend of Straight Whiskies." This type is reputedly the best for general use if obtainable in good quality.
(10) Spirit Whiskey. A mixture of neutral spirits and whiskey,

bottled at a minimum of 80 proof, and containing at least five per cent whiskey.

(11) Canadian Whiskey. Produced in Canada in compliance with Canadian laws, containing no distilled spirits less than two years old. Canadian whiskey that contains neutral spirits must be labeled, "Blended Canadian Whiskey."

(12) Blended Scotch-Type Whiskey. A mixture of whiskey and neutral spirits produced outside of Great Britain, containing at least 20 per cent of 100 proof malt whiskey. May be labeled "American Blended Scotch Whiskey."

(13) Blended Irish-Type Whiskey. A mixture of whiskey and neutral spirits produced outside of the United Kingdom or the Irish Free State, containing at least 20 per cent of straight malt whiskey. May be labeled "American Blended Irish Whiskey."

The term "bottled in bond" means that a straight whiskey of 100 proof has been stored in a charred oak barrel in a warehouse under the supervision of the United States Government for a period of four years or more. Such a specification *does not in any way guarantee the quality of the whiskey*. In fact, the Treasury Department, which controls the bonded warehouses, states in no uncertain terms that the "bottled in bond" stamp in no way guarantees the purity or quality of the spirits. It is merely proof of four years' storage in a government-controlled warehouse. The stamp is the same as the post mark on a letter; it has nothing to do with the contents of the container on which the stamp is placed.

In the yeasting process of making whiskey, some whiskies are yeasted by using a freshly developed batch of yeast for each mash. This is known as a "sweet mash" whiskey. Other whiskies are yeasted by using a small amount of the aforementioned mash plus an additional amount of new yeast. This is known as "sour mash" whiskey. The yield per bushel of grain is likely to be greater for sour mash than for sweet mash whiskey but both types may be of high or low quality, depending on the other processes of whiskey making.

Scotch Whisky. Scotch whisky is light-bodied and smoky-flavored. The grain is dried over open peat fires and the smoky quality does not leave the whisky during its entire making and bottling.

Almost all Scotch whisky is blended rather than straight. The blend includes all of the four Scotch-producing regions—the Highlands, the Lowlands, Campbeltown, and Islay. It is usually aged in Sherry barrels and the age is indicated on the bottle. One should not make the mistake of believing, however, that age is an absolute guarantee of quality. The cautious purchaser will soon learn that a *poor Scotch whisky retains its poor quality regardless of age.*

Liqueur Scotch whisky, very fine to begin with, has a mellow and distinctive flavor. Usually such Scotch is at least 12 years old. However, caution must be used in assessing the value of this designation on a bottle. It is sometimes used indiscriminately.

Irish Whiskey. Many people still take seriously the outworn joke that Irish whiskey is made from potatoes. This is completely erroneous and without foundation in fact. Irish whiskey is made in the same manner and with the same ingredients as Scotch whisky. The only difference is that the grain of Irish whiskey is dried over a closed fire instead of an open fire. Hence the smoky flavor of Scotch is absent.

Irish whiskies are sometimes blended whiskies but more frequently they are straight, pot-still whiskies. All Irish whiskies shipped to this country are at least seven years old and are usually of very fine quality.

Rums. Rum is distilled from the fermented juice of sugar cane products. It is not rum if it is mixed with any other spirits. The two principal types in greatest use at the present time are the light-bodied and the full-bodied rums.

Light-bodied rums sold in the United States hail mostly from Puerto Rico and Cuba. Both of these sources sell their rums under two labels—the white and the gold, corresponding roughly to the general coloring of each type due to the amount of caramel coloring added to the gold label rums. These light-bodied rums are more tart than the full-bodied rums.

Most of the full-bodied rums imported into the United States come from the Island of Jamaica in the West Indies. Other Caribbean areas produce full-bodied rums but they are not as well known as those from Jamaica. The latter are noted for their mellowness.

Caution should be taken in purchasing little-known rums of the full-bodied variety since there are quite a number of these that are familiarly called "monkey rums" in the trade. This is because of their "explosive" or "fiery" taste due to improper ageing and inferior ingredients.

Brandies. Brandy is a distilled spirit derived from a fermented mash of fruit and aged in the wood. Unless otherwise specified, brandy is generally taken to mean grape brandy, although excellent brandies are also made from apples, cherries, apricots, and plums.

Cognac is a type of grape brandy that obtains its name from the Cognac region of France and is generally regarded as brandy at its best.

This is due not only to the special process of distillation used in the Cognac district but also to the ideal combination of soil, climate, and growing conditions. Other areas may have some of these qualities but none of them have ever approached the superlative brandy of the Cognac district.

Although brandy from any other part of the world cannot be classified as Cognac, there are merchandising "angles" sometimes used which can be very misleading. One subterfuge is to make the label look like a Cognac label and the name sound very similar. In the labeling of Cognac, there are several abbreviations that have a specific significance and should be familiar to anyone purchasing this product. The abbreviations and their represented qualities are:

E—Especial	S—Superior
F—Fine	P—Pale
V—Very	X—Extra
O—Old	C—Cognac

Thus, the letters VSOP mean Very Superior Old Pale.

Stars on a bottle mean nothing of special significance. Each firm sets its own standards. Three stars for one company may mean something quite different from another's three-star product.

Cognac will improve while ageing in the wood for about 50 to 55 years. Obviously, this extremely long period of storage ties up capital and will increase the price considerably. For this reason, relatively little Cognac is aged for longer than a generation. It must be realized also that Cognac will not improve with age, once it is bottled. It can stay in the bottle for 50 years without any improvement. Bottles that have been made to look as though they were a century old are just an attempt to fool the credulous purchaser. A good quality Cognac, aged in the wood properly for six to 10 years, will be quite suitable for consumption. The best age for Cognac is between 20 and 40 years, if it has been aged in the wood for that period of time. A method of testing the quality of Cognac is to pour it into a glass and observe the glass 24 hours after the Cognac has been emptied out of it. If the glass still bears noticeable traces of the bouquet, the Cognac may be considered of high quality.

Of the French brandies, other than Cognac, Armagnac enjoys a favorable reputation in this country and one or two brands will be found on high-grade drink lists. Spanish brandy is generally sweeter than French brandy and is highly regarded by some patrons.

Another popular sweet brandy is Metaxa, a product of Greece. It is well known and is often found on the drink lists of fashionable establishments.

California produces a large quantity of excellent brandy for beverage purposes, though the demand for any brandy has been increasing very slowly. California's production, almost exclusively from grapes, represents two-thirds of the total brandy production of this country. Outside of California, the brandy made in the United States is mostly from fruit other than grapes.

Apple brandy is more commonly known in this country as "Apple Jack". It is quite extensively used in some regions. Calvados is a French cousin of our American Apple Jack and near the end of World War II, following the invasion of Normandy, it became a favorite of many American soldiers. It is normally aged for a longer period than Apple Jack.

Fruit brandy is not defined as precisely in Europe as in the United States. In this country, Federal regulations have established rigid standards for the use of the term "brandy" on a label. It must be made from the fermented juice or mash of the fruit.

Fruit liqueurs are made by infusing a fruit flavor into a brandy through a process of immersing the fruit in brandy for several months. Strictly speaking, such liqueurs are not a true brandy and cannot be bottled as such in the United States. In European countries, fruit liqueurs are indiscriminately bottled as fruit brandies without any legal restrictions. Great care should be used in buying these products.

Gins. The process for making gin is the simplest of all the spirits. This fact makes gin generally less expensive. It is potable alcohol that has been flavored, usually by the juniper berry. The higher the quality of the alcohol, the better the quality of the gin. Ageing does not improve gin and for that reason it is not stored in wooden casks but in earthenware or glass-lined vats.

Flavoring is accomplished through two different methods—distillation or compounding. Distilled gin is labeled as such. Compounding is the old "bath tub" method so prevalent during prohibition days.

The English make a dry gin, an "Old Tom" gin which is sweet, and a sloe gin which is actually a liqueur.

American gins are made from neutral spirits which are distilled at a very high proof, often at 190 proof, and reduced to the desired level.

American fruit-flavored gins are compounded and generally artificially flavored.

English and American gins are used almost entirely for mixed drinks. Holland's gin is generally consumed as a straight drink since it is too heavy for mixing.

Liqueurs. Some liqueurs are processed by secret formulas that have never been made public but most liqueurs, or cordials as they are frequently called, are made by either the infusion or the compounding method. A spirit of some kind, most frequently a brandy, is infused with flavoring in excess of two and one-half per cent of the volume.

Outstanding and world-famous liqueurs have been copied to the point where the market is often flooded with cheap and undesirable substitutes. Tricks in misleading labeling should be carefully watched.

A fine assortment of high-quality liqueurs lends a great deal of "tone" to the wine list and attracts a discriminating clinetele. The most popular liqueurs are:

Anisette
Apricot Liqueur
Benedictine
Blackberry Liqueur
Chartreuse, Yellow or Green
Cherry Heering
Cointreau
Cordial Medoc
Creme de Cacao
Creme de Menthe, White or Green
Creme de Cassis
Curacao
Drambuie
Grand Marnier
Kümmel
Maraschino
Peach Liqueur
Sloe Gin

Occasionally Southern Comfort is listed under this grouping although it is much higher in proof than any of those on the list and equals the proof of some whiskies.

In the liqueurs that are worth handling, there are no bargains. Some are such cheap substitutes that they are likely to produce "hangovers" or other disorders that will reflect against the establishment serving them. It is advisable to indicate clearly on the drink list the brand name of liqueurs when they might come from more than one source. The genuineness of these products should be stressed because the public has been sorely tried by inferior products of this particular type.

Miscellaneous Spirits. Certain drinks which are practically national drinks in some countries have developed considerable popularity in various parts of the United States. The most prominent of these include Akvavit from the Scandinavian countries, Vodka from Russia, Tequila from Mexico and Okolehao from Hawaii.

Akvavit, or Aquavit, as it is sometimes spelled, is made from grain or potatoes and flavored with caraway seeds and other flavoring agents. It is always served ice-cold.

Vodka is made from wheat and has no noticeable flavor. It is, therefore, very suitable for mixed drinks. It is always chilled when served. Domestic Vodka is generally regarded to be of very satisfactory quality.

Tequila is made from the hardy century plant. It has an extremely fiery quality. Because of this, half of a lemon or lime, plus a small pinch of salt are generally used as mace-bearers to clear the way for this potent drink.

Okolehao is derived from sugar cane molasses. It is most commonly used as an ingredient for mixed drinks, some of which are served in cocoanut rims.

CATERING TO A BRAND-MINDED PUBLIC

A large percentage of patrons have distinct likes and dislikes when it comes to brands of their favorite beverages. They may be quite naive about brand names generally, but they are "wedded" to certain brands for their own consumption. Substitutes will only annoy them, particularly inferior substitutes. A wise purchaser will avoid inferior brands because he will find, if he is successful in "working them off" that this process will back-fire in the form of lost patronage.

Regional Preferences. There are distinct regional preferences in types of liquor. The beverage purchaser should learn the extent of local trade compared with trade from some distance. In a hotel, a geographical breakdown of a list of guests will tell him what percentage hails from a radius of less than 200 to 250 miles. These guests are likely to have tastes that conform to his own local conditions. However, if a substantial percentage comes from greater distances, an inquiry to trade papers will probably give him information regarding regional preferences.

Consultations with Bartenders. Every beverage purchaser should have frequent meetings or chats with the bartenders working in the establishment. They will generally know what the customers are requesting. Waiters and captains should also be consulted. While it may be possible to determine from the perpetual inventories what products are being used, it is extremely important to know whether customers are making requests that cannot be filled. It may be found advisable, if the impressions of the waiters appear to be vague, to institute a procedure whereby every waiter or bartender records the requests that cannot be filled and what happened to such requests. It is important to know whether a patron ordered something else or just didn't order at all. These records cannot be kept perfectly, due to the pressure that comes with peak business, but even partial records prove more illuminating than none at all.

Listing Ingredients of Cocktails. The necessary tie-in purchases made during the war resulting in huge quantities of slow-moving stock brought about a regular jig-saw puzzle of queer sounding names for cocktails. In order to move some burdensome stock, a new cocktail would be invented as well as a new name. In some places, such practices may have proved highly satisfactory and continued after the need to push dead stock had passed. This is a matter of house policy. However, one way of testing the wisdom of such a practice is to list on the menu the ingredients of some of the more intricate cocktails while other well known cocktails go unlisted. After a period of time, the sales of the two types should be analyzed. This may establish customer tendencies and point the way to suitable merchandising practices. The person in charge of the bars of an establishment should make a periodic review of this angle of the operation.

Chapter XIX: WINE CELLAR OPERATION

WHEN MANY PRESENT-DAY establishments were built, the plans for the wine cellar were left completely out of the blueprints or treated inadequately. In either case, these architectural errors have increased the difficulties of efficient wine cellar operation. However, good working procedures and effective supervision will tend to overcome some of these difficulties. They are necessary, even in the most perfectly laid-out wine cellar, if haphazard operation is to be avoided.

PHYSICAL REQUIREMENTS

A wine cellar should have three separate units:

(1) The major unit, maintained at a temperature of 50 to 60 degrees.
(2) A smaller unit, maintained at a temperature of 40 degrees, to be used for the storage of sparkling wines. This chamber will also serve for pre-chilling other wines prior to serving.
(3) A storage room for beer, mineral waters and empty bottles on which deposits have been paid. Although this unit should be removed from boilers or furnaces and without hot water pipes, refrigeration to keep it at a low temperature is not necessary. It is most important that temperature control in the other two units be rigidly controlled.

Since delicate white wines and sparkling wines should not be chilled for a period exceeding a week, the unit used for pre-chilling should be checked carefully and restocked frequently.

The lock on the door of the chill room should have a handle on the inside to permit opening the door from that direction. This prevents anyone from being locked in the chill room accidentally. It also is a protection against raising the temperature of the room when the wine cellar attendant is in there procuring various beverages. Raising the chill room temperature or increasing the power to offset temperature decreases will prove more costly than the installation of an inside handle on the door.

Ventilation and Cleanliness. Wine cellars for many years were in a deplorable condition as regards ventilation and sanitation. Because so many historically famous wine cellars in Europe were dark, damp, and unsanitary, custom dictated that wines were best stored in such an environment. Modern science, however, has restored the need for the circulation of pure air in wine cellars. A dry, clean cellar prevents the growth of fungi which will in time permeate the corks of the wine bottles and contaminate the wine.

Par Stock. Every wine cellar should have a definite par stock based on the actual needs of the establishment and approved by the manager. This par stock and the proportions of the different items carried, such as spirits, wines, beers, etc., will vary with the geographical location of the establishment, its clientele, and its standards of service. For the average operation, however, the ratio for the various types of beverages will not deviate too much, in dollar value, from the following breakdown:

Wines	10%
Beer	10%
Rye and Bourbon	30%
Scotch	30%
Brandies, Gins, and Cordials	15%
Mineral Waters	5%

For example, if the total value of the inventory amounts to $5000, approximately $500 will be invested in wines, $500 in beer, $1500 in Rye and Bourbon, $1500 in Scotch, $750 in brandies, gins, and cordials and $250 in mineral waters.

Comparison of Stocks on Hand with Sales. The issues from the wine room will, in time, give an accurate picture of the demand for certain items. The percentage ratios of sales should be checked against the percentage ratios of the inventories. For example, if the sale of Scotch, over a period of time, has dropped off to 10 per cent of total sales, the inventory should not continue to show Scotch as 30 per cent of the total but only 10 per cent. This frequent check of ratios will avoid the accumulation of slow-moving or "dead" stock.

THE RECEIVING CLERK

Blind Purchase Orders. As with food, the care of incoming merchandise for the wine cellar starts with the receiving clerk. To make certain that he will count the number and size of cases and bottles of each kind of beverage received, he should be given "blind purchase orders" such as the one illustrated on page 106 for the food storeroom. This is merely a list of the items ordered with no figures as to the quantities or sizes.

Standard Weights of Cases. Counting the cases received is not enough as some cases might have missing or broken bottles. The receiving clerk should be obliged to weigh cases of each brand and size received until he has accumulated a complete table of standard weights. He can then spot-check the weight of incoming cases to catch those with missing or broken bottles. If a shortage occurs frequently, all incoming cases should be weighed and checked against the list of standard weights. If the cases of one particular vendor are short beyond a reasonable number, an investigation should be made. This may be no fault of the vendor directly, but his truck-driver may be careless or dishonest or both.

Standard Weights for Beer Kegs. Standard weights for incoming kegs of beer should be set up in the same way and all kegs weighed and checked against these standards. The weights should then be recorded on the receiving ticket. Spillage in filling the kegs or shortages due to other reasons cannot easily be detected in any other way.

Breakage Reports. Reliable vendors will not be guilty of short measure, broken bottles, or missing merchandise. However, the desirability and value of this type of merchandise encourages all sorts of mishaps in transit. The receiving clerk must report all discrepancies or leakage to the accounting department. Filling out the necessary forms for credit memoranda may be irksome when the clerk is busy but failure to do this means loss the same as money taken from the cash drawer. If his report on shortages does not reach the accounting department at regular intervals, an inquiry as to the reason should be made.

STORAGE

Methods of Storing Wines. Bottles containing table wines, those whose alcoholic content is less than 14 per cent, should be stored on their sides. This keeps the cork wet and tight in the bottle, preventing air from entering through the cork, which is porous when dry. Otherwise, acetification or oxidation may result.

Bottles containing fortified wines, such as dessert wines, and spirits, may safely be stored in an upright position. They will not be noticeably affected by the air which enters through the cork, since their alcoholic content is higher.

Sparkling wines, white wines, and beers should be stored near the floor where the cooler temperatures prevail. Red wines should be placed on the middle shelves with dessert wines and spirits above. All wines should be delivered several days before they are to be used so that the sediment, if any, in the bottles will have an opportunity to settle before serving.

Size of Shelves and Bins. The upright partitions of the storage bins should be spaced so that the base of each section will contain a specified number of bottles. This will facilitate counting while taking inventory. Bottle sizes vary considerably. The bin size that seems to accommodate the most frequently used bottles with least waste space is 22 inches wide by 14 inches high by 18 inches deep. The lowest shelf should be four inches or more above the floor.

The most satisfactory height for shelves in the wine cellar is seven and one-half feet. If they are higher it means too much climbing up and down ladders to put away stock and fill requisitions. When a case is opened, either two men must be used to place stock on the high shelves or one man must run up and down the ladder at the risk of breaking some of the bottles.

Small, wooden triangular wedges should be used to hold in position the wine bottles that are kept on their sides.

Handling Wines. Wines should be handled as little as possible while being issued and after removal from the wine cellar. Employees must be instructed in the necessary care, particularly as regards sensitive red wines. Careless handling will disturb the sediment which may be present in these wines and their clarity will be lost.

Fine Burgundies or other choice wines should be stored horizontally in wooden or metal racks that are inserted or built into the bins. When withdrawn, they should be set carefully in wicker wine baskets and carried directly to the patrons' tables.

Care of Beer. Beer kegs should be handled as little as possible. They must not be moved or jostled for at least 24 hours before being tapped or excessive foaming is certain to result. "Wild" beer also occurs when the temperature is too high. If it is kept between 40 and 50 degrees it will maintain its sparkle and vitality. If the temperature drops much below 40 degrees the beer becomes flat.

After draught beer is brought to the bar, the pressure should be watched closely. Too little pressure will cause "flat" beer while too much makes the beer "wild"—excessively foamy.

Locks and Keys. The keys to the wine cellar should be entrusted to one person only so that responsibility for shortages may be easily traced. The person responsible for the bar should not have the key to the wine cellar. This is an insurance against the temptation to charge off to spillage and evaporation any shortages he may incur. When the person responsible for the keys leaves the employ of the hotel, the locks of the wine cellar should be changed. This relieves the absent employee of any suspicion for missing merchandise.

There will be occasions when a patron orders a bottle of champagne or some other item that is not available at the bar. One or two procedures may be followed, depending upon the volume of such sales. If the establishment is open for late supper business, the bar should be equipped with a cooler and a par stock maintained for filling these orders. Where sales of champagne are relatively small, the wine cellar keys may be kept in a signed and sealed envelope in the manager's office or some place designated by the manager, where they are available for use by a qualified employee. He will be charged with the responsibility of supervising the opening of the wine cellar and of sealing a new envelope containing the keys.

An emergency set of keys should be kept in a sealed and dated envelope and placed in the safe where it is available only to the management. A signed and witnessed record should be kept of any use of these emergency keys. This type of emergency protection is mainly to safeguard the employee who is primarily responsible for any losses occurring in the wine cellar.

Equipment for Opening Cases and Kegs. The minimum requirements in the way of tools for a wine cellar are a wire cutter, a carton-cutter, a nail puller in good condition, and a strong hammer. A small hatchet may also prove handy though it should never be used in place of a wire puller. These tools are simple and inexpensive but they can save many man-hours of time.

When wine cases are packed, baling wires or strands are stretched taut. When these wires are cut, the cut ends spring apart very suddenly. For this reason, it is best to cut the wire on the sides of the cases rather than the top, so they cannot spring up and injure the eyes or cut the face. Employees should be cautioned to wear gloves when opening cases.

Wire Baskets. A supply of flat wire baskets should be available when the cases are opened, large enough to accommodate one bottle lying flat on its side. These baskets will keep old red wines in this position from the time they leave the case until they are served to the patrons. They also add showmanship to the wine service.

Requisitions. The controls over liquor stock should be just as rigid as the controls a bank maintains over the money in its vaults. Money cannot be drawn from a bank without checks; liquor should not be taken from a wine cellar without a proper requisition. There are times when a bar may be short-handed and an unexpected amount of business pours in. At such times, employees are prone to issue items from the wine cellar and fill out the requisitions when they have more time. This is particularly true in small establishments where employees are often close friends and have no reason to doubt the integrity of the other fellow. At such times they should remember that, although bank tellers are frequently very close friends with depositors, sometimes next door neighbors, no matter how long the line before a teller's window, he must have the check before he issues the money. Unless these rules are strictly observed, no adequate control can be maintained.

Schedule of Hours. A regular schedule of hours should be established for the wine room. There is even less reason for the wine room to be open at all hours of the day than for the food storeroom, since the number of different items is smaller and it is an easier matter for the bar man to maintain all necessary stock at the bar. Only rarely will items be ordered which should necessitate a visit to the wine room. The hours will depend upon the individual establishment and the hours the bar is open for business.

Cooks' Beer and Cooking Wines. Just as all petty cash disbursements are accounted for, so should a strict accounting be made of the cooks' beer and cooking wines. If these items are issued without regular requisitions, accurate control is difficult if not impossible. The cooks' beer should, of course, go through the wine cellar. This obvious statement is made because, in many cases, cooks' beer is not handled through the wine cellar, but turned over to the food storeroom for issue with little or no record keeping. The manager should authorize the number of bottles of beer to be issued from the wine cellar each day and this issue should only be made upon the receipt of a properly authorized and executed requisition signed by the chef. Cooking wines should be handled in the same way—stored in the wine cellar and issued to the kitchen upon receipt of a requisition made out by the chef. The filling of these requisitions soon becomes a matter of routine but they allow the accounting department to have a full set of facts at its disposal.

INVENTORIES

Bin Cards. These cards—see illustration on page 399—presumably carry an accurate count of the items in each bin. Their value lies in having this information easily accessible to the wine steward, keeping him posted as to the stock on hand. However, they do mean a duplication of effort since this same information must be kept in the perpetual inventory. Also, the monthly inventory must be taken by physical count. Since bottles at the back of the shelves are often not easy to reach, there might be a tendency on the part of inventory takers to accept the figure on the bin cards as accurate. This may result in incorrect inventories since there could be incorrect entries on the bin cards.

If it is possible for the wine steward to have access to the perpetual inventory books in the accounting office to check the amounts on hand, thought should be given to the possible elimination of bin cards.

Independent Monthly Inventories. The perpetual inventory maintained by the accounting office is the basic instrument of control. Here all purchases and issues are recorded. As has been said, a full-scale physical count of items in the wine cellar should be made at the end of each month. Periodic test checks during the month are advisable. When the perpetual inventory does not tally with the month-end physical count, a re-check of purchases and issues should be made as well as a re-count of the stock. The reasons for any shortage may be due to one or several causes—breakage, mistakes in filling requisitions, faulty receiving records, unauthorized consumption, and/or poor key control. In any event, all shortages should be thoroughly investigated.

It is advisable to arrange the pages of the inventory book in the same order that the stock is arranged in the wine room. This saves time in taking the inventory and lessens the possibility of overlooking either a page in the inventory book or a section of the wine cellar. Each page and each section is checked off in order.

Empty Bottle Control. Every year, establishments handling bottled beverages lose thousands of dollars by the haphazard way they handle empty bottles, beer cases and kegs. These items represent a considerable investment on the part of the establishment and their handling and control should be adequate to protect this investment. The vendors certainly keep strict records of bottles delivered and returned and their customers should do the same.

The only way to save the investment in deposits on bottles or other containers is to have a regular bottle room where the empty bottles are received from within the establishment, to be stored, placed in the proper cases and regularly returned for credit. The accounting department should carry an "over and short" account on these bottles and when any appreciable shortage appears, necessary steps should be taken to learn the reason.

Inspection. Once a wine cellar has been established and satisfactory controls set up, periodic inspections should be made to see that the rules are followed and order maintained. A review of the methods used for opening cases, storing bottles, controlling empties, and maintaining proper temperatures will impress on the storeroom personnel the importance of strict adherence to the rules. A check on cleanliness and ventilation will reduce laxity in this respect.

Chapter XX: BANQUETS

THE BANQUET SECTION of a restaurant operation often combines the qualities of a "star-boarder" and a "problem-child."

In operations where banquets are numerous and the sales volume high, the rest of the food department is sometimes severely neglected, or it may be overloaded with some of the expenses which rightfully belong to the banquet department. If room service waiters, for example, are used as part of the banquet service staff, it is possible that no allocation is made for that portion of the room service waiters' payroll that should be charged to banquets. Sometimes, when overtime payments become necessary solely because of banquet needs, allocation of expenses may be made on a straight-time basis without due consideration of the overtime payments. This gives a distorted picture of the earnings of the banquet section.

PERSONNEL DUTIES

The Banquet Manager. The position of the banquet manager is an important one but because of his training along certain lines, he is sometimes difficult to control. Generally he is either a former salesman or promotion man with a wide following among the local people, or he may have been a head waiter. Only rarely has he come up through the kitchen where he would have gained training in food preparation. For this reason, he is prone to stress volume of sales, or good service, without taking into consideration the value of fine food or the cooperation necessary from the kitchen to deliver the banquet he has sold.

The banquet manager is responsible for the selling, booking, arranging, and serving of all banquet functions. These include dinners, luncheons, suppers, special breakfasts, dances, teas, weddings, anniversary parties, meetings, fashion shows, commercial displays, pageants, and various civic functions. He is responsible for arranging local publicity stories after he has the permission of the people arranging for the banquet. This should be done at the time the arrangements are made. Frequently, the patrons will prefer to send out their own publicity.

The banquet manager is all too often more interested in selling the banquet than in making certain that the food preparations that are promised can fit into the available kitchen facilities. He must realize that the patrons in the regular dining rooms are the bread-and-butter business and these patrons must be served as well as the banquet guests.

Unless every detail of the agreement made between the hotel and the chairman of the banquet committee is in writing, misunderstandings are bound to arise. The man who sells the banquet should see to it that there is a contract or letter embodying these details, signed by the chairman of arrangements or some equally responsible person. Copies of the menu selected should be distributed to the manager, chef, pastry chef, banquet head waiter, beverage department and accounting department, head checker, and steward. These menus should include all special arrangements which have been made to forestall or minimize the possibility of error or omission.

For example, arrangements may have been made for floral displays, wedding canopies, ice cream service parades, multi-colored spotlights, patriotic motifs, public address or photographic equipment, radio or television hook-ups, or other special requirements. All these details should be listed on the function sheet and sent to the various department or sub-department heads concerned with making the necessary arrangements.

A chronological cross-check file of special arrangements is advisable to make certain that adequate preparations have been made sufficiently in advance to insure proper delivery and installation time. Such a file might read:

February 1
Check Pastry Chef on wedding cake for Feb. 3, Smith-Brown wedding.
Check flower order of Feb. 2, Collegiate Dance.
Check ordering of flags for French Consulate dinner of Feb. 5.

Weekly lists of functions should be prepared and despatched to all appropriate department heads. Signatures should be received to insure the actual receipt of these lists. *Daily* function lists should be delivered to all department heads concerned as a reminder, and to permit them to make last minute arrangements. These schedules for advance notification should be spelled out carefully to avoid friction resulting from last minute details.

The final arrangements for every function should be inspected by the banquet manager or an assistant responsible to him. Approval of arrangements should be initialed by the banquet manager or a delegated representative for future reference.

Banquet Head Waiter. The duties of the banquet head waiter are considerably more complex than for the same position in an ordinary dining room. Each function has different arrangements and personnel requirements. He must draw up the floor plan and notify the housekeeper of the room and equipment requirements. He must also check linen supplies, floral decorations, special menu cards, programs, place cards, and ticket collecting arrangements, if tickets are used. His major problem is, of course, the food service. Engaging extra waiters, captains, and bus help is his responsibility as is the maintaining of their time records and the authorizing of payment vouchers for wages due.

The banquet head waiter must obtain a verification of the number of persons served from the head checker and present the check for payment or signature. He must determine in advance, on information received from the credit manager, whether cash payment is required. He must collect for all checks not approved in advance for credit.

Serving the food is the difficult part of his job. Timing the courses so that all guests are served at approximately the same time, and finished at the same time, is no simple trick and requires complete cooperation from everyone concerned.

Chef. The chef must estimate the required amount of food sufficiently in advance to permit proper purchasing. He must arrange a time schedule for food deliveries to his department and prepare his requisitions accordingly. Supervision of all preparation details and the service to the waiters is his responsibility. If he will need extra help in his department for the banquet, he must engage them after appropriate approval has been given, maintain time records, and authorize wage vouchers.

Steward. The steward must supervise the supplying of all special banquet equipment and check refrigerators for storage of items prepared in advance of service. Control over warewashing, storage of leftovers, and restoration to its proper place of all equipment used for the banquet, are also his responsibility.

INTER-DEPARTMENTAL FUNCTIONS

The banquet menu differs from the dining room menu in that it is "custom-tailored" while that for the dining room is "ready-made." In a banquet, the menu is adjusted to the customer; in a dining room the customer adjusts himself to the menu. Usually the banquet menu is made up weeks ahead of time in an office that is far removed from the kitchen. This creates problems, since it is difficult to determine so far in advance, market conditions or kitchen problems. With proper co-ordination between departments, these difficulties can be greatly reduced.

When the banquet manager discusses arrangements with a prospective customer, he should have at his finger tips a complete list of all functions booked for the date under discussion. When the same group has patronized the hotel on previous occasions, those menus should be reviewed to prevent repetitions. The purchasing agent, steward, or food cost accountant can provide the banquet manager with a list of seasonal price fluctuations of various items. This will serve as a guide to proper pricing of menus weeks or months in advance. The chef should make a list of certain dishes that will mean a need for extra kitchen personnel and if these dishes are chosen, they will naturally increase the price. Preparation problems of all kinds of dishes should be card-indexed for easy reference. If the banquet manager keeps a list of banquet problems and their history, this will help him also. This history should contain all the difficulties encountered in every banquet function and how they were met.

As has been stated, the banquet manager may be inclined, under pressure of the possible loss of a booking to a competitor, to disregard or minimize kitchen problems. However, he *must* bear in mind that a kitchen taxed beyond its capacity will mean poor service and loss of future business.

The housekeeping department must carry on its busy daily schedule regardless of other business in the house. Sometimes certain housemen are designated as banquet housemen, but unless banquet bookings are sufficient to keep them busy all the time, their production is likely to be almost nil between banquets. Also, they are responsible to the housekeeper for their time records, and to the banquet manager for their assignments. This dual control is not a good working arrangement. It is wiser to loan them on a temporary basis to the banquet department and during dull periods in that department, they can take over their work for the housekeeping department. The housekeeper will also have to cooperate in the matter of service elevator use during banquets and other special functions.

The supervision of the check room must be delegated to a responsible employee unless it is handled by a concessionaire. If the use of the check room facilities has not been included in the cost of the function, and gratuities are permitted, the accounting department must be consulted on the engaging of check room girls. These girls must be issued proper working instructions. The supply of checks and hangers must be checked in advance and provisions made for the proper identification of umbrellas and rubbers in case of wet weather.

The superintendent of service must be held responsible for instructing all uniformed employees what information to give patrons who make inquiries regarding the location of a function. The assistant manager in charge of the front office must similarly be charged with the responsibility of giving these same instructions to all front office employees. The selection of a spot near each street entrance for the posting of a daily-events bulletin will minimize the number of questions that need be answered. The bulletin board should provide complete information. First, the room location; any such designation as the "Blue Room" is not sufficient. Second, the information on the board should also state whether an elevator may be used or whether a convenient stairway is available and where it is located.

The chief engineer must be notified of all the requirements that are under his jurisdiction. Any special electrical, carpentry, or painting work should be specified in writing. The expected schedule of each function should be included in the notification to the chief engineer so that a responsible employee in his department can be assigned to the operation of lighting equipment.

The head house officer must be notified in advance of the type of function and the need for special protection from the local police department, if this is warranted.

The beverage department must be informed of the beverage requirements so that extra help may be engaged in advance. Supervision of banquet beverage service is extremely important to prevent errors or faulty handling. Quantity mixing of standard cocktails must be safeguarded against dilution.

The accounting department must provide beverage checkers to control the service of individual beverage orders.

Supervision of inter-departmental functions in medium-sized or large hotels will generally be handled best by an assistant banquet manager. Since this work must take in several departments that have other tasks to perform, specific authority of this employee should be carefully charted.

Minimum Guarantee. If possible, the banquet manager should require a guarantee of the minimum covers to be served. If he cannot secure a minimum guarantee, some arrangement should be made for additional covers that may be requested after the time limit has passed. The stipulation should provide that these last-minute covers will not necessarily receive the identical menu served to the others. This will eliminate overproduction. It will also prove a boon rather than a hardship to the arrangements committee. People who cannot decide until the last moment whether they will attend or not are problems to the committee as well as to the hotel. A simple statement by the committee to its own members that they cannot be guaranteed the same menu after a certain time will help them decide. At least it will remove the cause for discontent if a substitution is made.

Consultations. There should be close cooperation between the chef and the banquet manager. Periodic consultations will result in lowering the preparation costs for banquets. Certain fixed policies affecting the workload of the preparation staff should be established in these consultations.

It may be deemed advisable to prepare a "code" containing preparation arrangement guides for the banquet sales office. Such guides might read:

Avoid parfaits for parties of more than 75 because of melting and storage problems.

Avoid Chicken Pot Pie for parties of more than 100 since they tend to tie up the baking facilities.

Try not to sell oysters and clams to large parties exceeding 100 unless there is an adequate staff of oystermen.

Don't push Baked Alaska or Cherries Jubilee for parties in excess of 25, because of service and preparation difficulties.

Avoid Parisienne Potatoes for parties of more than 75 because of the man-power requirements for scooping out each potato and also the waste.

Try to sell Candied Sweets with Turkey because of the ease of preparation.

Try to sell Minced Creamed Chicken on Holland Rusk for large parties—easier preparation and service.

These are but a few of the possibilities that can be worked out in consultations between the chef and banquet sales manager.

Supervision of Extra Employees. Banquets of any size require extra help in the kitchen for preparation and dishwashing and in the dining room for service. Since these "extras" are not regularly employed, their work is usually not on a par with the regular employees. They are not as alert and, therefore, bear close watching. This means that there should be an adequate staff to supervise banquet service. The crew of captains is often reduced to a minimum since the more there are, the less each waiter's share of gratuities. Unless there are specific union requirements, the man in charge of food operation should be the only one to decide the ratio of the number of captains to the number of covers. Failure to observe this point can result in poor service and loss of repeat business.

In the absence of definite union requirements, decisions regarding the proper number of captains will depend largely on the menu, type of service expected, and the architectural features of the dining room. To achieve outstanding service, it is advisable to have one captain for every five or six waiters. For less elaborate service, one captain may be able to supervise adequately, eight or ten waiters but certainly no more.

Extra employees engaged for banquets are usually paid for the hours they work which, as a rule, is something under four hours. They should report early enough to be thoroughly briefed before the meal so that they will know the menu and where everything is kept that they will need.

SEATING SPACE FOR PATRONS

Excessive crowding in a banquet is a frequent cause for complaint by patrons. This is one phase of banquet operation where fairly specific formulae can be set forth as a guide.

If circular tables approximately eight feet in diameter are used to seat 10 to 12 patrons each, a definite minimum of 10 square feet per patron is a safe guide to avoid over-crowding.

If rectangular tables, four by eight feet or similar measurements, are used, seating eight to 10 patrons, the absolute minimum should be eight square feet per patron. Knowledge of the square footage of any room will indicate the reasonable seating capacity.

READY-REFERENCE BANQUET-PRICING TABLE

The banquet manager should have available a ready-reference banquet-pricing table, established by the food cost accountant and revised every 30 to 60 days to reflect serious changes in the market prices of the foods purchased.

This table can be set up in two sections for most convenient reference. One section should indicate the various entrees in different price ranges, these prices being dependent upon the accompanying dishes. The other section is the make-up menus of these accompanying dishes offered at various price levels. With key letters in the first section indicating the various make-up menus in the second section, the banquet sales staff can

ENTREE SELECTIONS	Portion Size	PRICE RANGE $1.25	$1.50	$1.75	$2.00	$2.25	$2.50	$2.75	$3.00	$3.25
Chicken a la King	2½ oz.	A	B	C	D	E	F	G	H	I
Chicken Patty	5 oz.	A	B	C	D	E	F	G	H	I
Half Broiled Chicken	½ each				A	B	C	D	E	F
Breast of Chicken or Capon	½ each						A	B	C	D
Half Roast Stuffed Chicken	½ each				A	B	C	D	E	F
Roast Stuffed Turkey	6 oz.							A	B	C
Filet of Sole	5 oz.			A	B	C	D	E	F	G
Broiled Scrod	6 oz.	A	B	C	D	E	F	G	H	I
Baked Halibut	6 oz.				A	B	C	D	E	F
Poached Salmon	6 oz.				A	B	C	D	E	F
Sea Scallops Saute	4 oz.		A	B	C	D	E	F	G	H
Broiled Cape Scallops	4 oz.			A	B	C	D	E	F	G
Baked Lobster Thermidor	4 oz.								A	B
Broiled Chopped Sirloin Steak	8 oz.		A	B	C	D	E	F	G	H
Broiled Salisbury Steak	8 oz.		A	B	C	D	E	F	G	H
Yankee Pot Roast	6 oz.						A	B	C	D
Roast Top Sirloin of Beef	5 oz.				A	B	C	D	E	F
Broiled Hip Steak	8 oz.								A	B
London Broil on Toast	5 oz.				A	B	C	D	E	F
Roast Leg of Lamb	6 oz.							A	B	C
Lamb Chop Mix Grill	6 oz.							A	B	C
Roast Stuffed Shoulder of Lamb	6 oz.			A	B	C	D	E	F	G
Grilled Pork Chop	6 oz.		A	B	C	D	E	F	G	H
Roast Loin of Pork	7 oz.					A	B	C	D	E
Baked Sugar Cured Ham	6 oz.						A	B	C	D
Broiled Ham Steak	8 oz.						A	B	C	D
Roast Leg of Veal	6 oz.							A	B	C
Scalopine of Veal	4 oz.				A	B	C	D	E	F
Breaded Veal Cutlet	5 oz.					A	B	C	D	E
Roast Stuffed Shoulder of Veal	5 oz.				A	B	C	D	E	F

ENTREE SELECTIONS	Portion Size	PRICE RANGE $3.50	$3.75	$4.00	$4.25	$4.50	$4.75	$5.00	$5.25	$5.50
Half Broiled Chicken	½ each	G	H	I						
Breast of Chicken or Capon	½ each	E	F	G	H	I				
Half Roast Stuffed Chicken	½ each	G	H	I						
Roast Stuffed Turkey	6 oz.	D	E	F	G	H	I			
Filet of Sole	5 oz.	H	I							
Baked Halibut	6 oz.	G	H	I						
Poached Salmon	6 oz.	G	H	I						
Baked Lobster Thermidor	4 oz.	C	D	E	F	G	H	I		
Yankee Pot Roast	6 oz.	E	F	G	H	I				
Roast Prime Ribs of Beef	10 oz.						A	B	C	D
Roast Sirloin of Beef – U.S. Good	8 oz.					A	B	C	D	E
Broiled Hip Steak	8 oz.	C	D	E	F	G	H	I		
London Broil on Toast	5 oz.	G	H	I						
Roast Leg of Lamb	6 oz.	D	E	F	G	H	I			
Lamb Chop Mix Grill	6 oz.	D	E	F	G	H	I			
Roast Stuffed Shoulder of Lamb	6 oz.	H	I							
Roast Loin of Pork	7 oz.	F	G	H	I					
Baked Sugar Cured Ham	6 oz.	E	F	G	H	I				
Broiled Ham Steak	8 oz.	E	F	G	H	I				
Roast Leg of Veal	6 oz.	D	E	F	G	H	I			
Scalopine of Veal	4 oz.	G	H	I						
Breaded Veal Cutlet	5 oz.	F	G	H	I					
Roast Stuffed Shoulder of Veal	5 oz.	G	H	I						

ENTREE SELECTIONS	Portion Size	PRICE RANGE $5.75	$6.00	$6.25	$6.50	$6.75	$7.00	$7.25	$7.50	$7.75
Roast Prime Ribs of Beef	10 oz.	E	F	G	H	I				
Broiled Filet Mignon	8 oz.								A	B
Roast Sirloin of Beef – U.S. Good	8 oz.	F	G	H	I					
Roast Sirloin of Beef – U.S. Choice	8 ox.				A	B	C	D	E	F
Broiled Sirloin Steak – U.S. Good	8 oz.	A	B	C	D	E	F	G	H	I

		$8.00	$8.25	$8.50	$8.75	$9.00	$9.25	$9.50	$9.75	$10.00
Broiled Filet Mignon	8 oz.	C	D	E	F	G	H	I		
Broiled Sirloin Steak – U.S. Choice	8 oz.		A	B	C	D	E	F	G	H

MAKE-UP MENUS OF ACCOMPANYING DISHES

MAKE-UP MENU (A)

Grapefruit Juice — Tomato Juice — Vegetable Juice
Potatoes du Jour — Vegetables du Jour
Cole Slaw — Mixed Greens
French Dressing

Pudding du Jour
Fruit Jello with Whipped Cream — Ice Cream Slice (Brick Ice Cream)

Rolls and Butter — Coffee

MAKE-UP MENU (B)

Tomato Juice — Half Grapefruit — Grapfruit Juice
Fruit Cup — Vegetable Juice

Potatoes du Jour — Vegetables du Jour

Cole Slaw — Lettuce and Tomato
Mixed Greens — Salad Dressing — Chef's Salad

Fruit Jello, Whipped Cream — Pudding du Jour
Ice Cream Slice (Brick) — Layer Cake
Apple Pie (9 Cut)

Rolls and Butter — Coffee or Demi-Tasse

MAKE-UP MENU (C)

Orange Juice — Pineapple Juice
Grapefruit Juice — Vegetable Juice
Fruit Cup — Half Grapefruit
Antipasto — Seafood Cocktail Copley
Tomato Juice — (No Shrimp or Crabmeat)

Parsley, French Fried or Whipped Potatoes

Carrots and Peas — Corn Saute — String Beans
Carrots Vichy — Green Peas

Hearts of Lettuce — Tossed Green Salad
Lettuce and Tomatoes — Combination Salad
Mexican Slaw, French or Russian Dressing

Fruit Jello with Whipped Cream — Pudding du Jour
Ice Cream Slice (Brick Ice Cream) — Layer Cake
Apple Pie (9 Cut) — Fruit Compote

Rolls and Butter — Coffee, Demi-Tasse, Tea or Milk

MAKE-UP MENU (D)

Tomato Juice — Grapefruit Juice
Orange Juice — Pineapple Juice
Antipasto — Vegetable Juice
Orange and Grapefruit Cup — Half Grapefruit
Fruit Cup — Seafood Cocktail Copley
Chilled Celery and Olives

Potatoes: Parsley — French Fried — Whipped
O'Brien — Hashed Brown — Rissole

Carrots and Peas — Garden Spinach — Green Beans
Green Peas — Corn Saute — Carrots Vichy
Macedoine Vegetables

Hearts of Lettuce — Lettuce and Tomato
Tossed Green Salad — Fruit in Aspic
Chiffonade Salad — Combination
French, Russian or 1000 Island Dressing

Fruit Jello with Whipped Cream — Pudding du Jour
Ice Cream Slice — Layer Cake
Apple Pie — Fruit Compote
Bisquit Tortoni — Cherry Sundae

Rolls and Butter — Coffee, Demi-Tasse, Tea or Milk

MAKE-UP MENU (E)

Fresh Fruit Cup — Half Grapefruit
Antipasto — Orange and Grapefruit Cup
Small Shrimp Cocktail — Seafood Cocktail Copley
Avocado and Diced Celery Dressing
Celery - Radishes - Olives

Consomme — Chicken Broth with Rice

Potatoes: Whipped — Delmonico — French Fried
Hashed Brown — O'Brien — Rissole

Buttered Green Peas — String Beans Orientale
Buttered Macedoine of Vegetables — Carrots Vichy
Buttered Lima Beans — Garden Spinach
Whole Kernel Corn — Buttered Brussel Sprouts

Chef's Salad — Combination Salad
Chiffonade Salad — Lettuce and Tomato Salad
Fruit in Aspic — Floridian Salad
French, Russian or 1000 Island Dressing

Ice Cream Slice (Brick) — Apple Pie
Layer Cake — Cherry Sundae
Biscuit Tortoni — Sheraton Parfait
Sheraton Ice Cream Pie

Rolls and Butter — Coffee, Demi-Tasse, Tea or Milk

MAKE-UP MENU (F)

Fresh Fruit Cup en Port — Orange and Grapefruit Cup
Antipasto — Half Grapefruit Maraschino
Avocado with Diced Celery Dressing — Seafood Cocktail
Celery — Radishes — Olives — Copley

Consomme Pastina — Chicken Broth with Rice
Chicken Gumbo Creole — Fresh Vegetable Soup
Tomato Bouillon en Tasse

Potatoes: French Fried Julienne — Hashed Brown
Whipped — Delmonico — Au Gratin — O'Brien

Buttered Green Peas — String Beans Orientale
Buttered Mixed Vegetables — Buttered String Beans
Buttered Lima Beans — Carrots Vichy
Whole Kernel Corn — Braised Celery — Garden Spinach

Chef's Salad — Tossed Garden Greens
Chiffonade — Lettuce and Tomato
Fruit in Aspic — Combination Salad
Cottage Cheese and Pear — Floridian
French, Russian or 1000 Island Dressing

Ice Cream Slice — Fruit or Cream Pie
Layer Cake — Ice Cream Sundae
Biscuit Tortoni — Sheraton Parfait
Sultana Roll — Sheraton Ice Cream Pie
Ice Cream Eclair — Chocolate Sauce

Rolls and Butter — Coffee, Demi-Tasse, Tea or Milk

MAKE-UP MENU (G)

Fresh Fruit Cup en Port — Half Grapefruit Maraschino
Antipasto — Orange and Grapefruit Cup
Avocado with Diced Celery — Seafood Cocktail Copley
Dressing — Shrimp Cocktail (4) (20 Size)

Celery — Radishes — Olives

Consomme Pastina — Chicken Broth with Rice
Chicken Gumbo Creole — Tomato Bouillon en Tasse
Cream of Tomato

Potatoes: Hashed Brown — Rissole — Julienne
Delmonico — Long Branch — Oven Brown
O'Brien — French Fried — Au Gratin

Buttered Green Peas — String Beans Orientale
Buttered Mixed Vegetables — Buttered Green Beans
Buttered Lima Beans — Carrots Vichy
Whole Kernel Corn Mexican — Garden Spinach
Buttered Brussel Sprouts — Braised Celery

Chef's Salad — Sheraton Salad Bowl
Chiffonade — Combination
Fruit in Aspic — Lettuce and Tomato
Cottage Cheese and Pear — Floridian

(*Continued on next page*)

MAKE-UP MENUS OF ACCOMPANYING DISHES—Continued

Waldorf Salad - Mayonnaise   Tossed Green Garden
French, Russian or 1000 Island Dressing

Cream or Fruit Pie   Ice Cream Slice
Layer Cake   Sheraton Ice Cream Pie
Biscuit Tortoni   Nesselrode Pudding
Ice Cream Sundae   Sheraton Parfait
Sultana Roll   Ice Cream Eclair - Chocolate Sauce

Rolls and Butter   Coffee, Demi-Tasse, Tea or Milk

MAKE-UP MENU (H)

Fresh Fruit Cup en Port   Half Grapefruit Maraschino
Avocado with Diced Celery Dressing   Shrimp Cocktail
Seafood Cocktail Copley   Orange and Grapefruit Cup
Antipasto   Assorted Canapes
Celery - Radishes - Olives

Consomme Pastina   Chicken Broth with Rice
Chicken Gumbo Creole   Tomato Bouillon en Tasse
Cream of Tomato

Potatoes: Delmonico   Hashed Brown   Au Gratin
O'Brien   Lyonnaise   Oven Brown
Baked   Long Branch   French Fried   Julienne

Buttered Green Peas   String Beans Orientale
Buttered Mixed Vegetables   Buttered Green Beans
Buttered Lima Beans   Carrots Vichy
Whole Kernel Corn Mexicaine   Garden Spinach
Buttered Brussel Sprouts   Braised Celery
Buttered Asparagus

Chef's Salad   Tossed Green Garden
Chiffonade   Floridian   Sheraton Salad Bowl
Fruit in Aspic   Waldorf   Combination Salad

Cottage Cheese and Pear   Lettuce and Tomato
French, Russian or 1000 Island Dressing

Fruit or Cream Pie   Sultana Roll   Nesselrode Pudding
Layer Cake   Frozen Pie   Sheraton Parfait
Biscuit Tortoni   Sundae   Ice Cream Slice (Brick)
Ice Cream Eclair   Chocolate Sauce   Sheraton Ice Cream Cake

Rolls and Butter   Coffee, Demi-Tasse, Tea or Milk

MAKE-UP MENU (1)

Fresh Fruit Cup en Port   Half Grapefruit Maraschino
Avocado with Diced Celery Dressing   Shrimp Cocktail
Seafood Cocktail Copley   Assorted Canapes
Antipasto   Orange and Grapefruit Cup
Celery   Radishes   Olives

Consomme Pastina   Chicken Broth with Rice
Chicken Gumbo Creole   Tomato Bouillon en Tasse
Cream of Tomato

Potatoes: Hashed Brown   Julienne   French Fried
Delmonico   Lyonnaise   Oven Brown
Baked   O'Brien   Long Branch   Au Gratin
Petit Pois au Beurre   String Beans Orientale
Buttered Mixed Vegetables   Buttered Green Peas
Buttered Lima Beans   Carrots Vichy
Whole Kernel Corn Mexicaine   Garden Spinach
Buttered Brussel Sprouts   Braised Celery
Buttered Asparagus

Chef's Salad   Sheraton Salad Bowl
Chiffonade   Floridian   Combination Salad
Fruit in Aspic   Waldorf   Lettuce and Tomato

Cottage Cheese and Pear   Tossed Green Garden Salad
Choice of Salad Dressing

Fruit or Cream Pie   Ice Cream Slice (Brick)
Layer Cake   Sheraton Ice Cream Pie
Biscuit Tortoni   Sultana Roll   Ice Cream Cake
Ice Cream Sundae   Baked Alaska   Sheraton Parfait
Glace Meringue   Bombe Glace
Ice Cream Eclair   Chocolate Sauce

Rolls and Butter   Coffee, Demi-Tasse, Tea or Milk

quote prices without the need for irksome, time-consuming calculations. An example of these two sections may be seen on pages 308, 309, and 310.

SELLING PUBLIC ROOMS

In hotels and catering establishments and now, more and more, in commercial restaurants, there is the problem of selling the ballrooms, banquet halls and private party rooms as part of a planned program rather than a hit-and-miss proposition.

Profitable Business. For the most part, the use of these facilities for banquets, luncheons, meetings, and dances has resulted in profitable business, perhaps more so than the regular restaurant operation. This has proven true to such a degree that some operators give as the reason for low profits from food and beverages a competitor's advantage through more and better banquet space and facilities.

While the foregoing may be true, yet caution is advised in recommending or approving the creation of additional public spaces without first determining the usage to which the existing facilities are being put.

As has been said on many occasions: "Nothing is more perishable than a hotel guest room." This is equally true of unused banquet and party rooms, and it is one of the Banquet Department's important functions to analyze this situation and direct its selling efforts accordingly.

Checking Productivity. Those operations which are fortunate enough to have adequate function rooms should record their occupancies in the same manner as is done with hotel guest rooms, that is, show a daily "Percentage of Occupancy of Function Rooms." Thus, it will be possible to check the productivity of the banquet selling, not only in terms of dollars and cents but, equally as important, in terms of the sale of units available to be sold.

While it is important to maintain the function book so as to provide spaces for each meal in each room each day, and thus avoid double bookings and show available vacancies, there is no reason why reports on a week-to-week basis of available function rooms for the next succeeding week should not be made. Thus, banquet sales efforts may be directed to fill in these gaps. Monthly records are also important to study day-by-day sales of particular meals in certain rooms. A good form to use for this purpose is illustrated below:

1953	BALLROOM					RED ROOM					"A"					"B"				
JAN.	B	L	D	M	DC	B	L	D	M	DC	B	L	D	M	DC	B	L	D	M	DC
1																				
2																				
3																				
4																				
5																				
6																				
30																				
31																				
Total																				

Legend: B—BREAKFAST; L—LUNCHEON; D—DINNER; M—MEETING; DC—DANCE

As will be mentioned later, this form may also be used by the accounting department in controlling banquet revenue.

Thus armed with applicable statistical data, it is only fair to examine the selling tools to determine whether the banquet selling personnel is properly equipped to do a job (assuming necessary professional ability).

Banquet Sales Office. Is it a sales office or a conglomeration of desks, telephones, typewriters, and office personnel?

It is important to separate the banquet business office from the banquet sales office. Thus a prospective banquet customer, who feels that his or her banquet is the "one in a million," is treated as though this were the only banquet that the hotel was ever going to serve.

Are there sufficient brochures, three-dimensional natural-color photographs of table settings, wedding cakes, parties in progress, buffets, ice carvings, etc., to give the guest almost "real life" evidence of what he or she may expect to be served? Are there scrap books of clippings and photographs of previous functions held at the hotel, complimentary letters on file from prior clients?

Are there display cabinets of service china, glassware, silverware, tea service, etc?

Are there facilities for offering afternoon tea or serving cocktails?

Is a *sales* person available during evenings to accommodate persons making inquiries after the day's working hours? Outside of metropolitan areas, evening shopping, especially by engaged couples, is most frequent.

Are forms set up to give the impression that *this* party will be "made to order"? Does the customer feel that the hotel is endeavoring to anticipate all his wants and desires—that the hundred and one details so necessary to a successful party are being taken care of? The form on this page has proved successful for this purpose. It also will be later

FUNCTION ______ CONTRACT NO. ______

DATE ______ DEPOSIT OF $ ____ DUE ______

ROOM ______ PRICE PER COVER $ ______ CHARGE TO ______

COVERS { GUARANTEED ______ / SERVED ______ RENTAL $ ______ ADDRESS ______

ADDITIONAL OR INCLUDED ITEMS

ITEM	ADDIT.	INCL.	ITEM	ADDIT.	INCL.	ITEM	ADDIT.	INCL.
MUSIC			PUBLIC ADDRESS			WEDDING CAKE		
FLOWERS & DECORATIONS			SPOTLIGHT					
			CARD TABLES & CHAIRS			WINES & LIQUORS		
CANOPY			PLATFORM					
CIGARS			DRESSING ROOM			BEER		
CIGARETTES								
SPEAKERS AMPLIFIERS						MINERALS		
AMPLIFIED MUSIC			TIPS					

DATE	EXPLANATION	FOLIO ✓	DEBITS	DATE	EXPLANATION	FOLIO ✓	CREDITS

discussed in the section concerning control of banquet revenue.

Index Files. Are there chronological (and alphabetical) files of previous years' functions? Has follow-up correspondence been instituted?

Clipping Service. Does the hotel subscribe to a clipping service for social notices and follow-up thereon for future wedding business, etc?

A source of profitable business is the "outside caterer." Many hotels have made arrangements whereby the hotel furnishes space; linens; china, glass and silver; service personnel; food-warming facilities, and the caterer provides the food. The hotel sells the beverages, bills and collects from the banquet customer, and pays the caterer a stipulated amount per cover served.

Control of Banquet Revenue. The banquet form mentioned earlier is usually incorporated into the banquet contract, using a standard legal form of contract. Execution of this form by both parties concerned puts in motion the start of the accounting control of the particular function.

All contracts and acceptances are carefully checked for advance deposits. Whenever deposits are required, the amounts are lodged with the cashier and are identified by the serial number of the banquet receipt voucher presented to the patron by the banquet department. These deposits are listed individually on the cash sheets, and the amounts are credited to the proper banquet accounts in the accounting department. In some instances, contracts provide for a series of deposits in advance of the date the functions are to be held. Control sheets should be prepared in the accounting department for reminder purposes and any such advance deposits not received on their due dates should be reported to management and/or the banquet manager.

Banquet checks should be made up in triplicate and be serially controlled. At the conclusion of a function, the banquet department prepares the check from information contained in the contract and related data, as well as the actual service. It is then signed by a responsible representative of the engagor. The check is distributed as follows:

Original copy—Auditing department
Duplicate copy—Banquet guest
Triplicate copy—Banquet department

On page 314 is a suggested form of banquet check.

The accounting department should check daily to ascertain that for every function listed, a charge has been made in accordance with the function contract.

No cash disbursements chargeable to the engagors' accounts should be permitted without detailed explanations in support thereof and then only on proper authority. This has been a subject of misuse and abuse and requires constant and careful scrutiny.

Aids for Control of Banquet Revenue. There are several aids to use in assisting the accounting department in controlling banquet revenue.

HOTEL BANQUET DEPT.		NO. ______
Contract No.	Room	Date
CHARGE TO		
RENT		$
Covers at $		
Cake Boxes		
Beverages		
Flowers		
Music		
Cigars		
Cigarettes		
Tips		
	City Sales Tax	$
Folio	Total	
	Less Deposit	
	Balance	$

- -

HOTEL ______ BANQUET DEPT.	NO. ______

These revolve about the activities of the housekeeper and/or assistant managers in hotels. Just as a careful check is made of guest rooms occupied through maids' and housekeepers' reports, so should the function rooms be checked. Some hotels have the housekeeper submit daily to the auditing department a list of banquet and private rooms occupied or used the preceding day. From this data, a check may be made to ascertain that such spaces have been charged for through the banquet journal. On occasion, the banquet department will fail to prepare a check for these room rentals.

Another way to control banquet revenue is through the use of a special form which would be filled out by an assistant manager several times a day, say at 10:30 A. M., 12:30 P. M., 3:00 P. M., 7:00 P. M., and 10:00 P.M., or any other schedule suitable to management.

When the inspection report is completed it should be delivered to the auditor. In the accounting office each report should be checked to ascertain that the occupancy of the function rooms agrees with the function list for the particular day and, more important, that the proper revenue is received for each room shown as occupied at the agreed-upon charges for the type of service rendered. Any variations should be traced immediately and, if not reconciled, reported to management. The form on this page may be used for this purpose.

HOTEL U. S. A.
FUNCTION ROOM INSPECTION REPORT

Day ________ Date________ Time________

ROOM	B	L	D	M	DC	OTHER	ENGAGOR	✓
Ballroom								
Red Room								
White Room								
Blue Room								
"A"								
"B"								
"C"								
"D"								
"E"								
"F"								
"G"								

When Completed Deliver to Auditor

Legend:
B-Breakfast; L-Luncheon; D-Dinner
M-Meeting; DC-Dance

Signed ________ Position________

In the accounting department, the banquet or function check is reconciled with the contract provisions as recorded in the banquet ledger account to determine that all chargeable items have been included on the check.

A further check is made by comparing the number of covers served, as furnished by the chef, with the actual number charged for. It is also most helpful to have a representative or representatives of the accounting department (food and beverage checkers or others) on hand to assist in the checking of food and beverages served.

Before completion of the determination of the number of covers to be charged, minimum guarantees must be verified, and changes made when a function falls short of the number of covers contracted for. Management may decide to waive all or a part of the additional covers to be charged for. In any event, it is important to make the full charge and then issue a properly approved allowance, if necessary, with a complete history of the transaction.

Verification of all invoices and/or charges against the hotel for flowers, music, and entertainment, cigars, cigarettes, tips, etc., and of their charges to specific functions must be made before they are approved for payment.

From all the foregoing it becomes obvious to the reader that banquets can play an important part and contribute much to the success of a restaurant operation. Functions of this type are usually productive of greater gross profits than ordinary dining room sales and serve as an important source of wine and liquor business. Consequently, it is incumbent upon those who have the responsibility of selling, preparation, and service to cooperate to the fullest extent to the end that high volume is maintained, that the patrons are pleased with the quality of the food and its service, and that adequate profits result.

Chapter XXI: MUSIC AND ENTERTAINMENT

SINCE MUSIC AND ENTERTAINMENT mean a relatively large expenditure, a careful analysis is necessary to determine, (1) the most profitable policy, (2) when changes in that policy are advisable because of special features, and (3) what steps should be taken to gain the maximum advantage from the expenditure. With these precautionary measures, music and entertainment, in certain types of operations, can stimulate food and beverage sales; without them, the expenditure can become a millstone dragging the catering operation down to failure.

TYPES OF ENTERTAINMENT

There are four types of music and entertainment to be found in hotels and restaurants: (1) feature acts, (2) dance music, (3) individual instrumentalists, and (4) incidental music.

Feature Acts. These consist of one or more performers whose names are usually featured in various forms of promotion, in addition to the musicians. When these performers are well known nationally, an extensive external promotion campaign will stimulate patronage from all parts of the city and from the suburban districts. This means newspaper advertising locally and in suburban newspapers and nearby city dailies. To this may be added billboard advertising.

When the individual performers are not well known, the promotion is usually confined to internal advertising and the use of mailing lists.

Dance Bands. Many hotels and restaurants feature a dance band without any individual performers. These bands play during dinner and continue until sometime after midnight. In some communities, afternoon dance music starts with luncheon; others have found afternoon tea dances on Saturdays to be profitable. Afternoon music may bring in business otherwise completely lost, particularly in those places removed from theaters or other evening entertainment features and possibly located in shopping or commercial centers.

Where lunch business is brisk without the added expense of music, this business may be carried through the afternoon lull from three o'clock on through the cocktail hour by the addition of dance music. Each establishment must experiment and carefully analyze its own situation in this respect.

Frequently, in places featuring dance music, a simple fundamental in showmanship is completely overlooked. When a vocalist, male or female, sits with the band and rises from time to time to sing, the audience rarely applauds. However, if that same singer is introduced by name and the title of the song is announced, the patrons will notice her and generally applaud. This simple expedient transforms unnoticed singing into a show.

Individual Instrumentalists. Such performers often attract additional patronage, particularly in cocktail lounges, before and after dinner service. Organists, pianists, accordionists or guitarists are the ones most usually employed. With a large repertoire of familiar music and an engaging personality, these instrumentalists may attract a large repeat trade.

Incidental Music. By incidental music, reference is made to that which is "piped in" over a loud speaker. The cost is nominal and the reaction of patrons, particularly those dining alone, indicates an approving response. It is possible to merchandise this music by having a program printed on table tent cards. Many people will remark favorably on this service. Such music lends dignity and tone to a room, particularly during the dinner hour.

NET COST

The net cost of music and entertainment should have the closest scrutiny because, without specific knowledge of just what is meant by "net cost," even capacity business may prove unprofitable.

"Gross cost" is the amount paid for music and entertainment *without regard to the cover charge*. Where there is no cover charge, the gross cost automatically becomes the net cost. Where there is a cover charge, since patrons are obviously paying it because music and entertainment are furnished, it appears logical that the total sum of the cover charge is directly attributable to music and entertainment. This revenue should, therefore, be deducted from that expense to determine the *net cost*.

The cost of music and entertainment is not always the basic contract cost. Here is where the *small print* comes in. Usually there is the expense for rehearsal time which can vary greatly with each artist. This item is negligible where an artist carries his or her own band. One factor which can boost the cost of rehearsal time is the lack of planning on the part of the band management in the matter of instrument set-up, microphone placement, and lighting. Where continuous entertainment is the house policy and the business is attracted more on the basis of the entertainment than on the quality of the dance music, it has proven good policy to have a house orchestra trained in show accompaniment. Because many dance bands cannot do an adequate job of accompanying, such a plan would result in shorter rehearsals and aid in improving the artist's performance.

A large gross expenditure for music and entertainment does not necessarily mean a large percentage of the revenue dollar if the volume is considerable, and the cover charge revenue is substantial. Conversely, a relatively modest gross outlay may impose a heavy percentage burden on every revenue dollar if the volume is light and the cover charge income small or non-existent.

THE BREAK-EVEN POINT

It is extremely important to establish exactly at what point entertainment becomes either a drag on the revenue dollar or gives it a boost. Any costs above that point mean a loss; any costs below mean a profit. The determination of this break-even point is important, not only for the best reason in the world—that of profit—but also because sufficient basic information, readily available, can facilitate any desired or necessary change in policy.

A schedule giving the net cost of each booking on a week-to-week basis, will readily indicate to the management which entertainers constitute a heavy drain on every revenue dollar and which permit a profitable return. A form for this purpose appears below.

WEEKLY ENTERTAINMENT SHEET

Week of	Entertainer	Total Revenue	Food and Beverage Sales	Cover Charges	Music Cost	Entertainment Cost	Gross Total Music and Entertainment	Net Music and Entertainment Cost (less covers)	% of Net Music and Entertainment Cost To Food and Beverage Sales
9/10-16		$	$	$	$	$	$	$	$
9/17-23									
9/24-30									

With additional columns for payroll, advertising, and other expenses and the corresponding percentage breakdown, the complete picture of the breakdown of the revenue dollar becames available on a week-to-week basis. Getting these same figures on a monthly basis only may easily give a misleading picture and certainly cannot show the effect of individual groups of entertainers unless each group is engaged for a period of a month. This, as will be pointed out, is not a desirable arrangement. Furthermore, calculations on a weekly basis permit the consideration of various special events and holidays which strongly affect revenue.

Increases in volume will not have a marked bearing on cost of sales of food and beverages, unless there is a wide range between food and beverage cost percentages, and an appreciable increase in the beverage sales. This could affect the percentage that the cost of sales bears to total sales. For example, if food and beverage sales each amount to $1000 with food cost $350 or 35 per cent of sales, and beverage cost $270 or 27 per cent of sales, the total cost of merchandise sold would be $620 or 31 per cent of the total sales. If food and beverage sales were each doubled, making a total revenue of $4000 and total costs of $1240, the percentage between cost of sales and total sales would still be 31 per cent. However, if food sales only increased to $1500 and beverage sales to $2500, total sales would still be $4000 but the costs would be $525 for food and $675 for beverages, making a total of $1200 or 30 per cent of the total sales.

Advertising expense will not bear any fixed percentage relationship to volume as a rule, but will vary considerably, depending upon the type of campaign in progress.

Payroll percentages of the revenue dollar should show a decrease with increased volume of sales, although not in direct ratio since some additional help will usually be needed which will reduce the percentage of gains.

Each operation must develop its own break-even point for every type of entertainment since food costs, payroll costs, and entertainment costs vary in different parts of the country and, because of varying standards of service, even within the same city. Also, there will be variations between different volume ranges within the same establishment. It is important, however, to develop an entertainment history file for ready cross-reference purposes.

An example of a break-even point follows: *

Cost of food and beverage sales	30%
Payroll—direct operating staff	30
Employees' meals	2
China, glass, silver, and linen	3
Uniforms and guests' supplies	2
Music and entertainment	11
Fuel and laundry	2
Menus and miscellaneous	3
Advertising	4
Heat and light	3
Rent or equivalent space charge	10
Total	100%

* These figures are not to be construed as satisfactory operating norms. They are used solely for illustrative purposes.

It is obvious that if any of these costs materially increase so that the total is in excess of 100%, deficit operation will result. If this situation continues for any length of time, a change in policy is clearly indicated. If the reverse is true and by good management these percentages are decreased without any serious sacrifice of quality or service, then the break-even point has been lowered.

SCHEDULE PROBLEMS

Length of Engagement. Determining the most advantageous length of time for each engagement requires careful study. When entertainers are engaged for more than one week at a time, comparisons of each week's volume of business should be made. Some entertainers may build up volume as time goes on; with others the volume falls off. The third week of any entertainer's engagement will bear close study as by this time interest seems to have reached a saturation point. Even though the results of such study may be inconclusive, it may be well to form a policy of limiting engagement to two-week periods with options or return engagement later in the season if it seems advisable. This policy is better than to risk costly experiments that go beyond the point of patron interest. This is particularly true where performers have a set show routine with no new material to add to it. Major artists usually are in a position to present virtually a new show even weekly if required.

In making these weekly comparisons, allowance must be made for the season of the year, holidays, or the dates of national sports events, competition, program content, and the weather.

Special Dates. Booking entertainment without one eye on the calendar can prove costly. There are some seasons when expensive talent is not necessary since capacity business is practically assured; there are other seasons when business is slack and entertainment should be geared to meet this situation.

In many hotels and restaurants, business is practically assured on New Year's Eve. Entertainment is necessary at that time, but expensive entertainment seems a waste of money. When arrangements are made for entertainment for this occasion, past records should be studied for at least the two previous years. Consideration should be given to the fact that almost universally, a seven-to-ten-day lull sets in directly after New Year's Eve. Before final booking decisions are made, each day's business during that period should be studied for the past two years. To be tied up with a costly contract during a dull period can prove disastrous.

Christmas Day is traditionally a home holiday. Many hotels and restaurants close their dining rooms for that day because business is so slow. Even on Christmas Eve the normal run of attractions may not prove of interest. It might be advisable to engage local talent to sing or play Christmas carols. This also gives an opportunity for strong local publicity.

Before engaging talent for the holiday season, find out on what day of the week Christmas falls as it may be possible for one engagement to end on December 24th and a new one to begin December 26th.

An effort should be made to obtain the exact dates of all major sports events as far in advance as possible and bear them in mind when entertainment is booked. Those events held at night usually have a marked effect on business from 8:00 until 11:00 P.M. Some special arrangements may be necessary. This subject is treated more fully later in this chapter. Sports events held in the daytime tend to stimulate the volume of business in dining rooms featuring entertainment. Some afternoon sports events are so well attended that New Year's Eve conditions are almost duplicated. Food and beverage revenue statistics during prior events of a similar nature should always be on hand when bookings are made for entertainment on these dates.

Conventions have a variety of influences on the volume of business, depending upon the character of the conventions and where they are housed. During some conventions, people prefer the privacy of their own rooms for get-togethers or small meetings. In this case, the volume of room service business will be large while the volume in the dining room featuring entertainment may actually show a decline. When a convention of this type is booked it is advisable, if the entertainment is not already engaged, to study revenue statistics of such previous conventions. The convention days should be compared with the same days of the most recent non-convention week. For example, if a convention was booked from Monday through Friday of the fourth week of October, the third week of October of the same year, if no convention was booked, should be used for comparison to determine the effect of the convention on revenue.

It is of extreme importance that the entertainers be notified well in advance of the particular type of a convention. One song or specialty number of significance to the convention group may very easily stimulate business. If a convention is booked after entertainment has been arranged, correspondence details can usually be made through the booking agent. The entertainers then have sufficient advance notice of any preferences or suggestions the convention arrangements committee may have.

Entertainers prefer to perform before capacity audiences; booking agents prefer this also. Convention committees usually like to have something that is specially arranged for their entertainment. All these people can be pleased if the one in charge of housing the convention will find out what is wanted and give the entertainers sufficient advance notice. It is unfair to expect entertainers to learn of a convention's existence when they arrive. They have the ordinary problems of rehearsing their program without being expected to whip up something at the last moment that will meet their usual standard and professional style. Foresight along these lines may mean a long remembered convention and considerable extra business.

There is almost invariably a pre-Christmas lull when business is in the doldrums. This may extend for a full two weeks before Christmas, depending upon what day of the week Christmas occurs. This is due to shopping and other pre-holiday preparations. The week before Christmas is reputedly the low point in all entertainment fields during the entire season, extending from early fall to late spring. It is doubtful if the most expensive entertainer could lure many people into a public dining room during this time of the year. Therefore, attention should be given to a policy of retrenchment at this time with, possibly, programs of local interest.

The week between Christmas and New Year's Day generally produces a high volume of business followed by a post-New Year's lull unless a large convention is booked, or some special events are taking place. This lull may be caused by physical exhaustion or depleted funds. Whatever the cause, it is important that booking arrangements for this period be made with full cognizance of this situation. This is not just another winter week but a very "tough" week.

The period of Lent and Holy Week (the week before Easter) require special attention in nearly all communities. Since the calendar date of Easter is variable, it is well to determine when Lent occurs, particularly if entertainment arrangements are made during the preceding autumn. A change in policy may be advisable during this time, making it a sort of "holding" period with less expensive entertainment than usual. However, communities differ, and testing out different ideas may prove successful.

The summer season necessitates marked changes in the entertainment policy. Air-conditioned entertainment rooms are a *must* during this season. Competition has seen to that. Parking facilities are of nearly equal importance. Summer entertainment operations attract a motor trade—people from outlying communities who will not travel to town during the winter. To build up and retain this trade, parking facilities near at hand are necessary. Furthermore, "convenient parking" should be an important part of every advertisement.

Many sections of the country have their own regional holidays such as the Rodeo in Gallup, New Mexico; Cherry Blossom Time in Washington, D. C., or the Mardi Gras in New Orleans. These all have a marked influence on the volume of business as they are of national interest and attract many visitors from outside the community. Many of these special occasions do not have a set calendar date. Hence, their exact dates should be determined well in advance and their influence on revenue estimated so that bookings for entertainment may be made accordingly.

SELECTION OF ENTERTAINMENT

Suitability. It is frequently very difficult to determine from photographs and descriptions whether a single entertainer or a group will be suitable for a given location but suitability has a very direct bearing on the volume of business. Entertainers whose brand of humor or type of entertainment is not in keeping with the tone of a dining room or the character of the patronage are apt to have an adverse effect on local or repeat business. The general public is fairly lenient in its appraisal of sophisticated entertainment but anything that is crude or in poor taste is likely to be resented.

Architectural Features of Entertainment Rooms. In many public rooms some forms of entertainment are scarcely visible to a large number of patrons, due to pillars or insufficient elevation of the floor in remote parts of the room. Acts that require close visual attention and which cannot be seen will make some patrons very indignant because they feel left out of things, since they are paying for something which they cannot enjoy. When such architectural drawbacks cannot be corrected, it is best to secure entertainment that has primarily an auditory appeal.

Competition. To plan entertainment attractions successfully, the planner should be aware of the offerings of competitive establishments and the results achieved. There are no set rules for accumulating this data but brief notes of pertinent data can be extremely helpful at times. Such notes should give the name of the group, the type of entertainment, the date of their appearance, and the apparent results. They might also include suggestions for improvement or glaring faults that should be remedied. These notes may be of more help in learning what to avoid than what to sign up as there seems to be no certainty that a group will duplicate its success in a different location.

Patron Preferences. Pleasing the patrons is a basic rule and their preferences must be taken into account. Various forms of market research can be used to ascertain patrons' preferences. Table tent cards inviting opinions or suggestions will indicate a trend. If space is left on their cards for signature and address, this is one good way of adding to the mailing list. The head waiter often has an opportunity to query the patrons diplomatically. The waiters themselves often overhear comments about the entertainment.

Week-End Volume. In some communities, it is extremely difficult if not impossible to maintain a profitable entertainment program throughout the week. A study should be made of the daily business, Monday through Thursday, and compared with Friday and Saturday. Where the differential in volume is large between the week days and the week-end, it may be wise to limit the entertainment to the week-end only. The difficulty here will be to obtain talent only for week-ends. However, in a community large enough to support such dining rooms featuring entertainment, there is usually sufficient local talent that will perform on this basis. This policy can serve as a compromise between having no entertainment at all and entertainment that cannot pay for itself throughout the week.

Calculating Capacity. When nationally famous headline attractions are being considered, some thought should be given to the capacity of the dining area. There is no profit in attracting thousands of patrons if only hundreds can be served. The possible revenue from the available capacity should be calculated. Against this should be placed the costs, to determine whether there is a possibility of profit.

SCHEDULE ALTERATIONS

If a night baseball game or boxing exhibition or other attraction virtually annihilates business, entertainers on a fixed schedule will be performing to empty chairs. The usual starting time for most dining room entertainment is 8:30 to 9:00 P.M. but sporting events or other evening attractions start about that time also. An earlier dinner show, beginning at 6:45 or 7:00 P.M., will enable people to have dinner, see the entertainment and still get to their game or theatre or wherever they may be going. Most business people leave their offices before 6:00 P.M., usually at 5:00 or 5:30, and would probably welcome an earlier dinner hour. As a matter of fact, where some of them now go home for dinner they might stay in town or downtown if this arrangement were possible.

When such schedule alterations are made to provide early dinner entertainment, the fact should be extensively advertised and space should be secured in the daily papers as near as possible to the advertisement of the event itself. Direct-mail announcement to nearby commercial organizations might also be advisable. Hand-out posters to persons waiting for street cars or busses might prove effective if given out the night before the event when plans are still subject to change.

SPECIAL TRANSPORTATION

All persons attending large public gatherings become concerned about transportation. Some who are uncertain about the amount of time that should be allowed will rush through their dinner to make certain they will not be late, only to arrive a half-hour ahead of time. This time might have been spent enjoying a good dinner and entertainment if they were sure of reaching their destination in time. It does not require great effort to make arrangements with a taxi company, or even a bus company, to have sufficient vehicles available to carry these people to wherever they are going. Guests can be asked to make their request for transportation at the beginning of their meal so that arrangements can be made for sufficient vehicles to be ready for them when their dinner is finished. If bus facilities are not available for this purpose, certainly taxi transportation can be on call. Charter bus service can be advertised as being available to patrons making arrangements a day in advance.

When special events produce great emptiness in a dining room, such unusual arrangements are necessary to induce patrons to have an early dinner in the hotels and restaurants.

Ticket Facilities. Whenever possible, arrangements should be made for the sale of tickets somewhere on the premises to any sporting or other special event. This fact should be included in the advertisement previously mentioned. People coming to a place to buy tickets mean additional traffic, and this usually results in more business.

An entertainment policy is not something which can be embarked upon casually. Every angle must be studied—the type of patronage, the physical properties of the building, the location of the establishment, and its immediate surroundings. If all of these factors make an entertainment program seem wise, once having embarked upon it, the results must be analyzed just as carefully as the menu is, or should be, analyzed. Such a policy can be the right move in some cases, but a very wrong move in others.

Chapter XXII: BUDGETING FOR A FOOD AND BEVERAGE OPERATION

DURING THESE TIMES of high unit costs for merchandise and labor, as well as for the other items of supplies, expenses, and services involved in a food and beverage operation, it has become more than ever essential that management budget its operations to a desirable or, at least, necessary goal.

The preparation of budgets too often takes the form of the setting down of income and expense figures experienced in a prior period, with a passive acceptance of an inadequate end result projected, resignation to a sense of the inevitable, and a trust in providence or in just plain luck, that some unforeseen circumstances will bring increased volume and thereby cure all of the projected deficiencies and inadequacies of such a budget.

For the purpose of this discussion of budgeting theory, an entirely different and positive approach is used. Naturally, in any illustration or discussion of a principle, a set of hypothetical circumstances must be used and certain assumptions made as to basic governing conditions. Drawing upon our very considerable experience in the industry, we have, however, tempered the purely theoretical exposition of budgeting principles with the practical applicability of the end result, as actually demonstrated in a great many food and beverage operations throughout the country.

THE PRIME PURPOSE OF BUSINESS

The first step in the building of the budget should be recognition of the prime purpose of the business itself—an earnings return on the required investment of capital funds, and a profit return for successful management effort. The basis or end purpose of the budget is, therefore, realization of the amount representing the accomplishment of these two purposes. To illustrate:

Our hypothetical set of circumstances presumes that the investment in furniture, fixtures and equipment of the restaurant, in this instance, requires $200,000 of capital funds. We will assume further that the minimum amount representing a satisfactory return on this capital investment, together with a minimum satisfactory amount of operating profit, would be equivalent to 10% of the investment, or at the rate of $20,000 per year. This figure would be before consideration of taxes on income. Next, recognition must be given to the gradual using up of the investment in fixtures and equipment and the necessity for their replacement in a going business. Using an estimated useful life of twelve and one-half years for such fixtures and equipment, the operations should provide $16,000 annually for that purpose. Occupancy costs, whether they consist of maintenance, taxes and insurance for an owned building, or of rent payable to a lessor, are assumed for this purpose to amount to $24,000 per year.

Under this set of assumed circumstances, then, the hypothetical food and beverage operation must produce a total profit of $60,000 for the year, in order to cover rent, recovery of principal (depreciation), a moderate return on capital funds invested, and a minimum profit for management effort.

In order to fix in mind the different components and amounts of this all-important start in budgeting, these are tabulated as in the following:

BASIS OF BUDGET		
Investment—Furniture, Fixtures and Equipment	$200,000.00	
Budgeted Profit before Income Taxes, at 10% of Investment		$ 20,000.00
Depreciation—Computed at a 12½ Year Life of Fixtures and Equipment		16,000.00
Occupancy Costs		
Rent, Property Taxes, Fire Insurance, Etc.—Assumed to be		24,000.00
TOTAL OPERATING PROFIT REQUIRED TO COVER RENT, DEPRECIATION, AND RETURN ON INVESTMENT		$ 60,000.00

SALES VOLUME REQUIRED

Next in the process of building the budget, is the projection of the minimum volume of sales required, under good management, to produce the necessary operating profit. Again drawing upon our experience with many restaurant operators, we find that a profit result of 15% of gross sales, while neither a minimum nor a maximum measure of profit performance, represents one which is regularly attained by a great many operators, under good management. For our purposes, then, we can compute the minimum gross volume of sales which, producing a 15% operating profit, will result in the required $60,000 operating result projected by the budget. As $60,000 represents 15% of $400,000, the latter figure is used as the sales volume requirement.

As the hypothetical food and beverage operation would include both classes of sales, with their widely divergent direct prime cost factors, it is necessary to project a division of this sales volume as between food and beverages. These proportions vary widely in actual business but, for the purposes of this illustration, it is assumed that the operation will be primarily an eating establishment with the beverage department somewhat secondary in volume importance. Assuming that beverage sales will run 25% of the total, the budget projections will provide for food sales of $300,000 and beverage sales of $100,000 for the year.

AMOUNTS AVAILABLE FOR COSTS AND EXPENSES

Now that the amounts of required sales and operating profit have been determined, we can arrive at the number of dollars available for all other costs and expenses of doing business—for food and beverage costs, pay roll, and all other operating expenses.

COST AND EXPENSE BUDGET

	Amount	%
Sales	$400,000.00	100.
Less: Operating Profit Required (As Above)	60,000.00	15.
Balance—Available for Food and Beverage Cost, Pay Roll, and Other Operating Expenses	$340,000.00	85.

Thus, we find that $340,000, or 85% of the total sales, remain to be spread over the costs and expense of furnishing food and drink to customers.

With eighty-five cents of each dollar of sales remaining to be spread over the costs of merchandise, pay roll, supplies, management, business overhead, advertising, heat, light and power, and maintenance expenses, it is now necessary to appraise carefully either the existing style and scale of operations, or the plans in this respect in the case of a new operation. Prices, type of service, hours of service, etc.—all must be established before entering into the next phase of building the budget.

For the purpose of our illustration, we will assume that the restaurant in question is not an extremely high-priced, top luxury operation, but that it is more than a medium-price operation and that the staff, decor, and service are in keeping with such a price level.

Bearing in mind that we have eighty-five cents of each dollar of sales to spread over all operating costs and expenses, it now behooves us to set down first the types or groups of such costs and expenses to be provided for.

(1) Cost of food and beverage sales
(2) Operating pay roll
(3) Other direct operating supplies and expenses
(4) Management compensation
(5) Other administrative expenses
(6) Pay roll taxes and employee relations
(7) Advertising and promotion
(8) Heat, light and power
(9) Repairs and maintenance

Filling in the budget allowances for those items or groups of cost, about which we might have some opinion based on experience, we might budget 1½% of sales as a necessary expenditure for advertising and promotion to *maintain* a satisfactory sales volume. We might conclude that management compensation should be equivalent to 2% of sales and provide such a figure in the budget of expenses. Knowing that the "cost of doing business" conservatively runs around 6% of sales would enable us to fill in the other administrative expense budget at 4% of sales—a total of 6% for all administrative business expense, including management. Next, and using the experience of others in the same type of business at about the same sales volume, we might budget 2% of sales for heat, light and power expenses, and about the same amount for necessary recurring ordinary repairs and maintenance expenses.

This first series of steps in planning the expense budget based, realistically, upon knowledge of ordinary business considerations and requirements, results in tentative establishment of this part of the budget, as follows:

	Amount	*% to Sales*
Management compensation	$ 8,000.00	2.0%
Other administrative expenses	16,000.00	4.0
Advertising and promotion	6,000.00	1.5
Heat, light and power	8,000.00	2.0
Repairs and maintenance	8,400.00	2.1
	$46,400.00	11.6%

Acceptance of this part of the budget as practicable, would leave $293,600 or 73.4 cents of each dollar of sales remaining for the balance of the budget, comprising by far the heaviest items of cost. Specifically, this 73.4 cents of each dollar of sales must provide for the raw cost of food and beverages served to customers, wages of employees engaged in preparation and service, direct operating supplies and charges, and the increasingly cost-wise important taxes on pay rolls and fringe benefits for employees.

Pay Roll Cost. Tackling first the matter of operating pay roll cost, we take into account that prior to the planning of the budget, the standards and type of service have been established and menu policy decided upon. With those matters settled, the experienced operator can very readily determine the number of operating personnel needed to service the anticipated volume of sales, and it becomes a relatively simple matter of calculation with going wage rates to arrive at the total dollars of cash operating pay roll. We assume that the operator in this instance has done so and arrived at a figure of $108,000, or twenty-seven cents of each dollar of gross sales. Measuring this against other well-operated restaurants in the same class, we find it acceptable and feasible for use as a budget figure in this instance.

Having established the dollars of pay roll cost for the budget, it is a simple matter to apply pay roll tax rates, workmen's compensation rates, etc. to arrive at the required budget figure for pay roll taxes and employee relations expenses. We find that these will amount to about $5,600, or 1.4 cents of each dollar of sales, a figure which again compares with the experience of other successful operators, based on available statistical and operating data.

Direct Operating Supplies Cost. There remains one more group of expenses to be provided for in the budget, other than food and beverage cost. This is that group of direct operating supplies and expenses comprising the cost of such items as uniforms, laundry, cooking fuel, licenses, menus, sundry supplies, linens, china, glass and silverware, etc. We might project limits of amounts for these various items of expenses in this group, but the more realistic approach would again be to use the general experience of successful operators in the same approximate type of business, with respect to allowance in dollars, and in cents per dollar of gross sales, for the entire group of these expenses. Accordingly, an allowance of 7.5 cents per dollar sale, or $30,000, is budgeted for this group of expenses.

Again, it is time to cast up the accounts and measure the progress we have made toward realization of our budget goal—and to see if we have remaining out of the total budget sufficient dollars to provide adequately for the raw cost of food and beverages.

OPERATING EXPENSE BUDGET

	Amount	*% to Sales*
Operating Pay Roll	$108,000.00	27.0%
Other Direct Operating Supplies and Expenses	30,000.00	7.5
Management Compensation	8,000.00	2.0
Other Administrative Expenses	16,000.00	4.0
Pay Roll Taxes and Employee Relations	5,600.00	1.4
Advertising and Promotion	6,000.00	1.5
Heat, Light and Power	8,000.00	2.0
Repairs and Maintenance	8,400.00	2.1
Total	$190,000.00	47.5%

We now find that our cost of sales must be limited to 37.5 cents of each dollar of sales, for a total of $150,000 of the projected sales volume, if our calculations and estimates of requirements for other costs and expenses are to be accepted as realistic projections of requirements. To measure the feasibility of such a budget limitation on raw material cost, we will have to project the potentials, separately, for food cost and beverage cost. As discussed heretofore, it is assumed that menu policy has been established, price ranges set, portion and service standards determined. With that specific data at hand, it becomes possible to compute the theoretical potential cost per dollar of sale. Such calculations of potential cost for measurement against actual recorded cost are regularly made on a daily basis in a great many operations using the Pre-Cost Pre-Control System. This tool for management becomes increasingly popular year by year.

Raw Food and Beverage Cost. With the division of total gross sales at 75% for food and 25% for beverages, as discussed heretofore, we find that a combination of a 40% food cost and a 30% beverage cost would average out to a total of $150,000 for cost of sales or 37.5 cents per dollar sale. As this is within the limits established as a result of the prior steps in budgeting the operation, we need not go back over these steps to see where revisions in estimates must be made in order to stay within the overall budget limitations. However, there still remains the necessity of appraising these cost ratios as to their feasibility for budget purposes. First, comparison of these ratios with other successful operations of the same approximate type and class would indicate that they are well within the realm of attainment. Second, we will assume that they have been measured against calculated potentials based upon the menu and price policy and that we can accept these figures for sales costs as realistic and entirely possible of achievement.

COST OF SALES BUDGET

	Amount	%
Sales	$400,000.00	100.0
Division of Sales		
Food	$300,000.00	75.0
Beverages	100,000.00	25.0
Total	$400,000.00	100.0
Cost of Sales		
Food	$120,000.00	40.0
Beverages	30,000.00	30.0
Total	$150,000.00	37.5

With that step in the budget planning, we have completed a projection or plan of the operation to a desired goal. That is, a plan for the accomplishment of the primary reason for the existence of the business operation—the earning of a return on investment and a profit on management efforts.

The entire budget can now be put together in form recognizable as a statement of food and beverage operations and in form susceptible to comparison with actual performance.

A RESTAURANT COMPANY
SUMMARY OF BUDGET
FOR THE YEAR ENDING

	Amount	%
SALES		
Food	$300,000.00	75.0
Beverages	100,000.00	25.0
	$400,000.00	100.0
COST OF SALES		
Food		
Cost of Food Consumed	$129,000.00	43.0
Less: Credit for Cost of Employees' Meals	9,000.00	3.0
Net Cost of Food Sold	$120,000.00	40.0
Beverages	30,000.00	30.0
Net Cost of Food and Beverage Sales	$150,000.00	37.5
GROSS PROFIT	$250,000.00	62.5
OPERATING EXPENSES (Schedule 1)	190,000.00	47.5
OPERATING PROFIT	$ 60,000.00	15.0
RENT or PROPERTY TAXES, AND FIRE INSURANCE	24,000.00	6.0
PROFIT BEFORE DEPRECIATION	$ 36,000.00	9.0
DEPRECIATION	16,000.00	4.0
PROFIT BEFORE INCOME TAXES	$ 20,000.00	5.0

A RESTAURANT COMPANY
BUDGETED OPERATING EXPENSES
FOR THE YEAR ENDING

	Amount	*% to Sales*
OPERATING EXPENSES		
Direct Operating Expenses		
Salaries and Wages—Preparation, Service, Storeroom, Cashiers, Checkers	$108,000.00	27.0
Employees' Meals Uniforms Laundry Cooking Fuel Licenses Menus Ice Supplies Flowers and Decorations Replacements—Linens, China, Glass, Silverware Sundry	30,000.00	7.5
	$138,000.00	34.5
Administrative and General Expenses		
Management	$ 8,000.00	2.0
Salaries and Wages—Office Employees' Meals General Insurance Stationery and Office Supplies Telephone Legal and Auditing Services Subscriptions and Dues Contributions Sundry	16,000.00	4.0
	$ 24,000.00	6.0
Pay Roll Taxes and Employee Relations		
Federal Retirement Taxes Federal and State Unemployment Taxes Workmen's Compensation Insurance Retirement Benefits Paid Union Dues Sundry	$ 5,600.00	1.4
	$ 5,600.00	1.4
Advertising and Promotion		
Advertising Newspaper Outdoor Signs Car Cards Due Bills Entertaining Other	$ 6,000.00	1.5
	$ 6,000.00	1.5

A RESTAURANT COMPANY
BUDGETED OPERATING EXPENSES
FOR THE YEAR ENDING (Continued)

	Amount	*% to Sales*
OPERATING EXPENSES (continued)		
Heat, Light and Power		
Salaries and Wages—Engineers Employees' Meals Electricity Fuel Water Electric Bulbs and Supplies Engine Room Supplies	$ 8,000.00	2.0
	$ 8,000.00	2.0
Repairs and Maintenance		
Salaries and Wages— Mechanics, Painters, Carpenter, Plumber, Etc. Employees' Meals Hardware Supplies Decorating Supplies Contract Decorating Sign Maintenance Elevator Maintenance Inspection Fees Repairs Building Mechanical Equipment Furniture and Fixtures Refrigeration Air-Conditioning Other	$ 8,400.00	2.1
	$ 8,400.00	2.1
TOTAL OPERATING EXPENSES	$190,000.00	47.5%

The budget plan for this hypothetical operation provides for a net profit equivalent to five cents for each dollar of gross sales, before consideration of income taxes. In relation to return on investment, this profit of $20,000 represents a return of 10%, also before consideration of income taxes.

With these narrow margins of net remaining profit obtainable only through, first, careful planning of the operation, and second, faithful and effective execution of the plan in actual management of the operation, it has become increasingly necessary that the food and beverage operator pilot his business ship with the aid of tested and proven charts and instruments. The budget, when intelligently planned, charts the course toward financial success.

Chapter XXIII: KITCHEN PLANNING

THE EDITORS do not plan in this chapter to present a series of typical layouts of kitchens, perhaps the perfect kitchen. Generally speaking, there is no such thing as a typical kitchen, let alone a perfect one. Since this effort is directed toward every class of operation—the commercial restaurant, hotel, motor hotel, club, hospital, in-plant feeding, college and school, and related types of operation, it would not be feasible to attempt to include herein, detailed descriptive material relating to each class of operation. However, they are discussed in a most general manner.

It is a fallacy not to acknowledge that each of the aforementioned food and/or beverage operations has its own problems to solve in the matter of kitchen layout and equipment. Too often, failure to recognize this truism has resulted in inefficient layouts, excessive costs, and additional and unnecessary outlays to correct errors. From the luncheonette to the very largest type of feeding operation, there is the same problem except in degree, of proper advance planning to meet the requirements of a specific type of operation.

For example, take such a simple thing as glassware. In hospitals and institutions, the variety of glasses could be limited to a half dozen or so and the handling and storage would be quite simple; in a hotel having both bar and food service glasses, there might easily be 20 or more different types of glasses in use. This affects the clean glass storage space as, in the latter case, considerably more would be needed. It also affects the dishwashing area where additional space is necessary for sorting both soiled and clean glasses. Although the trend is toward the use of only one dishwashing machine for washing glasses, china, and silver, this may not prove satisfactory where a greater variety of glassware is in use, particularly when ample sorting tables for soiled and clean glassware is not provided. The result is usually confusion and greater breakage.

If anything in this chapter seems redundant, it has been written that way purposely because it is intended here to emphasize the necessity of sound business practices in an area of business that can't always boast of such practices.

At this point it might be wise to dispose of one area of food operation where the kitchen or service layout might conceivably be typical. This is in diners, some drive-ins with minimum menu selection, and others where the precise size and perimeter limitations are constant. To a very material degree, feeding facilities falling into these categories are virtually in the prefabricated class. This is certainly true of diners and now there are on the market prefabricated restaurants of the counter type. Even these, to a lesser degree, may be purchased subject to buyers' changes. But, by and large, one of the principal advantages in this type of unit is the pre-planning that the manufacturer has contributed, based on his own background and experience.

For the most part, it is assumed that readers of this book have two main objectives regarding kitchen layouts: (1) the planning of a new facility, or (2) the rehabilitation and/or modernization of an existing one. Consequently, it was felt that the greatest good would be served if, in this chapter we discuss the practical philosophy behind the planning of kitchens. The editors will have considered their time well spent and their efforts rewarded if those interested in the problems are alerted to the pitfalls that may be encountered.

First, to clarify our terminology, we are setting down a few definitions:

Meal Pattern—includes the meals to be served during a 24-hour period. This could be limited to one meal—breakfast, luncheon, or dinner; or it could include all three meals, or two meals, plus in-between snacks. For example, there are hotel kitchens that service coffee shops, formal dining rooms, banquet rooms, and room service. These would be required to be ready for service from early morning until past midnight. On the other hand, there are specialty restaurants that are open only for dinner and supper. Hospitals and institutions fall into the three-meals-a-day category. Industrial cafeterias usually limit their service to one meal although in some instances they operate practically on a 24-hour basis when three shifts of workers are to be fed.

Menu Pattern—the framework of the menu. There is a different menu pattern for each meal of the day—for breakfast, luncheon, dinner, supper, for afternoon tea, the soda fountain, etc. It answers the questions of what is served, the number of courses, etc. For example, the framework of a breakfast menu would include the number and price of club breakfasts and the number of a la carte items. In institutional feeding, the menu pattern could be extended to include weekly menu patterns. For example, the number of times juice or fruit appeared on the menu over the period of a week, etc.

Peak Load—This refers to the number to be served during the largest shift when the number refers to industrial cafeterias, or the greatest number to be served during a specific time which would vary with the individual operation. Some refer to a peak load during a meal period in which case it would probably last from one-half to one hour. Others might refer to the entire meal period. For example, if a restaurant served 200 for breakfast, 800 for lunch, and 300 for dinner, the peak load would be considered the 800 for lunch and the kitchen would be prepared to handle this number.

Seating Capacity—This is easier to calculate for industrial cafeterias than for restaurants since a close estimate of the number of people to be served can be obtained and the length and number of lunch periods can be determined and controlled. To determine the seating capacity of a restaurant is more complicated since it must be of a given size in order to make it a profitable operation. Furthermore, the number of turnovers that can be expected would depend to a large degree on the type of restaurant. A high-priced restaurant may only expect less than 1½ turnovers per seat, whereas lower priced restaurants must get 2½ or more turnovers per seat to make the operation profitable. Counter seat operations must have a much greater seat turnover. The range is generally from eight to as high as twenty or more depending on the length of the serving hours.

Seating Space—This refers to the number of square feet required to accommodate the number of seats determined upon, plus the traffic aisles. The normal range is from a low of eight square feet per person—obtained only by the use of long banquet tables—to as high as 17 or 20 square feet in formal dining rooms. Most seating, exclusive of counter seats, falls within the 12 to 15 square feet range.

Whether creating a new facility or modernizing an existing one, there are certain basic planning routines that should be followed. At least, these are the ones we have set down as a work program for the Project Directors of our Management Advisory Services Staff. They are as follows:

1. Type of persons to be fed.
2. Number of meals per day by categories:
   a. Potential (new operation)
   b. Actual from past records (alterations)
3. Average price customers can afford to pay.
4. If meals are gratis, how much subsidy is provided?
5. Menu and meal pattern.
6. Number of employees.
7. Length of serving periods.
8. Availability and intended use of various processed foods:
   Frozen, dehydrated, partially prepared foods, etc., in view of eliminating or modifying some production equipment.
9. Number of persons served during peak load.
10. Type of restaurant.

11. Size of restaurant. In a new operation the size may be fixed by the limits of the building. In the case of alteration, the area may be fixed and further restricted by the location of plumbing and heating connections, flues and ventilation.
12. Type of food served and quantities prepared. Consider to-order, ready-cooked foods, size of batches, etc.

ALL-INCLUSIVE AREA

Kitchen planning cannot be confined only to the kitchen proper with its receiving, storage, preparation, and service areas. It must also include and make provision for all related departments such as the dining rooms, including the employees' dining room, cafeteria counters, snack bars, coffee shops, banquet rooms, bars, service bars, the handling of clean and soiled dishes, silver, and glassware in all these areas, as well as linen and uniform rooms, locker rooms and janitors' closets.

Regardless of their final location, the entire food and/or beverage operation must be considered as a whole. One cannot concentrate on the kitchen proper and forget the other parts since they are too inter-related.

With continued and mounting labor and operating costs, food service operators are constantly forced to find ways and means of operating more efficiently. This is not always possible in some of the older buildings which were erected when labor was cheap and plentiful. Also, the character of the operation may have undergone a change. This means that modernization is a "must," if the business is to continue.

Evolving the most effective plan for the kitchen and having the right equipment correctly placed can best be done with the application of the principles of motion economy or job simplification. These are as follows:

Find the weak spots by analyzing the job—what has to be done?

Next come the answers to the questions why, what, where, how, who, and when. These answers will help to eliminate, combine, simplify and rearrange. Ask yourself these questions: Why is this necessary? What is this for? How should it be done? Who should do it? When should it be done? When you have the answers to these questions you are in a better position to find a solution to your problems. Very often, after answering why and what, it is found that some detail is not necessary and may be eliminated. Answers to the other questions often make it possible to combine two jobs, simplify others and completely eliminate still others. The question is, how to accomplish these changes? How to do it the best way with the least cost?

The answer to this question always involves equipment, sometimes new equipment, sometimes a change in position of old equipment so that everything is at the point most convenient for the persons using it. This is most important in working out the details of shelving at various work areas or determining the location of dish storage areas. These two important details are often ignored.

SPACE DETERMINATION

Because of the many factors to be considered in planning a kitchen, it is impossible to give an overall figure in square feet that can be used in calculating the total space requirements for all types of restaurant operation. A rule-of-thumb guide which has been found satisfactory under normal conditions allows an equal amount of space for the kitchen and its related areas as for the dining areas. This measure may be used as a rough estimate of space requirements but should not by any means be considered final.

The most satisfactory way is to work out each department of the kitchen, showing the equipment and the amount of aisle and work space needed and fit these together in such a way as to permit the flow of supplies from receiving on through storage and preparation to the service of the finished product as indicated on a flow chart, at the same time fitting into the building space the mechanical and structural requirements.

Space for Workers. The required work area for each worker in the kitchen is determined by the specific duties or work he is to perform. If at a fixed station, such as salad or sandwich preparation, the proper work area is that space within the arcs formed by the arms of a person seated or standing in a comfortable position. At the same time, equipment, tools, and shelves must be placed within easy reach of the worker, thereby eliminating unnecessary walking, bending, stretching, or straining. We have seen instances where steam table attendants and sandwich-making personnel have had to stand on their toes and stretch unduly to place orders on the serving shelf because it was set too far forward. There are also instances where the upper deck of a roast oven is so high that the worker has to stretch considerably to place or remove anything from it. These cases not only present accident hazards but cannot be classified as proper work areas. These are just two of the points that should be worked out carefully on the drawing board.

It is very often a good idea to seek help from the worker on the job.

They often have good ideas on details that may not be noticed by the supervisory personnel but can be an annoyance in the daily work routine.

Space in the Dining Room. The number of square feet required for the dining area is determined by the number of people to be seated within a specified time, taking into consideration the number of turn-overs expected, the aisle space, the shape of the dining room, the type of operation, and the type of chairs and tables used. The general range is from 8 to 15 square feet per seat. Banquet seating can be brought down to from 8 to 10 square feet per seat. Dining rooms average from 13 to 15 square feet per seat and even higher in some of the de luxe hotel dining rooms. Cafeteria dining rooms, exclusive of the service counter area, average from 13 to 17 square feet per seat and higher, particularly, with the present tendency of using smaller tables and allowing ample aisle space.

GENERAL PRINCIPLES OF LAYOUT

As we have stated, we cannot, in one chapter, cover all factors to be considered in planning kitchens for the varied types of food operation. We shall merely attempt to list the basic principles applicable to all and some characteristics of the more popular types.

Since a food operation may be likened to an industrial plant because it receives raw materials, processes, prepares, and sells the finished product, the individual work units should be planned in relation to the sequence of food production operation.

Types of Food Operation. Only when the type of food operation is known can the planning be intelligent. The requirements for a commercial service type of restaurant or a hotel kitchen are quite different from a hospital kitchen. School lunch feeding is quite different from a city luncheon club operation although both are one-meal operations. Unless one has an understanding and knowledge of the many factors involved, the type of food presented on the menu, the preparation, and the type of service, it is impossible to make the proper selection of equipment or to lay it out for efficient operation. Let us state briefly some of the points that affect space requirements and the layout of equipment that must be considered in planning various kitchens.

TYPES OF RESTAURANTS

To give some idea of the scope of food service operations, we list the more popular and better known ones below, each one requiring some special kind of equipment for the service given. Each one and its required equipment must be considered separately in planning the kitchen.

Airline	Commissary	Hotel
Camps	Convalescent home	Luncheonette
Cafeteria	Convent	Motel
Church	Counter operation	Railroad
Club—city	Department store	Restaurant
country	Drive-In	Specialty restaurant
beach	Employee feeding facility	Retreat
Coffee shop	Federal and State	Schools
College	Institutions	Steamship line
	Hospital	

The specialty restaurants below require more specialized equipment and close attention to detail in planning their kitchens:

Barbecue stand	Grill	Snack bar
Dairy lunch	Hamburger shop	Steak and chop house
Donut shop	Nationality restaurant	Vegetarian restaurant
Fountain	Seafood house	Waffle house

Next we present a partial classification, according to the type of service given, which affects the kitchen layouts:

Cafeteria	Table
Drive-In	Automat
Counter	Buffet
Airline type	Commissary
Open kitchen type	School lunch

Centralized or decentralized service in hospitals.

The major types of kitchen layout under which the leading food operations fall are:

Service kitchens as found in service restaurants and hotel coffee shops.
Combination service and preparation kitchen found in large hotel kitchens having several dining rooms, a coffee shop, banquet rooms, room service, and an employees' cafeteria.
Cafeteria (preparation kitchen).
Hospital kitchen (preparation or service or both).
Industrial food service with central kitchen (preparation)
with commissary (preparation).

SERVICE KITCHEN—COMBINATION SERVICE AND PREPARATION KITCHEN

(Hospitals excluded)

The service kitchen, in smaller operations, or the combination service-preparation kitchen in large operations are the type of kitchens found in service restaurants, hotels, motels, coffee shops, luncheon clubs, and city and county clubs. In such operations, waiters and waitresses come into the kitchen, pick up the food at the various units from the persons who prepared it, and then serve it directly to the patron.

The service type kitchen layout is based on the principle of a hollow rectangle, with service going counter-clockwise where serving units are also preparation units. In this layout it is important that ample space is provided for the waiters or waitresses assembling their food orders, as well as for dish trucks distributing clean china, glassware, and silver to the various points of service. It is also of utmost importance that ample tray rests be provided for assembling orders. Additional dish warmers and storing facilities are also needed, the amount depending upon the type of service given and the menu offered. If silver hollow-ware and fancy buffets are used, additional storage space will be required for this bulky type of equipment.

Whereas the cafeteria kitchen prepares food according to a set menu and in batches to meet the requirements of the service counter, service restaurants more often specialize in cooked-to-order items and require equipment that is more flexible in order to meet sudden demands.

Food checkers are usually employed in hotel and deluxe restaurant kitchens and the placement of these is important, particularly when there is more than one exit from the kitchen to the various dining rooms or other service areas. In planning the location of the checkers, consider also the placement of the service bar, so that if possible, one checker could check both the food and beverages.

A hotel kitchen can be a simple or a very complex operation depending on the extent and size of the food and beverage operation. In addition to the main dining room, the hotel kitchen often has exits to two or three different dining rooms, as well as a coffee shop, room service, banquet rooms and the employees' cafeteria. Although final preparation and service may be from a banquet kitchen, the bulk of the food preparation is usually done in the main kitchen.

One preparation and serving unit characteristic of hotel and deluxe restaurant kitchens is the garde manger. Also characteristic of these type operations, and for which provision must be made in the kitchen near the exit or exits to the dining rooms of service areas, is the checkers, or sometimes a combination checker-cashier.

CAFETERIA OR PREPARATION KITCHEN

In a cafeteria or preparation kitchen, the food is prepared and delivered in bulk to the points of service. The service personnel does not come into the kitchen to get the food but it is usually transported to a point within easy reach for them to place on the counter. Suitable cabinets for holding hot and cold food are desirable for temporary storage until it is placed on the counter.

In this type of kitchen, the large circulating area is not needed since there should be no traffic through the kitchen. But it is of primary importance to bring the preparation area as near as possible to the point of service so that the hot and cold food may be placed easily in the hot and cold pass-through cabinets placed in the wall between the cafeteria counter and the kitchen. Where space is limited and these pass-through cabinets cannot be used, the cook's table may be placed along the cafeteria wall, with ranges parallel and an opening provided to serve as a pass-through where the cooks pass the food directly to the counter personnel as it is needed. This same arrangement may be used at the cold section.

In locating the dishroom, consideration must be given to the flow of clean dishes to replenish the service areas, which would be the service counter, with limited quantities to the salad preparation area as well.

HOSPITAL KITCHENS

In planning hospital kitchens, there are factors not applicable to other feeding operations which must be considered as follows:

1. The type of service, whether centralized or decentralized.
2. The method of assembling trays and loading them on the food trucks.
3. Space for storing the food trucks between meal periods.
4. Space for washing the food trucks.
5. Food in hospitals must be prepared in large quantities and the food trucks loaded within a comparatively short time. Therefore, more equipment is sometimes needed than in a restaurant serving the same number of meals as a hospital and with a comparable menu.

6. Although the trend is away from providing special diet kitchens in newly constructed hospitals as they were set up years ago with their own ovens, ranges, broilers, etc., there is still need for an area where special formulas and other special diet foods can be prepared and kept refrigerated until delivered to the floors for distribution. If the pantry area is to be responsible for this work, more work space and additional refrigeration will be required. Also, in some cases, there is the problem of storing and washing the formula bottles, etc.

7. When a hospital is operating a snack bar, has public dining facilities, gives special service to private patients, and has feeding facilities for the doctors and nurses, these services must all come under consideration when analyzing the menu and the type of service given. It can be seen that feeding facilities in a hospital can be very simple or very complex and can become increasingly so, if food has to be transported greater distances to various buildings.

Following are some of the more pertinent questions to be answered before starting on the initial planning of a new hospital kitchen, or where changes are contemplated in an existing one.

1. Number of beds? Is expansion contemplated? To what extent?
2. Type of menu? Selective? Fixed?
3. Number on staff? Contemplated increase?
4. Centralized or decentralized service?
5. Diet kitchen? What percentage of patients are on special diets?
6. If decentralized service is used at present which is to be changed to centralized service, a complete study must be made of every phase. Include in this study the cycle of serving hours, the number of food carts used; the number of floor pantries and the equipment in each and how the food is served. Run time studies of the present cart deliveries, the method of handling soiled dishes and the staffing of the pantries including the truck boys. Consider the location of dumb waiters and/or elevators. What would be the potential income from the areas gained in converting from one type service to another? What potential payroll savings?
7. Analyze the feeding facilities of the staff including the doctors. Must separate doctors' dining room be provided?
8. Will there be a coffee shop or fountain or canteen? If so, who will operate it? Review the menu to determine the equipment needed. The type of operation and the menu will determine the equipment required.

9. Consider the size of the trays when purchasing the dishwasher. If they cannot be put through the dishwashing machine they will have to be done by hand, resulting in costlier dishroom operation and more trays will be needed. Also, the size of the trays is important when considering the use of conveyors or subveyors.

SPECIALTY RESTAURANTS

The kitchen layout and selection of equipment for a specialty restaurant must be carefully planned because there is less flexibility with that type of equipment. For example, there are many specialty restaurants serving fried foods. In these, one would find griddles and fryers predominant with perhaps only one range. Space requirements for such an operation could be very limited because food is cooked to order and the turnover is rapid. The equipment is also of the lighter type and would not require as much space.

We have not tried to cover all the types of operations but have cited those most typical and most complex.

PREDETERMINED NUMBER OF MEALS

School kitchens, offering simple menus and with the number of persons to be served at any meal virtually predetermined, should be planned without difficulty. Although hospitals have their service problems, the meal count can be pretty closely predetermined since it is based on the number of occupied beds plus the staff and the employees. In inplant and industrial feeding, the number to be served and the menu pattern for all practical purposes are usually known in advance. Therefore, the food can be planned accordingly. In a commercial cafeteria, the number of seats which probably have been determined in order to make it a profitable operation, plus the type of meal pattern, will form the basis on which to plan the kitchen.

However, kitchen planning is not an exact science. From the foregoing examples it can be seen that one set of space requirements would not be applicable to all kitchens. It is true that rule-of-thumb square foot areas have been established for service type restaurants. Kitchen area coefficients based on meal loads have also been established for cafeteria operations, but these should not be accepted as final.

It is wiser to take the time at the very beginning of new construction or alterations and work out the plan in detail for the individual restaurant since, as we have seen, there are so many variable factors affecting space requirements. For example, if the space for the kitchen is long and narrow or of an unusual shape, or broken up with large columns, space requirements will have to be increased considerably since equipment cannot be located as advantageously as in a large square area with no columns. Furthermore, the type of operation and the type of service—cafeteria, hospital, waiters or waitresses, or a combination of several—the menu, the geographical location, whether the plan is for a new building or for alterations in an existing building (which could present many problems) —all of these factors have a very direct bearing on the kitchen plans and such planning should be carefully reviewed since any change after the installation of equipment is very costly.

The first step is to learn everything you can about the particular type of operation you have in mind. Read and collect articles and plans of similar operations. Visit outstanding new operations to see the type of installation they have. Try to formulate a clear picture of the entire operation. Determine exactly in your own mind how every step in the preparation and service of food is to be carried out. Work up a list of the equipment needed.

Flow Chart. Next, in the preparation of the preliminary layout, work out a flow chart showing the progression of the incoming raw materials to the storeroom, to the refrigerated storage areas, to the preparation areas, and finally to the service areas.

Next, trace the flow of soiled dishes from the various dining areas to the dishroom and the return of the clean dishes to their place of use, which will be quite different between a service kitchen and a preparation kitchen.

Next, trace the handling of waste material, rubbish, and garbage, if a garbage disposal unit is not to be used. See also that space is provided for the washing and storing of garbage cans.

Now you are ready to fit the various preparation and service sections into their respective places as noted on the flow chart, giving careful consideration to work and service aisles so that there is ample clearance in front of ranges and bake ovens. Also, as near as possible, avoid cross traffic for carts. Each work station should be large enough to accommodate the number of workers needed.

After you have worked out a good preliminary plan and you have what you want and what you feel is necessary, it is time to get some help from a food facilities engineer and/or consultants in the field. They will help you with the layout, drawings, advise you on the selection of equipment, write the specifications, and advise you with respect to the cost and efficiency of fuel and power, involving availability and provision for gas, electricity, steam power, water, and the handling of ventilation and lighting. Your food engineer will also work with the architect on building construction, insulation, floors, walls, ceiling, etc.

LAYOUT PITFALLS TO AVOID

Following are a few fundamental principles of kitchen layout frequently overlooked which ultimately affect the efficiency of the operation as well as the quality of the food and its service:

1. *Inadequate space for the entire kitchen* because space requirements for equipment were not carefully analyzed in the preliminary stages of planning.
2. *Inadequate work space* for the number of workers needed at a work station or preparation area.
3. *Work aisles too narrow* to permit easy passage of workers without interference.
4. *Work aisles too wide,* necessitating extra steps.
5. *Lack of landing space near steamers, ovens, or refrigerators* on which materials may be placed.
6. *Inconvenient location of equipment,* so placed that server must be constantly turning back and forth.
7. *Lack of tray rests* on which waiters or waitresses may rest trays while assembling orders.
8. *Poor location of reach-in refrigerator.* It should be so placed that its constant use by a worker will not interfere with or annoy another worker.
9. *Work aisle too narrow.* Not sufficient clearance for a person standing in front of the refrigerator when the doors are open.
10. *Work and traffic aisles too narrow,* particularly when dish and food trucks are used.
11. *Garbage and trash rooms only accessible through the kitchen.* These rooms should not be accessible *only* through the kitchen, particularly when persons from other departments must use them.
12. *Central ice-making room only accessible through the kitchen or heavy traffic area.* Where it is necessary to plan on a central ice-making room, it should be so placed that it is accessible to other departments without going through the kitchen; also, it should not open into heavy traffic in the service or work areas.
13. *Inadequate receiving space.*
14. *No receiving scales or located inconveniently* so they are not used.
15. *Inadequate walk-in and reach-in refrigerators.* This can be costly, resulting in food spoilage and making it impossible to keep the refrigerators clean and orderly. There must be sufficient space to shift the food about. Lack of space here will also require more frequent deliveries which can affect the purchasing policy.
16. *Storeroom with inadequate space and poorly ventilated.* Poor ventilation

can also result in food spoilage; inadequate space requires more frequent deliveries and affects the purchasing policy as well as making it impossible to keep the storeroom clean and orderly.

17. *No provision for a work table in the storeroom.* This is needed for assembling orders and on which to place small packages.

18. *No scales in storeroom.* Counter scales are needed.

19. *No hand or utility sink for storeroom personnel.* This is particularly important where produce and meats, as well as canned goods and staples are in one storeroom. The storeroom personnel find it necessary to wash their hands after handling produce and other foods. There is also the possibility of spillage, etc.

20. *Improper size and capacity of equipment.* It is just as inefficient and wasteful to have the equipment too large as too small. This applies particularly to steam-jacketed kettles, vegetable steamers, meat choppers, and dishwashers.

21. *Inadequate and improperly placed work tables or work space* for each kitchen worker. This causes the worker to take many unnecessary steps in preparing or handling food.

22. *Cross traffic,* especially in congested areas.

23. *Improper floor and wall finishes* of such material that the high standards of cleanliness and sanitation cannot be maintained. This also applies to flooring materials, particularly, around steam kettles and drains.

24. *Floor drains and grills in kettle areas improperly placed* causing spillage onto floor when kettles are draining.

25. *Incomplete work units.* Everything that is needed for the preparation or service of any particular item of food should be easily accessible to that work area and worker.

26. *Inadequate dish storage space.*

27. *Sinks without drainboards.*

28. *Inadequate number of sinks.* This encourages poor work habits and lower standards of sanitation. It may also prove costly in the time lost by workers waiting to use a sink.

29. *Only one piece of a certain type of equipment when two are necessary.* The use of a certain piece of equipment by workers from two different work areas can result in friction and lost time unless its use is carefully scheduled.

30. *Poor location of equipment in original planning.* This results in many unnecessary steps.

31. *Inadequate facilities for properly storing cleaning utensils and equipment.* This includes such simple things as racks for brooms and mops to keep them off the floor.

32. *Inadequate space and lack of ventilation and lighting* in the janitors' closets.

33. *Inadequate locker and wash room facilities,* particularly for service personnel who should be well groomed.

34. *Lack of labor-saving devices.*

35. *Failure to provide for self-service whenever possible.*

36. *Inadequate facilities for holding hot and cold food* in relation to service counter.

37. *Inadequate soiled dish table space.*

38. *No vestibule or baffle* to keep the noise of the kitchen from the dining room.

39. *Poor lighting throughout the kitchen.*

40. *Inadequate ventilation throughout the kitchen and service areas.*

41. *Poor construction of equipment and its installation* making it difficult to clean and maintain high standards of sanitation.

CHECK LIST FOR PRE-PLANNING

Number of Serving Areas. This definitely affects the operation. In hotels, the serving areas may range from one dining room and a coffee shop to a complexity of dining facilities as we have outlined—several dining rooms, a coffee shop, and banquet facilities for several hundred or thousand distributed on several floors. Restaurants also may have one or more dining rooms distributed on various floors.

An industrial feeding operation may have one or more cafeterias or mobile units or canteens. This service may be very extensive depending upon the number to be fed, hours of work, the number and the distances of the distribution points and other factors.

Distance from Kitchen to Serving Areas. This factor also affects the equipment requirements. In cafeterias with a hot and cold pass-through from the kitchen to the serving counter, the required equipment is at a minimum. If food must be transported to various floors, there would probably be need for more hot and cold food-holding cabinets, both of the fixed and mobile type.

Meal Pattern and Serving Hours. Although the one-meal luncheon is the simplest type of operation, this does not mean that the menu is always simple. City clubs offer a varied selection of quality food comparable to that found in the deluxe restaurant or hotel dining room. The length of the serving period and the number of turnovers must be known so that quantities to be prepared can be determined.

Many resort hotels offer the modified American Plan meals which include breakfast and dinner. The tendency of guests in these hotels to sit down all at one time requires a large dining room, kitchen, and pantry.

Many restaurants, particularly in cities, are open only for lunch and dinner; others for the three meals including between-meal snacks. This is also true of hotel dining rooms where the hours of service may extend from seven in the morning until one or two o'clock the next morning.

Menus. The kind of menu and the portion sizes are important factors in planning and, with known quantities to be served, form an important guide in selecting the proper units of equipment for a particular type of service. After required equipment is decided upon, space requirements can be determined.

Storage. Some knowledge of the availability of supplies, the nearness of markets and expected deliveries must be considered since these affect the amount of refrigerated and dry storage space needed. For how many days' inventory is space required? This varies with the location and type of operation. Another thing to remember is that in the city storage space is at a premium. Here it is possible to have more frequent deliveries and it is wise to keep a low inventory where the per square foot of storage space is costly on a rent allocation basis.

Resort hotels may stock up for the season on many items since outlying areas are far from the markets and there are fewer deliveries. Hotels in island areas where import is necessary need even greater storage space, particularly of the refrigerated and freezer type. Shipping rates are lower on larger weights and shipments are dependent on sailing, and there is always the possibility of a shipping strike.

Butcher. Is the operation to use fabricated (i.e. oven-ready and portion-cut) meats or do its own butchering? The trend is more and more toward the use of fabricated meats although the larger and de luxe hotels and restaurants continue to do their own butchering and use few fabricated meats. Institutions, in-plant feeding operations, hospitals, schools, and numerous restaurants, however, are using more and more of the fabricated cuts.

Ice Cream. Is the operation to buy or make ice cream? In most instances, ice cream is purchased. If ice cream is to be made, local Health Department regulations should be checked so that all requirements will be met. Among the equipment which may be required, depending on the variety of flavors to be made, are the following:

Tilting kettle
Work table
Mixing bowls
Supply cabinet
Ice cream machine
2 1/2 gallon containers
Rack for storing ice cream containers.
Place to store frozen fruits and other items used in making ice cream.
Sink and facilities for sterilizing equipment.
Hardening cabinet for storing.
Place for storing ice cream molds, and various types of decorations.

Frozen Fruits and Vegetables. The extent to which frozen foods will be used must also be considered and planned for accordingly.

Garbage. The use of garbage disposal units should be considered wherever possible. A check should be made to see if their use is permitted since it is possible that there may be local restrictions due to local sewage systems. This may obtain in large cities as well as in small communities or in outlying operations having their own sewage systems. A garbage disposal unit is now available which does not interfere with any waste line. It grinds the garbage and waste into a pulp, extracts the liquid from it and empties the pulp into bags or specially built trucks for removal.

Ice Making. Is ice to be purchased or made? What type will be needed—cubed or crushed ice or both? The quantities needed of each will determine the kind and size of ice machine selected. We have found that the use of small units placed at the points of use rather than one large unit that requires the ice to be re-distributed results in savings of both time and labor. Also, in case of a mechanical breakdown of one unit, others are available.

Consider where cubed ice is to be used—in the dining room for drinking water? At the bars? At counters? In a cafteria having a chilled water fountain, cubed ice will not be needed but crushed ice could be needed for the cold pans at the serving counter. Pantries and garde manger stations in service kitchens often need crushed ice for ice pans, for the service of sea food and for the supreme dishes.

Water lines and floor drains for ice-making machines should not be put into a closed area if at all possible and should be placed well away from the walls. If the ice making machine is walled in on three sides, follow the manufacturer's advice on the amount of space allowance between the machine and the walls. Place the ice machine so that it is easily accessible for the removal of ice and for making repairs. However, in some instances it will be necessary to provide locking facilities so that the issue of ice can be controlled.

Refrigeration. Wherever remote units are installed, space for the compressors must be provided.

Soda Fountain. Space for the compressor and the CO^2 tanks will be needed.

Circulating Ice Water. Where will it be used?

Bulk Milk Dispenser. Is the installation of this equipment permitted or do local health department regulations prohibit its use?

Steam. Will steam be available from its own boiler room or from the building? If so, what is the pressure?

Water. What is the temperature of available hot water? What is the supply? Has the water been analyzed to determine its degree of hardness or the presence of harmful minerals? Is the taste affected? It should be tested also for its effect on dishwashing?

Fuel. Complete information must be gathered on fuels—electricity, gas, and oil—their availability, costs, etc.

DISHWASHING AND SILVER CLEANING

Although it is desirable to have the dishwashing area near the dining room, this is not always possible. Sometimes, due to the physical layout of the building, the dishwashing area must be located on a different floor from the dining room. Also, where central dishwashing is employed in larger restaurants, hotels, and hospitals, dishes sometimes must be transported several floors.

In an operation where waitresses do their own bussing of soiled dishes, it is desirable to have the dishwashing area to the right as one comes out of the dining room. Where bus boys are employed, this area may be somewhat removed from the dining room door and service areas brought nearer.

In cases where one dishwashing area serves two or more dining rooms, the amount of traffic, the hours of operation, and the type of service given must be considered in determining the best location. If central dishwashing is considered and dishes must come greater distances or from different levels, then efficient means must be provided for carrying the dishes to and from the dishwashing department. Conveyor systems, if on the same floor, and subveyors, if the dining room is on a different floor, are being successfully used in many installations. This is particularly true in industrial cafeterias where self-bussing is employed and the trays of soiled dishes are placed on conveyor belts by the individual and thus carried to the kitchen.

In any type of dishwashing layout, it is important that ample soiled dish table space be provided to receive the soiled dishes and for sorting, scraping, and stacking the china and separating the silver and glasses. Crowded conditions hamper the loading and unloading of the dish machine and prevent its operating at capacity. Most breakage occurs on the dish tables, not in the dishwashing machine.

In determining the amount of soiled dish table space to provide, the following factors must be taken into consideration:

1. The type of business.
2. The type of service.
3. The manner in which the soiled dishes come to the soiled dish table.

(a.) by service personnel who would unload their trays and do some, all, or none of the sorting of dishes, glasses, and silver
(b.) in a dish box, sorted or unsorted. For example, in counter service, some waitresses are trained to separate and sort dishes, glasses, and silver into separate dish boxes; others may put all three into one dish box, unsorted;
(c.) on individual trays. This would be in cafeterias where self-bussing is used.

4. The flow of dishes and extent of the meal period.

In a school lunch offering a simple menu, the number of dishes and silver flatware per person is considerably less than in a service restaurant or in a de luxe hotel dining room where hollow-ware may also be used in the service.

Where the soiled dishes are brought to the dish table on large trays by the service personnel, a tray rest should be provided along the front of the dish table. There are various ways of accomplishing this but one important thing is to eliminate the three-inch high rolled edge usually found around dish tables and provide instead a flat surface on which to rest the trays and which slopes into and becomes a part of the dish table. This prevents trays from tipping and spilling the contents onto the dish table.

There should be provided an overhead slanting shelf extending the full length of the soiled dish table and on which may be placed racks for glasses, cups, and other items one wishes to keep off the dish table. This helps to expedite the sorting and handling of these items and reduces breakage. Whether this slanting shelf is to slant outward or toward the dish handler depends upon who is to do the sorting of the glasses and cups into the racks.

Some provision should be made for the deposit of silver flatware into a soak sink or pan. In addition there are always some dishes, casseroles, and such, that require soaking and for these some provisions should be made. Instances where soak sinks have not been provided usually result in confusion and additional work.

When trays of soiled dishes are brought to the dish table by means of a conveyor belt, a longer dish table is needed so that the trays can be stripped as they move along, each dish handler picking off certain items.

If the dishes are bussed in the dining room and carefully sorted and stacked into dish boxes, eliminating these processes at the dish table, considerably less soiled dish table space is required.

With respect to the clean dish table, with a rack type dish machine, it is desirable to have the clean dish table long enough to accommodate a minimum of four dish racks. With the flight type dish machine, clean dishes are stacked directly onto portable dish carts. A portable sorting table has been found useful and is usually placed along one side of the take-off for clean dishes.

Regardless of the size of the operation, space for sorting the clean silver must also be provided, both flatware and hollow-ware, if the latter is used. These can be portable units but are definitely needed. The flatware sorting table should be large enough to hold several boxes for silver, the number again depending upon the size of the operation and the number of distributing points.

The washing of glassware cannot be overlooked in the planning of the dishwashing area. The tendency at present is to put all glasses, china, and silver through one machine. However, before deciding on the warewashing facilities, several things must be taken into consideration. In hospitals, schools, cafeterias, and the average-sized restaurant, this presents no problem, since the various kinds of glasses used are kept to a minimum usually including water, milk, juice, and ice tea glasses and perhaps some glass fruit or ice cream dishes.

However, hotels and specialty service restaurants generally use a greater variety of china, glassware, and silver. In addition, there are the bar glasses. Although a busy bar might have its own glass washing set up, a certain number of bar glasses will be returned from the dining room, from room service and from other sources.

If one considers that there are on an average 20 to 25 different bar glasses in use, and adds the food glassware in service, it may not be practical to put them through one dish machine, particularly since considerable space is needed for sorting the glasses, both before and after washing. As a rule, this space is not available in a dishwashing area and would cause considerable confusion and breakage. In planning a glass-washing section, soak sinks and glass brushes, as well as a sink with a fine strainer for emptying glasses, is needed.

Another thing which cannot be overlooked in operations where silverware is used—both hollow-ware and flatware—is to provide facilities for cleaning and burnishing. The amount of space required will depend on the extent of the silver service. Where flatware alone is used, a silver burnishing machine and a two-compartment sink with drainboards, as well as some additional table space on which to sort the silver will be needed. However, with the use of hollow-ware considerably more space will be needed, a second burnishing machine, more work space and storage space for silver to be cleaned and silver that has been cleaned, since it cannot be collected and distributed piece by piece or per machine load.

Where hollow-ware is used or even in larger operations using flatware only, it is advisable to have a separate silver burnishing room with an adjoining silver storeroom, both of which should be locked when the silver man is not on duty.

One thing often overlooked in planning the dishroom is the washing of trays. In a cafeteria operation, feeding several thousand persons during a meal period, one must consider that for every person served there will be a tray. If a rack type machine is used, check to see that the machine will take the size trays to be used; also consider that a rack will hold only eight or nine trays. Divide that number into the total number of persons served to get the number of racks which will be needed to handle trays alone. Add this to the estimated number of dishes or racks that a machine will have to handle per hour or per meal period.

The large oval trays or even some of the larger rectangular trays used by waiters are too large for the dishwashing machines and will, therefore, have to be done by hand. For these, a two-compartment sink with drain-boards, with the sink compartments of ample size to handle the trays, should be provided.

In the foregoing, we have tried to show the simplicity of some operations as against the complexity of others and some of the many things that must be considered in planning the dishwashing department.

LOCKER ROOMS AND WASH ROOMS

Too often locker rooms are neglected in planning. Yet they may have a definite effect on the type of employees that can be attracted to the restaurant. As the public rest rooms reflect the character of an operation, so too do the employees' locker rooms.

Following are some of the things to be considered in planning:

1. Provide ample space so that each employee may have his own locker. Also provide space for a bench so that employees may be seated when changing their shoes.

2. In service restaurants when it is not known in advance whether waiters or waitresses will be employed, or the number of women employees, if any, to be in the kitchen, it is advisable to provide two wash rooms and a minimum of three locker rooms so arranged that two could be used with one wash room. Employees should not have to walk through the kitchen area to get to their lockers.

3. It is desirable to provide separate locker and washroom facilities for all supervisory personnel, the extent to which this is carried out is determined by the type and size operation.

4. Have lockers wide enough to hold winter clothing and high enough for a full length coat.

5. Provide good ventilation, lighting, and other facilities.

6. In a waitresses' locker room, it is desirable to provide space for a powder room which should have a full length panel mirror in addition to the wall mirror. Also, space for an ironing board should the waitresses have occasion to freshen their uniforms between meals. Provide a uniform rack.

7. Provide lounge space for service and kitchen personnel for rest periods unless some other area is provided. This is particularly needed in large operations where most of the employees are on full time. Sometimes the employees' dining room is available for this purpose.

8. Toilet and washroom facilities must be in accord with the safety code for industrial sanitation with which the architect is familiar.

OFFICES

Depending on the size of the operation, offices will be required for the manager, chef, receiving clerk, the steward, the food and beverage controller, and other assistants such as the dietitian. Each office should be large enough to provide space for a desk, two chairs, and a file cabinet, shelving for books, periodicals, etc. Allow privacy for the manager, steward, dietitian, and the purchasing agent if the latter is located in the office area.

Chapter XXIV: SOME ASPECTS OF FOOD CONTROL

THERE ARE MANY misconceptions concerning the true functions and purposes of a "Food Cost Accounting System" or "Food Control," as it is more commonly called. This system is definitely not to be considered an automatic cure-all, relieving management of the responsibility for making necessary decisions. However, the reports rendered by the food cost accountant are more like "fever-charts" that inform management of weaknesses requiring attention and curative measures.

DEPARTMENTAL INTER-RELATIONSHIPS

There should be nothing fundamentally mysterious or hidden about the work of the food controller insofar as the various department heads are concerned.

Practical food cost accounting should serve to help the several department heads achieve an economically sounder approach to the various phases of their work. The records and material prepared by the food controller should always be available to the chef, steward and banquet manager, but the food control office should never be permitted to become subject to the supervision of anyone directly concerned with the operation of the food department. The reason for this is obvious. No department can effectively control itself.

To give the food controller the proper degree of independent detachment, this functionary should not be permitted to direct the activities of, or be directed by, any employee in the food department. The food controller gathers facts for and makes recommendations to management, but does not tell anyone in the food department what to do or what not to do.

Various methods of food control or cost accounting have been in use for many years. The primary objective of effective control must be the providing of useful, informative operational data *as quickly as possible* to management so that corrective measures, if needed, can be taken in time. Figures that are purely historical and reach management too many days after the close of an operating period do not serve the purpose for which they were intended—that of a current operating tool.

Each system has its own particular features and benefits and should be judged on its direct usefulness to management.

Under certain set-ups, a sales value is assigned to the various components of a meal, such as the appetizer, main dish, dessert, and beverage. Costs are assigned to a grouping of the different types of sales. In some cases the sales information is supported by the number of portions sold, which is compared with the number of potential sales possible on the basis of the yields of each type of purchase. With this method, it is possible to determine which commodity groups are not producing a desired return and hence the need for menu changes. In large operations, the development of desired information can prove slow, cumbersome, and expensive.

The type of system best suited to a particular operation cannot be selected hastily.

Avenues of Control. A sound food control system should comprise seven forms of control. These are listed in the following table together with the sources of the basic data required:

Form of Control	Source of Data
(1) Purchasing	Purchasing Agent or Steward
(2) Receiving	Receiving Clerk
(3) Storing	Storeroom Man
(4) Issuing	Storeroom Man
(5) Production	Chef
(6) Inventory	Food Controller
(7) Sales	Accounting Department

PURCHASING CONTROL

There are two primary types of food purchases, the Daily or Direct purchases for immediate consumption and the Stock or Storeroom Purchases for future use. The former consist mainly of perishable items, while the latter are composed of merchandise purchased in bulk and can be stored.

The most common deficiency in regard to the handling of Direct Purchases has been the predisposition to place fixed or "standing orders" for certain quantities of milk, cream, bread, and other perishable items without proper regard to the daily sales expectancy.

Standing Orders. If a suitable cost accounting system is in operation, the purchases of such items can be tied in directly to the anticipated volume of sales for each day. Where such a system is not used, past sales records can be compiled and sales averages established for each day of the week for each month of the year. On this basis, flexible "standing orders" could be used. These might take the following form:

JANUARY

	LIGHT CREAM	MILK	BREAD	ROLLS
Sunday	20 quarts	40 quarts	10 loaves	30 doz.
Monday	35 "	70 "	18 "	50 "
Tuesday	45 "	90 "	22 "	65 "
Wednesday	45 "	90 "	22 "	65 "
Thursday	45 "	90 "	22 "	65 "
Friday	40 "	80 "	20 "	60 "
Saturday	30 "	60 "	15 "	45 "

Exceptions must be made for holidays. Direct reference to prior sales histories for each particular holiday is necessary to make proper adjustments in the orders. Adequate consideration must also be given special occasions and unusual banquet business.

Stock Purchases. In regard to non-perishable bulk purchases, the major controls revolve around two operational procedures. They are:

(1) Competitive buying.
(2) Standard Purchase Specifications.

While it is manifestly clear that the lowest price does not always mean the best buy, it is nevertheless quite apparent that a lower price will usually indicate a better purchase most of the time, if standard purchase specifications are used. Competitive buying for a food service establishment requires the obtaining of competitive bids from several vendors before placing orders. This subject is discussed in detail in the chapter on Food Purchasing Guides.

It is the duty of the food controller to verify for management whether orders have gone to the lowest bidder, except when special considerations dictate otherwise in certain situations. He should ascertain that the merchandise received is in accordance with the established specifications.

All food purchases should be divided into two categories:

(1) Purchases requiring the issuance of authorized purchase orders. These will generally be non-perishable items that can be stored.
(2) Purchases not requiring the issuance of purchase orders. These are perishable items generally used shortly after receipt.

Copies of all purchase orders must be dispatched to the food controller, who checks them against the related invoices and these, in turn, against the list of standard purchase specifications.

RECEIVING CONTROLS

It is incumbent upon the food controller to spot-check receiving procedures from time to time. The food controller's authority to perform this function should be carefully spelled out by management and the accounting department.

Where standard purchase specifications are in use, it is the receiving clerk's duty to check all incoming shipments against the applicable purchase specifications. It is likewise the responsibility of the food cost accountant to determine whether this practice is adhered to. Spot-checking the actual weight of incoming merchandise, together with rigid checking of invoices against purchase specifications, will minimize the likelihood of sub-standard shipments being accepted by the receiving clerk.

The food controller should check whether the following receiving routines are properly handled:

(1) Each item purchased by weight should be weighed *separately*. Exception can be made for 100 pound bags of merchandise, providing the weight of these bags is spot-checked occasionally.
(2) Items purchased individually should be counted.
(3) Items purchased in cases should be opened on a test basis to ascertain that the *entire* case contains merchandise as labeled.
(4) All items should be inspected as to quality.
(5) All items should be checked against standard specifications, if these are used.
(6) Weights and counts, as determined by the receiving clerk, should be compared with the invoices or shipping tickets accompanying the merchandise.
(7) Where weight or count is deficient, or where inferior quality necessitates a return of merchandise, a "Request for Credit Memo" must be made out and handed to the deliveryman.

It is to be expected that the average receiving clerk will not be sufficiently expert to pass upon the quality of all food received. In cases of doubt, he should summon the chef, steward, or assistant steward to determine whether the merchandise is of acceptable standard. The food controller should ascertain whether the receiving department requests expert opinion, when necessary, or follows the line of least resistance and accepts merchandise of dubious quality.

A function of the receiving department is the preparation of adequate receiving records for use by the food controller and the accounting department. This involves compiling a "Receiving Clerk's Daily Report" or "Receiving Sheet," as it is more generally called. The record constitutes a complete list of all incoming food shipments. The explicit details of this type of work will be found in the chapter on "Receiving Procedures."

All incoming food shipments must be listed on the receiving sheet as either Direct Purchases, which are sent to the kitchen for use usually the same day, or Stock Purchases, which are sent to the storeroom for subsequent usage. It is important that the food controller check for any errors in recording shipments received. A Direct Purchase item erroneously charged to Stock Purchases would overstate the storeroom inventory, while, conversely, a Stock Purchase entered in error in the Direct Purchase column would understate the storeroom inventory. Either type of error would distort the daily consumption figures.

As soon as meat and poultry items are received and individually weighed by the receiving clerk, he should attach a perforated meat tag to each piece showing:

(1) Date received
(2) Dealer's name
(3) Type of cut
(4) Weight
(5) Price per pound
(6) Extension

One-half of the meat tag should remain attached to the meat and one-half, containing identically the same six-point data enumerated above, should be retained for the food cost accountant.

In larger establishments, it is advisable for the food cost accountant to maintain a meat-tag book containing the following six columns:

(1) Serial number of the meat-tag
(2) Date received
(3) Type of cut
(4) Weight
(5) Price per pound
(6) Date issued

This type of record proves of material aid to the food controller as a cross-check for inventory purposes.

STORING CONTROLS

Storing controls consist mainly of systematized procedures to guard against losses through pilfering or spoilage.

These two channels of potential waste require properly outlined duties for the personnel involved, plus periodic inspection by the food cost accountant.

Pilferage Control. Three cardinal principles must be observed if storeroom pilferage is to be eliminated. They are:

(1) Keeping the storeroom door locked.
(2) Safeguarding the storeroom keys when not in use.
(3) Prohibiting entrance into the storeroom by unauthorized persons.

Nothing less than the most rigid observance of these three rules will prevent storeroom pilferage.

To facilitate the filling of requisitions, Dutch doors should be used. In this type of door, the top half can remain open, while the bottom half remains securely locked.

The food controller should review the extent to which these rules are followed.

Spoilage Control. Improper storage facilities can cost any restaurant operation substantial sums of money. Spoilage is brought about by two major causes—internal and external. Internal spoilage is generally caused by excessively long periods of storage, improper ventilation, or inappropriate temperatures. External spoilage may be caused by vermin, rodents, leaky pipes, dirt, dust, broken containers, or sundry foreign substances.

Slow-moving stock can easily be hidden, misplaced or forgotten. Inventory positions on all stock should be carefully reviewed by the food controller to guard against having slow-moving items turn into dead stock. Recommendations in writing for the need of working-off slow-moving stock and for the need of remedying causes of spoilage are a sound contribution that an alert food controller can make regarding this problem, after a thorough inspection of the shelves, refrigerators and other storage areas.

A thorough review of all storage conditions that can produce external spoilage should be made by the food controller at least once every month.

ISSUING CONTROLS

No food stock of any kind should ever be issued without a properly executed requisition. These requisitions can be simplicity itself as far as format is concerned. However, they must contain a complete list of all food items requested and the signature of an employee authorized to request such merchandise. It does not mean that the employee signing the requisition should actually appear in person to obtain the desired food items. A requisition is simply a "food-check" and should be handled exactly as though it were a check for monetary funds.

The importance of the daily requisition slips cannot be overstressed. They are the major key to reconciling inventories and consumption. Any inaccuracies or omissions in the requisitions will distort the reports on consumption and costs. The food controller is obliged to insist upon reasonable accuracy, thoroughness and legibility. These requisitions must be priced by the storeroom attendant to determine the true value or cost of the items requisitioned. A sample requisition form appears in the chapter on Issuing Food.

During the period of a month or any other length of time used to compute operational costs, the following formula will determine consumption:

Opening Inventory
+ Purchases
= Total Available
− Closing Inventory
= Consumption

Another way of stating this same equation follows:

Consumption = Purchases + Opening Inventory—Closing Inventory

Theoretically, the value of all requisitions should agree with the foregoing consumption figures. However, in actual practice shrinkage, spoilage and mispricing of requisitions will create certain discrepancies.

If these discrepancies exceed 1 per cent of the total amount of the issues for a particular period, something is wrong. Pilferage or slip-shod issuing procedures may be responsible.

The food cost accountant must check the pricing of the requisitions and then extend the calculations.

Where meat tags are in use, the food cost accountant must check them against the requisitions. If a meat tag book is also used, all meat tags must be entered as issued after being checked to the requisitions.

PRODUCTION CONTROLS

Production, or preparation, control centers around the "leftover" problem. A certain amount of "leftovers" is inevitable, since no one person or group of persons can ever anticipate precisely what all the patrons will want. However, the extent to which these items can be kept within reasonable limits and subsequently "worked-off" with a minimum of waste and spoilage, will often spell the difference between profit and loss in a restaurant operation.

Food production controls are specific procedures governing the preparation of food to reduce waste and eliminate portion inequalities. Many restaurant operators overlook the advantages to be gained from the employment of a satisfactory system of production controls. Chefs may be inclined to look askance at this type of control the first time they encounter it, but those who have used it know that it represents the only practical means of combating overproduction and waste.

There are many refinements in this type of control but they all involve the following three basic phases:

(1) Planned Preparation
(2) Standard Recipes
(3) Standard Portion Sizes

It will be instantly recognized that the foregoing are nothing more or less than extensions of modern manufacturing methods into the restaurant field. Many of those who have adopted these methods soon begin to wonder how they ever attempted to operate a profitable business without knowing how much merchandise should be "manufactured"; what measures of which ingredients went into their products, and the standard size of the products they offered for sale.

Planned preparation involves the proper interpretation of past experiences in the sales of various menu items. Sound analysis of sales histories is an indispensable guide. It eliminates guess-work.

The chapter on Pre-Cost Pre-Control Procedures illustrates how this function becomes an important step in controlling the food cost percentages "before they happen."

In any establishment where "Pre-Control" is not in use, the minimum data required for the maintenance of an adequate sales analysis record are the following for each item offered for sale:

(1) Date
(2) Day
(3) Meal
(4) Number of Portions Prepared
(5) Number of Portions Sold
(6) Ratio to Total Sales

Menu combinations are important. Broiled pork chops might be a leading seller if it were the only "solid meat" dish offered. However, if a veal cutlet appeared on the same menu, the proportion of pork chop sales would unquestionably decrease, unless there was a substantial price disparity.

It is therefore quite obvious that a complete file must be kept of all menu offerings for each meal to provide simple means of cross-reference regarding menu combinations.

The use of standard recipes is of primary importance in maintaining standards of quality. There can be, and there have been, lengthy discussions regarding the impact of standardized recipes on the artistry of cooking. Good recipes are those which are written in such a manner as to reflect the methods and ingredients actually used in the kitchen for which the recipes are intended. It is almost impossible, and very imprudent, to ask any chef to accept a set of pre-determined recipes, but most any progressive chef will work with management in preparing recipes covering their own food preparation.

It is not the function of the food cost accountant to prepare standard recipes, but it is essential that he or she has a set of standard recipes for costing purposes. It is therefore advisable for the food cost accountant to work with the preparation department in formulating and recording the standard recipes on appropriate filing cards.*

The use of standard portions is one safeguard against patron dissatisfaction. It is extremely annoying to any patron to see someone else being served a larger portion, or for him to be served a portion smaller than the last time the same dish was ordered.

Standard portions are the only means of preventing favoritism or antagonism between service personnel on the one hand and preparation personnel or patrons on the other. Adherence to standard portion sizes assures standardized service to all patrons regardless of any personal factors that might be involved. Treating all patrons alike will please more people more of the time than any other method.

* See chapter on Pre-Cost Pre-Control Procedure for a specimen standard recipe.

A reasonable review of adherence to established standards lies within the scope of duties of the food cost accountant. Perfection is not to be expected but glaring deviations should not be overlooked.

INVENTORY CONTROLS

The food cost accountant's responsibility in regard to inventories is complete. The normal accounting department food inventorying duties are assumed by the food cost accountant, who must supervise the taking of all physical inventories and maintain such perpetual inventory records as are necessary.

In most restaurant operations, financial statements are issued on a monthly basis. This, therefore, necessitates the taking of monthly physical food inventories to ascertain accurately the cost of food sold.

The inventory books must be priced, extended and totalled by the food cost accountant, or his assistant, and turned over to the accounting department for recording in the books of account.

It is quite unusual for any restaurant of considerable size to maintain perpetual inventory records of all food stocks. Some establishments maintain a partial perpetual inventory of the high-priced items, while others maintain a rigid control over the meat tags as previously described in this chapter and which constitutes a form of perpetual inventory control of meat items.

It is advisable for the food cost accountant to maintain a perpetual inventory in terms of total value of all food stocks. In this type of set-up, the total value of each day's storeroom purchases are added to the opening inventory, and the day's storeroom issues are deducted. At the end of the month the closing book-inventory is compared with the value of the actual physical inventory and all sizable discrepancies must be investigated. These usually result from the following:

(1) Illegible Requisitions
(2) Incorrect Pricing
(3) Arithmetical Errors
(4) Shrinkage
(5) Spoilage
(6) Pilferage

As previously mentioned, discrepancies exceeding 1 per cent of the total issues should be regarded as worthy of thorough investigation. It is not sufficient that variations even below 1 per cent be accepted without comment. All employees should be made acquainted with the fact that management is alert to these conditions, so that nothing will be taken *for granted*.

DAILY FOOD COST CONTROL SHEET

There is a prevailing belief that small restaurant operations cannot obtain adequate food cost data, especially where the major food deliveries are likely to be on a weekly or semi-weekly basis. There is, therefore, a tendency to wait until the end of the month, and the closing of the books to obtain food cost data. This is not necessary. A relatively small amount of work by the bookkeeper each day will provide workable food cost data on a cumulative basis without undue delay. A simplified food cost control sheet follows on page 370.

It will be noted from the foregoing control sheet that the taking of a physical inventory at any time during the month would provide accurate consumption figures with relatively little extra effort, if such data were required.

SALES CONTROL

The food cost accountant does not have the responsibility of verifying sales. This function rests within the scope of duties of the accounting department. The usual procedure is the maintenance of the following threefold control:

(1) Food checkers maintain a rigid control over all food items leaving the kitchen by recording the sales value of each item on a guest check.

(2) Food cashiers maintain control over guest check revenue by receiving and registering cash or approved charge account checks.

(3) Income or revenue controllers (or bookkeepers) audit and reconcile the daily work of the checkers and cashiers.

The food cost accountant uses the sales figures produced by the income or revenue controller, but exercises no authority over the checkers, cashiers, or income controllers. However, it is apparent that any serious shortcomings on the part of the checkers or cashiers would distort the sales figures, and, likewise, the food cost accounting. It is to be expected that the food cost accountant will satisfy himself or herself that the checkers and cashiers are performing their work-tasks in a reasonably satisfactory manner. Any irregularities should be discussed with the chief accountant.

If sales analysis records are maintained, it is the ultimate responsibility of the food cost accountant to obtain the appropriate sales data from the

A study of this report will indicate that it is simple to prepare yet provides valuable information on a daily and cumulative basis.

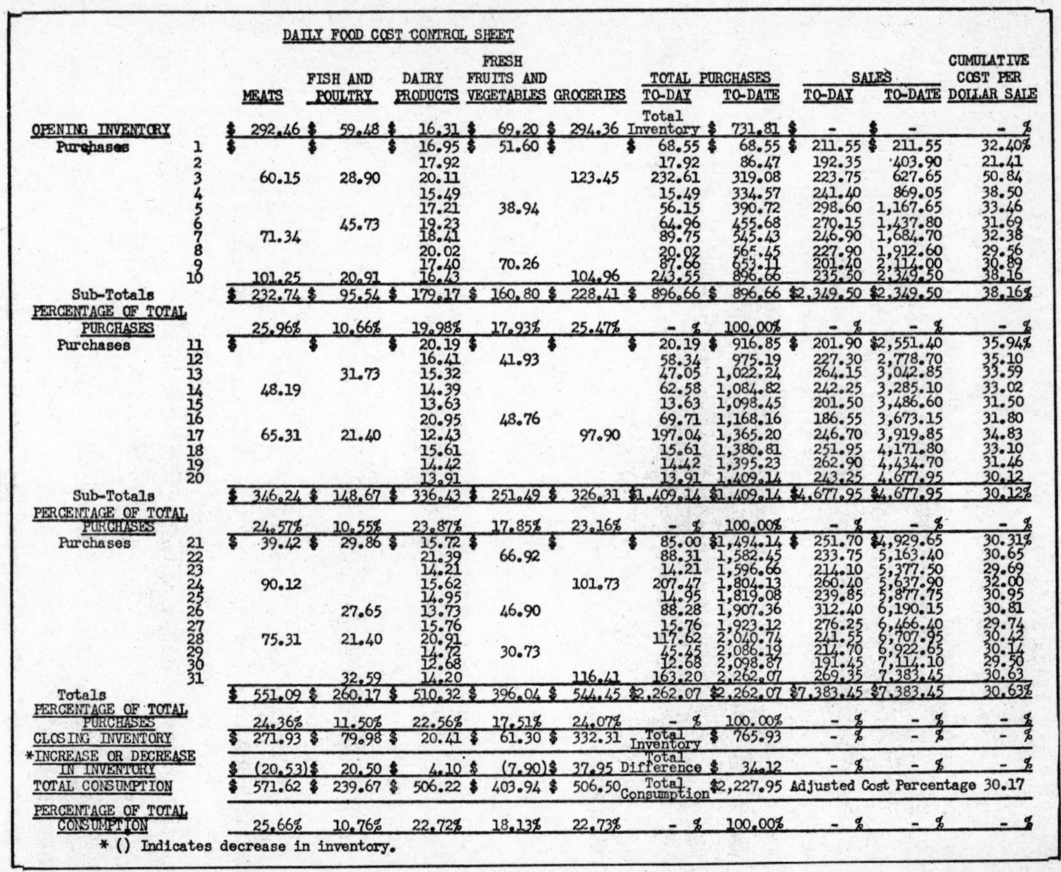

DAILY FOOD COST CONTROL SHEET

		MEATS	FISH AND POULTRY	DAIRY PRODUCTS	FRESH FRUITS AND VEGETABLES	GROCERIES	TOTAL PURCHASES TO-DAY	TOTAL PURCHASES TO-DATE	SALES TO-DAY	SALES TO-DATE	CUMULATIVE COST PER DOLLAR SALE
OPENING INVENTORY		$ 292.46	$ 59.48	$ 16.31	$ 69.20	$ 294.36	Total Inventory	$ 731.81	$ -	$ -	- %
Purchases	1	$	$	$ 16.95	$ 51.60	$	$ 68.55	$ 68.55	$ 211.55	$ 211.55	32.40%
	2			17.92			17.92	86.47	192.35	403.90	21.41
	3	60.15	28.90	20.11		123.45	232.61	319.08	223.75	627.65	50.84
	4			15.49			15.49	334.57	241.40	869.05	38.50
	5			17.21	38.94		56.15	390.72	298.60	1,167.65	33.46
	6		45.73	19.23			64.96	455.68	270.15	1,437.80	31.69
	7	71.34		18.41			89.75	545.43	246.90	1,684.70	32.38
	8			20.02			20.02	565.45	227.90	1,912.60	29.56
	9			17.40	70.26		87.66	653.11	201.40	2,114.00	30.89
	10	101.25	20.91	16.43		104.96	243.55	896.66	235.50	2,349.50	38.16
Sub-Totals		$ 232.74	$ 95.54	$ 179.17	$ 160.80	$ 228.41	$ 896.66	$ 896.66	$2,349.50	$2,349.50	38.16%
PERCENTAGE OF TOTAL PURCHASES		25.96%	10.66%	19.98%	17.93%	25.47%	- %	100.00%	- %	- %	- %
Purchases	11	$	$	$ 20.19	$	$	$ 20.19	$ 916.85	$ 201.90	$2,551.40	35.94%
	12			16.41	41.93		58.34	975.19	227.30	2,778.70	35.10
	13		31.73	15.32			47.05	1,022.24	264.15	3,042.85	33.59
	14	48.19		14.39			62.58	1,084.82	242.25	3,285.10	33.02
	15			13.63			13.63	1,098.45	201.50	3,486.60	31.50
	16			20.95	48.76		69.71	1,168.16	186.55	3,673.15	31.80
	17	65.31	21.40	12.43		97.90	197.04	1,365.20	246.70	3,919.85	34.83
	18			15.61			15.61	1,380.81	251.95	4,171.80	33.10
	19			14.42			14.42	1,395.23	262.90	4,434.70	31.46
	20			13.91			13.91	1,409.14	243.25	4,677.95	30.12
Sub-Totals		$ 346.24	$ 148.67	$ 336.43	$ 251.49	$ 326.31	$1,409.14	$1,409.14	$4,677.95	$4,677.95	30.12%
PERCENTAGE OF TOTAL PURCHASES		24.57%	10.55%	23.87%	17.85%	23.16%	- %	100.00%	- %	- %	- %
Purchases	21	$ 39.42	$ 29.86	$ 15.72	$	$	$ 85.00	$1,494.14	$ 251.70	$4,929.65	30.31%
	22			21.39	66.92		88.31	1,582.45	233.75	5,163.40	30.65
	23			14.21			14.21	1,596.66	214.10	5,377.50	29.69
	24	90.12		15.62		101.73	207.47	1,804.13	260.40	5,637.90	32.00
	25			14.95			14.95	1,819.08	239.85	5,877.75	30.95
	26		27.65	13.73	46.90		88.28	1,907.36	312.40	6,190.15	30.81
	27			15.76			15.76	1,923.12	276.25	6,466.40	29.74
	28	75.31	21.40	20.91			117.62	2,040.74	241.55	6,707.95	30.42
	29			14.72	30.73		45.45	2,086.19	214.70	6,922.65	30.14
	30			12.68			12.68	2,098.87	191.45	7,114.10	29.50
	31		32.59	14.20		116.41	163.20	2,262.07	269.35	7,383.45	30.63
Totals		$ 551.09	$ 260.17	$ 510.32	$ 396.04	$ 544.45	$2,262.07	$2,262.07	$7,383.45	$7,383.45	30.63%
PERCENTAGE OF TOTAL PURCHASES		24.36%	11.50%	22.56%	17.51%	24.07%	- %	100.00%	- %	- %	- %
CLOSING INVENTORY		$ 271.93	$ 79.98	$ 20.41	$ 61.30	$ 332.31	Total Inventory	$ 765.93	- %	- %	- %
*INCREASE OR DECREASE IN INVENTORY		$ (20.53)	$ 20.50	$ 4.10	$ (7.90)	$ 37.95	Total Difference	$ 34.12	- %	- %	- %
TOTAL CONSUMPTION		$ 571.62	$ 239.67	$ 506.22	$ 403.94	$ 506.50	Total Consumption	$2,227.95	Adjusted Cost Percentage		30.17
PERCENTAGE OF TOTAL CONSUMPTION		25.66%	10.76%	22.72%	18.13%	22.73%	- %	100.00%	- %	- %	- %

* () Indicates decrease in inventory.

restaurant checks. However, everyday practice in many establishments has proven the feasibility of having the cashiers or checkers assist in listing the sales of items either from the guest checks or from the trays of the service personnel.

DAILY REPORTS

The major portion of the records necessary for any system of food cost accounting is prepared by employees other than the food cost accountant. The task of correlating the material and presenting the salient operational facts to management through the medium of reports must be performed by the food cost accountant. The sources of the data used by the food cost accountant are as follows:

Data	Source
Purchase Orders	Purchasing Agent
Market Quotation Sheets	Purchasing Agent
Daily Food Receiving Sheet	Receiving Clerk
Food Invoices	Receiving Clerk
Storeroom Requisitions	Storeroom Attendant
Record of Sales	Accounting Department

It is necessary for the food cost accountant to establish a daily routine that embraces all the necessary checking and integration of data.

Invoices or delivery tickets must be checked against the receiving sheet, which is then cross-checked to the purchase orders to make certain incoming shipments have been properly authorized.

The prices charged by the dealers must be checked with the quoted prices as shown on the quotation sheets.

Invoices that are checked against the receiving records and verified as to arithmetical accuracy must be dispatched promptly to the accounting department for recording and payment.

The receiving sheet entries must be checked as to proper distribution, either as direct or storeroom purchases, and accurate cross-footing.

Storeroom issues must be priced at cost and extended. The total of all storeroom issues for each day plus all direct purchases will equal the daily consumption cost.

From the foregoing data, the food cost accountant is able to prepare the Daily Food Cost Report. The delineation of sales can be as simple or as detailed as management requires. Commercial restaurants will usually have a minimal breakdown of dining room sales to individuals and banquet sales to groups. Hotels may have room service sales listed separately. If a Pre-Control system is in effect, more detailed reports are mandatory. The reader is referred to the chapter on Pre-Cost Pre-Control Procedure for the type of daily food cost reports used under that system.

A simple daily food cost report appears below.

DAILY FOOD REPORT

DATE June 2 DAY Friday

EXPLANATION	TO-DAY	TO DATE THIS MONTH	LAST MONTH	LAST YEAR
SALES:				
Dining Room	$1,500.75	$2,982.55	$3,011.40	$3,145.20
Banquets	185.00	325.00	370.00	440.00
Total Sales	$1,685.75	$3,307.55	$3,381.40	$3,585.20
COST OF FOOD SOLD:				
Direct Issues	$ 139.53	$ 270.11	$ 286.51	$ 301.20
Storeroom Issues	483.16	941.12	1,001.17	1,092.64
Total Issues	$ 622.69	$1,211.23	$1,287.68	$1,393.84
Employees' Meal				
Credit	87.50	173.50	167.00	181.50
Cost of Food Sold	$ 535.19	$1,037.73	$1,120.68	$1,212.34
NET COST PER DOLLAR SALE	31.7¢	31.3¢	33.1¢	33.8¢

It is advisable that the foregoing simplified form of Daily Food Cost Report be in the hands of management by noon of the day following the day reviewed.

MONTHLY REPORTS

Monthly reports are compiled for the guidance of management. Hence, they should be as condensed or comprehensive as management desires.

Most of the data presented in the monthly reports should afford a comparison of the *current month* with the *prior month* and also *same month of prior year.*

FOOD PURCHASES AND INVENTORY TURNOVER

The breakdown of food purchases, together with the inventory turnover, is contained in the table below.

FOOD PURCHASE DISTRIBUTION AND INVENTORY TURNOVER (*)

	CURRENT MONTH	RATIO TO TOTAL	PRIOR MONTH	RATIO TO TOTAL	SAME MONTH OF PRIOR YEAR	RATIO TO TOTAL
Meat	$ 2,388.96	30.60%	$ 2,509.34	30.66%	$ 2,149.80	29.29%
Poultry and Game	992.73	12.72	932.23	11.39	658.50	8.97
Fish	965.85	12.37	1,131.60	13.83	733.44	9.99
Eggs	199.76	2.56	292.11	3.57	324.03	4.42
Butter	270.39	3.46	297.81	3.64	284.79	3.88
Milk and Cream	349.91	4.48	398.45	4.87	517.42	7.05
Vegetables	653.77	8.37	563.49	6.89	584.03	7.96
Fruits	399.33	5.11	328.05	4.01	425.82	5.80
Groceries	1,587.53	20.33	1,730.32	21.14	1,661.97	22.64
Total Purchases	$ 7,808.23	100.00%	$ 8,183.40	100.00%	$ 7,339.80	100.00%
Gross Food Cost	$ 7,913.19		$ 8,092.89		$ 8,613.58	
Average Inventory	$ 2,777.68		$ 2,948.12		$ 4,274.59	
Inventory Turnover	2.85 Times		2.75 Times		2.02 Times	

(*) These figures are taken from an actual operation and are used solely for purposes of illustration. They are not intended to be construed as a satisfactory norm or measure for other operations.

Seasonal changes in the purchase distribution are to be expected, but sharp shifts in the ratio in one or more categories of purchases will provide a suitable avenue of investigation. When used in conjunction with the information provided by the daily and monthly "Pre-Control" reports, these figures can be useful in correcting serious defects in the distribution of the purchase dollar.

PURCHASE PRICE COMPARISON

The food cost accountant should include in his monthly report to management, a Purchase Price Comparison, in which should be shown the range of high and low prices paid for all major purchases. If desired, this type of comparison can be issued twice a month. A sample of such a report is shown on page 374.

PURCHASE PRICE COMPARISON

	UNIT	CURRENT MONTH HIGH	CURRENT MONTH LOW	PRIOR MONTH HIGH	PRIOR MONTH LOW	SAME MONTH PRIOR YEAR HIGH	SAME MONTH PRIOR YEAR LOW
BEEF:							
Short Loin	Pound	$ 1.05	$ .98	$ 1.18	$ 1.10	$ .82	$ .80
Shell Loin	"	1.20	.85	1.00	.98	.83	.82
Corned Brisket	"	.74	.72	.74	.65	.63	-
Filet	"	1.52	1.45	1.55	1.46	1.45	1.40
Bottom Round	"	.64	.60	.60	.58	.62	.58
Rib of Beef	"	.78	.62	.87	.60	.63	.61
LAMB:							
Racks	"	.84	.80	.77	.76	1.00	.85
Chucks	"	.38	.35	.40	.35	.50	.42
Legs	"	.62	.54	-	-	.66	.60
VEAL:							
Liver	"	1.19	-	1.19	-	1.20	-
Shoulder	"	.44	.39	.42	.37	.46	-
PROVISIONS:							
Bacon	"	.45	-	.47	.46	.62	.52
Sausage	"	.42	-	.42	-	.55	.44
Loin of Pork	"	.39	.38	.42	.38	.54	.52
Smoked Ham	"	-	-	.51	-	.55	-
POULTRY:							
Broilers	"	.36	.35	.38	.33	.42	.38
Fowl	"	.34	.29	.33	-	.45	-
Turkey	"	.42	.37	.43	.39	.60	.59
SEA FOODS:							
Lobster, Live	"	1.40	.81	1.28	.60	1.20	.76
Shrimp	"	.80	.76	.82	.75	.78	.77
Boston Sole	"	.35	.20	.45	.27	.30	.16
VEGETABLES:							
Cabbage	50# Bag	2.50	1.60	2.25	1.75	2.75	1.75
Carrots	Bushel	2.75	2.50	2.70	2.90	2.50	1.35
Celery	Crate	5.15	3.50	4.50	3.35	5.50	3.50
Potatoes	100#	3.40	3.30	3.40	3.30	4.90	4.85
Mushrooms	Basket	1.65	1.40	1.60	-	2.25	1.60
Tomatoes	Till	2.10	1.25	1.30	1.10	1.70	1.55
FRUIT:							
Apples	72's	6.00	4.75	5.25	4.50	8.00	5.50
Grapefruit	54's	5.85	5.25	6.00	5.25	6.50	4.75
Lemons	360's	7.50	5.75	7.50	5.90	8.25	8.00
Oranges	216's	6.85	6.35	7.60	6.85	6.40	5.75
DAIRY PRODUCTS:							
Butter, Salt Print	Pound	.67	.66	.67	.66	.67	.65
Eggs, White	Dozen	.49	.48	.58	.47	.63	.58

This "market barometer" will indicate whether major decisions regarding menu structure are advisable in the light of unusual market conditions. This type of summary keeps management informed of the basic costs of the various food ingredients.

FOOD COST ANALYSIS

The minimum requirements for a satisfactory food cost analysis are contained in the tabulation below.

FOOD COST ANALYSIS	MONTH REVIEWED	PRIOR MONTH	SAME MONTH PRIOR YEAR
NET SALES	$21,868.66	$21,546.14	$22,123.63
COST OF FOOD SOLD (1)	7,121.87	7,290.47	7,597.87
GROSS PROFIT	$14,746.79	$14,255.67	$14,525.76
COST PER DOLLAR SALE	32.57%	33.84%	34.34%
OPENING FOOD INVENTORY	$ 2,907.89	$ 2,988.34	$ 4,958.93
NET PURCHASES	7,652.76	8,012.44	7,244.89
TOTAL AVAILABLE	$10,560.65	$11,000.78	$12,203.82
CLOSING INVENTORY	2,647.46	2,907.89	3,590.24
COST OF FOOD CONSUMED	$ 7,913.19	$ 8,092.89	$ 8,613.58
LESS: EMPLOYEES' MEALS AND CREDITS	791.32	802.41	1,015.71
COST OF FOOD SOLD (1)	$ 7,121.87	$ 7,290.48	$ 7,597.87

It will be noted that the excessive inventory position of the prior year was corrected and brought into line. An inventory reduction of approximately 30 per cent represents a substantial thinning down of slow-moving and dead stock.

A relatively simple array of salient operating data will often lead to speedier recognition of the necessary remedial steps than a lengthy, detailed report. However, since this analysis is intended to be an aid to management, the form of the report must be amplified or condensed as best suits the needs of any particular operation.

Chapter XXV: PRE-COST PRE-CONTROL PROCEDURES

"PRE-CONTROL" NOW IS THE familiar name in the restaurant trade for the Pre-Cost Pre-Control Food Accounting System. It is a tool designed to make use of modern merchandising practices in the restaurant field. It is the answer to repeated requests by alert management for a method whereby the everyday procedures in use in various mercantile fields could be applied to the restaurant industry.

Management wanted sound measuring rods of the sales appeal of various menu items offered to the public. It sought up-to-the-minute purchasing techniques and insisted upon planned production. To meet the persistent demands by management, "Pre-Control" was designed to fill these needs. However, like all tools, its maximum serviceability depends upon the manner in which it is used. When it is properly utilized, it produces beneficial results. It promotes efficiency, provides sound sales data, coordinates purchasing and preparation, reduces over-preparation and helps iron out elusive merchandising wrinkles in the menu structure. Above all, it reduces food costs.

Listed in the tabulation on page 377 are the "before" and "after" sales and costs of a large, nationally-famous, mid-western restaurant operation:

"Pre-Control" is not, and was never meant to be, a "straitjacket" to restrict any employee. On the other hand, it cannot be an automatic "insurance policy" against waste or inefficiency.

It cannot be an effective instrument unless it has the complete cooperation of Management, the Chef, Steward, Maitre d'Hotel, Head Checker and Food Cost Accountant. There must be a reasonable harmony of interest or "team-work" among these key employees for "Pre-Control" to yield the maximum results.

In some restaurant operations, the "control" employees and the "operating" employees have definite misunderstandings about the place of each in the scheme of things. To the men and women charged with the responsibility of buying, preparing, and serving food, the "controller" often seems to be a hard-headed constable constantly pointing an accusing finger in all directions. To the food cost accountants, who endeavor to exercise some degree of "control" over the all-important factor of food costs, the operating department heads sometimes seem to be hypersensitive "traditionalists" who allow themselves to become overwhelmed by their desire to maintain everyone's "good-will," literally at all costs.

	BEFORE INSTALLATION		AFTER INSTALLATION	
	NET SALES	COST PER DOLLAR SALE	NET SALES	COST PER DOLLAR SALE
January	$ 131,462.03	45.15	$ 130,211.23	37.23
February	125,721.16	43.02	131,645.92	36.55
March	135,611.71	42.92	144,127.16	36.14
April	142,170.20	41.64	146,216.39	36.37
May	139,289.16	42.37	137,778.85	37.42
June	136,437.55	41.89	129,039.47	35.29
July	95,189.47	48.23	93,882.16	39.84
August	98,836.42	47.84	96,640.79	39.31
September	132,914.92	46.38	130,990.52	38.41
October	144,973.01	44.83	140,353.63	39.23
November	143,002.86	47.32	140,501.94	37.45
December	148,194.29	44.16	142,364.00	38.64
Total	$1,573,802.78	44.23	$1,563,752.06	38.09

The average saving of approximately 6 cents per dollar sale was accomplished without any basic reduction in the volume of sales, other than an extremely nominal amount which was attributable to the trend of the times. The decline of less than 1 per cent in the volume of sales was considerably less than the national or regional trends. On the other hand, this result was accomplished without sacrifice of quality of food or character of service.

While it is unquestionably true that a conscientious controller may occasionally appear to resemble a "walking Geiger-counter," constantly "looking for trouble," and that some department heads may tend, under pressure, to be insufficiently mindful of wasteful practices in their departments, the all-important fact remains that sound operation in a highly competitive field requires the best of understanding and mutual helpfulness on all sides.

No department head in any sizable restaurant operation has an easy job. With competitive price squeezes on all sides, uncertainties about customer preferences, inadequately trained employees and the extreme perishability of certain foods, the work-duties of chef or steward are unquestionably difficult. That is why they are entitled to all possible assistance in their efforts to navigate the tricky cross-currents of public whim and fancy.

"Pre-Control" helps tie together many of the difficult aspects of planning the writing of menus and the purchasing and preparing of food. In the daily forecast meetings, all useful information is pooled, minimizing the haphazard influence of chance or the personal "hunch" of any single individual. If there is a predisposition on the part of anyone to overemphasize what is considered to be the purely "artistic" side to the actual detriment of commercial success, the operational cost of this tendency soon comes to light. This is particularly true in some hotels where commercial decisions of considerable importance are sometimes based on the inertia of tradition or the imperfect recollections of previous sales histories.

The General Manager of a hotel has a special problem since he or she is usually not a technical food expert and is often forced to rely on the "business" judgment of the department heads, with no practicable means of checking on the dollars and cents wisdom of these decisions except through scrutiny of the month-end food cost percentages and operating results. Comparison with previous months or with other hotels may reveal discouraging facts, but will not indicate which constructive, corrective steps should be taken in time to prevent a repetition of similar results.

Calling department heads "on the carpet" to express extreme displeasure over the high food cost does not solve problems, since it does not get at the root of the difficulties. Demanding better results on the basis of an "or else" ultimatum is not constructive, but merely shifts the feeling of frustration from the manager's shoulders to those of the department heads. The end result of such an encounter is often the determination to "make a showing" even though it might mean "cutting corners" with the customers.

Cutting quality or portion sizes is not the answer to better costs. Anyone who believes in these "solutions" will generally be proved shortsighted through diminishing volume of business.

The solution to high food cost problems is to be found in taking decisive steps before the actual damage is done. No one can cure faulty purchasing, excessive spoilage or overpreparation merely by being indigant or "hitting the ceiling" after it has happened. Over-preparation and other wasteful practices can be controlled only by adequate planning and predetermination of purchase and preparation requirements *before* the actual purchasing or preparation commences.

Before any procedures of the Pre-Cost, Pre-Control System of Food Accounting may be instituted, it is extremely important that the ordinary, basic or "understood" controls are in effect. By these controls are meant competitive purchasing; receiving checks by quality, weight, and quantity; requisition control over the storeroom; proper sales check storage and distribution, along with effective checking, cashiering, and proving of food register readings.

With these controls in operation, it is possible to prepare the foundation for Pre-Cost, Pre-Control Food Cost Accounting. Following are the preliminary steps of the actual installation.

RESTAURANT PORTION SALES HISTORY

(1) This basic phase is the record of portions sold of luncheon and dinner entrees and the major a la carte items in the various restaurants. This is accomplished by either the checkers and or the cashiers "keeping score" on the menu copy of the number of portions sold in the several categories mentioned above. Where available, multi-counter machines may be utilized for this purpose. At the end of each meal period the marked menus are sent to the food cost accountant for recording in the Sales Analysis Book.

A typical menu for a restaurant in the modest price brackets is seen on page 380.

(2) The Sales Analysis Book should be divided into separate sections for each restaurant. Each section should be further sub-divided into luncheon, dinner, luncheon a la carte and dinner a la carte sub-sections, and as many other sub-sections as may be necessary. The following information should be shown in this record:

1. Date
2. Day of Week
3. Weather
4. House Count
5. Special Events
6. Total Meals Served
7. Remarks

(3) For purposes of illustration, the columnar arrangement of a segment of a typical Sales Analysis Book is shown on page 381.

(4) With such a record for guidance, the determination of expected portion sales is placed on a sounder commercial basis. A minimum of a thirty-day period is generally required for determining properly the various sales expectancies and the related projection of the purchase and preparation of food supplies.

FORMAT OF SALES RECORDS

The form in which the sales records are kept is of secondary importance. It is essentially a matter of individual choice or convenience.

A continuing, chronological arrangement of a 28, 29, 30 or 31 column

Appetizers

Sliced Banana and Orange Cocktail 25 Chilled Vegetable Juice 15
Old Fashioned Potato Chowder 20
Clear Beef Bouillon with Melba Toast 15

LUNCHEON SUGGESTIONS
CLUB LUNCHEON INCLUDES DESSERT AND BEVERAGE

A LA CARTE		CLUB LUNCHEON
50	Noodles and Fresh Mushrooms au Gratin	75
70	Frankfurters with Boston Baked Beans *Brown Bread and Butter*	95
1 00	Fresh Calf's Liver with Smothered Onions *French Fried Potatoes, Tomato Slice*	1 25
65	Fresh Vegetable Plate: Baked Sweet Potato with Marshmallow *Buttered Broccoli, Succotash*	90
90	Irish Lamb Stew with New Vegetables *Pickled Beet and Sliced Egg Salad*	1 15

Hot Bread and Butter Served with Above Orders

Desserts

*Fresh Orange Bavarian Pudding with Orange Sauce 20
*Fresh Apple Pie 20 *Chocolate Cream Puff 20 *Silver Nut Layer Cake 20
Creme de Menthe Sundae 25 *Elberta Peaches in Juice 20
*Jell-o with Whipped Cream 20 *Danish Pastry 15
*Fruit Sherbet 15 Dessert Cheese with Toasted Crackers 30
Peanut Ice Cream Ball in Chocolate Sauce 25
*Vanilla, Chocolate or Strawberry Ice Cream 20

*CLUB LUNCHEON DESSERTS

Beverages

Pot of Tea 15
Coffee .... 10 Buttermilk 10
Cup of Postum .... 10 Milk 10

book for each month indicates quite clearly the companion offerings for a given day and the extent of repetition of any one item.

At the beginning of each month, the first day's offerings for a given meal are listed in sequence. The second day's menu items follow, then the third day's until the end of the month. After the first few days, items that are repeated will have to be located when the postings are made. This is its one real disadvantage. When sales histories are required, the individual item desired must be sought out from the entire listing to date. However, there is always the definite advantage of having the entire month's picture at hand.

COFFEE SHOP LUNCHEON		DATE	5/1	5/2	5/3	5/4
		DAY	M	TU	W	TH
		WEATHER	RAIN	CLEAR	CLEAR	CLOUDY
		HOUSE COUNT	607	720	701	685
		MEALS SERVED	343	356	364	350
		SPECIAL EVENTS	NONE	NIGHT BASEBALL	FLOWER SHOW	NONE
PORTION COST	ITEM	SALES PRICE	PORTIONS SERVED			
20	Noodles & Mushroom	50	22/42			
25	Frankfurter & Beans	70	53/48		34/38	
39	Calf's Liver	100	12/29			
20	Vegetable Plate	65	17/14			
33	Irish Lamb Stew	90	42/47			34/40
15	Poached Egg on Codfish Cake	80		21/49		
20	Chef's Salad Bowl	70		28/25		
23	Patty of Sweetbread	85		20/28		
18	Ravioli	75		31/19		
22	Chicken Croquettes	90		27/33		
27	Filet of Sole	80			20/11	
28	Lamb Kidney on Toast	95			15/13	
21	Chicken Salad	85			21/38	
16	Baked Macaroni	60			37/44	
23	Smoked Whitefish	85				13/16
17	Patty of Chicken a la King	80				21/23
26	Ham & Eggs	85				31/39
18	Omelette	60				21/30

A card index file is the other method of recording the menu sales histories. Each item is listed on a separate card that is filed alphabetically under the various headings such as Beef, Veal, Lamb, Provisions, Poultry and Seafood. Posting is generally somewhat faster by this method, as well as the location of any particular menu items. However, there is no way of knowing what companion items were offered on a given day, except by additional reference to a file of menus.

RATIO OF SALES

There are two very important sales ratios that have a marked effect on reducing overpreparation and on strengthening the average receipt per check. The ratio of each entree sold to the total of all du jour sales will give a very valuable clue as to relative sales appeal of any dish. If any entree that has sold on certain given days within a range of 15 to 20 per cent of the total du jour sales, suddenly jumps to 30 per cent or falls to 10 per cent, there is almost invariably a reason within the menu structure for such a drastic change. Either the type of companion offerings is inappropriate or the price structure has been inadvertently altered. In either case a change may be highly advisable. Under "Pre-Control" such gyrations can easily be checked and something constructive done in time.

The ratio of the total du jour selections to the total number of covers served for a given meal is very important. If the percentage of the total du jour to the total covers served falls below 80 per cent, close scrutiny

MONDAY							TUESDAY							WEDNESDAY							THURSDAY						
PRICE	COST %	W	DATE	NO. L	NO D	RATIO	PRICE	COST %	W	DATE	NO. L	NO. D	RATIO	PRICE	COST %	W	DATE	NO L	NO D	RATIO	PRICE	COST %	W	DATE	NO. L	NO. D	RATIO
																					170			1/5	18		15%
																								1/19	14		12
																								2/2	11		10
																					175			2/16	15		20
																								3/2	13		11
																								3/16	22		15
																					170			3/30	20		16

80-8 ITEM ROAST LEG OF LAMB ROOM CHRYSTAL

of the menu structure is advisable. In such instances it becomes necessary to determine why more than 20 per cent of the customers ignored the du jour selections. This percentage represents more than the reasonable amount of so-called "sandwich trade." Inspection of the checks of the patrons who did not order from the du jour section may be advisable. The menu offerings may not have been attractive enough and considerable revenue may have been lost.

VARIATIONS OF THE DAYS OF THE WEEK

The first thing that a comprehensive sales history indicates is the relative selling strength of the different days of the week. In most commercial establishments Sunday sales are virtually a law unto themselves, bearing no resemblance to other days of the week. Standing orders of perishable food supplies and the general menu structure must be related to the demonstrated selling power of the Sunday meals.

In some establishments such merchandising features as Brunch or Buffet are advisable. All new experiments in selling techniques or menu structure must be properly recorded in the sales histories.

For many establishments, Monday is often a rather unique sales day. Excessive indulgence over the week-end by any substantial portion of the patronage makes advisable the judicious offering of relatively simple "hangover" dishes. Lean purses due to week-end extravagances reflect themselves in the type of dishes selected by the patrons.

Tuesdays, Wednesdays and Thursdays in many establishments will bear a certain resemblance to each other. The sales history of any one of these days is likely to be quite similar to that of the other two days.

Friday is a pre-week-end day that may feature poor dinner dishes. It is a "fish" day in many communities. In some localities, it is also college student night.

Saturday bears close watching, especially where a five-day work week is prevalent. Saturday luncheon may be very light in a commercial neighborhood. It is a frequent occurrence, on close examination of the sales histories of previous Saturdays, to find that a menu may be too strong for the expected trade. Too many good sellers, when only a moderate trade can reasonably be expected, can easily result in overpreparation.

Pay Days. It is advisable to determine, if possible, when pay days occur in the various establishments from which restaurant trade may be expected. It will be abundantly clear to anyone perusing sales records that business is generally brisk on pay days. "Pay-day specials" of attractive dishes will quite often bring in a much higher average receipt per check. Gearing the menu to the customers' pay days is good selling and will easily be apparent in the type of selections made by some of the customers. By the same token, the two or three days before pay day, especially where payrolls are on a bi-weekly or semi-monthly basis, are the occasions when budget specials will move briskly. However, some establishments have experienced a relatively poor volume of luncheon sales on pay days, especially in neighborhoods catering to a predominantly feminine trade, where there is often a predisposition to hurry through a quick luncheon in order to go shopping.

CUSTOMER LIKES AND DISLIKES

An adequately maintained sales history will clearly indicate, without any guess-work, what the customers want. The extent and proportion of their interest in certain dishes, and the prices they are willing to pay, become quite clear. Experimentation is possible, within easy-to-control and easy-to-watch limits. Profit positions can be constantly improved by selling customers the dishes they have demonstrated they want and by eliminating items they do not wish to buy.

Variety Versus Monotony. There will always be a running, fluctuating battle between the adherents of *variety* and the proponents of *monotony*. Either can be costly if carried to extremes. Variety, if it is overdone, can easily mean dead stock in the storeroom, spoilage and left-overs. Monotony can mean added business for someone else's restaurant. A happy balance between these two extremes must be sought. A sound sales history will readily highlight any dangerous tendency in either expensive direction.

DIARY OF SPECIAL EVENTS

If the events that have a direct bearing upon additions to or subtractions from the volume of business are numerous, it is a sound practice to obtain a diary and list all such items. Thus, a rain that fell during lunchtime but cleared by night-fall would be listed.

Special events in the community that might bring in trade or divert it elsewhere should be listed. All special features in competitors' establishments should be included.

SELL-OUT TIME

Whenever pre-prepared dishes sell out, the checkers should be required to note on the menu the time this occurred. A history of these sell-out times can be a very useful bit of additional information. Thus, if Roast Duckling sold out at 1:10 at luncheon, it is entirely probably that anywhere from 20 to 40 per cent more orders of this item might have been sold. Subsequent sales histories of sold-out items bear special scrutiny. New, experimental dishes should be prepared on the basis of an early expected sell-out. The time of the sell-out gives a clear indication of the extent of the increase in the production quota the next time the same dish is offered.

STANDARD PURCHASE SPECIFICATIONS

The establishment of standard purchase specifications is the basis of the pre-costing of menus and the serving of standard portion sizes. Proper trim and quality are of prime importance in maintaining an efficient and economical food operation.

Some examples of standard purchase specifications will be found in the chapter on Food Purchasing Guides.

Computing Portion Cost Factors. The Butcher Test Card is the primary record for computing portion cost factors and completing the cost calculators. The component parts of each cut of meat must be weighed and recorded properly as butchered to show the yield and the prepared cost per portion. Dividing the purchase cost per pound into the prepared cost per portion, results in the portion cost factor.

The portion cost factor may be applied to fluctuating market prices to arrive at the portion cost without resorting to additional testing. Further importance of standard purchase specifications is evident since the cost factor should only be utilized when the standard purchase specifications are being followed as to weight range and trim.

An illustration of a Butcher Test appears on page 386.

The top portion of the Butcher Test Card is self-explanatory. It merely shows the purchase statistics of the particular cut of meat, but it must include more specific identifying information than merely the name of the cut. The flank trim can make an appreciable difference in the final cost of the portion served.

The front of the Butcher Test Card shows the weights of the component parts. Credit for the by-products such as bones, fat, hamburger meat, short ribs, or grenadin of beef is applied at the purchasable market prices. The remaining cost of $28.58 in the illustrated sample form is assigned to the oven-ready rib.

The cost factor per pound or portion is determined by dividing the original purchase price into the cost per pound or portion. Once it has been determined, the cost factor per pound or portion is multiplied by any new purchase price to determine cost per pound or portion. Having this information immediately available makes for rapid re-costing of menu items, particularly during periods when prices are controlled by governmental regulation.

STANDARD PORTION SIZES

Successful operation of the Pre-Cost Pre-Control system of Food Accounting depends in a large measure upon strict adherence to standard portion sizes. Changes in portion sizes should only take place after thorough tests have proven the portion size to be uneconomical to the hotel, by reason of size, popularity, or competitive situations.

As an aid to the butcher in cutting uniform portions, a 16 or a 32

FORM NO. PC PC-1b HKF & CO.

BUTCHER TEST CARD

ITEM PRIME RIB OF BEEF-7 CUT- 10 INCH FLANK TRIM SHORT SKIRT GRADE CHOICE DATE 3/28-29

PIECES 1 WEIGHING 36 LBS. 4 OZ. AVERAGE WEIGHT

TOTAL COST $ 31.90 AT $ .88 PER LB SUPPLIER SMITH HOTEL SUPPLIERS

BREAKDOWN	NO.	WEIGHT		RATIO TO TOTAL WEIGHT	VALUE PER LB.	TOTAL VALUE		COST OF EACH		PORTION		COST FACTOR PER	
		LB.	OZ.					LB.	OZ.	SIZE	COST	LB.	PORTION
OVENREADY RIB		22	13	62.8%	1.25	$28	58						
SHORT RIBS	5	3	7	9.3	.37	1	27	.37	.023	10 oz	.25	.42	.27
GRENADIN OF BEEF	5	2	13	7.6	.48	1	35	.48	.03	8 oz	.24	.55	.27
HAMBURGER	2		10	1.5	.45		28	.45	.028	5 oz	.23	.51	.27
FAT		4	0	11.7	.08		32						
BONES		2	9	7.1	.04		10						
TOTAL		36	4	100.00%	$ .88	$31	90						

ITEM PORTION SIZE PORTION COST FACTOR

COOKING LOSS

COOKED 4 HOURS 0 MINUTES AT 350 DEGREES

HOURS MINUTES AT DEGREES

BREAKDOWN	NO.	WEIGHT		RATIO TO TOTAL WEIGHT	VALUE PER LB.	TOTAL VALUE		COST OF EACH		PORTION		COST FACTOR PER	
		LB.	OZ.					LB.	OZ.	SIZE	COST	LB.	PORTION
Original Weight		36	4	100.0%	$ .88	31	90					1.0	
Trimmed Weight		22	13	62.9	1.25	28	58					1.4	
Loss in Trimming		13	7	37.1		3	32						
Cooked Weight		19	0		1.50	28	58					1.7	
Loss in Cooking		3	13										
Bones and Trim		4	8										
Loss in Slicing													
Salable Meat		14	8	40.0	1.97	28	58	1.97	.123	10 oz	1.23	2.2	1.4
Salable Meat													

REMARKS:

ITEM ROAST PRIME RIB PORTION SIZE 10 OZ PORTION COST FACTOR 1.4

ounce portion scale should be provided, so that he will be able to measure each portion as it is cut. The cooks should be instructed in the proper serving spoon to use and the quantities to be served.

DAILY PRICE BOARD

In order to pre-cost the menus at current market prices it is necessary always to have them available.

A wall blackboard listing the main meat, poultry, and fish items with a column for the latest purchase price is utilized for the purpose of obtaining the current costs. The board should be posted daily. Thus a person may pre-cost a menu by merely glancing at the Price Board for his item price and referring to the proper price line on the Cost Calculator for the portion cost.

STANDARD RECIPE CARD

The standard recipe card should be completed to show the recipe accepted for use by the hotel.

All ingredients used must be listed and the cost determined for the quantity produced. From this information the cost of a portion may be computed. The recipes will be re-costed when a cost factor or the market prices reflect substantial changes.

For a typical "Standard Recipe Card" see page 388.

Recipe Conversion Tables. To aid in the costing of recipes, it is advisable to have "Recipe Conversion Tables" easily available. These facilitate rapid conversion from purchasing units to recipe units.

A sample of such conversion table follows:

RECIPE UNIT	ITEM	PURCHASE UNIT
1 Cup	Flour	4 Ounces
1 Cup	Powdered Sugar	6½ Ounces
1 Cup	Sugar	8 Ounces
2 Tablespoons	Sugar	1 Ounce
6 Teaspoons	Sugar	1 Ounce
1 Cup (8 Ounces)	Milk	½ Pint
1 Quart	Canned Tomatoes	1¼ Pound—Fresh
2 Quarts	Cooked Noodles	10 Ounces—Raw
1 Quart	Cooked Macaroni	8 Ounces—Raw
1 Cup	Diced Ham	½ Pound
1½ Pound	Chopped Hard Cooked Eggs	1 Dozen
1 Quart	Cooked Lima Beans	6 Pounds in Shells
1 Gallon	Shredded Carrots	8 Pounds
1 Gallon	Mushrooms	8 Pounds

COST OF MAKE-UP COURSES FOR TABLE d'HOTE MEALS

In addition to the cost of the main dish, the cost of the other courses such as the appetizer or soup, vegetable, potato, salad, dessert, beverage,

Form No. PC-2 H.K.F. & Co.
2M449

STANDARD RECIPE CARD

DATE ______

ITEM Browned Beef Stew AMOUNT PRODUCED 8 3/4 GAL COST PER (GAL) $2.73

NUMBER OF PORTIONS 140 PORTION SIZE 8 oz. 4 oz MEAT PORTION COST .18 HOTEL STYLE

QUANTITY	UNIT	INGREDIENTS	PURCHASE PRICE	UNIT PRICE	TOTAL COST	QUANTITY	UNIT	INGREDIENTS	PURCHASE PRICE	UNIT PRICE	TOTAL COST
35	LB	Boneless Chuck	.56		$19 60			Total Brought Forward			$23 57
5	oz	Salt	.02		01	1	ea	Bay Leaf	–		01
3/4	oz.	Pepper	.40		02	1	LB.	Flour	04		04
1½	oz	Paprika	.82		07	1½	gal	Brown Sauce	.20		30
1½	LB.	Shortening	36		54			Total Cost			$23 92
7	LB.	Onions (cut coarsely)	094		67						
4	LB.	Celery (cut coarsely)	076		30						
7	LB.	Carrots (cut coarsely)	.085		60						
6	LB.	Turnips (cut coarsely)	.032		19						
20	LB.	Potato (Large Dice)	.053		1 01						
4	kernels	Garlic (Finely Chopped)			02						
1	#10	Tomatoes	.54		54						
		Total Carried Forward			$23 57						

(FRONT)

PREPARATION AND SERVICE

METHOD: (Procedure, Time, Temperature, Remarks)

Season meat with salt, pepper and paprika.

Place shortening in roasting pan in hot oven, add meat and cook until brown, add flour and cook 20 minutes. Remove to another kettle and add hot brown sauce and tomatoes; stir and let simmer.

Cook vegetables; when meat is nearly done add vegetables, potatoes last, and cook 30 minutes.

Season to taste.

(BACK)

rolls and butter must be computed. Since the majority of the pre-costing concerns the table d'hote meal or forms of it, it is necessary to have the cost of the "surrounding" courses for each restaurant. It is best to compute the average cost of the "surrounding" courses and add the total to the entree cost.

"FORECAST" SECTION OF MENU PRE-COST AND ABSTRACT

The work of Pre-Cost Pre-Control food accounting is divided into two phases: that which is done three days prior to the menu serving day and that which is completed on the day following the menu serving day.

The chef's menu copy for luncheon, dinner and major a la carte items is received three days prior to the menu serving day and the menu items and selling prices are transcribed to the "Menu Pre-Cost and Abstract."

A separate abstract is used for each restaurant, listing the luncheon, dinner, and a la carte items, or when the same menu is for more than one restaurant, a three-column abstract is used.

The pre-costing of the menu begins with reference to the Portion Size, Cost Calculators, Standard Recipe Cards, Daily Price Board, and Average Cost of surrounding items. Thus, the cost of each menu item is determined and the anticipated cost per dollar sale computed.

The next step is the proper evaluation of all factors having a bearing on the sales of each offering. These factors will generally include:

(1) Conventions in town.
(2) Special sports or theatrical events.
(3) Comparative prices of various offerings.
(4) Type of food.
(5) Type of preparation.
(6) Weather.
(7) Ratio to total sales.
(8) Season of the year.
(9) Day of the week.
(10) Holidays.
(11) Holiday eves.
(12) Ratio of total entree sales to total covers served.

Certain "slow-movers" can be eliminated by appropriate analysis of the previous sales history.

The forecasted portions are applied to the individual costs and sales and the anticipated revenue and the cost for the day is arrived at, as well as the anticipated cost per dollar sale for the day.

Desired changes in the menu structure to eliminate certain offerings that are pulling the food cost percentage out of line can be made at a Forecast Meeting. Participants in these meetings should be the Chef, Steward, Maitre d'Hotel, Head Checker, Food Cost Accountant and management's direct representative. Expected sales figures are reviewed and analyzed. In the light of their direct experience, those attending these meetings will often suggest adjustments in the number of portions to be prepared. When there is agreement as to the number of portions to be prepared, the Food Cost Accountant leaves a carbon copy of the "Menu Pre-Cost and Abstract" with the Chef for his guidance in requisitioning food for that day and his order to the butchers and cooks for the number of portions to prepare. By close cooperation between the Chef and the Food Cost Accountant in this phase, unnecessary preparation with its subsequent waste can be prevented.

Close adherence to the accepted portions to be prepared must be reflected in the requisitioning of foods by the Chef. While this in no way prevents the carrying of a "normal inventory" for "maison plat" and the usual a la carte items, it does limit the excessive prior preparation that proves so costly.

On page 391 is a "Forecast" Menu Pre-Cost and Abstract:

"Actual" Section of Menu Pre-Cost and Abstract. The "Actual" Section of the "Menu Pre-Cost and Abstract" is then completed from the marked menu copy received from the checkers and/or cashiers. The number of portions sold are entered in the "Portions Sold" column and extended for cost and sales. When the abstracts for all rooms have been completed, the meal totals by rooms are entered on the "Daily Summary of Food Costs and Potential Savings."

The "Portions Sold" of the various entrees are now posted to the Sales Analysis Book and become part of the Restaurant Portion Sales History.

On page 392 is an example of a completed Menu Pre-Cost and Abstract.

DAILY SUMMARY OF FOOD COSTS AND POTENTIAL SAVINGS

The "Daily Summary of Food Costs and Potential Savings" is prepared from the completed "Menu Pre-Cost and Abstract," "Preliminary Food Cost Report," and the Controller's Daily Revenue report. From the "Menu Pre-Cost and Abstract" the actual totals of portions sold, total revenue, and total cost are entered for luncheons, dinners, and a la carte entrees for each restaurant. The total breakfast covers and sales are transcribed from the Controller's Daily Revenue report. The cost of breakfasts is determined by applying the cost per dollar sale of the breakfasts in the various restaurants which are pre-costed periodically.

The total covers and total sales for the dining room are entered and the difference in sales between the breakfast, luncheon, dinner, and a la carte entree sales and the total sales is entered as "a la carte other." The cost of the "a la carte other" sales is either calculated at the over-all cost per dollar sale of the breakfast, luncheon, dinner and a la carte entrees, or is costed on the basis of periodic calculations of the actual cost of the items served. The above procedure is followed for all restaurants.

Form No. PC-PC 6A, HKF&CO.

HOTEL Metropolitan

DAY & DATE Sat. 6/10

HOUSE COUNT

MENU PRE-COST AND ABSTRACT

WEATHER

Entree	Cost Per Ptn.	Forecast				Cost %	Actual Sales			Cost %	Ratio to Total*
		No.	Total Cost	Sales Price	Total Sales		No. Sold	Total Sales	Total Cost		
CLUB DINNERS											
Cheese Omelette	.40	3	1.20	1.25	3.75						
Broiled Striped Bass	.52	10	5.20	1.40	14.00						
Baked Ham	.57	18	10.26	1.50	27.00						
Breaded Sweetbreads	.63	5	3.15	1.50	7.50						
Roast Leg of Lamb	.78	17	13.26	1.55	26.35						
Casserole of Capon	.66	9	5.94	1.80	16.20						
Assorted Cold Cuts	.57	5	2.85	1.45	7.25						
Total		67	41.86		102.05	41.01					
A LA CARTE											
Special Prime Rib of Beef	.91	10	9.10	1.95	19.50						
Chef's Salad Bowl	.29	8	2.32	.95	7.60						
Fruit Salad	.24	15	3.60	.85	12.75						
Half Spring Chicken	.60	3	1.80	1.50	4.50						
Calf Liver & Bacon	.43	6	2.58	1.25	7.50						
Total		42	19.40		51.85	37.42					
GRAND TOTAL		109	61.26		153.90	39.81					100.00

* Popularity Index Ratio.

Banquet cost is computed on the basis of the actual menu served.

The total of the pre-costed restaurants and banquets is the "Potential Net Cost" for the day. This is compared with the "Actual Net Cost" for the day as shown on the "Preliminary Food Cost Report." The excess of the "Actual Net Cost" over the "Potential Net Cost" represents the "Potential Savings" for the particular kitchen involved.

The Food Cost Accountant must discuss with the Chef daily the "Potential Savings" in order to arrive at the reasons therefor, the object being to narrow the "Potential Savings" down to as small an amount

Form No. FC-FC 6A, HKF&CO.

DAY & DATE Sat. 6/10

HOTEL Metropolitan

HOUSE COUNT 275

MENU PRE-COST AND ABSTRACT

WEATHER Clear - Hot

Entree	Cost Per Ptn.	Forecast				Cost	Actual Sales			Cost	Ratio to Total*
		No.	Total Cost	Sales Price	Total Sales	%	No. Sold	Total Sales	Total Cost	%	
CLUB DINNERS											
Cheese Omelette	.40	3	1.20	1.25	3.75		4	5.00	1.60		3.16
Broiled Striped Bass	.52	10	5.20	1.40	14.00		12	16.80	6.24		10.61
Baked Ham	.57	18	10.26	1.50	27.00		20	30.00	11.40		18.95
Breaded Sweetbreads	.63	5	3.15	1.50	7.50		4	6.00	2.52		3.79
Roast Leg of Lamb	.78	17	13.26	1.55	26.35		20	31.00	15.60		19.58
Casserole of Capon	.66	9	5.94	1.80	16.20		9	16.20	5.94		10.24
Assorted Cold Cuts	.57	5	2.85	1.45	7.25		6	8.70	3.42		5.50
Total		67	41.86		102.05	41.01	75	113.70	46.72	41.09	71.83
A LA CARTE											
Special Prime Rib of Beef	.91	10	9.10	1.95	19.50		8	15.60	7.28		9.85
Chef's Salad Bowl	.29	8	2.32	.95	7.60		8	7.60	2.32		4.80
Fruit Salad	.24	15	3.60	.85	12.75		19	16.15	4.56		10.20
Half Spring Chicken	.60	3	1.80	1.50	4.50		1	1.50	.60		.95
Calf Liver & Bacon	.43	6	2.58	1.25	7.50		3	3.75	1.29		2.37
Total		42	19.40		51.85	37.42	39	44.60	16.05	35.97	28.17
GRAND TOTAL		109	61.26		153.90	39.81	114	158.30	62.77	39.65	100.00

* Popularity Index Ratio.

as possible by corrective action. Among the factors to be checked will be adherence to Standard Purchase Specifications and to Standard Portion Sizes.

For an example of a completed "Summary of Food Costs and Potential Savings," see below.

The total potential cost represents the "Pre-Controlled" cost as approved by management or management's direct representative. This is what the meals served should have cost if all of management's decisions were carried out to perfection. Perfection can never exist, but the margin of disparity between existing and ideal conditions can now be measured in terms of dollars and cents.

DATE April 22
DAY Saturday
WEATHER Fair

	To-Day				This Month to Date			
	Number Sold	Actual Sales	Calculated Cost	Cost Per Dollar Sale	Number Sold	Actual Sales	Calculated Cost	Cost Per Dollar Sale
Coffee Shop:								
Breakfast	214	$ 176.45	$ 56.46	32.0	5,366	$ 4,566.40	$ 1,461.27	32.0
Luncheon	92	86.45	28.18	32.6	2,902	2,710.05	907.80	33.5
Dinner	108	121.25	39.43	32.5	2,701	3,745.80	1,235.74	33.0
Buffet	-	-	-	-	743	1,671.75	977.75	58.5
A La Carte Entrees	84	89.95	36.68	40.8	1,480	1,352.15	449.58	33.2
A La Carte Others	53	170.10	53.75	31.6	1,178	3,751.93	1,203.14	32.1
Total	551	$ 644.20	$ 214.50	33.3	14,370	$17,798.08	$ 6,235.28	35.0
Cafe:								
Luncheon	59	$ 81.25	$ 22.16	27.3	1,363	$ 1,919.80	$ 552.24	28.8
Dinner	62	147.60	49.18	33.3	1,602	3,447.80	1,185.82	34.4
A La Carte Entrees	56	207.63	79.31	38.2	1,592	5,222.89	2,004.52	38.4
A La Carte Others	45	126.52	43.78	34.6	850	2,204.82	776.83	35.2
Total	222	$ 563.00	$ 194.43	34.5	5,407	$12,795.31	$ 4,519.41	35.3
Dining Room:								
Dinner	180	$ 589.90	$ 186.87	31.7	2,060	$ 6,702.35	$ 2,313.71	34.5
Supper	44	103.75	35.90	34.6	372	880.60	302.24	34.3
A La Carte Entrees	58	212.75	102.42	48.1	664	2,252.70	1,045.45	46.4
A La Carte Others	17	348.05	127.04	36.5	423	3,371.40	1,226.71	36.4
Total	299	$1,254.45	$ 452.23	36.1	3,519	$13,207.05	$ 4,888.11	37.0
Room Service:								
Breakfast	81	$ 124.10	$ 37.47	30.2	1,499	$ 2,174.30	$ 658.99	30.3
Luncheon	2	2.70	.66	24.4	114	174.35	44.56	25.6
Dinner	21	54.00	17.50	32.4	298	707.90	239.91	33.9
A La Carte Entrees	56	132.93	52.51	39.5	1,223	2,802.93	1,083.30	38.6
A La Carte Others	30	71.52	24.75	34.6	634	1,388.72	476.38	34.3
Total	190	$ 385.25	$ 132.89	34.5	3,768	$ 7,248.20	$ 2,503.14	34.5
Total Dining Room Potential Cost	1,262	$2,846.90	$ 994.05	34.9	27,064	$51,048.64	$18,145.94	35.5
Banquets	1,240	4,527.50	1,121.76	24.8	9,690	37,099.60	10,336.18	27.9
Total Potential Net Cost	2,502	$7,374.40	$2,115.81	28.7	36,754	$88,148.24	$28,482.12	32.3
SUMMARY								
Total Gross Cost-Actual	2,502	$7,374.40	$2,500.38	33.9	36,754	$88,148.24	$36,206.32	41.1
Less: Employees' Meals			265.00	3.6			5,736.58	6.5
Total Net Cost-Actual	2,502	$7,374.40	$2,235.38	30.3	36,754	$88,148.24	$30,469.74	34.6
Total Net Cost-Potential	2,502	$7,374.40	$2,115.81	28.7	36,754	$88,148.24	$28,482.12	32.3
Total Potential Savings			$ 119.57	1.6			$ 1,987.62	2.3
Net Dining Room Cost-Actual	1,262	$2,846.90	$1,113.62	39.1	27,064	$51,048.64	$20,133.56	39.4
Net Banquet Cost-Actual	1,240	$4,527.50	$1,121.76	24.8	9,690	$37,099.60	$10,336.18	27.9

J. J. Jones
Food Cost Accountant

The total potential savings represent the aggregate sum of excess cost due to failure to purchase according to specification, waste, overproduction, mysterious disappearance, spoilage, and other factors. The potential cost is the responsibility of management. The variation between the potential and the actual cost is the joint responsibility of the chef, steward, and catering manager.

It will readily be seen that Pre-Control helps to measure that part of food cost pre-determined by management's policies, and the part of food cost resulting from the execution of those policies by the department heads. With these methods, then, management could not only direct the operation to the desired over-all profit result, but would have positive means of measuring any deviations and fixing responsibility for such deviation.

RECAPITULATION OF PRE-COST PRE-CONTROL

RESULTS IN THE FOOD DEPARTMENT

FOR THE MONTH OF FEBRUARY 1950

	Number Sold	Actual Sales	Calculated Cost	Cost Per Dollar Sale	Ratio to Total Net Sales
LOUNGE					
Items Pre-Controlled					
Luncheon	3,994	$ 5,172.45	$ 1,898.66	36.7%	7.59%
DINING ROOM					
Items Pre-Controlled					
Breakfast	4,808	$ 4,466.85	$ 1,320.52	29.5%	6.55%
Luncheon	4,904	5,937.65	1,853.48	31.2	8.71
Dinner	2,736	7,276.29	2,962.85	40.7	10.67
Other Items	2,931	5,414.91	1,732.72	32.0	7.94
Total	15,379	$ 23,095.70	$ 7,869.57	34.1	33.87%
ROOM SERVICE	3,734	$ 6,833.40	$ 2,114.86	30.9%	10.02%
BANQUETS	9,379	$ 33,500.44	$ 10,130.58	30.2%	49.14%
TOTAL POTENTIAL COST			$ 22,013.67	32.2%	
ALLOWANCES		($ 423.85)			(.62%)
ADJUSTMENT TO COST					
Expenditures Over Potential Cost			1,006.37	1.5	
GRAND TOTAL	32,486	$ 68,178.14	$ 23,020.04	33.7%	100.00%

In devising the Pre-Cost Pre-Control system or procedures, the practices of industry in budgeting and planning production and sales, were borrowed from liberally. While these same techniques have been used for many years by expert food men and survey analysts in their studies of food department operations, until now these techniques were highly complicated and involved, and were not generally applicable to the daily operation without extensive assistance of such experts. After much experimenting for several years, the Pre-Cost Pre-Control procedures have been refined and simplified to the point where they have been operating in small as well as large establishments with uniformly gratifying results.

It must be realized that no system will, in itself, accomplish all that is desired. The sum total effort and cost involved in the installation of a system and in the daily accumulation of data, will be fruitless unless such data are used by those responsible for the direction and results of the food department. It is, therefore, essential that top level management in restaurants, hotels and other feeding institutions, understand the principles involved and the uses of the material produced by the system, if the maximum profit results are to be obtained. While it is also necessary that the chef, or other operating head of the food department, be thoroughly conversant with the theory and principles of the system, the final responsibility rests with management. The system in no way supplants artistry in cookery, a flare in service, ability in merchandising, or to successfully supervise personnel. It is basically a management tool with which the direction of a food operation can be handled from the business office of the institution.

Stated in its simplest terms, the procedures provide advance information as to how much to buy of what and when, and how much to prepare of what and when. In other words, buying for use rather than for stock, and producing for sale.

Chapter XXVI: WINE AND LIQUOR CONTROL

ALL PURCHASES OF WINES AND LIQUORS should be made by the manager, purchasing agent, or wine steward on written purchase orders. It is not advisable to delegate this responsibility to others.

Purchase Orders. Verbal purchase orders are too often unreliable. Unless an establishment has a rigid policy of written purchase orders, overambitious salesmen or faulty telephone connections can "accidentally" cause slow-moving stock to find its way into a wine cellar.

Verification of Invoices. The purchaser of wines and liquors should be responsible for personally approving every invoice before payment is made. Otherwise, the door is open to all sorts of errors, disputes, and irritations.

BEVERAGES

Date	Distributor	Bin No.	Items	CASE GOODS				Total Cost Per Case	Total Cost Per Unit
				No. of Cases	Size of Units	Units Per Case	Total No. of Units		
	B-F Brewery		Pabst Beer	15	12 oz	24	360	3 00	45 00
			Returns						
	G-G Brewery		Beer	20	12 oz	24	480	2 20	44 00
			Returns						
	Smith & Brown		Pommery Sec NV	10	26 oz	12	120	40 75	407 50
	International Bev. Co.		Bellows Rye	10	26 oz	12	120	37 08	370 80
	"		H & H 5 Star	10	26 oz	12	120	53 52	535 20

Wine Steward

When invoices are examined by the accounting department or beverage controller, four points should be checked:

(1) Proper purchase authorization;
(2) Comparison of prices with prior purchases;
(3) Likelihood of over-stocking;
(4) Arithmetical accuracy.

Comparison of prices with prior purchases is advisable to assure proper investigation of any serious price increases and to uncover vendors' possible errors. Checking the arithmetical accuracy of every invoice is an absolute necessity. A re-check of present and past inventory positions on items arriving in substantial quantities will prevent overstocking.

RECEIVING

Appropriate Records. The receiving of all beverage shipments should be handled by a receiving clerk, directly responsible to the chief accountant. This insures effective, independent control. Beverage deliveries should be segregated from the foodstuffs and separate receiving records maintained.

RECEIVED

Date March 20

No. of Units on Hand at Arrival	Average Cost Per Unit	Total of Invoice	Deposits		Net Purchases				
			Charges	Credits	Wines	Champagnes	Spirits	Beer Ale	Minerals
	12½	45 00	9 00					45 00	
				6 60					
	9½	44 00	15 00					44 00	
				11 25					
	3 40	407 50				407 50			
	3 09						370 80		
	4 46	906 00					535 20		
		1402 50	24 00	17 85		407 50	906 00	89 00	

S D Williamson
Receiving Clerk

The receiving sheet is a basic instrument in the proper maintenance of a beverage control system. All liquor entering the delivery door should make its first recorded appearance on a receiving sheet.*

PURCHASE ORDER

THIS ORDER NUMBER

№ 8268

must appear on your invoices and packages

To Jones Weezer, Incorporated
523 West 79th Street
New York, New York

New York March 20, 195

Please supply the following. and

Mark for WINE Dept.

QUANTITY	DESCRIPTION	Price	Amount	
2 cs.	St. Marceaux	72.96	145	92
3 cs.	Pommery Sec NV	40.75	122	25
	Immediate Delivery Confirmation Requested			

Ace Restaurant

Invoice must accompany delivery or be mailed at time of shipping. All packages accepted subject to count, weight and examination.

per R. M. Jones

All deliveries should be checked against a copy of the properly authorized written purchase order. Any discrepancy should be brought to the immediate attention of the wine steward or his assistant for corrective action.

Invoices and delivery tickets should be sent to the accounting department after the proper entry has been made on the receiving sheet.

To avoid confusion due to the pronunciation of the names of foreign wines, all items should be assigned numbers. These numbers should appear on the bins and on the wine lists. This is a help to patrons in ordering and to the waiters in filling the orders. If this is done, neither the customer nor the waiter need be a linguist to give or understand an order for De Vauzelle; Cuvee de Reserve, Brut; Veuve Ambal Burgundy or Haut Medoc, when No. 114, 181 or 212 will accomplish the same result.

Standard Weights. Liquor has an amazing propensity for "evaporating" even when it is in bottle form. Bottles can easily vanish into thin air unless every reasonable receiving safeguard is established and observed.

A list should be compiled of every standard case weight and be kept by the receiving clerk for handy reference. Every major brand should

* See illustrations, pages 396 and 397.

be weighed in case form and recorded. Weighing each case and checking its weight against the list will eliminate dozen-lots that somehow consist of only 10 or 11 bottles.

STORING

The wine cellar has within its four walls the most valuable products of any similar space in the restaurant. It should be thought of as being comparable to a vault in which coins or currency are kept, for each of the bottles on the shelves in the wine cellar represents a definite sum of money.

Bin Cards. The wine steward will often find it desirable, in order to establish purchase requirements, to maintain his own perpetual inventory record of all items received in the wine cellar. This record is compiled from the incoming deliveries and the issues to the bars or kitchens. For this purpose, a book record, or bin card arrangement, is generally employed. This set of records should be completely independent of perpetual inventory records maintained by the Beverage Controller or accounting department, although monthly comparisons are advisable. Bin cards, similar to the sample form illustrated below, are often kept in or alongside the bin containing the actual stock.

BIN CARD

No. 315 Size FIFTHS

Name JOHNNY WALKER - RED LABEL

Date	Rec'd	ISSUED TO BAR NO. 1	2	3	4	5	Total	Balance
3/1	24							24
3/2		2	3				5	19
3/4		3	1				4	15
3/6		2	2				4	11
3/7	12	1	1				2	21

The perpetual inventory records maintained by the beverage controller or accounting department should contain information showing the item, date of receipt, quantity received, amount issued, balance on hand, and other pertinent data regarding dealer, price paid, date ordered, and condition of stock.

Temperature Control. The temperature of the wine cellar should be under close scrutiny at all times, with periodic inspections and notations of the temperature made in an appropriate book. The temperature should be controlled at about 55 degrees. Recording the temperatures and maintaining a permanent record thereof, from time to time, is the only sound method of insuring against spoilage or deterioration. Ventilation is also vitally important. The wine cellar should be well ventilated to prevent losses.

ISSUING

Requisitions. It must be a strict rule that issues from the wine cellar are to be made only by units on approved requisitions. These requisitions should be made out in triplicate, the original and duplicate to be signed by the employees issuing and receiving the stock. This should take place at the time the requisition is filled.

SERVICE BAR-KITCHEN No. 2035

Date 3/15

Quantity	Size	List No.	DESCRIPTION	Unit Cost	
2	1/5	221	Canadian Club		
4	1/5	235	Four Roses		
1	1/5	315	Old Grandad		
3	1/5	447	Haig & Haig 5 Star		
3	1/5	482	Johnny Walker Red		
2	1/5	486	Teachers		

Requisitioned by: Henri Sommelier   Issued by: J Jones   Received by: Wm Stevens

The original requisition should be forwarded to the accounting department, the duplicate retained in the wine cellar, where it may be used for inventory record purposes. The triplicate should be kept by the person in charge of the station receiving the merchandise.

The first of the sample requisition forms illustrated on page 378 represents the typical appearance at the time the order is filled. The second form indicates its appearance after the requisition has been priced, extended, and totalled by the beverage controller or accounting department.

If a "Selling Price Control" system is used, the requisition should include two extra columns for Unit Sales Value and Total Sales Value for each item. In the form on page 402, if Canadian Club were served in one and one-quarter ounce portions, twenty and one-half drinks would be obtained from a fifth. If the selling price for each individual drink were 60 cents, the Unit Sales Value for each bottle would be $12.30 and the Total Sales Value for the two bottles of Canadian Club would amount to $24.60. The over-all Grand Total Sales Values for a

SERVICE BAR-KITCHEN Nº 2035

Date 3/15/5

Quantity	Size	List No.	DESCRIPTION	Unit Cost		
2	1/5	221	Canadian Club	4	41	8.82
4	1/5	235	Four Roses	3	44	13.76
1	1/5	315	Old Grandad	5	33	5.33
3	1/5	447	Haig & Haig 5 Star	4	46	13.38
3	1/5	482	Johnny Walker Red	4	48	13.44
2	1/5	486	Teachers	4	47	8.94
						63.67

Requisitioned by: Henri Sommelier — Issued by: J Jones — Received by: M M Stevens

given period would immediately indicate the expected or potential revenue. Adjustments must be made for mixed drink sales, bottle sales and inventory differentials before comparing with actual sales. These adjustments are explained in the section dealing with Selling Price Control.

Separate requisitions should be used for mineral waters. Requisitions for food items will, of necessity, be separate forms, since they will be sent to the storeroom instead of the wine cellar. Requisitions for mineral waters and food will contain only the cost value and never the sales value.

Banquet Procedures. All requisitions for banquets should be prepared by the banquet manager, using separate sets of requisitions for each banquet. These should indicate, aside from the date and time of day, the room in which the banquet is to be served and the name of the person or organization to whom the charge is to be made. This will greatly facilitate the all-important matter of sales reconciliation and collection of the banquet accounts.

BAR INVENTORY AND REQUISITION No. 2611

BAR No. Service DATE 3/15/5

LIST NO.	SIZE	DESCRIPTION	REQUISITION QUANT.	UNIT COST	TOTAL COST	UNIT SALE VALUE	TOTAL SALE VALUE
221	F	Canadian Club	2	4 41	8 82	12 30	24 60
235	F	Four Roses	4	3 44	13 76	10 25	41 00
315	F	Old Grandad	1	5 33	5 33	14 35	14 35
447	F	Haig & Haig 5 Star	3	4 46	13 38	12 30	36 90
482	F	Johnny Walker Red	3	4 48	13 44	12 30	36 90
486	F	Teachers	2	4 47	8 94	12 30	24 60
					63 67		178 35
			Differential				6 65
							171 70
			BOTTLE		9 80		20 00
			DRINK		53 87		151 70

REQUISITION BY: Henri Sommelier — ISSUED BY: J Jones — RECEIVED BY: M M Stevens

Close control is particularly necessary in the case of banquets because there are so many opportunities for abuse. Patrons may be charged for champagnes and other expensive liquors that are never served or they may be charged in excess of the amount actually consumed. The resultant ill-will, especially at banquets where an arrangement committee is likely to maintain a strict tally of consumption, is bound to be extremely harmful.

The return of unused wines and liquors from the banquet department to the wine cellar requires close attention. These returns must be handled properly to guard against accidental or deliberate errors. After each banquet, a credit memo should be drawn up for the return of all full bottles that were not used. This type of memo should contain the name of the banquet, the date, the total amount issued, and the number of full bottles returned. Partially used bottles or those on which the seal has been broken, are not to be returned to the wine cellar but should be transferred to another bar. The credit memo for full bottles returned and transfers of bottles with broken seals should be made out in duplicate. The original should be sent to the accounting department with the duplicate retained by the wine steward.

BOTTLE SALES AND DIFFERENTIAL:

BAR Service DATE 3/15/51

	Bin No.	Amt.	Unit Cost	Total Cost	Unit Drink Price	Total Drink Value	Bottle Sales Price	Total Sales	Differential
Old Grand-Dad	315	1	5.33	5.33	14.35	14.35	11.00	11.00	3.35
Teachers	486	1	4.47	4.47	12.30	12.30	9.00	9.00	3.30
				9.80		26.65		20.00	6.65

Bottle Sales. The management must determine what the mark-up on bottle sales should be to regular customers and for special sales, commonly known as Stewards' sales, in order to avoid confusion about pricing. It is necessary that all bars handling bottle sales forward to the accounting department all records of such sales so that the proper breakdown of sales and costs can be maintained; also in order that the bars will be given proper price adjustments if a selling price control is used.

As an added precaution against inexplicable bottle disappearances, all bottle sales should be filled only on the basis of a special slip, signed by the waiter placing the order. These bottle sale slips, which are forwarded to the accounting office, serve as vouchers to substantiate the bartenders' reports of bottle sales. They should be numbered serially so that a control of their usage can be easily maintained. In addition to the serial number, they should specify the bar from which the sale was made, the bin or menu number of the bottle sold, the number of bottles sold, the sales price, and the waiter's signature. This is another instance of *dollars converted to merchandise,* where employees often fail to exercise proper care and control.

BAR CONTROL

Bar control is of two major types—Selling Price Control or Ounce Control. The first is based on comparison of issues with sales potentials. The second requires a complete analysis of all sales in terms of ounces of consumption of the various ingredients.

Bar control in a large operation is an absolute necessity. In a small establishment, it may seem a bit of a luxury, but it is definitely desirable. Without bar control, temptation may be too great to overcome. In one small establishment enjoying a fine reputation in the community, the bartender decided to become an "unofficial partner." He brought a bottle or two to work and sold its contents to the customers, keeping the entire return. He had no overhead and no salaries to pay and his profit was very high—eating into the establishment's legitimate return. Unless management has a clear-cut picture of what the beverage cost really is, and should be, sooner or later someone is likely to be tempted to "share" the profits.

Standard Bar Portions. Once a bottle has been opened, there is always the possibility that some part of its contents might very easily be "diverted" unless strict precautions are observed. Any type of accidental diversion is bound to hurt the establishment, directly or indirectly. If fewer drinks are served to customers because of "excessive evaporation," the beverage cost climbs up unnecessarily and diminishes the potential return. If smaller drinks are served, to offset "bottle shrinkage," the customers will be dissatisfied and loss of patronage is likely to result.

In the service bars the head bartender should be supplied with a chart showing how many unit sales he is expected to obtain from each bottle. These units priced at selling prices will constitute the charge against the bar for the purpose of a selling price control. This, however, does not apply to fresh fruits, fruit juices, milk, eggs, carbonated waters, peanuts, or other gratis items which will be handled as overhead expenses. There is no specific control over these items but requisitions for undue quantities should be investigated.

The service bar should be stocked with a standard quantity of bottled goods. If a daily inventory is used, the employee in charge should take this inventory in order to bring the stock back to standard or par. It is the duty of the incoming bartender to make certain that he starts the day with a par stock.

If a daily inventory is taken, a combination inventory and requisition form can be used containing the items of stock and the standard quantities set for each, with due allowance for the addition of other items. This form should provide space for filling in the inventory and the quantity necessary to bring the stock back to par. A space for pricing to facilitate selling price control is advisable. This form should be printed in triplicate. One copy is retained at the bar, one copy used by the wine cellar as the requisition form for the issuance of replacement stock, and the third copy directed to the accounting department for selling price control. This form requires the signature of the head barman, the storekeeper issuing the stock, and the bartender receiving the goods, in addition to the approval of the wine steward.

The re-stocking of the service bar to bring it up to par cannot always be exact. Some open goods, such as whiskeys, may show a half-empty bottle and yet the attendant will requisition a full bottle. In another case, a bottle may have been used for a few drink sales and the attendant may not deem it necessary to replenish the stock for that day. The procedure for re-ordering should be on a common sense basis.

The control of the public bars takes fundamentally the same form as that outlined for the service bar. The major exception pertains to the method of recording sales, since they will not always be charged on restaurant checks as is the case in service bars. In some instances, a type of cash register may be used that throws out a check showing the total amount of the sale. Payment of the check may then be made either to a cashier or to the bartender.

There are obvious disadvantages in having a higher-salaried bartender doing the work of a cashier. Unless the volume is extremely low, or severe space limitations make it impractical, it is desirable to separate the function of sales-making and cash-handling. Where cashiers are employed there should be in operation the usual controls as between the register readings and the actual cash receipts. Regardless of whether the bartender or a cashier receives the cash, a locked box with a slot should be provided wherein all checks should be deposited as they are paid. Often this slot is on the flat top of the cashier's desk, the checks dropping into a locked drawer beneath. This is to restrict the possible practice of using the same check more than once.

In a cocktail lounge where bar waiters as well as bartenders may present checks to a cashier for payment, it is advisable to have a perforated stub attached to the check, known as the waiter's receipt. This portion should be torn off from the main body of the check and handed to the waiter or bartender. This is a further means of preventing re-use of a check.

Some establishments may find it advisable, in public bars, to use a regular restaurant check on which the bartender or checker records, by a checking machine, the amount of the sale. It will be found advisable, with rare exceptions, to have a checker record all orders served on waiters' checks in a differently colored ink from that used for recording food sales.

Where a bartender does receive cash, it is advisable to establish a fixed routine to minimize "check-mishaps." Reduced to a dozen steps, the requirements can be summarized as follows:

(1) Obtains order from customer.
(2) Takes check and pencil.
(3) Writes down order on check.
(4) Leaves check face up near guest.
(5) Mixes drink.
(6) Serves drink.
(7) Picks up check.
(8) Registers price on check.
(9) Returns check to customer.
(10) Collects from customer.
(11) Registers receipt of cash.
(12) Deposits paid check in locked box.

It is not to be inferred that the bartender is to demand payment for each round of drinks. However, it is prudent to require the bartender to close the cash drawer of the cash register after each transaction.

Par Stock for Bars. The use of a Par Stock Beverage Control System is the most practical method of controlling the re-stocking in bars. A suitable par for each item is established. The quantity used on the busiest day of the year plus a 50 to 75 per cent safety factor for extraordinary situations should suffice. If a daily inventory is not taken, requisitions for stock should be made only on a "bottle for bottle" basis. A count of empty bottles automatically determines the amounts to be requisitioned.

Glass Size Uniformity. In large operations where there are several bars or bartenders, it is rather surprising how often the drink glasses will vary in size. Obviously, it is difficult to control costs properly if there are different size glasses used for the same purpose. It is advisable that the uniformity of glass sizes be checked by actual measurement at least once or twice a year.

SELLING PRICE CONTROL

Daily selling price control consists of comparing the actual sales for the various selling stations during a given period of seven, ten or fifteen days with the value, at selling price, of the issues from the wine cellar. It must be realized, when a par stock system is used, that these comparative figures for a single day's sales do not take into account the differences in partly sold bottles. They are based solely on the sales value of the bottles issued per requisitions.

Sales Potentials. A standard should be set for the number of drinks to be obtained from each bottle. This standard is multiplied by the selling price per drink to arrive at the potential sales value of each bottle. If all drinks were sold as straight drinks or highballs, no adjustments would be necessary. However, beverages are sold in bottle form and as mixed drinks, such as cocktails. If requisitions are filled out to indicate total potential sales values, it is necessary to deduct the difference between the sales value by the drink and the sales value by the bottle from the daily total of the potential sales value. A simple workpaper can be used for this purpose, as illustrated on page 402.

The adjustment for mixed drinks, if any, is deducted from the Drink Total Sales Value, which, in the illustrated form, is $151.70. This adjustment for Manhattans is determined on the basis of the number of bottles of sweet vermouth that were used, computing the rye * consumption according to the mixing formula. Thus, if one bottle of sweet vermouth had been consumed, and the mixing formula called for two ounces of rye to one ounce of vermouth, it would be taken for granted that two bottles of rye had been used for Manhattans. If Manhattans sell for 50 cents, the sales value for a fifth of rye, containing 25.6 ounces, would be 12.8 times 50 cents, or $6.40. If the highball sales value of rye is $10.25, the credit adjustment for Manhattans would be $10.25 less $6.40 or $3.85 for each fifth of rye used for Manhattans. This would be deducted from the Drink Total Sales Value, which is shown as $151.70 in the illustrated form.

When the potential sales value has been established for the merchandise used, it is necessary to compare these figures with the actual revenue received for the period under consideration. The primary importance of selling price control is the margin of the differential with the actual sales. Minor variations are to be expected; major ones should be investigated. The sales potential indicates what money should have been received. The revenue figures indicate what was actually received. A

* In certain sections of the country Bourbon is the principal ingredient in Manhattan cocktails.

comparison of the two indicates how close to normal the operation is faring. Actual revenue in excess of the sales potential warrants investigation. It may mean the customers have very likely been served substandard drinks.

Periodic Summary of Operations. At the end of each month, the accounting department or beverage controller should prepare a summary of the selling price control for the month. This summary should be based on the actual requisitions from the wine cellar for the various selling stations, priced at the unit selling prices for the respective stations. After proper credit has been given for any returns to the wine cellar, the net issues from the wine cellar should be added to the inventories on hand at the beginning of the month, priced at unit selling prices. The total of the net issues plus the opening inventory represents the total amount available for the particular period. From the total amount available, there must be subtracted the physical inventory at the end of the month

PERIOD MARCH 16-31, 195

SUMMARY OF BEVERAGE OPERATIONS

	TOTAL BARS		MEN'S BAR		SERVICE BAR	
	THIS PERIOD	TO DATE	THIS PERIOD	TO DATE	THIS PERIOD	TO DATE
TOTAL SALES	21,256.35	49,860.25	4,737.30	10,228.00	16,519.05	39,632.25
FULL BOTTLE SALES	4,344.32	10,704.42	19.50	55.05	4,324.82	10,649.37
DRINK SALES	16,912.03	39,155.83	4,717.80	10,172.95	12,194.23	28,982.88
POTENTIAL SALES	21,049.87	48,957.66	4,638.05	9,978.95	16,411.82	38,978.71
BARS (OVER) OR SHORT	206.48	902.59	99.25	249.05	107.23	653.54
% OF (OVERAGE) OR SHORTAGE THIS MONTH	.98 %	1.84 %	2.14 %	2.50 %	.65 %	1.68 %
% OF (OVERAGE) OR SHORTAGE LAST MONTH	3.02 %	2.94 %	2.86 %	3.09 %	3.11 %	2.86 %
COSTS OF:						
FULL BOTTLE SALES	1,820.76	4,437.77	9.09	23.74	1,811.67	4,414.03
DRINK SALES	5,514.96	12,608.98	1,552.78	3,316.36	3,962.18	9,292.62
TOTAL SALES	7,335.72	17,046.75	1,561.87	3,340.10	5,773.85	13,706.65
COST PER DOLLAR OF SALE PERCENTAGES:						
FULL BOTTLE SALES	41.91 %	41.46 %	46.62 %	43.12 %	41.89 %	41.45 %
DRINK SALES	32.61 %	32.20 %	32.91 %	32.59 %	32.49 %	32.06 %
TOTAL SALES THIS MONTH	34.51 %	34.19 %	32.97 %	32.65 %	34.95 %	34.58 %
TOTAL SALES LAST MONTH	34.82 %	34.18 %	30.89 %	32.52 %	34.63 %	34.44 %
TOTAL SALES LAST YEAR	34.60 %	33.99 %	31.07 %	31.61 %	34.84 %	34.71 %
PERCENTAGE OF TOTAL SALES:						
FULL BOTTLE SALES	20.44 %	21.47 %	.41 %	.54 %	26.18 %	26.87 %
DRINK SALES	79.56 %	78.53 %	99.59 %	99.46 %	73.82 %	73.13 %

DESIGNED BY HARRIS, KERR, FORSTER & CO.

in order to arrive at the monthly potential sales. Before an effective comparison with actual sales is made, due allowance must be made for any bottle sales or special sales at lower than ordinary selling prices per drink. All such sales must be supported by appropriately approved memoranda. After applying all the special sales, the net result will yield the overage or shortage of the retail selling price control for the period. The following represents a simple formula of the foregoing:

Requisitions — returns + inventory on hand at beginning of month = amount available.

Amount available — inventory at end of month = monthly potential sales.

Monthly potential sales — bottle sales = potential drink sales.

If reports are rendered on a 15-day basis, one interim report will be rendered each month, while reports on a 10-day basis means two interim reports every month in addition to the month-end report.

Interim reports do not necessarily require pricing the entire inventories at the beginning and end of the period. Only the inventory difference need be priced and extended. If the closing inventory is less than the opening inventory, the operation has in part "lived off" or used up a portion of the inventory. Therefore, the inventory difference must be added to the issues for the period. However, if the closing inventory is greater than the opening inventory, the inventory position has been increased or "built up" and therefore the difference is deducted from the issues for the period to determine the exact consumption.

INVENTORY CONTROL

Perpetual Inventory. A perpetual inventory record should have a separate page for each brand, size, and vintage. The number given to each item should correspond to the bin number and the line number appearing on the wine list. This record may be similar to, but independent of, the inventory record maintained in the wine cellar.

The perpetual inventory should indicate the date of receipt, quantity received, amount issued, balance on hand, dealer, and price paid for each item. The data used in maintaining the perpetual inventory should be obtained from approved invoices, signed requisition, return memos, and credits for breakage or spoilage. The requisitions should be posted by brands and quantities as a credit to the wine cellar, and in turn be charged against the service bar, public bar, or banquets. Any returns to the wine cellar are to be handled in the reverse manner; namely, charged to the wine cellar and credited to the station that originally received the merchandise.

It is obviously impractical to maintain a perpetual inventory control over wines and liquors after their issuance from the wine cellar. The control at the bars can best be maintained by means of the selling price control as already indicated.

Physical Inventories. At the end of each month, a complete physical inventory of the stock in the wine cellar should be taken by the chief accountant or beverage controller and the wine steward, with the stock being priced at cost for accounting purposes. Similarly, the same individuals should take the inventories in the various bars, which should be priced at cost and selling price—the cost value to be recorded in the accounting records to arrive at cost of sales and the sales value to be used as part of the selling price control.

At frequent intervals, the accounting department should make actual inventory tests of various bins to see that the quantities indicated in the perpetual inventory record are actually in the wine cellar. In the service and public bars, frequent tests should be made to determine whether the standard stock is on hand. Without such tests, it is impossible to ascertain whether the standards are being maintained.

When physical inventories are taken, it is advisable that the bin cards be removed from the actual bins to insure an absolutely valid, independent count. When bin cards are too easily accessible, there is always the possibility that figures for hard-to-reach shelves or bins might be taken from the bin cards rather than from an actual count of the units. It is sound policy, for the periodic check-up inventories, that part or all

BIN NO. 273 ITEM H r H 5 Star UNIT Fifths

RECEIVED							ISSUED						
DATE	QUAN.	UNIT	DEALER	PRICE	AMOUNT	REC'D	DATE	QUAN.	AVERAGE PRICE	DEP'T	B.O.H.	INVENTORY	REMARKS
4 10	2 cs	F	Universal	5 38	129 28	24			538		24		
							4 10	1		Cafe	23		7893
							4 18	1		Service	22		7919
							4 20	1		Service	21		7942
							4 30					21	
							5 2	2		Cafe	19		8011
							5 6	1		Service	18		8043
							5 11	6		Banquet	12		8115
5 12	1 cs	F	Ajax	5 28	63 36	12			533		24		
							5 15	1		Cafe	23		8230
							5 19	2		Service	21		8317
							5 20	2		Cafe	19		8472
							5 31					19	

of the stock be counted on some calendar date other than at the end of a month.

Verification of Inventories. The beverage controller must check every item of the physical inventory with the perpetual inventory records. Any breakage must be accounted for on the basis of the actual broken bottles and clearly indicated when credit is given. Any other discrepancies should be investigated since they can be caused only by errors in the requisitions or by pilferage. All breakage credits should be supported by actual sales memoranda as though they were Steward's sales. These memoranda, drawn up at the end of each month, should contain signatures attesting to the destruction of the revenue stamps. These signatures should include those of the wine steward, auditor and beverage controller.

Verification of Bin Contents. Independent of the accounting department, the wine steward should make daily inventory tests of as many bins as possible. Any discrepancies between the quantities on hand and those called for by his own inventory control should be immediately investigated.

It should be automatic for the wine steward to send a report to the accounting department indicating losses resulting from leaky, spoiled or broken bottles, so that the wine cellar stock records may be appropriately adjusted.

Container Control. Where there is a deposit on containers, this factor must be taken into consideration and properly handled by the accounting department. A form of perpetual inventory is the best method of controlling the calculations of the value of quantities on hand. The size of the containers in comparison to the relatively small sum of money on deposit for each container encourages carelessness in handling or control. This is inexcusable. The purveyors manage to mantain a sound container control. There is no valid reason why a restaurant cannot do the same.

SUMMARY OF CONTROL PROCEDURES

In the following tabulation there are set forth in summary form the procedures necessary to effect proper control of wines and liquors. They may be amplified to meet existing conditions but it is not recommended that there be any relaxing of these basic requirements.

1. Check each invoice against the receiving sheet. (See receiving sheet, pages 397 and 398.)
2. Check extensions and additions of invoices.

3. Call attention to *discount bills.*
4. Check footings of total purchases on receiving sheet to totals of distribution of the types of purchases. (See receiving sheet, pages 396 and 397.)
5. Maintain daily summary of container charges and credits to tie in to month-end inventory. (See receiving sheet, pages 396 and 397.)
6. Post receipts of merchandise and requisitions in perpetual inventory book. (See perpetual inventory, page 410.)
7. Fill in on all requisitions unit cost and total cost; also unit sales value and total sales value, if selling price control is used. (See requisitions, pages 401 and 402.)
8. Compile bottle sales summary. Deduct bottle sales differential and also mixed drink adjustments from total of requisitions. (See bottle sales and differential form, page 403, requisition, page 402.)
9. Add reductions in inventory to, or deduct additions in inventory from, total of requisitions for 7, 10 or 15 day period to determine net consumption. (See summary of beverage operations, page 408.)
10. At end of month and every 7, 10 or 15 days, take physical inventory to verify consumption for the month. (See section on physical inventories.)
11. Make adjustments for issues to food department, such as cooking wines, and requisitions from food department, such as lemons, oranges, cream, and olives.
12. Compare actual and potential sales. (See summary of beverage operations, page 408.)
13. Develop cost percentages for each outlet. (See summary of beverage operations, page 408.)

FEDERAL, STATE AND MUNICIPAL REGULATIONS

Not all states in the United States permit legalized sales of liquors, wines, and beer. In fact, even within some states that permit such sales, municipalities have what is known as "local option." This means that it is within the rights of the citizens of these municipalities to decide whether or not there shall be legal sales of wines, liquors, and beers. To put it simply, there is no uniformity among the states and cities with respect to sales of alcoholic beverages.

In most states where alcoholic beverages are sold, there is a State Authority or Board which promulgates the regulations under law for these sales. Here, too, there is no uniformity, as a wide range in the degree of control and enforcement exists. In addition, of course, there is the over-all general law of the Federal government relating to the taxing of alcoholic beverages and the granting of licenses for their manufacture, distribution, and sale.

Because of the lack of uniformity in the regulatory provisions, as indicated above, the reader is put on notice to become well acquainted with the laws and regulations in his own state and city regarding the sale of alcoholic beverages. Many require special bookkeeping procedures. Some specify dates on which liquor bills must be paid. Others limit the number and locations of bars in a restaurant. Still others regulate the number and type of advertising signs and even the personnel. It is obvious therefore, that there must be strict adherence to all of the governmental requirements in order to insure peaceful possession and operation of the beverage facilities in any restaurant. Failure of compliance may mean revocation of license, penalties, and loss of a substantial investment in bar and restaurant equipment.

Chapter XXVII: PAYROLL ANALYSIS

IN A RESTAURANT OPERATION payroll costs are quite often the largest expense item, not excluding cost of food. It is, therefore, quite evident that this major expenditure is deserving of analysis and control.

Any conscientious effort to keep payroll outlays in a restaurant operation within reasonable limits requires a search for specific answers to certain key questions. It is important to know the average work-load that various employees are required to handle from day to day; the staff coverage at all work stations throughout the work-day and the amount of work that can be shifted to ease the peak periods of activity.

ANALYZING WORK-LOADS

Percentage Standards and Their Limitations. In many restaurants, particularly chain establishments controlled from a central office, great stress is placed on the percentage of payroll costs to total sales revenue. While this figure has certain value in focusing attention on a "high" payroll cost as against a moderate or comparatively low payroll expense, there are certain major deficiencies in using this form of analysis alone.

The major defects in using the percentage scale exclusively, are:

(1) Food and beverage payroll costs are often merged or subject to arbitrary allocation and the resulting percentages can be grossly misleading.

(2) Percentages are usually calculated on a monthly basis and cast no light whatever on variations of productivity from day to day or during various hours.

(3) Summer deviations are too readily ascribed to vacation pay and volume slump, with no analytical basis for remedial action.

(4) Menu price and wage rate changes, and shifts in volume of business distort the percentage figure without indicating which work stations may be understaffed or overstaffed.

Work Units Produced. Calculation of work units produced gives a clearer indication of shifts in the work-load and points to avenues for remedial action. It is important to note that no two operations are identical, and each establishment must be studied individually.

Joint Use of Percentage and Work-Unit Standards. In reviewing an operation, the use of percentage ratios and analysis of work units produced are by no means mutually exclusive. They can easily be employed and studied jointly. The important point to remember is that the work unit scale is more definitive and more specific in analyzing weaknesses in an operation.

METHODS OF ANALYSIS

The crux of any form of payroll study is the method whereby the most fruitful use of payroll time can be achieved. This fundamental task requires, as a primary pre-requisite, an analysis of the existing productivity of the available employees. A sound measurement must be made of the amount of work there is for the various employees to do—and when they must do it. Then there must be an appropriate evaluation of the number of employees that are required to handle the varying workloads.

The volume of work changes from one day to another and also during the various hours of the day. Tabulations should be set up to determine what these changes are and whether staff coverage is adequate, insufficient, or excessive.

Understaffing can be extremely wasteful in the long run. To be shorthanded will cause poor quality of preparation or service, which will, in turn, result in lost business. If the bartenders, waiters, salad-makers, or any other group of employees are short-staffed, the customers will be forced to wait much longer than necessary to be served. Sooner or later, a substantial number of patrons are likely to grow weary of waiting and go elsewhere. Short-staffing will inevitably have an adverse effect on the volume of business. On the other hand, the wastefulness of excessive staffing is self-evident.

Every restaurant or restaurant unit should maintain reliable statistics that indicate the number of covers served for breakfast, luncheon, dinner, and supper.

A test period of five to ten weeks should be used to determine the average number of covers served for each meal during each day of the week.

This test should be made for the summer season from June 15 or July 10 to August 31; the autumn season from September 10 to December 10;

the winter season from January 10 to March 31; and the spring season from April 1 to June 15.

As a minimum, the summer and winter seasons should be analyzed separately, since the autumn and spring seasons will normally bear a certain resemblance to the winter season in most commercial establishments, resorts excluded.

The sample tabulation below shows the average number of covers served.

By dividing the number of employees on duty into the average number of covers, the average daily productivity of each employee will be determined.

If there are extremely sharp fluctuations in the volume, an effort should be made to determine the specific causes. It may easily be possible to staff for average business and to obtain extra help when sharp rises in volume can be anticipated. If the fluctuations are marked, it may be necessary to gear work-loads in terms of 10 per cent less than the highest volume, rather than the average for a given test period.

ANALYSIS OF COVERS SERVED FOR SUMMER FIVE-WEEK TEST PERIOD (*)

	SUNDAY	MONDAY	TUESDAY	WEDNESDAY	THURSDAY	FRIDAY	SATURDAY
BREAKFAST COVERS SERVED							
WEEK OF:							
July 11-17	112	233	286	257	295	273	236
July 18-24	117	258	309	287	283	245	180
July 25-31	141	263	301	302	306	252	224
August 1-7	108	243	311	315	303	257	213
August 8-14	120	235	282	271	313	269	209
Total for Test Period	598	1,232	1,489	1,432	1,500	1,296	1,062
Average for Test Period	120	246	298	286	300	259	212
LUNCHEON COVERS SERVED							
WEEK OF:							
July 11-17	247	262	264	291	318	285	259
July 18-24	261	277	325	303	293	285	253
July 25-31	328	253	254	285	286	245	272
August 1-7	276	264	314	326	299	272	231
August 8-14	302	281	280	297	290	251	244
Total for Test Period	1,414	1,337	1,437	1,502	1,486	1,338	1,259
Average for Test Period	283	267	287	300	297	268	252
DINNER COVERS SERVED							
WEEK OF:							
July 11-17	135	230	224	227	235	223	175
July 18-24	124	205	216	211	222	206	184
July 25-31	142	193	182	225	195	190	189
August 1-7	194	223	257	243	219	203	197
August 8-14	153	211	209	231	191	181	169
Total for Test Period	748	1,062	1,088	1,137	1,062	1,003	914
Average for Test Period	150	212	218	227	212	201	183
SUPPER COVERS SERVED							
WEEK OF:							
July 11-17	49	63	104	160	120	152	174
July 18-24	56	51	81	117	96	105	127
July 25-31	42	57	120	126	112	141	180
August 1-7	49	70	96	158	88	108	158
August 8-14	63	64	111	156	104	139	149
Total for Test Period	259	305	512	717	520	645	788
Average for Test Period	52	61	102	143	104	129	158

(*) If fluctuations from week to week are considerable, a longer test period should be used.

The determination of work-productivity is shown in the chart below. Staff structure cannot be based solely on an arithmetical calculation of work-productivity. Other factors must be considered. These will include:

(1) Average receipt per cover.
(2) Type of food preparation.
(3) Kitchen layout and facilities.
(4) Distance from kitchen to dining room.
(5) Dining room facilities.
(6) Type of service.
(7) Volume of between-meal business.

WORK-PRODUCTIVITY ANALYSIS

	SUNDAY	MONDAY	TUESDAY	WEDNESDAY	THURSDAY	FRIDAY	SATURDAY
BREAKFAST							
Average Covers Served	120	246	298	286	300	259	212
Waiters on Duty	10	12	12	12	12	12	10
Average Covers per Waiter	12.0	20.5	24.8	23.8	25.0	21.6	21.2
LUNCH							
Average Covers Served	283	267	287	300	297	268	252
Waiters on Duty	10	12	12	12	12	12	10
Average Covers per Waiter	28.3	22.3	23.9	25.0	24.8	22.3	25.2
DINNER							
Average Covers Served	150	212	218	227	212	201	183
Waiters on Duty	11	14	14	14	14	14	14
Average Covers per Waiter	13.6	15.1	15.6	16.2	15.1	14.4	13.1
SUPPER							
Average Covers Served	52	61	102	143	104	129	158
Waiters on Duty	11	14	14	14	14	14	14
Average Covers per Waiter	4.7	4.4	7.3	10.2	7.4	9.2	11.3

Note: The foregoing are illustrative as to method only and are not to be considered as general standards.

(8) Prevailing wage scale.
(9) Portion of time spent in beverage service.

There are no automatically sound par figures for any work-station in any restaurant operation. Analysis and observation of the flow of work and materials under varying work conditions are indispensable necessities.

It is quite obvious that in an establishment where an unusually low wage scale is in force, the degree of efficiency that prevails in establishments paying a high wage scale is not likely to be readily forthcoming.

A low wage scale will generally attract marginal employees whose efficiency, work-comprehension, or temperament are such that a more leisurely work pace is the general result. Standards of work-productivity will inevitably be in sharp variance with other establishments.

STAFFING PROBLEMS

Major staffing problems that remain unresolved can mean financial losses for management and nervous exhaustion for the staff. Periods of idleness followed by periods of intense rushing are to be avoided as much as possible. An even work pace, whenever and wherever feasible, is the more profitable for management and more satisfactory to the staff. A certain amount of meal-time acceleration is inevitable, but everything possible should be done to facilitate the flow of materials and to minimize the feverishly hectic pace of rush-hour peaks.

Improper Scheduling. Some departmental executives seem to find it much simpler to have two shifts—the early and the late. The former services breakfast and luncheon while the latter takes care of dinner and supper. The "spanner" shift, wherein some employees might report for work at hours that span both the early and late shifts, is a great convenience that is all too often overlooked.

In the chart (page 419), there is depicted in the top section, the work schedule of a warewashers' station, for a typical weekday, wherein the two-shift system was used exclusively, regardless of the distribution of work-loads. The middle section of the chart indicates the hourly distribution of work-loads or covers served. The bottom section reflects the use of "spanner" shifts to conform to the pattern of the work-load distribution.

Arrangement of Days Off. All too often days off are arranged as a result of special requests or haphazard calculations rather than in accordance with specific work-load patterns. It is easily possible to have instances of over-staffing and under-staffing during different parts of the week. Both of these can be leveled off by proper study and re-adjustment of work schedules in most instances if proper regard is given to the varying work-load volumes for each day of the week. Quite often this will involve using a stagger system for different days of the week.

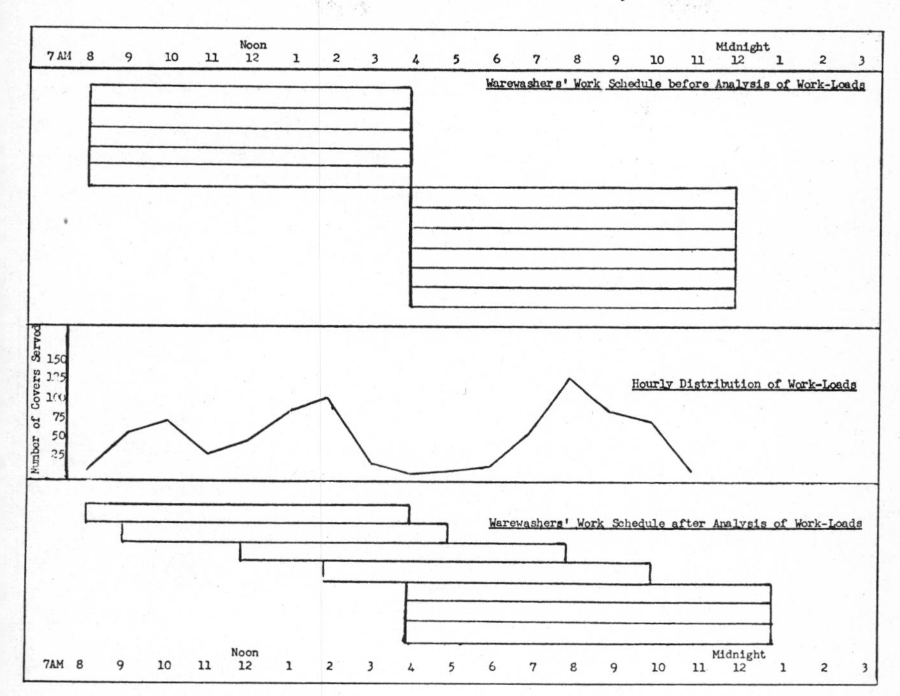

Stagger System for Hours of Arrival. Quite often some form of stagger system, whereby one or more employees report for work at different hours on different days, constitutes the only workable method of achieving proper distribution of work-loads.

There appears to be a fairly prevalent uneasiness among restaurant executives over the arrangement of having John Doe report for work at 8:00 A.M. on Tuesday, Wednesday and Thursday, and at 9:30 A.M. on Monday and Friday. Nevertheless, analysis of work-loads will often reveal that just such a plan will ease the pressure in many directions. It is admittedly easier to have a fixed schedule for all days of the week, Saturday and Sunday sometimes excepted, than a different schedule for each day of the week. However, a bar chart arrangement of employee schedules for each day of the week will almost invariably lead to a smoother work pace, better work-load distribution and better value for the payroll dollar.

Using the previous chart showing warewashing personnel, the table below shows the full week's work schedule and illustrates certain of the specific points discussed.

Inadequate Delineation of Duties. It is found that many establishments do not have a clear-cut arrangement regarding specific assignment of duties.

Inflexibility, wherein one employee will rest with arms folded while some other employee is overburdened, is not sound, but too much flexibility can easily mean a one-way ticket to a nervous breakdown for the operator and his sub-department heads. When assignments are on a catch-as-catch-can basis, some employees can develop an amazing talent

STAGGER SYSTEM FOR HOURS OF ARRIVAL.

WORK SCHEDULE

TIME CARD NO.	JOB TITLE	SUNDAY	MONDAY	TUESDAY	WEDNESDAY	THURSDAY	FRIDAY	SATURDAY
111	Warewasher #1	8:00 A.M. to 4:00 P.M.	X	X	X	X	Off	Off
113	#2	Off	9:00 A.M. to 5:00 P.M.	X	X	X	X	Off
114	#3	Off	Off	12:00 Noon to 8:00 P.M.	X	X	1:00 P.M. to 9:00 P.M.	1:00 P.M. to 9:00 P.M.
115	#4	2:00 P.M. to 10:00 P.M.	X	Off	Off	X	X	X
118	#5	5:00 P.M. to 1:00 P.M.	X	X	X	Off	Off	X
119	#6	Off	5:00 P.M. to 1:00 A.M.	X	X	X	X	Off
120	#7	Off	5:00 P.M. to 1:00 A.M.	X	X	X	X	Off
117	Relief #1	12:00 Noon to 8:00 P.M.	12:00 Noon to 8:00 P.M.	2:00 P.M. to 10:00 P.M.	Off	Off	8:00 A.M. to 4:00 P.M.	8:00 A.M. to 4:00 P.M.
121	#2	5:00 P.M. to 1:00 A.M.	Off	Off	2:00 P.M. to 10:00 P.M.	5:00 P.M. to 1:00 A.M.	5:00 P.M. to 1:00 A.M.	5:00 P.M. to 1:00 A.M.

Note: - Saturday and Sunday are lower volume days, permitting absorption of a portion of days-off without relief.
X - Denotes same working time as shown on first work day.

for not being "caught" too often. The sound middle-ground between both these undesirable extremes requires a maximum spelling out of specific duties with a reasonably flexible leeway for odds and ends of duties that cannot always be exactly anticipated.

Faulty Supervision. The supervisor who attempts to be "everywhere at the same time" will scarcely succeed. Sound supervision does require being everywhere but in a feasible sequence of time.

Proper supervision does not mean covering the maximum amount of ground at breakneck speed. Swiftness of movement is not an acceptable substitute for comprehensiveness. The hurried supervisor generally does not see very much and usually only one thing at a time. The "all-seeing" supervisor who is able to notice the maximum number of elements that require attention, and to take remedial action as needed, is the one who gets around with a swift eye and steady step. The trained eye can cover ground more quickly than the fastest feet.

Where supervision is faulty, the work performances of subordinate employees will almost invariably be faulty in one way or another. It is extremely rare to find poor supervision and top-notch subordinate work existing in the same department.

Sometimes supervision is weak simply because supervisors are driven by unreasonable and unreasoning superiors. Understanding the problems of supervisors, and taking remedial action in time when sound recommendations are made, will almost invariably yield smoother work-results than "driving" the supervisory employees.

Knowing what is possible and then requiring the best that is possible is more productive of excellent results than demanding the impossible and reaping alibis or high labor turnover.

Inadequate Layout of Facilities. There is probably no expense that is more unnecessary than the payroll dollars that go swirling down the drain of unchecked bottlenecks. Relatively simple layout problems such as inadequate dish-drop facilities for soiled dishes or insufficient side-tables will tie waiters and waitresses into knots. The deplorable part of inadequate facility layouts is the dual aspect of money loss—wasted time and loss of patronage due to slow service. There is scarcely a kitchen or dining room that does not have some major flaw or flaws that could easily be resolved by proper study and re-arrangement of facilities. There is almost invariably a determinable cause for every bottleneck or delay. In a large percentage of cases, they can be eliminated once the cause has been ascertained.

Every bottleneck imposes a heavy tax throughout the year, and often year after year. However, this is one tax that can be substantially reduced.

Absenteeism. Absenteeism can often be a far more expensive payroll item than is generally realized. There are two aspects of the problem of absenteeism that require consideration; namely, the causes and the effects.

When absenteeism is quite prevalent, there is always a reason or combination of reasons. It is not within the realm of probability that employees will be completely frank and state the real reasons for their absences. Certain reasons, such as post-week-end indispositions, reluctance to travel during unpleasant weather, job-seeking elsewhere, attendance at sports events, or job dissatisfaction are usually not offered as explanations of absence. However, in spite of these and other expected exceptions, it is advisable to require and record the reasons given for absences. Analysis of the patterns of absenteeism, comparisons of one department with another, will often cast considerable light on the basic causes for absenteeism. The exit interview at the time of severance from the payroll can also be extremely helpful in determining the real reasons for this schedule-disrupting problem. If a grievance committee exists for the purpose of airing bona fide grievances, this machinery can be used to provide better information as to the causes of absenteeism.

The importance of knowing the reasons of absenteeism is the advantage that this knowledge can provide in reducing the problem. Where absenteeism is a frequent occurrence, department heads will consciously and unconsciously strive to over-staff certain stations in order to avoid being caught short. Analysis will often reveal that 300 man-days of time are often added to a payroll structure to "cover" 20 or 30 man-days of absence during a year. If the 20 or 30 days could be reduced to 5 or 10, the problem would be greatly simplified. There would be fewer occasions when the departmental executives would be called upon to request the staff to set a hectic pace to make up for a missing employee.

Frankness in dealing with this problem can often be helpful. An employee may feel inclined to shrug off an absence as being no direct expense to management, since no pay is received. However, other employees may have the mistaken notion that absenteeism actually saves management money. There may be a marked disinclination on the part of the remaining staff to assume the duties of the missing employee, since the same work would be rendered by fewer employees for less money received. They feel they are "giving" management a man-day of work for nothing.

Few employees will concern themselves over or even be aware of the actual payroll expense of carrying an additional employee to cover frequently recurring absenteeism.

REMEDIAL MEASURES

After staff work-loads have been analyzed on a day-to-day as well as meal-to-meal basis, and special staffing problems have been properly studied, the steps toward sounder payroll structure can be taken.

Remedial measures, alleviating pressure points and uneven work-loads can be undertaken. It is only natural that if employees are required to work at an abnormally feverish pace for one or two hours a day, they may completely forget or not even care that the remaining six or seven hours of their day proceed at an extremely leisurely pace. It is always the effect of the "rough-spots" that leaves the greatest imprint on the mind and also takes the greatest physical toll of the employees.

It is, therefore, better for management and employees alike that remedial measures leading to a better distribution of the work-loads be undertaken and effectuated.

Distributing the Work-Loads. When a thorough study has been made of the staff coverage and work-productivity per employee at the various work stations for all the meal periods of the week, the uneven aspects of the work-loads will be immediately apparent. Generally; the work-loads, save in extremely exceptional cases, can be distributed on a much more reasonably even basis through appropriate rescheduling. Most of the problems can generally be ironed out through proper allocation of the days off and the advantageous use of "spanner" shifts and variable work schedules for some employees. When variable work schedules, involving different work-shifts on different days, are necessary, the factor of seniority should serve to determine the method of assigning these schedules, if a voluntary choice does not yield the required number of employees for these tours of duty. Experience has shown that quite often there are more than enough volunteers, who prefer a variable work schedule, especially when it permits late-sleeping and avoidance of rush-hour travel.

Reviewing Hours of Operation. An important by-product of work-productivity analysis is the opportunity provided for a thorough review of hours of operation. Where business is scant during certain days or hours, an hourly breakdown of business at the cashier's section will reveal whether any change of hours is desirable. On the other hand, contemplated expansion of hours can be subjected to controlled experimentation and analysis until the most advantageous schedule of operation is finally determined.

There are many communities where business after 8:30 P.M. is virtually non-existent except on Fridays and Saturdays. However, on these two days, opportunities for a steady snack business can easily be overlooked, because of the seemingly difficult scheduling problems. Where scheduling of work-hours is allowed to assume the necessary degree of flexibility, this "2-day problem" often ceases completely to be a problem and merely becomes a matter of judicious re-arrangement of work-schedules in a few required work stations.

Integration of Relief Schedules. The problem of relief scheduling for days off can be rather complex in smaller establishments. In a larger establishment where more than 5 or 6 employees are engaged in most of the sub-departments, the problem of days off tends to be absorbed since it becomes merely a matter of distributing the days off to conform to the volume pattern of business.

Some establishments operate on a 6-day work-week while others have adopted a 5-day week. Where a 6-day week is prevalent, it is necessary to have one employee cover the relief for the days off of 6 employees, unless part-time employees are available who are interested in working a lesser number of days. Where the 5-day week is in effect, there are distinct problems of scheduling. If one employee covers the relief schedule for 3 employees, there will be an extra work-day to be concerned about, unless the volume of business or integration with other work-stations permits the ready absorption of this extra day. However, even though there are additional problems, there are also additional opportunities for rearranging of work schedules, except in extremely small establishments.

At first glance, putting together suitable work schedules under these conditions will resemble the coloring of an intricate jig-saw puzzle. Quite frequently, the problems involved may seem insoluble, but once the jig-saw is put together, the end results will be more than worth the effort.

Revision of Facilities. Physical layout and type and condition of equipment have an important bearing on operating costs, particularly payroll expense.

To achieve an improved, workable layout of facilities it is necessary to ascertain, at the very least, the major work-steps performed by the various employees at the sundry work-stations. During meal-time peaks time lost because of poor layout and bottlenecks can generally be measured within reasonable limits. It is time that can never be recovered. Five seconds at one work-station and one minute at another quickly mount up to truly astonishing figures.

Offhand, it would seem that one man-minute per cover served does not represent a very great loss. Superficially, it might seem of no great consequence that a customer can complete a meal in 39 minutes instead of 40. But simple calculation reveals that the cumulative, persistent loss becomes quite enormous even in a restaurant of modest size.

The following illustration indicates the extent of loss of one man-minute per cover served when carried out over a period of one year in a restaurant serving 200 covers per meal, assuming a seven-day per week operation:

1 man-minute lost per cover served × 200 covers per meal = 200 man-minutes lost during each meal;
200 man-minutes lost × 3 meals per day = 600 man-minutes lost each day;
600 man-minutes lost per day × 365 days = 219,000 man-minutes or 3,650 man-hours or
456¼ man-days lost each year (based on 8 hour work day).

This total of man-days obviously represents a substantial monetary loss. The defect has more serious consequences when it becomes cumulative year after year.

This unnecessary expense does not take into consideration the possible loss of revenue. It is no longer merely a case of one customer eating in 39 or 40 minutes, but 200 times one minute means 3 hours and 20 customer-minutes saved. Five additional customers can be served in the time that is saved.

In the face of these figures, a seemingly large expenditure to eliminate a bottleneck is very likely to pay for itself within a year or less.

In addition to bottlenecks, where employees are obliged to stand inactively and wait for someone ahead of them to move on, unnecessary cross-traffic and improper location of supplies are the greatest wasters of time. Quite often, a discerning eye, given time to study the work-traffic problems can iron out many unnecessary kinks merely through rearrangement of facilities—without the purchase of new equipment.

In the light of the foregoing, it becomes self-evident that the existence of proper "in-the-dining room" facilities will save many steps and much time.

Summer Furloughs. One of the seemingly insuperable problems is the summer lull in many restaurant operations. In quite a number of large cities, a summer drop in volume of 40 to 50 per cent is not uncommon. Staffs are quite often kept practically intact even though there is scarcely half as much for them to do simply because seasonal diminution of staff structure might mean permanent loss of very good workers.

With fingers crossed and a heavy heart, many managers look upon vacations as a means of "easing the pressure." Frequently, this is not a satisfactory solution.

Many employees retain their city jobs during the summer even though they could procure seasonal jobs in a resort area that would yield better pay and a more satisfactory climate. They are reluctant to leave their permanent jobs since it would normally mean loss of vacation rights and possible loss of the permanent job.

Management is unhappy keeping more employees than are needed because satisfactory employees cannot be easily replaced in the autumn. The staff remains in the city during the summer because good jobs cannot easily be found again in the autumn.

There are many restaurant operations where a summer furlough with full vacation rights is the only sound solution. Under this procedure, the number of employees needed in terms of winter standards plus vacation replacements is determined. The excess number is given the privilege of taking a summer job and returning in autumn with seniority and all other rights preserved.

The employees can have their own vacation, take a more remunerative job in a resort atmosphere and return without loss of rights or opportunities.

Management gains because a smaller staff during the summer means less of a payroll burden during the months of depressed revenues. The only actual cost to management is the granting of 12 days of vacation for 9 months of work instead of 12 months. This means an outright granting of only 3 extra days of vacation, on a pro rata basis. The difference between 3 extra days of vacation and 3 extra months of payroll burden is considerable.

Chapter XXVIII: PAYROLL CONTROL

Effective payroll control must be geared to a sound measurement of daily staff requirements in terms of work-units to be produced. This method of payroll evaluation entails a departure from past concepts.

Traditionally, payroll costs have been regarded solely in terms of unit purchases of employees' time. The inherent inflexibility of this procedure has all too often caused extremely uneven work-loads. These, in turn, have produced excessive fatigue, breakage, and absenteeism on the one hand and expensive "payroll leakage" on the other.

Sound control requires the gearing of payroll "purchases" to specific need. This is somewhat similar to the practice, outlined in the chapter on Pre-Cost Pre-Control Procedure, of purchasing perishable food items in direct relation to the expected day-to-day volume of business.

The fact is quite obvious that payroll "purchases" are extremely perishable. Employees' time that is wasted can never be reclaimed. There are no rebates for partly-used hours.

THE BASIC STAFFING TABLE

A basic staffing table is a prime pre-requisite for the smooth functioning of a payroll control system. It must indicate the work-units of production per day or hour that can be reasonably expected as standards within the various staff categories. When these standards are applied to the anticipated volume of business for the various days and meals, a suitable work schedule can be established that will greatly diminish the peak and low volume days. Work-performances will tend to be formulated on a fairly consistent pattern, reducing fatigue, friction, and labor turnover.

If the basic staffing table is predicated on a sound analysis of work-loads, it provides a yardstick of comparison for the actual daily payrolls. This comparison will quite readily high-light any flaws in the staffing structure that require attention.

It must be borne in mind that there are no rigid standards of work-performance that can be applied to all establishments. Many variable factors must be taken into account. These include:

(a) Layout
(b) Facilities
(c) Type of business
(d) Off-hour volume of business

The basic staffing table for any establishment is, therefore, a purely individual matter.

Significance of Variations. When actual payrolls tend to vary repeatedly in either an upward or downward direction from the Basic Staffing Table, this will generally indicate that the departmental and sub-departmental work schedules have not been adjusted to conform to the general pattern of business volume.

The Payroll Analyst. In an establishment of sufficient size, the best results in the field of payroll control will usually be produced by centralized review of all payroll "purchases." One employee, answerable only to the top level of management, can usually do the best job of analyzing the fluctuating payroll needs from day-to-day and week-to-week.

If such an employee is engaged, it is his or her job to render a series of reports that will constantly reflect the proper measurement of the required staff structure. Should the relatively small size of an establishment eliminate the possibility of a full-time payroll analyst, the reports and functions described in this chapter can be taken over by the Accounting Department.

PRELIMINARY PROCEDURES

The first step taken by management and the payroll analyst should be to acquaint the department heads with the purpose and operation of the payroll control system. The reasons why they should cooperate, and exactly what is expected of them, must be made quite clear. This educational program can be accomplished by one or more of the following methods:

(1) Direct memoranda over the signature of the general manager.
(2) A departmental meeting with short talks by the general manager and the payroll analyst, followed by a discussion period.
(3) Informal talks between the payroll analyst and each department head separately.

(4) A follow-up letter to all department heads. A sample letter follows:

To All Department Heads:

Recently you have been given the daily and weekly total of standard man-hours for each section of your department.

These standards have been determined after careful study and evaluation of current and past work performance levels for each job classification, and with due consideration for present business volume. In some cases, which will be quite obvious to you, sharp fluctuations in business will alter the standards for certain job classifications, either upwards or downwards.

Some departments will find themselves well within the standards set, especially in certain job classifications, while others will find they are exceeding the standard man-hours. We can expect some day-to-day variations, but the final criterion for determining basic staffing will be the total man-hours worked in each department for the payroll week.

Using this guide for daily staffing will aid materially in keeping your payroll within satisfactory limits. If you find that you cannot meet the standards set for a specific job group, please see me about this at your earliest convenience. Further study and discussion may justify minor adjustments in some cases.

Unless adjustments are made and approved, each department will be expected to meet the weekly standards set forth in the departmental schedule.

Frequent conferences with the Payroll Analyst are indicated as a means to better payroll control within each department.

JOHN C. DOE
General Manager

THE DAILY PAYROLL REPORT

Under this system, the departmental executives must complete each day a daily payroll report. Attention must be paid to accuracy and punctuality in forwarding these reports to the payroll analyst.

A sample form appears on page 430.

All department heads must be furnished with an ample supply of these forms. A time and place must be established for submitting these completed forms each day.

When the reports have been collected the payroll analyst checks each for arithmetical accuracy. Any apparent discrepancies should be discussed immediately with the department head involved. When the payroll analyst has completed his examination of each report he should indicate this fact by placing a check mark in the space provided on the form.

DAILY PAYROLL REPORT

DEPT: Butcher DATE May 15 19__

JOB TITLE	HOURS WORKED			
	REGULAR	OVERTIME	TOTAL	PAR
Head Butcher	8	-	8	8
Chicken Butchers	16	1	17	16
Fish Butchers	16	-	16	16
Extras (Explain Below)				
Total	40	1	41	40

REMARKS:

DEPARTMENT HEAD: CHECK ☐

Receipt of each department's daily payroll report can be recorded by checking them off on a check sheet.

The information contained on the Daily Payroll Reports should be entered on a Master Control Sheet such as that shown on page 431.

The sub-departmental breakdown can be as varied as management desires. Some establishments may find it desirable to use the following categories:

Chefs and cooks
Butchers
Vegetable workers
Cashiers and checkers
Headwaiter and captains
Waiters and waitresses

Pastry shop
Kitchenmen and potwashers
Pantry
Steward and assistants
Warewashers
Bus help
Banquet department
Wine Steward and assistants
Bartenders
Cellarmen and bar porters

Where the number of hours worked is uniform throughout the establishment, listing the days worked in place of, or parenthetically inserted alongside, the number of man-hours worked may present a more graphic picture of the payroll structure.

MASTER CONTROL
HOURS WORKED

Month: May 19

DAY	DATE	CHEFS AND COOKS		VEGETABLE WORKERS AND RUNNERS		PASTRY		PANTRY AND STOREROOM		WAREWASHERS AND CLEANERS		DINING ROOM STAFF		BARTENDERS		OTHER BEVERAGE EMPLOYEES		EXTRAS		TOTAL	
		S	A	S	A	S	A	S	A	S	A	S	A	S	A	S	A	S	A	S	A
	1	184	188	40	40	24	24	64	60	160	152	176	168	32	32	88	80	0	0	768	744
	2	160	168	32	40	24	25	56	64	144	160	160	164	32	33	72	80	24	36	704	770
	3	160	160	32	32	24	24	56	56	144	152	152	148	32	32	72	72	0	0	672	676
	4																				
	5																				
	28																				
	29																				
	30																				
	31																				
TOTALS																					

KEY:
S: Standard Hours
A: Actual Hours

An important daily procedure is the checking of the *extras* shown on the daily payroll reports against the factors of unusual volume such as banquets or other special functions. If the number of *extras* used is out of line with the set standard for the size and number of functions held, the reason must be ascertained.

The Weekly Report. The first step to be taken in preparing the weekly summary is a comparison of the hours reported on the daily payroll reports for each department with the actual hours worked as shown on the payroll. If the hours are not equal the reason for discrepancies should be ascertained. Experience has shown that the error can be in the payroll records as easily as in the daily payroll reports.

A common source of error is found in the practice of totaling the time cards incorrectly. A card that actually totals 41 hours may be totaled as 45 hours, and a card totaling 45 hours is commonly totaled as 48 hours. This error is usually brought about by totaling the hours the worker *usually* works instead of the hours *actually* worked. An investigator from the New York State Department of Labor remarked that, in the course of his investigations of time cards, he discovered that this error occurred frequently.

After a reconciliation between Daily Payroll Reports and the Payroll Records has been effected, the weekly summary should be prepared. This

WEEKLY PAYROLL COST CONTROL REPORT

FOR WEEK ENDING JANUARY 14

The following departments exceeded the man-hours as set forth in the Basic Staffing Schedules:

DEPARTMENT	EXCESS HOURS	OVER-TIME	TOTAL EXCESS	EXPLANATION
Chefs and Cooks	24	0	24	Breaking in new Roast Cook
Pastry	8	0	8	Special Banquet order
Warewashers	16	0	16	Machine breakdown
Bartenders	0	1	1	Heavy rush at 7:00 P.M.
Extras				
Total	48	1	49	

This represents a decrease of 7 excess hours compared with the preceding week.

The following departments, exceeding the man-hours as set forth in the Basic Staffing Schedules for the preceding week, are now within the limits set:

1. Dining Room Staff
2. Other Beverage Employees

Conferences with the department heads involved have been arranged to discuss the excess hours and overtime hours shown above.

Respectfully submitted,

JOHN C. SMITH
Payroll Analyst

summary, in the form of a report to the general manager, should disclose the following information:

(1) Departments exceeding the man-hours set in the Basic Staffing Report.

(2) The number of excess man-hours for each department.

(3) The reasons for the excess hours.
(4) Use of overtime by departments.
(5) Progress made by each department towards achieving satisfactory payroll costs.

An example of such a report is on page 432.

The Monthly Reports. The monthly payroll control report should include a summary of the man-hours worked and a comparison with the established standards, as shown below.

In addition to this basic report, a supplemental section should be appended commenting upon:

(1) All overtime
(2) All extra time
(3) All special and cyclical factors affecting the over-all payroll structure.

MONTHLY PAYROLL SUMMARY

SUB-DEPARTMENT	STANDARD	ACTUAL	HOURS OVER	HOURS UNDER
Chefs and Cooks	5,040	5,084	44	-
Vegetable Workers and Runners	1,008	1,004	-	4
Pastry	744	752	8	-
Pantry and Storeroom	1,624	1,616	-	8
Warewashers and Cleaners	4,488	4,532	44	-
Dining Room Staff	4,880	4,840	-	40
Bartenders	992	998	6	-
Other Beverage Employees	2,392	2,424	32	-
Extras	168	180	12	-
Total	21,336	21,430	146	52

Overtime. The presence of overtime should always be investigated to determine its significance in each particular instance. Some overtime is unavoidable in meeting emergencies if the staffing is closely adjusted to normal requirements. However, it must be closely watched to prevent abuses.

Extra Time. Extra time must be correlated with banquets and special functions to determine whether it was required in the amounts indicated.

Additional commentary may be made upon the following:

(1) A summary of any payroll revisions made during the period.
(2) Anticipated revisions and adjustments, together with an indication of the factors upon which they are contingent.
(3) A summary of conferences with department heads and the results obtained.

EMPLOYMENT TURNOVER

Whenever an employee is hired or separated from the payroll, the payroll analyst must be notified. Standard procedure should require the initialling by the payroll analyst of all incoming or outgoing employment cards.

LABOR TURNOVER ANALYSIS

SUB-DEPARTMENT	TOTAL EMPLOYEES	NUMBER OF NEW EMPLOYEES	PERCENTAGE OF NEW EMPLOYEES TO TOTAL EMPLOYEES THIS MONTH	AVERAGE MONTHLY PERCENTAGE OF NEW EMPLOYEES TO TOTAL EMPLOYEES DURING TWELVE PRECEDING MONTHS
Chefs and Cooks	14	1	7.1	3.6
Vegetable Workers and Runners	4	1	25.0	17.4
Pastry	5	0	-	2.8
Pantry and Storeroom	7	1	14.3	9.6
Warewashers and Cleaners	9	4	44.4	52.1
Dining Room Staff	20	2	10.0	12.3
Bartenders	4	0	-	1.9
Other Beverage Employees	11	1	9.1	7.8
Total	74	10	13.5	24.3

A complete record of each payroll change must be maintained by the payroll analyst in order to make a proper determination of all payroll adjustments each month.

A tabulation of turnover by departments and a comparison with past periods is advisable. A sample form for this appears above.

Turnover Ratios. Analysis will often reveal that a steadily high or sharp upward trend in sub-departmental labor turnover ratios may be due to one or more of the following reasons:

(1) Unsatisfactory work-relationships between supervisor and employee.
(2) Inadequate wage structure.
(3) Improper working conditions.
(4) Poor employee morale.

Proper investigation of these factors will generally result in saving considerable money. High labor turnover is expensive. It is an expense that can be curtailed through analysis and remedial action.

Chapter XXIX: VENDING MACHINES AND FOOD SERVICE

TRADITION has long been king in the food-service field. What few changes have occurred have been a matter of refinement—gradual improvement of this or that technique—perhaps a displacement of some old mechanical marvel by a new one—so long as the new one produced the same end result—an adjustment to speedier service and increased business but without any noticeable change "out front."

These few changes have conformed to the same basic pattern. They have all served to sustain the old image, to observe the old rules rather than write new ones.

Since the industry exists to serve the basic needs of mankind, why has food service been so universally unresponsive to changes in human conditions and situations? Are the basic rules immutable?

For those who favor tradition, they are right in at least one respect; the ultimate purpose of food service must remain fixed. Despite the eons elapsed between man's discovery of fire and his invention of electronic cooking, food service principles have hewed to a necessary line: grow it or buy it; cook, serve, and sell it; start the cycle all over again. That much cannot and should not change. But the techniques employed throughout the cycle—the ways of doing things, the means of achieving the end—are another matter entirely.

Many developments have spelled change in the back-of-the-house but they have had no marked effect upon what the customer sees—upon the ways in which food service truly serves his needs. Among these developments are packaged foods, food frozen or canned for out-of-season use, readily available transportation for raw materials, the automatic dishwasher, the electric oven, and many others. It is in this area that the greatest challenge and opportunity lies for the food service operator. What are the changes afforded by modern technology? How can they be made to bring food service closer to the real needs of people in today's world?

For the food service operator, these opportunities grow out of a central fact. As the mobility of man steadily increases, people are ranging further and further from their homes to use their on-the-job skills. The dependence upon the home for shelter remains. But for food, the traditional link to the family (even if only for the family-packed lunch-pail) is rapidly being broken. The result for food service operators, particularly in our industrial society, means an opportunity to break away from traditional restaurants and institutional feeding situations, into a vast hungry and growing market.

How? One of technology's most promising new answers is vending. To know how to make a profit in food service by way of the vending route and to know what the possibilities are it is necessary to know, first, the history of vending machines from the first ones down to the present.

History of Vending Machines. As early as the start of the 17th Century, vending was a way of distributing merchandise. Snuff and tobacco machines appeared with some regularity during that period in English taverns and inns, and a number of devices came to the American colonies with early settlers. The first U.S. patent for an automatic merchandising device was issued in 1884, followed in one year by the first penny weighing scale—an import from Germany. But the real growth didn't begin until the end of the 19th Century, with the issuance of dozens of patents and the formation of automatic merchandising companies. Vending was becoming a known factor in merchandising, and an accepted and trusted one in the mind of the average man.

By 1961, in a volume commemorating the 75th anniversary of automatic merchandising on an organized scale in the United States, G. R. Schreiber, the industry's historian-without-portfolio, was able to call the vending machine "part and parcel of the 20th Century revolution in retailing—the silent salesman with built-in cash register which annually moves billions of dollars of goods and services to consumers."

An increasingly important part of those billions is being spent on food, as vending machines fill a vacuum in a way that is both responsible and responsive to the needs of the public for food service.

At the start of the 1960s, prepared foods for vending accounted for $44 million in annual sales—twice the share of the total food market held by canned foods. In all, total food vending—including prepared foods and canned foods served by machine, represented a business that had reached the $60 to $65 million level.

Potential for Vending. From one point of view, the growth to date is just a drop in the bucket. There is still a long way for vending to go and enormous opportunities for the food service operator seeking room for expansion. For example, the total food market in the industrial field alone, excluding vending, already adds up to between $800 million and $1 billion annually. That is volume any way you look at it. And, of that market which has in it the potential for fantastic growth, what portion do vending machines hold? Barely 15%! For the operator, the potential is obvious and worth reaching for.

Historically, as we have seen, food by machine is nothing new—far older even than the practical beginnings of the vending business in the United States, with the introduction, in 1888, of the ever-present Adams Gum Machine. What *is* new are the technological advances that make today's vending practical for complete food service. And today's vending equipment is a far cry from yesterday's, even a yesterday as recent as a year ago.

Advantages. Already on the market is a machine—first of its kind—capable of taking a platter of frozen food and reconstituting it to its original fresh-cooked, ready-to-eat, hot state, requiring only the insertion of a couple of coins for service.

On the way is even more advanced equipment, capable of doing the cooking and reconstituting job almost instantaneously—in twenty seconds as opposed to the present two hours. Result of this development will eliminate the need to load a machine and start it working early in the day, several hours before actual service is required.

No Guesswork. Further, the guesswork factor—classic bugaboo for operators of all kinds of food service, manual or automatic—will be avoided for the first time in history. No longer will there be any need to ask: "What will they want to eat today?" Operators won't have to take the pulse of the public, without seeing the patient, on the basis of "if" or "maybe" analysis, crystal ball-gazing, experience, luck, or last year's form charts. Instead, varied menus—running the entire gamut of food preferences—will be prepared in advance and frozen for service on demand, manually or automatically, in the way or combination of ways most suitable for the circumstances.

No Waste. Human fallibility (and food-service operators *are* human, just as customers, more often than not, are all-too-human) will be replaced by machines that make possible choice without waste, by cooking the individual customer's food, instantly and to order, after he has made his personal selection. Menu selections not in demand will remain frozen until chosen—with an almost indefinite shelf-life in the machine, and a well-nigh immeasurable saving of food that previously went into the waste-bin, taking the operator's profits with it.

Hot-platter equipment plus modern meal-freezing techniques mean that food service—all kinds of food service, not only food vending—has reached the break-through point.

Better Control. Quality and portions can be controlled. The operator can take advantage of the economic savings of bulk buying and centralized preparation. The skilled chef can deploy his talents—increasingly costly and hard to find—over millions instead of hundreds of meals. The kitchen can be taken out of the cafeteria, making it possible for food service to serve *people* wherever they are, requiring for minimal operation only several square feet for a machine and an electrical outlet into which it may be plugged.

The fully automatic cafeteria is a reality for industrial and institutional installations, for commercial buildings and office feeding, for public restaurants and retail stores. The 1960s will be the decade that justifies those early prophets who saw fantastic potential in food-by-machine.

The Industrial Market. If only because it is untapped to a large extent, the industrial market is the largest outlet for fully automatic food service. This is true because traditional food service methods require subsidy in many cases and rarely include the elements of control and the freedom from care that characterize vending.

Size of the Market. The size of the market is worth remembering:

(1) $800 million to $1 billion in annual food volume already, excluding existing vending.

(2) Some 65,000,000 employed and away from home during at least one meal hour every working day.

(3) Better than 6,000 manufacturing plants with 250 or more employees—about half the plants of this size in the United States—providing some type of regular on-premise food service facility for use of personnel, and most of the rest of industry interested, as the idea becomes an accepted standard.

(4) Around $260 million, or about 3% of the estimated wholesale cost of food handled by all away-from-home eating places—the yearly expenditure in terms of food used by U. S. manufacturing plants employing 250 or more persons.

Vending can serve them all—the plants that have food service and the plants that don't. In addition and very important, vending can serve the many, many industrial plants employing fewer than 250 persons where, in most cases, the only food service is traditional food service.

As in the institutional and commercial markets, in-plant feeding for industry requires what vending now has—hot food equipment, fresh-brewed coffee machines, soft drink machines (featuring ice as well as chilled beverages), candy, gum, tobacco, and specialty services, all kinds of salad and sandwich machines, self-contained equipment for maintaining pre-cooked foods at proper serving temperatures (steam tables in effect), ice cream and dessert service.

Even the industrial climate is right. For one thing, the trend toward building factories in suburban or rural areas is continuing, even accelerating. It is a trend that makes inescapable the problem of having clean, wholesome food available at reasonable prices and at the proper time.

For another thing, the tightening economy and profit squeeze is making industry look twice at such matters as subsidy for food-service, this despite the fact that management is well aware of the light in which employees increasingly view food-service. Properly operated automatic food service avoids the issue by making subsidy unnecessary.

By the same token, office buildings in heavily-congested urban centers have a need for food-service. They displace low-rent luncheonette-cafeteria locations and, at the same time, bring vast new populations to small areas. Cooking on the premises is often out of the question—for reasons of space, ventilation, handling, etc. Automatic service is an answer, and a newly-feasible one, particularly since it can readily be combined with manual service, making possible either a counter-plus-machine arrangement, or executive dining rooms and employee cafeterias under the management of the same operator, who can afford to run the quality service installation because he is efficiently and profitably running the mass-population, quick-turnover cafeteria.

Further to the above advantages add these: A vending operation can offer the plant manager quality products, at a reasonable price to employees, served under sanitary conditions in surroundings that make for a pleasant dining climate.

Food service, where it is automatic, is available around-the-clock—of significant value where industrial operations use two or three shifts as well as in such institutional situations as hospitals.

Automatic equipment can be located conveniently for employees, making feasible the maintenance of strict lunch-hour schedules and saving countless hours of time lost when feeding is on a hit-or-miss or personal basis (half-hour lunch periods, increasingly prevalent, encourage fully automatic cafeterias, since they put a premium on speed). Automatic installations can handle any number or any frequency of staggered meal hours. Automatic installations can handle more people in fewer square feet, since space that would otherwise be devoted to back-of-the-house functions is eliminated, in favor of room to handle demand.

Virtually all employees want greater variety as their pay increases, and automatic service makes it possible—along with the quality that Americans want more and more, as good tastes and preferences grow more sophisticated or "international" in flavor.

Is everything, then, gravy—or roses—for the food-service operator eying automation and contemplating a switch to take advantage of its opportunities?

No. The very basis of successful automatic food service—its stress upon volume, for example—is directly opposed to the traditional philosophies of the food service field. The "mom and pop" philosophy operative in so many food-service situations, for example, has no place in the vending picture. Vending requires expensive machinery, technical maintenance know-how, wide distributive facilities, complex food production centers capable of multi-million meal capacity. It is big business, serving big business—a fact that is underlined by the accelerating pace of mergers within the field.

Planning for Food Service Vending. Planning the automatic food service parallels in most ways the planning of any other type of feeding operation. The first fact to be determined is the number and nature of the customers. Naturally, this task is easier in a closed situation such as an industrial facility, than in the public place, such as a service station, where estimates of traffic and its nature must be projected. Once determined, however, it is still important to learn as much as possible about the present food services available at or near the location. The "captive" audience, except in a totally ex-urban location, hardly exists today with competition seldom further away than around the corner.

The number and nature of expected customers will determine the number and type of machines. To justify full-line vending, the customers should require at least one full meal a day, plus one or more regular refreshment breaks. Supplementary vending services, such as coffee or drink machines, should be considered where less than a full meal is desired on the premises.

Full-line vending today would include machines that dispense hot and cold entrees, salads, sandwiches, soups, hot and cold beverages, pastries, ice cream, prepared desserts, snacks, and side dishes. The choice of machines vending these items, or combinations of these items, is almost as varied as the choice of items themselves. There are machines that vend both hot and cold soup and coffee, sandwiches, salads, and snacks all in one. The choice should be based on the requirements of the menu. Since certain machines will best vend certain items, it would be wise to select only those that can do the best job for the particular items to be served. The same would be true for the number and type of change-making devices to be employed, and the decision on the inclusion of non-food vending items, such as cigarettes.

Merchandising. Although some items will not be on open display, as in the cafeteria line, merchandising for eye-appeal still pays off in vending. Many machines are designed to make their products visible to the patron. Where this is so, particularly with salads and sandwiches, it is wise to prepare these dishes with a maximum of eye appeal, employing colorful garnishes, fillings, and dressings. As for prepared entrees, it is important to make the package an attractive unit as it reaches the customer, compensating for the human element of "dishing out" with a smart, clean look and the precise eating temperature. The right feel to a package can make up in part the lack of intimacy in service. Once opened, however, it is vital that the package be artfully presented, contrasted in the color, texture, and shape of its elements, as well as nutritionally balanced. The gratification of the customer upon finding a pleasingly arranged dish before him is the same, whether the dish is served by a waiter, or taken from a vending machine.

Good food service design takes on greater than usual dimensions in vending. While pleasant atmosphere is always sought by the operator, in an automatic installation it is imperative. As long as the vending of food is still a rather new concept, everything must be done to instill feelings of familiarity, warmth, and congeniality. Intelligent use of color and lighting in both the vending and dining areas can help. The placement of the vending machines, to make for both convenience of service and esthetic appeal, is most important. Many machines are available in different outer designs. Some may be banked together along one wall; some may be installed in walls; others may be grouped under a single structural unit, such as a ceiling, or set off in the floor area. Whichever design is chosen, an integrated vending area, with accompanying service spots, will help gain quick acceptance for the facility.

Along with the design of the facility, the dishes, trays, utensils, and other ware used should be of integrated design if at all possible. Although these items are to be thrown away, the sense of hodge-podge created by unplanned elements detracts from the atmosphere of the unit. An integrated service promotes well-being in much the same way that proper linen, silver, and nice sets of china do in a fine restaurant.

Manager. For operation of the automatic cafeteria it is always desirable to have a manager in the facility. It is possible, of course, to plan a completely self-operated unit, to be serviced by roving personnel on a scheduled basis. Considering the delicate nature of food service, and the justifiable sensitivity of most persons in this regard, it is wise to have the manager at hand at all times, nor should his job be purely a customer-relations function.

The ideal manager should be thoroughly familiar with the workings of vending machines. In fact, he should be a qualified mechanic. Although mechanical failure is no more prevalent in vending equipment than in any other kind, occasional jams do occur that can be remedied quickly on the spot. A qualified mechanic should also be able to determine quickly when more serious work would be required.

In addition to his mechanical training, the manager should be experienced or trained in the basic operation of a food service facility, namely, ordering, maintenance, and housekeeping. It is up to the manager to determine which of the choices from the master vending menu, and in what quantity, are to be made available on any one day. He should be close enough to his audience to judge preferences and predict usage. In his ability to predict, his function is the same as that of any food service manager.

In addition to the manager, the facility should have one neat appearing person bussing tables and generally keeping the place tidy. Following these restaurant principles, the automatic facility can be as smart as the smartest manual food service.

If there is any fixed fact about vending and food service it is this: it is growing fast and, if anything, changing faster. Today's way of doing things may not be tomorrow's; today's machinery may be outdated by a discovery as yet unannounced. All that is certain is that there is a need and that equipment is filling that need; that within the pattern of automatic food service are lessons for the operator concerned with more traditional aspects of the food industry.

One such lesson is in the matter of economics; bulk-buying, centralized preparation, wide distribution—all fall into this category. The traditional food service operator can profit increasingly to the extent to which he can successfully use the lessons of automatic food service in his operations.

Another lesson is in the matter of marketing. Automatic food service is proving successful because it found a market that it is uniquely able to serve, and is filling that market's demands. The traditional food-service operator would be well-advised to explore his own concepts for his own area to see if, perhaps, there are not opportunities that are being overlooked, despite their profit potential, just because they are "different" or "off-beat."

A third lesson—and perhaps the most significant of all—is in the matter of service. Food service must *serve;* it must meet the customer on his own terms, with service when and where he wants it, up to quality standards, and at a price for value that is equitable.

Vending is realizing new profits for food service precisely because it is not bound by tradition. It is making new rules—and new sales—because it serves the demands of the changing times.

BIBLIOGRAPHY

Ahern, Edwin F. *Safety Training Manual.* Ahrens Publishing Company, Inc., New York, N. Y., 1955.

Barnes, Ralph M. *Work Methods Manual.* John Wiley & Sons., Inc., New York, N. Y., 1944.

* Benge, E. J. *How to Make a Morale Survey.* National Foremen's Institute, Inc., New York, N. Y., 1941.

* Berolzheimer, Ruth. *Two Thousand Useful Facts About Food.* Culinary Arts Press (for Culinary Arts Institute), Reading, Pa., 1941.

** Bird, William. *A Practical Guide to French Wines.* Paris, 1951.

* Blumenthal, Saul. *Food Manufacturing—Food Products.* Chemical Publishing Company, Inc., Brooklyn, N. Y., 1942.

* Boomer, L. M. *Hotel Management.* Harper & Brothers, New York, N. Y., 1938.

Breland, J. H. *Chef's Guide to Quantity Cookery.* Harper & Brothers, New York, N. Y., 1947.

Clawson, Augusta. *Equipment Maintenance Manual.* Ahrens Publishing Company, Inc., New York, N. Y., 1951.

Dahl, J. O. *Menu Making for Professionals—Restaurant Management.* Dahl Publishing Company, Stamford, Conn., 1945.

* ———. *Restaurant Profits and Management Methods.* Dahl Publishing Company, Stamford, Conn., 1945.

* Dana, Arthur W. *Kitchen Planning.* Harper & Brother, New York, N. Y., 1949.

Dardarian, Leo. *Put Profit on the Menu.* Ahrens Publishing Company, Inc., New York, N. Y., 1959.

Dietz, Susan M. *The Correct Waitress.* Ahrens Publishing Company, Inc., New York, N. Y., 1952.

Dukas, Lundberg. *How To Operate A Restaurant.* Ahrens Publishing Co., Inc., New York 17, N. Y., 1960.

* Faissole, Charles A. *The Restaurateur's Handbook.* Harper & Brothers, New York, N. Y., 1938.

Finance, Charles. *Buffet Catering.* Ahrens Publishing Company, Inc., New York, N. Y., 1958.

* Out of print.

** Published under the auspices of Centre National du Commerce, Exterieur, Comité National de Propagande en Faveur du Vin, Institut National des Appellations D'Origine, Comité Interprofessionnel du Vin de Champagne.

Fleischman, E. M. *Modern Luncheonette Management.* Ahrens Publishing Company, Inc., New York, N. Y., 1955.

Gamble, Margaret Turner. *To Market, To Market.* The Bobbs Merrill Company, New York, N. Y., 1940.

* ———. *Your Food Dollar.* World Publishing Company, New York, N. Y., 1942.

Gancel, Joseph. *Encyclopedia of Modern Cooking.* Radio City Book Store, New York, N. Y., 1918.

* Glaser, Comstock. *Administrative Procedure.* Public Affairs Press, Washington, D. C., 1947.

Grossman, Harold J. *Grossman's Guide to Wines, Spirits and Beers.* Charles Scribner's Sons, New York, N. Y., 1955.

———. *Practical Bar Management.* Ahrens Publishing Company, Inc., New York, N. Y., 1959.

Halsey, George D. *Supervising People.* Harper & Brothers, New York, N. Y., 1953.

* Hauser, Benjamin G. *Harmonized Food Selection.* Tempo Books, Inc., New York, N. Y., 1930.

Heine, Paul L. H. *Food Sales, Unlimited.* Ahrens Publishing Company, Inc., New York, N. Y., 1952.

* Herod, William P. *An Introduction to Wines.* Fortuny's, New York, N. Y., 1936.

Hoke, Ann. *Restaurant Menu Planning.* John Willy, Inc., New York, N. Y., 1940.

* Huntington, Richard T. *Bar Management and Beverage Profits.* Dahl Publishing Company, Stamford, Conn., 1938.

Knowles, A. S. and Thomson, R. D. *Management of Manpower.* Macmillan Company, New York, N. Y., 1943.

* Kosma, Andrew R. *The A. B. C.'s of Motion Economy.* Institute of Motion Analysis and Human Relations, Newark, N. J., 1943.

Lange, Howard F. *Catering.* Ahrens Publishing Company, Inc., New York, N. Y., 1955.

Lefler, Sack and Blanc. *The Waiter and His Public.* Ahrens Publishing Company, Inc., New York, N. Y., 1959.

* Lewisohn, S. A. *Human Leadership in Industry.* Harper & Brothers, New York, N. Y., 1945.

* Out of print.

** Published under the auspices of Centre National du Commerce, Exterieur, Comite National de Propagande en Faveur du Vin, Institut National des Appellations D'Origine, Comité Interprofessionnel du Vin de Champagne.

Little, R. Keith. *Kitchen Layout Logic.* Age Publications, Ltd., Toronto, Canada, 1959.

* MacDonald, Aeneas. *Whisky.* Henry & Longwell, Garden City, N. Y., 1930.

* Mehlig, Madeline C. *Kitchen Strategy.* Wilcox & Follette Company, Chicago, Ill., 1943.

* Metcalf, Henry C. and Urwick, L. *Dynamic Administration.* Harper & Brothers, New York, N. Y., 1942.

* Mooney, Paul. *Profitable Labor Relations.* Harper & Brothers, New York, N. Y., 1946.

Pfeiffer & Voegele. *The Correct Maid for Hotels and Motor Hotels.* Ahrens Publishing Co., Inc., New York 17, N. Y., 1960.

Prescott, Samuel C. *Food Technology.* McGraw-Hill Book Company, Inc., New York, N. Y., 1937.

* Reid, Margaret G. *Food for People.* J. Wiley & Sons, Inc., New York, N. Y., Chapman & Hall, Ltd., London, 1943.

* Reitell, C. *Training Workers and Supervisors.* The Ronald Press, New York, N. Y., 1943.

* Rorty, James. *Tomorrow's Food.* Devin-Adair Company, New York, N. Y., 1956.

* Schoonmaker, Frank and Marvel. *The Complete Wine Book.* Simon and Schuster, New York, N. Y., 1934.

Sherman, H. C. *Foods: Their Values and Management.* Columbia University Press, New York, N. Y., 1946.

* Simon, André L. *Wine and Spirits.* Duckworth & Company, London, 1919.

* Todd, William J. *Handbook of Wine.* J. Cape, London, 1922.

Todoroff, A. *Food Buyer's Information Book.* The Grocery Trade Publishing House, Chicago, Ill., 1950.

Urwick, L. *Elements of Administration.* Harper & Brothers, New York, N. Y., 1944.

Wenzel, George L. *Wenzel Menu Maker.* Austin, Texas, 1934.

* Wine Advisory Board of California. *The Sale of Wine in Restaurants.* California Wine Advisory Board, San Francisco, Calif., 1943.

Wolff, Jack L. *The Production Conference.* Houghton Mifflin Company, Boston, Mass., 1944.

* Out of print.

** Published under the auspices of Centre National du Commerce, Exterieur, Comité National de Propagande en Faveur du Vin, Institut National des Appellations D'Origine, Comité Interprofessionnel du Vin de Champagne.

INDEX

Absenteeism, 399
Accident prevention, 22
Accounting, controls, 11
  department, 9, 305
    responsibility, 105
Advantages of vending machines, 438
Advertising and promotion, 228
Advertising, analysis of potential market, 229
  appraisal of restaurant, 228
  billboard, 233
  budgets, 17, 241
  car and bus cards, 234
  coordination of, 240
  direct mail, 234
  internal merchandising, 237
  long-range planning, 240
  magazine, 231
  manager or agency, 243
  media, studying, 230
  neighborhood, 232
  newspaper, 231
  publicity suggestions for, 242
  radio, 236
  telephone directory, 233
  television, 237
  visitors' guides, 236
A la carte selections, 63
Ale, 283
American Plan, combined with European, 214
  dinner menu, 210, 212
  extra meal service, 222
  food checking, 217
  food cost percentages, 213
  food service, 219
  guest order check, 220, 222
  internal control, 227
  luncheon menu, 210, 211
  meal checking sheet, 220
  menu structure, 207
  menus, 210
  portion sizes, 212
  profit factors, 216
  room service, 226
  staff, 214
  table capacity, 214
  transient meal service, 224
American service, 154
American whiskeys, 281
Analysis,
  of comparative sales, 13
  covers served, 416
  food cost, 375
  job, 151
  menu, 28
  payroll, 414
  portions, 16
  sales, 29, 63
  work productivity, 417
Analyzing, work loads, 414
  training needs, 145
Annual sales, 437
Appearance of food, 36
Appetizers, 39
  menu listings, 40
Ash trays, 163
Atmosphere, restaurant, 62
Automatic equipment, 440

Bakery items, frozen, 143
Baking, 141
Balanced meals, 189
Banquets, 301
  check room, 304
  chef, duties of, 303
  consultations, 306
  control of revenue, 313
  employees, extra, 306
  guarantee, minimum, 305
  head waiter, duties of, 303
  houseman, duties of, 304
  interdepartmental functions, 303
  manager, duties of, 301
  menu, 31, 307
  pricing table, 307
  procedures, wine and liquor, 402
  sales office for, 311
  seating space, 307
  selling public rooms, 310
  sources of bookings for, 312
  steward, duties of, 303
  superintendent, duties of, 305
Bar, boys, duties of, 173
  control, 404
  glassware, 406
  par stock, 406
  porters, duties of, 174
  portions, 382
  service, 175, 404
  stand-up, 174
  waiters, duties of, 173
Bartenders, 291
  duties of, 173
Basic planning routine, 339
Basic needs, 436
Basic pattern, 436
Bechamel sauce, 140
Beef, 44, 84
  entrees, 44

Beer, 283
  brands, 283
  care of, 296
  cooks', 298
  kegs, standard weight, 295
  packaging, 284
  water content of, 283
Beverage, brands, 291
  department, 305
  inventory, 270
  overhead, 270
  purchasing guides, 269
  sales analysis, 271
  service, 173
Beverages, 52
  basic ingredients, 269
  distilled, 272
  fermented, 272
  menu listings, 53
Billboards, 233
Bin cards, 271, 298, 399
Blind purchase orders, 294
Blind receiving, 106
Blocked out menu, 31
Blue plate selections, 63
Bock beer, 283
Bottle control, 299
Bottle sales, 281
"Bottled in bond," 286
Brandies, 287
Brands, of beer, 284
  beverages, 291
Breakage reports, 295
Breakdowns, job, 150
Break-even point, entertainment, 319
Breakfast menus, 33, 64
  suggestions, 53
Breakfasts, club, 65
  late, 215
Brunch suggestions, 55
Budgeting, 327
  advertising and promotion, 17, 241
  basis of, 327
  costs and expenses, 329
    direct operating supplies, 331
    payroll, 331
    raw food and beverage, 332
  sales volume required, 328
Buffet service, 154
Bulk buying, 439
Burns, 22
Bus cards, 234
Bus help, in cafeterias, 183
  duties of 162
  for vended service, 443
Butcher, 352
Butchering tests, 82, 385
Butter, grades of, 89
  storage, 117
Buyer, 99
  food, 70
Buying, bulk, 439
  open market, 72
  procedures, 71
  quality, 76
  routine, 95
  specifications, 77

Cafeteria, bus help, 183
  food display, 182
  food stations, 182
  kitchen, 344, 345, 439
  portion sizes, 183
  service, 181
  silverware arrangement, 182
  tray removal, 183
  types of, 181
Cake, menu listings, 50
Canned foods, 96, 436
  fruit and vegetable grades, 90
  tests, 78
Capacity, seating, 339
Captains, duties of, 160
Car cards, 234
Cases, weight of, 295
Cash, handling in receiving room, 110
Cashier, 15
Catering department organization, 10
Ceilings, maintenance of, 252
Centralized and decentralized kitchens, 193
Centralized preparation, 439
Champagnes, 276
Changes in vended service, 443
Chart, flow, 341, 348
Charts, organization, 10
Check disputes, 176
Check lists, 20
  pre-planning, 357
  sanitation, 258
Check room, 304
  service payment of, 170
Checkers, 15, 169, 344
Checking for quality, 102
Checks, 165
Cheese, menu listings, 52
  storage, 118
Chef, duties of, 303, 439
  executive, 10
Chef-steward, 70, 303
Chicken Veloute, 140
Cleaning, time for, 255
  methods, 264
  silver, 354
Club, city, 205
  country, 201
Club breakfasts, 65
Cocktail lounge, 174
Cocktails, listing ingredients of, 292
Coffee service, 164
Cold meats, 47
Colleges, 201
Competition, 29
Computing portion cost factors, 385
Conformation of meat, 85
Contract purchasing, 73
Control, avenues of, 360
  banquet, 313
  bottle, 299

Control, *Cont'd.*
employees, 13
food, 359, 439
inventory, 368, 409
issuing, 365
payroll, 427
pest, 254
pilferage, 364
production, 366
purchasing, 360
receiving, 362
sales, 369
spoilage, 364
storage, 364
wine and liquor, 396
Cooking, fish, 131
meat, 132
soups, 138
temperatures, 135
vegetables, 136
Cooking tests, 82
Cooks' beer, 298
Cooperative associations, 74
Cost accounting, food, 359
Cost of food and beverages, 18
reports, daily, 15
Costs and profits, operating, 8
Counter service, 181
menus for, 181
order of, 184
order taking, 185
payroll for, 187
Covers served, number of, 18
Customer likes and dislikes, 384

Daily cost reports, 15
Daily food cost control sheet, 369
Daily market information, 99
Daily payroll report, 429
Daily price board, 387
Daily reports, 371
Daily summary of food costs, 390
Date stamp, 126
Days off, 418
Defrosting, 119
Departmental supervision, 5
Desserts, 49
Diary of special events, 384
Diet kitchen, 346
Dietician, 71
Diners, 338
Dinner menus, 33, 65
Dining room, 7
employees, duties of, 155
service, 153
space, 342
Direct mail advertising, 234
Discord, employee, 25
Dish removal, room service, 171
Dishes for proper service, 166
Dishwasher, automatic, 436
Dishwashing, 252, 354, 357
Display advertising, 231
Distilled beverages, 272
spirits, 284
Distributing work loads, 423
Drive-ins, 338

Economy, motion, 340
Egg entrees, menu listing, 46
Eggs, 46
frozen, 142
grades, 89
service, 164
storage, 116
Elevator, cards, 238
service, 9
Elevator vestibule posters, 238
Employees, attitude of, 215
control of, 13
discord among, 25
duties in dining room, 155
grievances, 26
hazards of, 22
health and hygiene, 245
recognition, 27
relations, 25
retraining of, 149
training of, 145
turnover, 257, 434
Employment in hotels, 2
Engineer, 10, 305
Engineering expenses, 17
English service, 154
Entertainment, types of, 317
Entrees, 42
beef, 44
eggs, 46
fish, 43
lamb and mutton, 45
miscellaneous, 46
pork and ham, 45
poultry and game, 45
seafood, 43
veal, 44
Equipment, automatic, 440
hot platter, 439
power driven, 24
receiving, 101
service, 166
Executive chef, 10
Exit interview, 27
Expenses, hidden, 20
undistributed, 17
Extra meal service, American Plan, 222
Extra time, 433

Facilities, influence on menu, 29
layout, 421
Factories, 440
Fats and shortenings, 141
Federal grading standards, 83
Feeding, industrial, 188
Fermented beverages, 272
Finish of meat, 85
Fish, 43, 94
cookery, 131
entrees, 43

Fish, *Cont'd.*
Veloute, 140
Flavoring, 142
Flies, 254
Floors, maintenance of, 252
kitchen, 22
Flour, 141
Flow chart, 341, 348
Food, appearance of, 36
area, 340
buyer, 69
care after cooking, 368
care during cooking, 249
care prior to cooking, 249
checkers, 13, 344
records of, 226
checking, American Plan, 217
control of, 359
cost accounting, 359
analysis, 375
control sheet, 369
percentages, American Plan, 213
costs, daily summary of, 390
hospital, 197
reasons for high, 8
solution to high, 378
display in cafeterias, 182
freezing techniques, 439
frozen, storage, 119
inventory control, 368
issues, supervision of, 125
market, 438
operations, manager, 70
types of, 342
poisoning, 257
preparation, 150
price of, 38
purchase and inventory turnover, 373
purchasing, 191
control, 360
purchasing guide, 68
quality of, 62
service, 62, 436
American Plan, 219
service, field, philosophies of, 441
stations in cafeterias, 182
storage, 111
sanitary, 247
stores, retail, 74
tests, canned, 78
raw, 78
Food and beverage cost, 18
Foods, canned, 436
frozen, 436
packaged, 436
Forced issues, 129
Format of menu, 57
Fountain, soda, 353
French service, 153
Fresh fruit and vegetable grades, 92
Frozen food storage, 119
fruits and vegetables, 352
Frozen foods, 436
Fruit, grades, canned, 90
fresh, 92
frozen, 352
menu listings, 51
mixes, 270
storage, 118, 120
Fuel, 354
Full-line vending, 441
Furloughs, summer, 425
Futures and contract purchasing, 73

Game and poultry, 45
Garage posters, 239
Garbage, 352
Gelatin, 51
Gins, 289
Glass, broken, 23
storage, 337
Glassware, 176, 337
Grades, of butter, 89
canned fruits and vegetables, 90
eggs, 89
Federal standards, 83
fresh fruits and vegetables, 92
meat, changes in, 86
choice, 86
commercial, 86
cutter and canner, 87
good, 86
prime, 86
selected, 87
poultry, 87
Gratuities, in counter service, 186
Grievances, employee, 26
Grocery items, 96
Guarantee, minimum banquet, 305
Guest order check, American Plan, 220
Guides, food purchasing, 68
visitors', advertising, 236

Ham and pork, 45
Hazards, employee, 22
Health and hygiene of employees, 245
Head waiter, duties of, 157
banquet, 303
Hidden expenses, 20
High food costs, reasons for, 8
solution to, 378
Hiring interview, 145
History of vending machines, 437
Holiday menus, 32
Hollandaise sauce, 140
Home style service, 209
Hospitals, 193, 357
food costs, 197
kitchens, 345
menu planning, 196
payroll, 197
service, methods, 195
types, 194
Hostess, duties of, 157, 166
Hot platter equipment, 439
Hotel and restaurant administration school, 2

Hotels, employment in, 2
problems peculiar to, 4
property of, 2
sales, 1
Hours of arrival, 419
Hours, for issuing, 127
of operation, 423
schedule for wine cellar, 298
serving, 351
Houseman, banquet duties of, 304

Ice cream, 352
menu listings, 51
Ice making, 353
Ice water, circulating, 353
Identification of stored items, 126
Industrial feeding, 188
between meals snacks, 190
controls, 192
kitchens, 193
market, 439
menu planning, 190
mobile units, 191
staggered schedules, 190
types of service, 188
Inspection, 20
wine cellar, 300
Institutions, 197
Inter-departmental relationships, 9, 303, 359
Internal control, American Plan, 227
Internal merchandising, 237
Interview, exit, 27
initial hiring, 145
Inventories, 120
beverage, 270
control, 368
wine and liquor, 409
perpetual, 272, 403
physical, 410
sales, 271
turnover, 373
verification of, 411
wine cellar, 298
monthly, 299
Invoice stamp, 108
Invoices, wine and liquor, verification of, 396
Irish whiskey, 287
Issues, forced, 129
supervision of food, 125
Issuing, controls, 343
hours for, 127
mechanics of, 125

Job, analysis of, 151, 340
breakdown, 150
classification, 19
deficiencies, 146
simplification, 340

Keys, storeroom, 114
wine cellar, 296
Kitchen, cafeteria, 344, 345, 439
diet, 346
equipment, sanitation of, 251, 253
harmony in, 168
hospital, 345
influence on menus, 35
layout, 166, 337, 338, 399
planning, 337
service, 344
tests, 80, 82
Kitchens, centralized and decentralized, 193
Knives, 23

Labor turnover, 257, 438
Lamb, 86
entrees, 45
and mutton, 45
Lamp, ultra violet ray, 116
Laws, 21
Layout, general principles of, 342
pitfalls, 349
Leftovers, use of, 30, 143
Licenses and permits, 21
Limited menus, 60
Liqueurs, 290
Lobby posters, 238
Local farmers and producers, 74
Local regulations, 21
Location, 7
restaurant, 62
Locker rooms, 357
Locks and keys, wine cellar, 296
Losses, operating, 8
Luncheon menus, 33, 65

Machines, vending, 436
Magazine advertising, 231
Maintenance and repairs, 10
kitchen, 252
Management responsibilities, 5, 189
Manager, 70
food operations, 70, 301
for vended service, 443
Manuals on sanitation, 255
Manufacturers and packers, 73
Market, 30, 75
food, 438
industrial, 439
information on, 99
offerings of, 75
quotations, 96
size of, 439
visiting, 75
Markets, municipal, 74
Meal pattern, 338, 351
checking sheet, American Plan, 220
Meals, balanced, 189
pre-determined, 347
Meat, cookery, 132
grading service, 83
shrinkage, 135
stamping procedure, 83
storage, 118
tag, 103
tagging, 126
thermometer, 136
Meats, cold, 47

Menu listings, appetizers, 39
beef entrees, 44
beverages, 52
blue plate, 63
breakfast suggestions, 33, 53, 64
brunch suggestions, 55
cake, 50
cheese, 52
desserts, 49
dinner, 33, 64
eggs, 46
entrees, 46
fish, 43
fruit, 51
gelatin, 51
holiday, 32
ice cream, 51
lamb and mutton, 45
luncheon, 33, 64
pies, 50
pork and ham, 45
potatoes, 48
poultry and game, 46
puddings, 50
seafood, 43
sherbet, 52
side salads, 49
soups, 40
souvenir, 64
supper, 33, 54
sweet potatoes, 48
veal, 44
vegetables, 48
Menu making, primary principles, 30
clubs, 203, 206
hospitals, 196
industrial feeding, 190
Menu pattern, 338
Menus, 7, 28, 39, 57, 351
a la carte, 63
American Plan, 207
analysis, 28
banquet, 31
blocked out, 31
copy for, 58
counter service, 181
flexibility, 60
format of, 57
kitchen influence on, 35
limited, 60
neighborhood influence on, 33
pre-cost, 389
pricing, 37, 61, 66
sales analysis, 63
structure, American Plan, 207
variety, 59
American Plan, 208
table d'hote, 63
wording of, 59
Merchandise, returned, 108
spoiled, 129
Merchandising, wine, 177
internal, 237
vended foods, 442
Methods, cleaning, 264
hospital service, 195
purchasing, 72
training, 149
Milk dispenser, bulk, 353
Minimum banquet guarantee, 305
Minors, 175
Mixes, 269
fruit, 270
Mobile units, 191
Modernization, 340
Monthly reports, 372
Monthly sales, 271
Monthly statements, 12
Motion economy, 340
Municipal market, 74
Music and entertainment, 317
break-even point for, 319
net cost, 318
schedule changes, 325
schedule problems, 321
selection, 324
Mutton and lamb, 45

Needs, basic, 436
Neighborhood advertising, 232
Neighborhood influence on menu, 33
Net cost of entertainment, 318
Newspaper advertising, 231
Number of meals, pre-determined, 347

Office buildings, 440
Offices, 358
On-the-job training, 146
Open market buying, 72
Operating costs and profits, 8
Operating losses, 8
Order clerk, room service, 170
Order taking, room service, 170
Orders, purchase, 98
standing, 96, 360
Organization, of catering department, 10
charts, 10
Oven, electric, 436
Overhead, beverages, 270
Overtime, 411

Packaged foods, 436
Packaging, beer, 284
Packers and manufacturers, 73
Par stock for bars, 406
for wine cellar, 294
Patronage, reasons for, 61
Pattern, basic, 436
Payroll, 19, 414
analysis methods, 415
test period, 415
analyst, duties of, 428
control, 427
counter service, 187
hospital, 197
reports, daily, 16, 429
monthly, 433
weekly, 431

Peak load, 338
Perishables, 95
Permits and licenses, 21
Perpetual inventory, 272, 409
Personnel, receiving department, 100
Pest control, 254
Philosophies of food service field, 441
Pies, 10, 166
Pilferage control, 364
Pitfalls, layout, 349
Planning for food service vending, 441
Planning routines, 339
Pork and ham, 45
Pork grades, 87
Porter and stout, 283
Portion, analysis, 16
  computing cost factors, 385
  sales history, 379
  size, American Plan, 212
    bar, 404
    in cafeterias, 183
    standard, 367, 386
Potatoes, 48
Potentials for vending, 437
Poultry and game, 45
  grades, 87
Pre-control, advantages of, 376
Pre-packaging, 126
Preparation and service kitchen, 344
Pre-planning check list, 351
Preparation, centralized, 439
  staff, 35
Price control, sales, 407
Price of food, 38
Price tag appeal, 66
Pricing, requisitions, 126
  menus, 61
Producers and local farmers, 74
Production control, 366
Profit, 19
Profit factors, American Plan, 216
Profits, operating costs and, 8
Promotion, *see* Advertising and promotion
Promotion of employees, 152
Public rooms, selling, 310
Public safety, 25
Publicity, suggestions for, 242
Puddings, 50
Purchase orders, 98
  blind, 294
  price comparison, 373
  suitability, 75
  wines and liquors, 396
Purchases, food and inventory turnover, 373
  stock, 361
Purchasing, contracts and futures, 73
  control, 360
  guides, 264
  methods, 72
  sealed bids, 72
  specifications, standard, 78, 385
Purchasing agent, 71
Purveyors, relations with, 74

Quality buying, 76
  food, 61
  meat, 85
Quotations, market, 96

Radio advertising, 236
Ratio of sales, 382
Raw food tests, 78
Raw materials, 436
Reasons for inadequate sales volume, 7
Receiving, blind, 106
  clerk, 99
    wine cellar, 294
  controls, 362
  department, function of, 100
    personnel of, 100
  equipment, 101
  mechanics, 101
  records, 107
  sheets, 107
  specifications, 103
  stamp, 108
  tests, 105
  tickets, 108
  wines and liquors, 375
Receiving room, handling cash in, 110
Recipe cards, standard, 365
  conversion tables, 387
Records, receiving, 107
  wines and liquors, 397
Refresher techniques, 148
Refrigerated units, 119
Refrigeration, 114, 353
  temperatures, 116
Refrigerator, 30
Refuse handling, 23
Regional preferences, 291
Regulations, Federal, state, and municipal, 412
  local, 21
Relief schedules, 424
Reports, breakage, 283
  daily, 371
  daily cost, 15
  monthly, 372
  payroll, daily, 16
    monthly, 433
    weekly, 431
Requirement for vending, 440, 441
Requisitions, 127
  liquor stocks, 297
  pricing, 128
  wines and liquors, 400
Restaurant, atmosphere of, 62
  location of, 62
  pre-fabricated, 338
  problems, basic, 4
  specialty, 347
  types of, 342
Retail food stores, 74
Retraining employees, 149
Returned merchandise, 108
Reviews, periodic, 21
Rodents, 254

Room cards, 237
Room service, 170
  American Plan, 226
  checks and payment, 172
  dish removal, 171
  order taking, 170
  telephone order clerk, 170
  waiter, 171
Rooms, department, 9
Rums, 287
Russian service, 154

Safety, public, 25
Salad dressing, 46
Salads, 144
  main dish, 46
  side, 49
Salaries and wages, schedule of, 19
Sales, annual, 437
  bottle, 403
  control, 369
  history, portion, 379
  inventory, monthly, 271
  potentials, for wine and liquor, 407
  ratio of, 382
  record, format for, 380
  variations in daily, 383
  volume, 7
    reasons for inadequate, 7
Sales analysis, 29, 63, 379
  beverage, 271
  comparative, 13
  menu, 63
Salesmen, 99
Sanitation, 245, 256
  check list, 258
  of kitchen equipment, 251, 253
  in food preparation, 247
  in food storage, 247
  manuals, 255
  standards, 255
Sauce, Bechamel, 140
  Brown, 140
  Hollandaise, 140
  White, 140
Saving space, 440
Scales, 101
Schedules, relief, 424
  staggered, 419
Schools, 198
  administration, 2
Scotch whisky, 286
Seafood, 43
Sealed bid purchasing, 72
Seasonal menus, 31, 65
Seating capacity, 339
  space, 339
  space, banquet, 307
Selected grades, 87
Selecting trainer, 148
Sell-out time, 484
Service, American, 154
  American Plans, features, 208
  bar, 175, 404
  beverage, 173
  buffet, 154
  cafeteria, 181
  coffee, 164
  counter, 184
  dining room, 153
  dishes for, proper, 166
  egg, 164
  food, 436
  English, 154
  equipment, 166
  French, 151
  home style, 209
  kitchen, 344
    and preparation, 344
  room, 170
  Russian, 154
  take-out, 186
  techniques, 163
Serving areas, distance from kitchen, 351
  hours, 351
  number of, 351
Shelves and bins, wine storage, 296
Shelving, storeroom, 112
Sherbet, 52
Shortening, 141
Shrinkage, meat, 135
Side tables, 164
Side towels, 164
Signs, *see* Advertising and promotion
Silverware, 163
  arrangement in cafeteria, 182
  cleaning, 354
Size of market, 439
Soda fountain, 353
Sorting tables, 337
Soup, 40, 138
  clear, 139
  stock, 139
    brown, 140
  thick, 41
Space in dining room, 342
  requirements, 341
  saving, 440
  seating, 339
  for workers, 341
Specification buying, 77
Specifications, receiving, 103
  standard purchasing, 385
Spoilage, 129
  control, 364
Staff, American Plan, 214
  basic, 427
  preparation, 35
  variations in, 428
Staffing problems, 418
  table, 427
Staggered schedules, 190, 419
Stamp, date, 126
  invoice, 108
  receiving, 108
Stamping procedure, meat, 84
Standard portions, 367, 386
Standard purchase specifications, 78, 385

Standard recipe card, 387
Standing orders, 380
Stand-up bar, 174
Statements, food and beverage, 12
Statistical references, 18
Steam, 353
Steward, duties of, 303
Steward's department, 11
Stock purchases, 361
Storage, 352
  butter, 117
  cheese, 118
  controls, 364
  eggs, 116
  food, 247
  fruit and vegetables, 118
  frozen food, 119
  glass, 357
  meat, 118
  utensils, 253
  wine, 295
  wines and liquors, 399
Storeroom, equipment, 112
  hours, 113
  keys, 114
  location, 112
  physical properties, 112
  shelving, 112
  size, 112
Structural defects, 23
Subsidy, 439, 440
Suitability of purchase, 75
Summary of wine and liquor operations, 408
Summer furlough, 425
Superintendent of service, 305
Supervision of food and beverage operation, 4
Supper, menu suggestions, 54
  menus, 33

Table cards, 239
Table d'hote meals, 388
  selections, 63
Tables, capacity, American Plan, 214
  service, 163
  side, 164
  sorting, 357
Tagging meat, 126
Take-out service, 186
Techniques, food freezing, 439
Telephone directory advertising, 233
Television advertising, 237
Temperature, cooking, 135
  refrigeration, 116
  wine cellar, 400
Tests, butchering, 82, 385
  canned food, 78
  cooking, 82
  kitchen, 78, 82
  raw food, 78
  receiving, 105
Thermometer, meat, 136
Tickets, receiving, 108
Towels, side, 164
Trainer, selecting, 148
Training, employee, 145
  induction, 147
  methods, 149
  needs, 145
  on-the-job, 146
  procedure, 147
Transient meal service, American Plan, 224
Tray removal in cafeterias, 183
Trays, 347
Trucks, 24
Turnover, food inventory, 373
  labor, 257, 434
Types of food operation, 342
  of restaurants, 342

Ultra violet ray lamp, 116
Undistributed expenses, 17
Uniform System of Accounts, 11
U.S. Meat-Grading Service, 83
Unsanitary conditions, 7
Utensil storage, 253

Variation in daily sales, 383
Veal, 44, 45
Vegetable platters, 47
Vegetables, cookery, 131, 136
  grades, canned, 90
    fresh, 92
  menu listings, 48
  storage, 118
Veloute, chicken and fish, 140
Vended food, merchandising of, 442
Vended service, bussing for, 443
  changes in, 443
  manager for, 443
Vending, 437, 439
  full-line, 441
  planning for food service, 441
Vending machines, 436, 438
  advantages of, 438
  history of, 437
  requirements of, 440, 441
Vermin, 254
Visiting market, 275
Visitors' guides, 236

Waiter, duties of, 161
  bar, 173
  room service, 171
Waitress, duties of, 161
Walls, maintenance of, 252
Washrooms, 357
Waste, controlling, 167, 438
  disposal, 254
Water, 353
Water content of beer, 284
Water, impure, 254
Whiskey, Irish, 287
Whiskeys, 285
Whisky, Scotch, 286
Wholesale supply houses, 73
Wine cellar operation, 293

Wine cellar operation, *Cont'd.*
- care of beer, 296
- cooks' beer, 298
- equipment, 297
- inspection, 300
- inventory, 298
  - bin cards, 298
  - bottle control, 299
  - monthly, 299
- locks and keys, 296
- par stock, 294
- receiving clerk, 294
  - blind purchase order, 294
  - breakage reports, 295
  - weights of cases, 295
- requirements, physical, 293
- requisitions, 297
- schedule of hours, 298
- shelves and bins, 296
- storage, 295

Wine and liquor control, 396
- banquet procedures for, 402
- bar control, 404
- bottle sales, 403
- inventory control, 409
- invoices, verification of, 396
- issuing, 400
- par stock, 406
- purchase orders, 496
- receiving, 397
- regulations, 412
- requisitions, 400
- sales potentials, 407
- selling price control, 407
- storage, 399
  - bin cards, 399
- temperature, 400

Wines, 272
- Alsatian, 276
- American, 280
- appetizer, 273
- Bordeaux, 274
- Burgundy, 276
- California, 281
- champagnes, 276
- dessert, 274
- European, 274
- French, 274
- German, 277
- Hungarian, 277
- Italian, 279
- red table, 273
- Spanish and Portuguese, 278
- sparkling, 274
- white table, 273

Work loads, analyzing, 314
- distributing, 423
- schedules, 418
- units, 414

Workers, space for, 341